Using Children's Literature
Across the Curriculum

ONE WEEK LOAN

A H ＇egies

Boston Columbus Indianapolis New York San Francisco Upper Saddle River
Amsterdam Cape Town Dubai London Madrid Milan Munich Paris Montreal Toronto
Delhi Mexico City Sao Paulo Sydney Hong Kong Seoul Singapore Taipei Tokyo

Vice President, Editor in Chief: Aurora Martínez Ramos
Editorial Assistant: Amy Foley
Marketing Manager: Amanda Stedke
Production Editor: Mary Beth Finch
Editorial Production Service: Omegatype Typography, Inc.
Manufacturing Buyer: Megan Cochran
Electronic Composition: Omegatype Typography, Inc.
Interior Design: Omegatype Typography, Inc.
Cover Administrator: Linda Knowles
Cover Designer: Jenny Hart

Standards for the English Language Arts, by the International Reading Association and the National Council of Teachers of English, are copyright © 1996 by the International Reading Association and the National Council of Teachers of English. Reprinted with permission. Available at www.ncte.org/standards

Library of Congress Cataloging-in-Publication Data

Using children's literature across the curriculum : a handbook of instructional strategies / Catherine O'Callaghan . . . [et al.].
    p. cm.
  Includes bibliographical references and index.
  ISBN-13: 978-0-13-171191-4 (paperbound)
  ISBN-10: 0-13-171191-1 (paperbound)
 1. Language arts (Elementary) 2. Reading (Elementary) 3. English language—Composition and exercises—Study and teaching (Elementary) I. O'Callaghan, Catherine M.
  LB1573.U85 2011
  372.6'044—dc22

2010018915

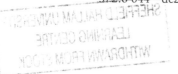

10 9 8 7 6 5 4 3 2 1   14 13 12 11 10

www.pearsonhighered.com

ISBN-10: 0-13-171191-1
ISBN-13: 978-0-13-171191-4

Authors

Catherine M. O'Callaghan is a professor of education and chair of the education department at Iona College. She entered the profession as an early childhood teacher in New York City and continued her career as a literacy specialist. Teaching in New York City within diverse settings afforded her a wide range of teaching experiences. She has published numerous journal articles and books including (with Patricia Antonacci) *Portraits of Literacy Development: Instruction and Assessment in a Well-Balanced Literacy Program K–3* (2004), *A Handbook for Literacy Instructional & Assessment Strategies K–8* (2006), and *Developing Content Area Literacy* (2010).

Patricia A. Antonacci is a professor of education and teaches in the literacy education program at Iona College. Antonacci entered the teaching profession as a classroom teacher for the elementary and middle grades and continued as a reading specialist. Her long career in public schools brought her a range of experiences as a teacher at all grade levels including a number of years working in diverse classroom settings. She has published numerous journal articles and books including (with Catherine O'Callaghan) *Portraits of Literacy Development: Instruction and Assessment in a Well-Balanced Literacy Program K–3* (2004), *A Handbook for Literacy Instructional & Assessment Strategies K–8* (2006), and *Developing Content Area Literacy* (2010).

Lucy Murphy is a professor of education and teaches methods in science education at Iona College. She entered the profession as an elementary teacher and continued her career as a chemistry/biology teacher on the secondary level. She is currently involved in recruiting diverse candidates into the teaching profession.

Florence D. Musiello is the former director of student teaching at Iona College. Her experiences as an assistant superintendent for curriculum and instruction afforded her a wide range of instructional methods to draw on across the content areas. Dr. Musiello entered the profession as a public school teacher in New York City. She continued her career at the middle school level in Westchester County. These diverse settings provided her with myriad ways to differentiate instruction.

Eugene Wolfson is an associate professor at Iona College and works with teacher candidates to develop their teaching methods in literacy and language arts, as well as utilizing and developing strategies in assessment. His experience as a childhood teacher in New York City provided him the opportunity to incorporate effective instructional strategies to meet the needs of diverse students in a variety of settings. As a literacy specialist at the middle and high school levels, he served students and content area teachers to improve literacy across the curriculum. Lastly, Dr. Wolfson spent many years as an administrator of an early childhood program that provided him with a complete developmental perspective of literacy through the grades.

Contents

CHAPTER 2 ■ Journeys   41

CHAPTER 5 ■ Connections   169

CHAPTER 6 ■ Choices   207

Preface

As we enter the second decade of the new millennium, it is important to take stock of our literacy curriculum and evaluate its effectiveness. According to the National Assessment of Educational Progress (2007), U.S. students today have shown progress in mastering basic literacy skills but are faltering in terms of critical literacy. *Critical literacy* is defined as the ability to use reading, writing, listening, speaking, and viewing of text to evaluate and to unravel its layers of meaning in regard to the author's purpose and sociocultural context (Leu, Kinzer, Coiro, & Cammack, 2004). Critical literacy requires that students make inferences, analyze text, and see patterns across literature. In order to develop fluency in this type of literacy, students must be exposed to quality literature across genres and be able to comprehend multilayered texts and to grasp "big ideas" (Walmsley, 2006). As society moves increasingly toward online text and students are required to evaluate the accuracy of online information, the demand for critical literacy will increase (Leu, 2006).

■ Purpose of the Text

The purpose of this handbook, *Using Children's Literature Across the Curriculum*, is to provide pre-service and in-service teachers with a guide to using multilayered texts to facilitate students' attainment of critical literacy. It is designed to be a *supplemental text* to guide teachers in designing literacy instruction. This handbook uses quality children's literature to implement six themes across grades K–8. The themes are based on concepts gleaned from the national curriculum standards and are presented through text sets that have been carefully selected to facilitate discussion, analysis, and critical thinking across the grades. The national curriculum standards utilized in this handbook are from the following sources:

- National Council of Teachers of English and International Reading Association's *Standards for the English Language Arts* (1996), available at www.ncte.org/standards
- National Council of Teachers of Mathematics' *Principles and Standards for School Mathematics* (2000), available at http://standards.nctm.org
- National Council of Social Studies Teachers' *Expectations for Excellence: Curriculum Standards for Social Studies* (1994), available at www.socialstudies.org/standards
- National Committee on Science Education Standards and Assessment and the National Research Council's *National Science Education Standards* (1995), available at www.nap.edu/catalog.php?record_id = 4962
- International Society for Technology in Education's *National Educational Technology Standards for Students* (1998), available at www.iste.org/Content/Navigation Menu/NETS/ForStudents/1998Standards/NETS_for_Students_1998.htm

Each theme is divided into primary (kindergarten to grade 2), intermediate (grades 3 to 5), and middle grade (grades 6 to 8) instructional samplers. The samplers illustrate how the theme is rooted in national curriculum standards. A selected text set of quality children's literature is used to implement the theme in a literacy block. The instructional sequence, outlined as a guide for the teacher to follow, includes the following components:

- Learner outcomes
- Focus lessons
- Mini-lessons
- Reading and writing workshops

The instructional sequence also includes collaborative inquiry activities across the curriculum to extend the theme to math, technology, science, and social studies. Teachers are shown how to incorporate family literacy with Home–School Connections and differentiate instruction for individual learners with On-Your-Own Activities. The theme concludes with a critical literacy activity that applies the content knowledge of the theme with collaborative inquiry. Each chapter concludes with a resource section that outlines bibliographies and extension activities for each grade level. A unique feature of the handbook is the emphasis on performance-based assessment, with each instructional sequence containing rubrics for the teacher to implement. The instructional sequences are meant as models for teachers to use in developing their own themes in order to facilitate critical literacy. These models can be adjusted to fit the reading level of the students as teachers become more familiar with the text's structure and their students' needs.

■ Making It Your Own

The following vignette about Kate Harron, a first-grade teacher in Brooklyn, New York, is used to illustrate how to make the sampler fit your own instructional needs.

Kate Harron teaches first grade in a culturally diverse school where the majority of students are recent immigrants to the country. Kate needs literacy lessons that address the low-level readers of her class as well as the few students who are reading on a second-grade level. After reading the sampler in Chapter 1 entitled Changes in the Family, Ms. Harron uses the graphic illustrated in Figure 1 to adapt the instructional sequence. The first step in the graphic organizer is to examine the text set to see whether it addresses the needs and interests of the students. The focus lesson uses the text *A Piece of Home;* Ms. Harron believes that because her students are also immigrants they will respond to the characters in the story. However, because a majority of her class are struggling readers, she will tape record the story for English language learners to follow along. She will also use *The Always Prayer Shawl* with the higher-level readers. The second step in the graphic organizer calls for a review of the curriculum. Ms. Harron consults the district curriculum guide and selects state as well as district standards that are aligned with the learner outcomes of the lesson. The final step is to determine the resources available for the text set. Texts such as *The Always Prayer Shawl* and *The Relatives Came* are available in the reading coach's resource room. However, other texts will be substituted for the lower-level readers. Ms. Harron has also decided to modify the writing workshop activity by asking the special education coordinator to supply a scribe to accommodate the needs

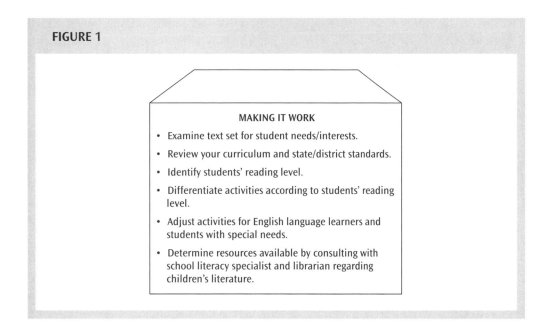

FIGURE 1

MAKING IT WORK

- Examine text set for student needs/interests.
- Review your curriculum and state/district standards.
- Identify students' reading level.
- Differentiate activities according to students' reading level.
- Adjust activities for English language learners and students with special needs.
- Determine resources available by consulting with school literacy specialist and librarian regarding children's literature.

of one of her students who has dyslexia. After planning the modifications, Ms. Harron is excited to begin her first instructional sequence.

As teachers become more proficient in using the handbook, they will become familiar with the necessary modifications for their class as each sampler is implemented. Gradually, teachers will be able to use quality children's literature across the curriculum as they help their students grasp "the big ideas" and develop advanced literacy skills to compete in the future.

What makes *Using Children's Literature Across the Curriculum* different from other literacy handbooks?

- *Using Children's Literature Across the Curriculum* outlines a complete instructional sequence that is rooted in national curriculum standards.
- Teachers are shown how to use text sets to facilitate critical literacy at the primary, intermediate, and middle grade levels.
- Assessment instruments are provided that are linked to instruction. Each instructional sequence contains a rubric for the instructional sequence and a holistic rubric to evaluate students' grasp of the theme.
- The diverse classroom of today is addressed and teachers are shown how to differentiate instruction and assessment for the twenty-first century classroom.

What are the special features of this handbook?

- Each sampler begins with graphic organizers that illustrate how the theme is implemented across the curriculum.
- Each chapter includes a primary, intermediate, and middle grade sampler so a theme can be implemented across grade levels.
- Each sampler shows how the theme is aligned to national curriculum standards and linked to assessment.
- Each sampler has an instructional sequence that outlines how to use the selected text set in a literacy block.

- Each chapter has a complete resource section that includes a bibliography for each grade level.
- Collaborative inquiry activities illustrate how the theme can be extended across the content areas.
- Family literacy is emphasized on every grade level with Home–School Connection activities.
- Assessment instruments linked to instructional strategies are included in every sampler.

Acknowledgments

We wish to thank all of our students and practicing teachers within our literacy programs at Iona College who tried out the text sets and instructional strategies in their classrooms and offered us valuable feedback. We also extend our gratitude to our reviewers: Cathy Blanchfield, California State University; Ward A. Cockrum, Northern Arizona University; Patricia DeMay, University of West Alabama; Stacey A. Dudley, Bowling Green State University; Deanna Gilmore, Washington State University; Amanda M. Grotting; Leslie Jacoby, San Jose State University; Margot Kinburg, National University; Peggy Rice, Ball State University; Barbara Smith Chalou, University of Maine; and Carolyn Spillman, Florida Gulf Coast University.

Finally, we are especially indebted to the wonderful team of editors at Allyn & Bacon who were responsible for this project from beginning to end. A special thanks to our editors, Linda Bishop and Aurora Martínez Ramos, who took the time to share their expertise with us.

References

International Society for Technology in Education. (1998). *National Educational Technology Standards for Students.* Eugene, OR: Author. Available at www.iste.org/content/NavigationMenu/NETS/ForStudents/1998Standards/NETS_for_Students_1998.htm

Leu, D. (2006). *The new literacies.* Paper presented at the International Reading Association's Research Conference, Chicago.

Leu, D., Kinzer, C., Coiro, J., & Cammack, D. (2004). Toward a theory of new literacies emerging from the Internet and other information and communication technologies. In R. Ruddell & N. Unrau (Eds.), *Theoretical models and processes of reading* (5th ed.) (pp. 1570–1614). Newark, DE: International Reading Association.

National Assessment of Educational Progress (NAEP). (2007). *The nation's report card: Reading 2007.* Retrieved August 1, 2009, from www.nces.ed.gov/nationsreportcard/pubs/main2007/2007496.asp

National Committee on Science Education Standards and Assessment & the National Research Council. (1995). *National science education standards.* Washington, DC: National Academies Press. Available at www.nap.edu/catalog.php?record_id=4962

National Council of Social Studies Teachers National Task Force for Social Studies. (1994). *Expectations for excellence: Curriculum standards for social studies.* NCSS Bulletin No. 89. Baltimore: Author. Available at www.socialstudies.org/standards

National Council of Teachers of English & International Reading Association. (1996). *Standards for the English language arts.* Newark, DE: Authors. Available at www.ncte.org/standards

National Council of Teachers of Mathematics. (2000). *Principles and standards for school mathematics.* Reston, VA: Author. Available at http://standards.nctm.org

Walmsley, S. (2006). Getting the big idea: A neglected goal for reading comprehension. *The Reading Teacher, 60*(3), pp. 281–285.

Change

The concepts of *time, continuity,* and *change* have been targeted by the National Council for the Social Studies (1994) as central themes for the new millennium. As students read and discuss award-winning literature with the theme of Change, they learn about the changes that occur within themselves, their families, and the world.

Chapter 1 facilitates this journey of change over time by presenting quality literature and instructional activities for primary, intermediate, and middle grade students. Instructional samplers or models are provided for each grade level, focusing on how families change due to conflicts or historical events. Students in the primary and intermediate grades are introduced to families that must leave their homeland and immigrate to America. The text selections *A Piece of Home* and *Maggie's Door* bring these families to life as students engage in the text. Students in the middle grades read and discuss *My Brother Sam Is Dead* to experience changes that are wrought by war. Although the text selections for each grade differ, the emerging theme is the enduring strength of the family unit throughout historical events and conflicts.

■ Primary Grades: Kindergarten–Grade 2

In *The Always Prayer Shawl* by Sheldon Oberman, a young Russian boy named Adam must leave his homeland behind and head for a new life in America with his family. Adam is allowed to bring his grandfather's prayer shawl with him to this strange new land. As he travels through the urban landscape of America, clutching his prayer shawl, Adam says, "I am always Adam and this is my Always Prayer Shawl. That won't change" (p. 12).

As students explore the theme of *change* in the primary grades, they will investigate how change affects their own families as well as the world around them. Children in the primary grades will relate new concepts to their own personal experiences. The primary grade sampler presented in this chapter facilitates this conceptual understanding by introducing children to change as it occurs in their own families.

In addition to the sub-theme Changes in the Family, illustrated in the graphic organizer, the students will read and write about books that examine how Animals Grow and Change, such as the metamorphosis of a caterpillar into a beautiful butterfly. In their immediate world, primary grade students will explore how families change due

PEOPLE WHO MADE CHANGES

Text Set

The Yellow Star
Dear Benjamin Banneker
Thomas Jefferson
Minty
Eleanor
Lives: Poems About Famous Americans

Outcomes

- Create a hand puppet of the person you admire who created change.
- Describe how you plan to change the world.
- Identify the character traits of Benjamin Banneker and Minty on a Venn diagram.
- Research someone living today who you feel is trying to make the world a better place.

SUDDEN NATURAL CHANGES

Text Set

Hurricane City
Magic School Bus Inside a Hurricane
Do Tornadoes Really Twist?
Hurricanes!

Outcomes

- Outline the states that tend to get hurricanes.
- Create a mural of a tornado in action.
- Research either a tornado or hurricane and present your information to the class in a panel presentation.
- Create a wall story of *Magic School Bus Inside a Hurricane*.

NEW FAMILY MEMBERS

Text Set

A New Barker in the House
Adoption Is for Always
The Memory Coat
When Jesse Came Across the Sea

Outcomes

- Write about a time you were new to a group and how it made you feel.
- Construct a character puppet of Jesse and dramatize her life story.
- Interview your family members about changes to your family.

World Changes

CHANGE

Family Changes

CHANGING OURSELVES

Text Set

The Human Body Explorer
Now We Are Six
When I Was Five
The Summer My Father Was Ten
Now I'm Big

Outcomes

- Construct a body outline and write how you will take healthy care of it.
- Measure your growth on a chart and check on progress each month.
- Retell the story *Now We Are Six* through a story board format.
- Write about your diet and exercise for one week and keep a chart of your progress.

Growth Changes

CHANGES IN THE FAMILY

Text Set

The Relatives Came
When I Was Young in the Mountains
The Patchwork Quilt
A Piece of Home
The Lotus Seed
The Always Prayer Shawl
Coming on Home Soon

Outcomes

- Write a letter to a grandparent about a family tradition.
- Construct a patchwork quilt that has symbols for the members of your family.
- Write a story about a family holiday or event like *When I Was Young in the Mountains*.

ANIMALS GROW AND CHANGE

Text Set

A Platypus Probably
Animals Born Alive and Well
From Caterpillar to Butterfly
Eliza and the Dragonfly
I See Animals Hiding

Outcomes

- Write a class wall story that retells how a caterpillar changes into a butterfly.
- Identify vocabulary words from the text set and use word cards to create sentences.
- Create your own picture book of animals and their young with research on each page.

to circumstances in the world or at home. Students will discover that, despite these changes, the customs and traditions that families celebrate remain.

The concept of family differs across today's society. Therefore, teachers need to be sensitive to the diversity of today's family units as they engage students in this sub-theme. A discussion of the many varied types of families would be a wonderful way to begin the sub-theme and invite students from nontraditional families to share their stories as well.

SAMPLER ▪ Changes in the Family

It is Monday morning in Ms. Harron's second grade class. Ms. Harron is introducing the students to the sub-theme Changes in the Family. She begins the read aloud by asking the students how they would feel if they had to leave their home. "I did leave my home!" yells Miguel. "Tell us what happened," responds Ms. Harron. Miguel begins his narrative with their drive from Mexico to Texas and how they left their grandparents and cousins behind. "The characters in our text set had very similar experiences to Miguel's," says Ms. Harron. She then begins the read aloud of *A Piece of Home.*

On the primary level, change is best studied by exploring how our families have evolved across generations. Grandparents today often describe the world of their childhoods and how it was very different from the technological society we enjoy today. As students explore their own family histories, they are making connections to their own lives and noting similarities among their fellow classmates. The primary grade subtheme of Changes in the Family allows the students to discuss why families change and how we share similar customs.

As students explore why some families have to leave their homelands, as in *A Piece of Home* or *The Lotus Seed*, they are learning the concept of *immigration.* This concept is introduced through family stories and provides a natural focal point to discuss how students' families came to America. As students explore their family histories and how their lifestyles have changed across generations, they are analyzing how societies and cultures share similar needs and desires (National Council of Social Studies, 1994).

The text set also explores traditions that are handed down across generations despite travel or the passage of time. In *The Always Prayer Shawl*, a young Russian boy treasures the prayer shawl given to him by his grandfather and later passes it on to his own grandson. A similar theme is presented in *The Patchwork Quilt*, as a family's story is revealed through a patchwork quilt. As students discuss the text set, they are learning to respect one another's cultures and traditions. In addition, the activities in the text set focus on our similarities as a society as we celebrate our own families' stories as well as that of the nation.

Primary grade students love to talk about their families and are interested in learning more about their history. This instructional sequence integrates the concept of Changes in the Family with students' developmental needs to discuss their families. The students will read and write about families from around the globe and across generations to discern how family customs and histories may change, but their own core values remain the same.

NCTE/IRA Standards for the English Language Arts

1. Students read a wide range of print and non-print texts to build an understanding of texts, of themselves, and of the cultures of the United States and the world.

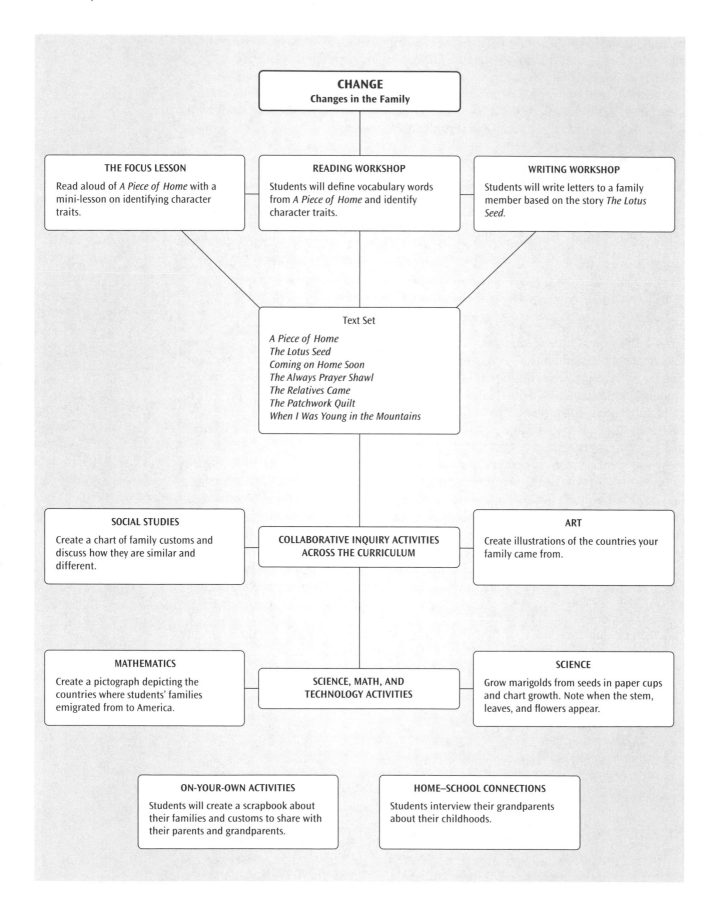

CHANGE
Changes in the Family

THE FOCUS LESSON
Read aloud of *A Piece of Home* with a mini-lesson on identifying character traits.

READING WORKSHOP
Students will define vocabulary words from *A Piece of Home* and identify character traits.

WRITING WORKSHOP
Students will write letters to a family member based on the story *The Lotus Seed*.

Text Set

A Piece of Home
The Lotus Seed
Coming on Home Soon
The Always Prayer Shawl
The Relatives Came
The Patchwork Quilt
When I Was Young in the Mountains

SOCIAL STUDIES
Create a chart of family customs and discuss how they are similar and different.

COLLABORATIVE INQUIRY ACTIVITIES ACROSS THE CURRICULUM

ART
Create illustrations of the countries your family came from.

MATHEMATICS
Create a pictograph depicting the countries where students' families emigrated from to America.

SCIENCE, MATH, AND TECHNOLOGY ACTIVITIES

SCIENCE
Grow marigolds from seeds in paper cups and chart growth. Note when the stem, leaves, and flowers appear.

ON-YOUR-OWN ACTIVITIES
Students will create a scrapbook about their families and customs to share with their parents and grandparents.

HOME–SCHOOL CONNECTIONS
Students interview their grandparents about their childhoods.

Learner Outcomes

Students will be able to do the following:

1. Identify and describe the elements of plot, setting, and character traits in a story.
2. Recollect, talk, and write about the story to make text-to-self connections.

Conduct a Focus Lesson

The focus lesson will engage students in a read aloud to explore differing family structures in the United States as well as across the globe. Children's literature that helps students identify character traits will be an integral part of the lesson.

Establish a Purpose   The text set for Changes in the Family includes award-winning literature that primarily focuses on how families change because of immigration or other situations that arise in the world. The focus lesson will feature *A Piece of Home* by Sonia Levitin, a story about a Russian family that leaves their home to join their relatives in America. Gregor's father tells the young boy that he can only take one item with him because the plane cannot carry everything they own. Gregor chooses the blanket that his great-grandmother made, because it makes him feel safe and secure. When he arrives in America, he is delighted to find that his cousin Elie doesn't think he is a baby for bringing his blanket—Elie has the same one from their great-grandmother proudly displayed in his bedroom!

The teacher will use a picture walk to begin the focus lesson and state the purpose of the lesson.

- The students will engage in a read aloud to hear about families from different cultures.
- The students will discuss how Gregor's family life changed when he moved from Russia to America.
- The students will identify Gregor's character traits and write about how they are similar or different from their own.

Engage in Read Aloud   The lesson begins with a read aloud of *A Piece of Home.*

- In order to prepare the students for the text set, the teacher conducts a brainstorming activity similar to Figure 1.1 to explore the theme of family change.
- After completing the chart and discussing their responses, the teacher begins the read aloud by conducting a picture walk. The students are shown a few pictures at the beginning, middle, and end of the story and asked to make predictions. The teacher can also ask the students what they think the title *A Piece of Home* means.
- As the teacher reads the text aloud, the students can use the picture clues and context of the sentence to define the words *garmoshka* (musical instrument) and *samovar* (Russian teapot). The students should also discuss how Gregor is feeling as the story unfolds.
- The teacher concludes the read aloud by asking the students to describe how Gregor and his family changed once they moved to America. The students will also be prompted to share similar experiences from their own lives.

Conduct a Mini-Lesson   After the read aloud, the teacher conducts a mini-lesson. The purpose of the mini-lesson is to describe the main character, Gregor.

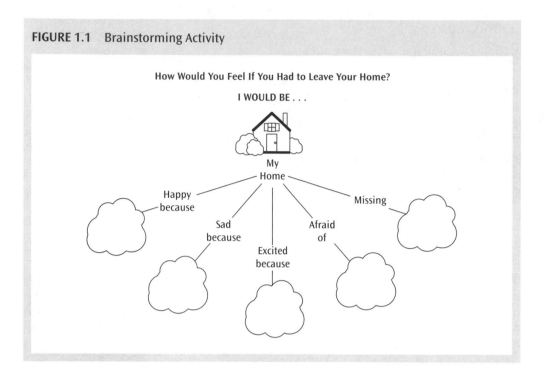

FIGURE 1.1 Brainstorming Activity

- The students can return to the focus question about leaving their homes and discuss how Gregor's family was able to adjust to their new life in America.
- The students will use adjectives to describe Gregor in a chart similar to Figure 1.2.
- As a summation of the lesson, the teacher selects students to come up to the chart to draw symbols for each character trait.
- After the students have completed the chart, they can create a character hand portrait by outlining a hand and writing Gregor's character traits on each finger (Antonacci & O'Callaghan, 2006).
- If students need a more challenging text, *The Always Prayer Shawl* can be used instead of *A Piece of Home.*

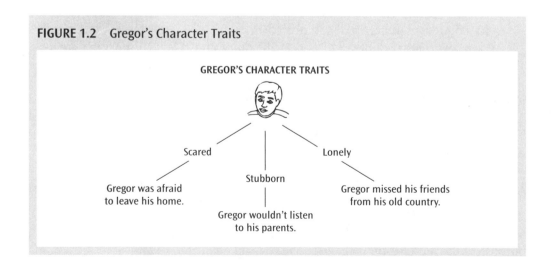

FIGURE 1.2 Gregor's Character Traits

Additional Mini-Lessons

Reading Comprehension

- Using the sketch to stretch strategy, the students draw their responses during and after the story.
- After they have finished drawing, students discuss their illustrations and how they represent their interpretations of the text.

Text-to-Text Connection

- After the students have finished the stories in the text set, they choose two main characters and compare their traits.
- The students then create a Venn diagram using the characters' traits.

ASSESS LITERACY

The rubric presented here may be used to focus the teacher's lens on student performance in the instructional sequence as the student identifies character traits. The rubric assesses the student's ability to describe character traits as well as to respond to the story.

Criteria	Independent	Proficient	Developing
Description of Character Traits	Student identifies several character traits and supports them with evidence from the text. (3)	Student identifies some character traits and supports them with evidence from the text. (2)	Student does not identify character traits and cannot cite evidence from the text. (0–1)
Student Participation	Student participates in discussion of character traits and focuses on the story. (3)	Student partially participates in discussion of character traits and focuses on the story. (2)	Student does not participate in discussion of character traits or focus on the story. (0–1)
Response to Story	Student provides a full response to the story and gives details about the plot and characters. (3)	Student provides a minimal response to the story and gives few details about the plot and characters. (2)	Student does not respond to the story and cannot provide details about the plot and characters. (0–1)
Analysis of Characters	Student compares/contrasts the character traits of the main characters in the text set. (3)	Student partially compares/contrasts the character traits of the main characters in the text set. (2)	Student does not compare/contrast the character traits of the main characters in the text set. (0–1)

Independent: 9–12
Proficient: 5–8
Developing: 0–4

- After completing the diagram, the students discuss the characters' similarities and differences.

Text-to-Self Connection

- Students write a journal entry in Gregor's voice as he arrives in America.
- Students then read aloud their journal entries and explain their interpretations of Gregor's character traits.

Conduct a Reading Workshop

The second text in the text set, *The Lotus Seed* by Sherry Garland, has a very similar theme to *A Piece of Home*. *The Lotus Seed* is about a Vietnamese woman who carries a lotus seed from the emperor's garden to her new home in America. When her grandson takes the seed and plants it in the garden, she is despondent—until one day it blooms and the whole family is given its seed in remembrance of Vietnam and the emperor.

In the reading workshop, the students apply their knowledge of how families change to the new story *The Lotus Seed*. Students will also be challenged to compare the character Gregor with the grandmother in *The Lotus Seed*.

Before Reading Before the students read, the teacher shows the students a picture of a lotus flower and asks them to describe the lotus flower and make predictions about the text. The students should also be shown Vietnam on the map and told that this is the setting for the first part of the story.

During Reading As the students are reading the text, the teacher stops to ask them to define the following words from context: *emperor, imperial, mother of pearl, ao dai (Vietnamese)*.

At the critical point when the lotus seed is lost, the teacher can ask the students to predict what will happen next in the story.

After Reading When the students complete their reading of the text, the teacher asks the students to recall their predictions. They then discuss the similarities between the grandmother in *The Lotus Seed* and Gregor in *A Piece of Home*. A Venn diagram can be drawn on chart paper to compare their character traits.

Conduct a Writing Workshop

The text set has several stories that show the main characters writing to family members to keep in contact. Therefore the focus of the writing workshop will be on letter writing.

Before Writing The writing workshop begins with a model of a letter from the grandmother in *The Lotus Seed* to her family back in Vietnam written on chart paper. The students are asked to come up to the chart to highlight the date, salutation and closing of the letter.

The students are then asked to select a family member they would like to write to and discuss their ideas for the content of the letters. The students are encouraged to write to relatives that have taught them about family customs or traditions.

During Writing Students may refer to the letter model when they need help in formatting their message. Some students may need to draw a picture first to generate text.

The teacher assesses the student's performance in reading workshop using this rubric.

Criteria	Advanced	Target	Developing	Needs Improvement
Making Predictions	Student uses prior knowledge to make predictions about and connections to the text. (4)	Student uses prior knowledge to make predictions about the text. (3)	Student uses prior knowledge to partially make predictions about the text. (2)	Student does not use prior knowledge to make predictions about the text. (0–1)
Defining Vocabulary Words	Student activates prior knowledge to define vocabulary words from context and continues to expand on definition. (4)	Student activates prior knowledge to define vocabulary words from context. (3)	Student, to some degree, activates prior knowledge to define vocabulary words from context. (2)	Student does not attempt to activate prior knowledge to define vocabulary words from context. (0–1)
Identifying Character Traits	Student uses prior knowledge and the text to compare and contrast character traits. (4)	Student uses the text to compare and contrast character traits. (3)	Student, to some degree, uses the text to compare and contrast character traits. (2)	Student does not use the text to compare and contrast character traits. (0–1)

Advanced: 10–12
Target: 7–9
Developing: 4–6
Needs Improvement: 0–3

They can also use their word journal or class word wall as reference tools for spellings. During the drafting and editing phase, the teacher works individually with students to help them to elaborate and use new vocabulary words.

After Writing   When the students have completed their letters, they can share them with a peer for editing. The teacher may want to encourage some students to share their letters with the whole class. After the letters have been revised, the students can address an envelope and mail their letters.

Collaborative Inquiry Across the Curriculum

The sub-theme of Changes in the Family has natural extensions to several different content areas integrating reading, writing, and critical thinking.

Extension to Mathematics   In *The Always Prayer Shawl*, the grandfather tells his grandson that even though he has changed a great deal over the years, his prayer shawl and traditions remained constant. As children discuss the countries of their families'

STANDARDS

Mathematics Standards
4. Measurement

ASSESS LITERACY

The teacher uses the following rubric to assess student work.

Criteria	Advanced	Target	Developing	Needs Improvement
Components of a Letter	Student is knowledgeable about components of a letter and applies them in creative ways. (4)	Student is knowledgeable about components of a letter and applies them. (3)	Student is somewhat knowledgeable about components of a letter and begins to apply them. (2)	Student is not knowledgeable about components of a letter and does not apply them. (0–1)
Planning	Student actively participates in planning letter and in discussing ideas in creative ways. (4)	Student actively participates in planning letter and in discussing ideas. (3)	Student is somewhat active in planning letter and in discussing ideas. (2)	Student does not actively plan letter and does not discuss ideas. (0–1)
Composing	Student uses the writing process, strategies, and reference material to compose letter. (4)	Student uses the writing process and some strategies to compose letter. (3)	Student, to a small degree, uses the writing process and some strategies to compose letter. (2)	Student does not use the writing process and strategies to compose letter. (0–1)
Editing	Student edits letter; reviews sentence structure, vocabulary, grammar, and spelling; and refers to sources to check content. (4)	Student edits letter and reviews sentence structure, vocabulary, grammar, and spelling. (3)	Student partially edits letter and reviews sentence structure, vocabulary, grammar, and spelling. (2)	Student does not edit letter or review sentence structure, vocabulary, grammar, and spelling. (0–1)

Advanced: 13–16
Target: 9–12
Developing: 5–8
Needs Improvement: 0–4

origins, they can begin to create a pictograph. The pictograph will display which countries the students' families came from, allowing students to see if anyone emigrated from the same location.

Extension to Science   In *The Lotus Seed*, the grandson plants a lotus seed and it blooms into a beautiful flower. The students can plant marigold seeds or lima beans in paper cups and record how long it takes for the stems, leaves, and finally the flowers to appear. After the students have completed their data charts, they can compare their findings and reach conclusions regarding the amount of time it takes a seed to blossom into a flower.

STANDARDS

Science Standards
Science as Inquiry,
Teaching Standard A1

FIGURE 1.3   Family Traditions Chart

Tradition	Description	Country of Origin
Paella	This is a dish my mother makes with rice and fish.	Spain
Polka	This is a dance I do with my grandparents.	Poland

Extension to Social Studies   The text set focuses on how families change as they become acclimated to American life. The stories also show that despite many changes, the families still retained some of their native customs and traditions. As students discuss the origins of their own families, the teacher can chart the countries where the family traditions originated, as illustrated in Figure 1.3. During collaborative literacy, the students can draw a picture of their family tradition next to each nation's flag.

Home–School Connections   The sub-theme Changes in the Family can be extended to the home through oral history interviews. The stories *The Relatives Came, When I Was Young in the Mountains,* and *The Patchwork Quilt* can be used as examples of family histories. The primary grade child can interview a grandparent or other elder in the community about a family tradition such as quilting. The students can report their findings in class and write a summary of the interviews in their journals.

On-Your-Own Activities   *Coming on Home Soon* by Jacqueline Woodson completes this text set and is an excellent choice for an independent literacy activity. It is about an African American girl whose mother has to work in Chicago on the railroad during World War II. The story depicts Ada Ruth's loneliness during this time, as well as her pride in her mother's achievements.

After the students have completed the text set, they can create a scrapbook on a family tradition to share with their grandparents or other elders. Students can include an illustration of themselves with their grandparent and a description of what they have learned from them. This activity helps the students value their own family customs and develop a sense of self as they study their family histories.

Critical Literacy

After completing the collaborative inquiry activities, it is important to help students synthesize their new concepts regarding change in families. As the theme is explored, students work with a partner to document their schema regarding change in families. At the completion of the unit, the students return to discuss how their schema regarding change in families has been deepened as they complete the critical thinking activity in Figure 1.4.

Collaborative Literacy

As a conclusion to the instructional sequence, the students can present a PowerPoint presentation on "How My Family Has Changed" for their parents and peers. The

STANDARDS

Social Studies Standards
II. Time, Continuity, and Change

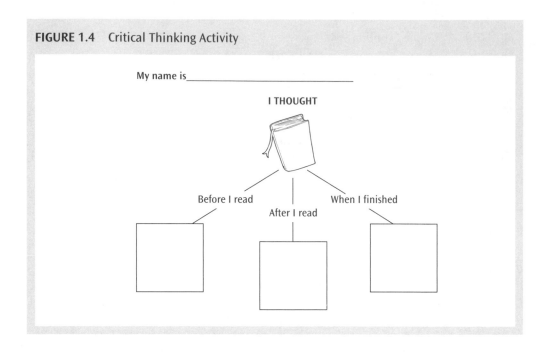

FIGURE 1.4   Critical Thinking Activity

My name is_____

I THOUGHT

Before I read

After I read

When I finished

students can describe how their families came to America and what customs they still practice in their homes. The presentation can also include the letter they wrote during writing workshop and the description of the family custom or tradition that they learned.

■ Intermediate Grades: Grades 3–5

With the stroke of her pencil, her dreams turn into pictures. Hollis Woods, who has spent all of her twelve years going from one foster home to another because she is a "mountain of trouble," longs for a family, but her attempts to become part of one place her in the midst of one crisis after another. In *Pictures of Hollis Woods* by Patricia Reilly Giff, students will see the dramatic change in Hollis as she connects to Josie, a foster mother who values the artistic instincts of her young charge. Josie, an elderly artist who accepts Hollis wholeheartedly and with honest affection, is also quite forgetful and somewhat eccentric, causing Social Services to remove Hollis to another foster home. Children will be able to connect to Hollis's challenge to fit into a loving family, and it is this very struggle that leads Hollis to the beginning of a deep personal growth.

In the intermediate grades, students will investigate the theme of Change by reading literature that is related to personal growth. Their explorations of the literature will deepen their own understandings of how people change and allow them to make connections to their personal lives as well as to others in their lives. They will begin to view personal growth as developing from a set of complex issues, rather than a simple change in one's life.

There are additional sub-themes within the theme Change that are illustrated in the graphic organizer. For example, the sub-theme Family Changes is key to the theme. Because of its significance in children's lives, this sub-theme is further developed through a study of three different causes for family changes—*famine, poverty, war,*

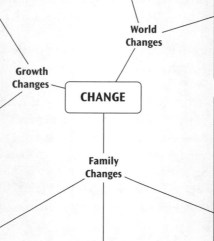

NATURAL CHANGES IN THE WORLD

Text Set

The Storm
Storm
Earth Alive!
The Day It Rained Forever
Night of the Twisters
Tornado!
Tornado
Lightning
Why Does Lightning Strike?
Quake!
Earthquake Terror
Why Do Volcanoes Blow Their Tops?

Outcomes

- Identify natural changes and the positive and negative effects that each have on the Earth, the people, and animals.
- Identify causes and effects of recent natural changes.

BECOMING COURAGEOUS

Text Set

Peeling the Onion
All By Herself: 14 Girls Who Made a Difference
Wringer
How Many Miles to Babylon?
Knots on a Counting Rope
Catch That Pass!
The Scared One
The Cat Who Escaped from Steerage

Outcomes

- Brainstorm ways fear was turned into courage.
- Retell a story involving personal courage.

INVENTORS WHO CHANGED THE WORLD

Text Set

Always Inventing: A Photobiography of Alexander Graham Bell
Benjamin Franklin: Printer, Inventor, Statesman
Girls and Young Women Inventing
Girls Think of Everything: Stories of Ingenious Inventions by Women
So You Want to Be an Inventor
TV's Forgotten Hero: The Story of Philo Farnsworth
Toilets, Toasters and Telephones: The Why and How of Everyday Objects

Outcomes

- Identify a problem that needs an invention for solution.
- Sequence possible steps and materials for invention.

GROWING-UP CHANGES

Text Set

All the Way Home
Pictures of Hollis Woods
Because of Winn-Dixie
The Tiger Rising
The Whipping Boy
The Hundred Dresses
Mr. Lincoln's Way

Outcomes

- Analyze a character from text set before, during, and after story.
- Identify personal changes.

World Changes

Growth Changes

CHANGE

Family Changes

CHANGES IN FAMILIES CAUSED BY FAMINE AND POVERTY

Text Set

A to Z: Ireland
Nory Ryan's Song
Maggie's Door
Katie's Wish
Black Potatoes
Potatoes, Potatoes
The Irish Potato Famine: The Birth of Irish America
Ashes of Roses
Streets of Gold
Under the Hawthorn Tree
Wildflower
So Far from Home
Potatoes

Outcomes

- Research Irish population growth during the famine.
- Create an Alphabet Book of facts about the Irish Famine.
- Conduct an experiment on growing potatoes.

CHANGES IN FAMILIES CAUSED BY HOMELESSNESS

Text Set

The Family Under the Bridge
Sophie and the Sidewalk Man
We Are All in the Dumps with Jack and Guy
Homeless Children
Family Pose
Monkey Island
Homecoming
The Midwife's Apprentice

Outcomes

- Research homelessness in the community and possible solutions.
- Brainstorm ways students can get involved in the fight against homelessness.

CHANGES IN FAMILIES CAUSED BY WAR

Text Set

I Am David
Number the Stars
The Orphans of Normandy
Lily's Crossing
Along the Tracks
Erika's Story

Outcomes

- Research current global conflicts and present information to class.
- Identify ways global conflicts have changed family life.
- Compare/contrast changes in families from text set with real life.

and *homelessness*. In addition to this sub-theme, students will also use literature to explore World Changes.

SAMPLER ■ Changes in Families Caused by Famine and Poverty

At first it seems that Nory and her friend Sean are playing like all 12-year-old children, by the cliffs of Maidin Bay on the west coast of Ireland, Sean has just finished searching for food to eat. With delight, he offers Nory a bit of purple seaweed. Nory's hunger causes her to eat this unsavory morsel with great delight. Early in *Nory Ryan's Song* by Patricia Reilly Giff, students learn why millions of Irish leave their families and their beloved Ireland. "We will be there one day in Brooklyn," Sean says to Nory as they both look at the bay. What happens to courageous Nory Ryan as she helps her family through the darkest days of starvation? The reader will again meet Nory and Sean in the sequel, *Maggie's Door.* Unable to endure the starvation, Nory and her family and friends embark on a perilous voyage to join her older sister Maggie in Brooklyn, New York.

Nory Ryan's Song and *Maggie's Door,* along with other informational and historical fiction books, help students to further develop their understandings of the conditions and causes that led to emigration from Ireland and the dangerous voyages taken by those who sought freedom in America. Extension activities will help students make important connections between the Great Irish Famine and those suffering from starvation within their own communities as well as in other countries. Further, during the instructional and independent activities, the teacher will help students see how famine and starvation can cause family changes.

The major focus of the instructional sequence is to deepen students' knowledge of the causes of emigration from Ireland during 1846 to 1852 as they develop literacy skills. Additionally, students are expected to learn the effects that famine had on the lives of Irish families who left for other countries. Through literature and related content-area activities, students will learn that the poverty, starvation, and death of so many people during this period of history resulted from a complex set of causes rather than one event, the failure of the potato crop. Students will learn that these causes not only changed families, but in many ways changed the course of Irish history.

NCTE/IRA Standards for the English Language Arts

1. Students read a wide range of print and non-print texts to build an understanding of texts, of themselves, and of the cultures of the United States and the world; to acquire new information; to respond to the needs and demands of society and the workplace; and for personal fulfillment. Among these texts are fiction and nonfiction, classic and contemporary works.

Learner Outcomes

Students will be able to do the following:

■ Participate in a shared reading to learn from firsthand accounts about the Irish famine during 1846 to 1852.
■ Relate firsthand accounts to their own experiences.
■ Write about how the potato famine caused the Irish to emigrate from their homeland.

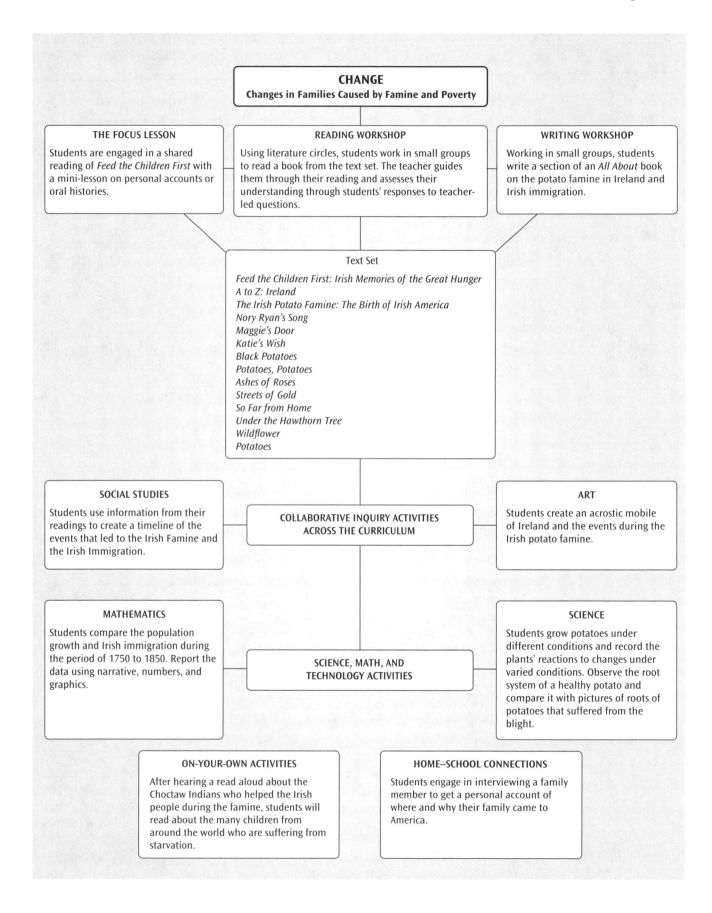

CHANGE
Changes in Families Caused by Famine and Poverty

THE FOCUS LESSON

Students are engaged in a shared reading of *Feed the Children First* with a mini-lesson on personal accounts or oral histories.

READING WORKSHOP

Using literature circles, students work in small groups to read a book from the text set. The teacher guides them through their reading and assesses their understanding through students' responses to teacher-led questions.

WRITING WORKSHOP

Working in small groups, students write a section of an *All About* book on the potato famine in Ireland and Irish immigration.

Text Set

Feed the Children First: Irish Memories of the Great Hunger
A to Z: Ireland
The Irish Potato Famine: The Birth of Irish America
Nory Ryan's Song
Maggie's Door
Katie's Wish
Black Potatoes
Potatoes, Potatoes
Ashes of Roses
Streets of Gold
So Far from Home
Under the Hawthorn Tree
Wildflower
Potatoes

SOCIAL STUDIES

Students use information from their readings to create a timeline of the events that led to the Irish Famine and the Irish Immigration.

COLLABORATIVE INQUIRY ACTIVITIES ACROSS THE CURRICULUM

ART

Students create an acrostic mobile of Ireland and the events during the Irish potato famine.

MATHEMATICS

Students compare the population growth and Irish immigration during the period of 1750 to 1850. Report the data using narrative, numbers, and graphics.

SCIENCE, MATH, AND TECHNOLOGY ACTIVITIES

SCIENCE

Students grow potatoes under different conditions and record the plants' reactions to changes under varied conditions. Observe the root system of a healthy potato and compare it with pictures of roots of potatoes that suffered from the blight.

ON-YOUR-OWN ACTIVITIES

After hearing a read aloud about the Choctaw Indians who helped the Irish people during the famine, students will read about the many children from around the world who are suffering from starvation.

HOME–SCHOOL CONNECTIONS

Students engage in interviewing a family member to get a personal account of where and why their family came to America.

■ Participate in a guided discussion of *Nory Ryan's Song* and respond to questions about the conditions in Ireland that caused immigration to America.

Conduct a Focus Lesson

Use a shared reading activity as the focus lesson to engage students in learning about how the Irish Potato Famine, poverty, and governmental rule instigated major changes in Irish families. *Feed the Children First: Irish Memories of the Great Hunger,* edited by Mary E. Lyons, is a unique informational book that combines art with personal accounts. It brings to life the Irish people and their customs; the famine, starvation, and poverty they endured; and the consequences of governmental rule that eventually caused thousands of Irish families to emigrate from their homeland. Mary Lyons accomplishes this through a collection of artwork and first-person accounts by those who remember the Great Hunger. The following shared reading activity will provide students with background knowledge of the Irish famine, the potato blight, and the concept of emigration from Ireland required for students' further readings. The mini-lesson following the shared reading will introduce students to first-person accounts and oral histories.

Establish a Purpose   Gathering the students together in a circle, the teacher begins by showing pictures of the Great Irish Famine from the book *Feed the Children First: Irish Memories of the Great Hunger.* The pictures provide a glimpse into the lives and tragic times of the Irish people during the Great Hunger. Using the pictures as a tool to begin discussion, the teacher relates the purpose of the lesson.

■ They will hear *first-person accounts, real stories,* or *oral histories* from many different Irish people who remembered the Great Hunger.
■ They will learn how the failure of the potato crop, religious persecution, and English rule over Ireland caused starvation and emigration from Ireland.
■ They will read and write about how the potato famine changed the lives of Irish families when they were forced to emigrate from the country they loved so much in order to save their lives.

Engage in Shared Reading   The teacher introduces the book by giving an overview of the genre and content of *Feed the Children First: Irish Memories of the Great Hunger.* During the book introduction, the emphasis is placed on the literary style utilized by the author, the use of first-person accounts to write about history. The table of contents provides the students with an overview of Irish history that is developed through oral histories: background for the Great Hunger (1845–1852); the people and their homes; the potato blight, famine, starvation, and searching for food; soup kitchens and evictions from their homes; and emigration from Ireland.

Having prepared the students to listen to this unique informational book, the teacher selects three short oral histories that will be read aloud: (1) "The Great Hunger (1845–1852)," including the role of government during the famine; (2) "The People" and how they survived through storytelling and music; and (3) "The Potato Blight." After reading each section, the teacher stops to engage students in a discussion, sharing their responses and interpretations of the reading. The teacher concludes with an emphasis on the academic vocabulary that was part of the readings and discussions.

Conduct a Mini-Lesson   *Feed the Children First* is a compelling story of the Irish Famine told through pictures and first-person accounts of those who remembered the Great

Hunger. Within this mini-lesson, the teacher focuses on the definitions of first-person accounts or oral histories and how they are used in this informational book to tell the story of the Irish Famine.

Reading a short section of the book called "Searching for Food" (pp. 18–19), the teacher tells how oral histories provide a personal understanding of "history in the making" by showing what can be learned about history from this first-person account. The teacher then models to the students a first-person account shared in his or her own family and asks the students to think about a true story told to them by an older person in their family. Students can share their family stories with the class.

Additional Mini-Lessons

Academic Vocabulary

- Select approximately 8 to 10 key words for understanding that will appear in most of the readings.
- Conduct an active discussion of each word to develop a class word web. Emphasize the contextual definition of the word.
- Encourage students to add new words from their readings to the word web and record new information they have learned about a word.

Activate and Build Prior Knowledge

- Prior to the discussion of the shared reading, ask students what they know about famine and list it on a K-W-L chart.
- Engage students in a discussion on what they want to learn about the Great Irish Famine and Irish families and have them list their ideas on the chart.
- After the reading, have them list all the new ideas that they learned from the reading.
- Encourage students to use the K-W-L strategy on their own during independent reading.

Text-to-Self Connections

- Invite students to make personal connections to the story, recording them on large chart paper.
- Encourage students to continue to make personal connections during their readings and to record them in their journals.

Conduct a Reading Workshop

The focus lesson provides the background knowledge of the Irish Famine that students need to read and understand the significance of the historical novel *Nory Ryan's Song*. The teacher works with a group of seven students who are reading *Nory Ryan's Song* while other students in different literature circles read related literature from the text set.

Before Reading   During the introduction of *Nory Ryan's Song*, the teacher makes a connection between historical fiction and informational books written as first-person accounts such as *Feed the Children First: Irish Memories of the Great Hunger*, which students heard during the shared reading.

The teacher begins by reading the epilogue aloud to the students that explains why the book was written and how the author gathered the information to write about a young girl who suffered through the Irish Famine. Why did one million of the eight million Irish people die from starvation? And why did over one million people leave their homeland? No one in her family spoke of those times, but author Patricia Reilly Giff knew that if her Irish grandmother were alive, she would tell her the story. Giff traveled to Ireland many times, seeing the places where her family lived as well as the memorials in Roscommon and Cobh, and asking people she met to tell her anything they remembered hearing about the Famine. With all of the bits of information from the many Irish who told their stories, the author tells how she saw the different characters in her story emerge. She saw the little cottages that might have been like the house where the old woman Anna and the Ryan family lived. The teacher's introduction of the epilogue helps students learn that the author's use of the myriad collection of memories of the Irish people creates a wonderful story of a family suffering through the Irish Famine and immigrating to Brooklyn, New York.

Prior to their reading, the teacher asks students to turn to the glossary containing nine words from the Irish language (Gaelic), including pronunciations and translations. The teacher begins a brief discussion of the meanings and the pronunciations of the words, making a request for similar words that are used in our language. Modeling how to use the glossary during reading, the teacher reads a sentence with a Gaelic word, turns to the glossary to show how to find its meaning, and continues to read to the end of the sentence.

The first three chapters focus on the hunger of Nory Ryan and her family and friends. The teacher will help students understand the setting by referring to "Searching for Food" in the shared reading, *Feed the Children First*. The teacher shows the students the picture from that section and tells them to think about the meaning of the picture to further understand the plight of the characters in *Nory Ryan's Song*.

During Reading   As the students begin to read the first three chapters of *Nory Ryan's Song* independently, the teacher reminds them that they will read about Nory Ryan's search for food for her family. Where does she look? Are there any dangers in her way?

After Reading   The teacher engages students in a guided discussion of their reading of the first three chapters by using the questions outlined in Figure 1.5. The purpose of the discussion is to elicit students' responses to the reading and to develop their knowledge of the conditions in Ireland that caused emigration from Ireland to America and other countries.

After the discussion, the teacher directs the students to pretend to be a friend of Nory and write a personal account of her hunger, fear, bravery, and search for food.

Throughout the week, the students engage in reading *Nory Ryan's Song* until its completion. The teacher will use the same format for literature circles described above:

FIGURE 1.5   Guiding Questions for Post-Reading Discussion

- How would you feel if you were Nory Ryan or her friend Sean? How would you feel if you had no food to eat?
- Find a part in the story that shows the hunger and poverty of the people and read it to us. Tell why you selected that passage.
- Why was Nory Ryan so frightened of Lord Cunningham?

ASSESS LITERACY

The teacher assesses the students' performances in literature circles, including (1) students' level of engagement during silent reading, (2) students' participation in discussions, (3) the nature of students' responses during the discussion, and (4) students' ability to raise questions about their readings. The teacher observes students' performances during post-reading discussion using the following rubric.

Criteria	Independent	Proficient	Developing
Silent Reading	Student is highly engaged during silent reading, remaining on task throughout the allotted time. (3)	Student is engaged during silent reading, remaining on task for most of the allotted time. (2)	Student is somewhat engaged during silent reading, remaining on task for some of the allotted time. (0–1)
Student Participation in Discussion	Student actively participates in discussions, is highly engaged in listening to group members, takes turns, and respond to others with respect at all times. (3)	Student participates in discussions, listens to group members, takes turns, and responds to others most of the time. (2)	Student participates in discussions to some degree, begins to listen to group members, takes turns, and respond to others some of the time. (0–1)
Discussion Responses	Student gives elaborate, accurate responses to teacher-led questions; frequently incorporates language from readings; at times, includes critical analysis within the response; and makes varied types of text connections. (3)	Student gives fairly accurate responses to teacher-led questions, at times incorporates language from readings, attempts to include a critical analysis within the response, and makes some types of text connections. (2)	Student gives very brief and minimally accurate responses to teacher-led questions, rarely incorporates language from readings in the response, and does not make text connections. (0–1)
Raising Questions	Student poses thoughtful and honest questions about the readings. (3)	Student poses some questions about the readings. (2)	Student does not initiate questions about the readings. (0–1)
Independent: 9–12 Proficient: 5–8 Developing: 0–4			

(1) prepare the students for reading, (2) direct students in a discussion after reading, and (3) provide students with an opportunity to respond in their journals.

Conduct a Writing Workshop

The teacher introduces the instructional activity *All About* Book, a class project for all students. They will co-author a book about Irish immigration and the Irish Famine

FIGURE 1.6   Topics for *All About Irish Immigration*

1. The Irish People
2. Location of Ireland and Its Land
3. The People Who Ruled the Irish People
4. The Houses and the Land of Ireland
5. The Potato Blight
6. The Great Hunger 1845–1852
7. Searching for Food to Feed Their Families
8. The Government and the Starving People
9. Those Who Tried to Help the Starving People
10. Dying from the Famine
11. Emigration to America

entitled *All About Irish Immigration.* Students work in pairs on a sub-topic and collaborate on writing their parts of the informational book. They gather ideas from their readings to write one or two pages that include illustrations.

Before Writing   The students brainstorm possible topics that they would like to write about. As the discussion begins, the teacher makes a list of topics the students request. The teacher keeps the discussion lively by directing their attention to their journals and the books that they are reading during reading workshop and independent reading. Figure 1.6 shows a list of possible topics.

The students choose a topic that they know well, have an interest in, and would like to write about. Working in groups of three, they use a web to begin the process of brainstorming ideas they already know about the topic. They then reread books, consult the Internet for relevant websites, and find new books to gather more facts.

During Writing   Working in small groups, the students begin to write their first draft. Conferring with groups, the teacher reminds students to follow the book guidelines, and most importantly, to write ideas that relate to their topic.

The teacher listens in to one group reading their interpretation of "The Potato Blight." One student insists on writing about the cause of the blight, because she has read a lot about the fungus that destroyed the potatoes. Another student goes back to rework the paragraph, adding the years for different blights that ruined the potato crops, and the third is busy drawing a healthy potato and a comparison illustration of one that has been attacked by the fungus. The illustrator asks help from the group as he works, labeling the parts of the potato on his drawings.

After Writing   Each small group of students works on the revisions for their part of the book. The teacher monitors their work so that each part provides a good fit for the class book, *All About Irish Immigration.* After each part is revised and edited, the sections are bound into one book.

STANDARDS

Mathematics Standards
  2. Algebra

Technology Standards
  5. Technology Research Tools

Collaborative Inquiry Across the Curriculum

Extension to Mathematics and Technology   A dramatic number of Irish people were forced to immigrate to America and Canada during the period of the Great Hunger (1845–1852). Starvation also caused many people to die, with few surviving and remaining in Ireland.

ASSESS LITERACY

The teacher uses the following rubric to assess students' work.

Criteria	Independent	Proficient	Developing
Content	Student integrates the content about the Irish immigration throughout the text. (3)	Student integrates some content about the Irish immigration in the text. (2)	Student does not integrate the content about the Irish immigration in the text. (0–1)
Planning	All parts are present, well-developed, and written in a logical sequence. (3)	All parts are present and written in a sequence that the reader can follow. (2)	Text does not have a logical order and parts are not easy for the reader to follow. (0–1)
Sentence Structure	Student employs varied types of sentences in writing, using some complex structures when appropriate. (3)	Student uses sentences that are somewhat simple, but accurate. (2)	Student uses sentence structure that is simple and not always accurate. (0–1)
Vocabulary	Student consistently uses content vocabulary throughout with a high degree of accuracy. (3)	Student uses some of the content vocabulary from Irish immigration; may use words incorrectly. (2)	Student does not use the content vocabulary from study of Irish immigration. (0–1)
Language Mechanics	No errors in language mechanics are present. (3)	Some errors in language mechanics are present but do not interfere with meaning. (2)	Many errors in language mechanics appear throughout. (0–1)

Independent: 11–15
Proficient: 6–10
Developing: 0–5

The teacher has the students use the Internet to locate the number of Irish people who remained in their country and the number that fled to North America from 1845 to 1852, as well as the number of people who died of starvation during that same time. Students present descriptive comparisons through the use of narrative text, bar graphs, line graphs, and pictographs. They complete the activity with summary statements that interpret the data and draw conclusions.

Extension to Science Students have learned about the fungus that attacked the potato plant through their readings. The teacher extends their knowledge by studying the growing conditions that support healthy crops and having the students read their science textbook. They also use two pieces of children's literature as resources, *Potatoes* and *Plant Fun: Ten Easy Plants to Grow Indoors*. The teacher shows students how to grow potatoes under different conditions by changing one or two variables for each

STANDARDS

Science Standards
Life Science, Content
Standards C1 and C3

plant. Students observe and carefully record in their science journals the plants' reactions to changes in the control variables of (1) water, (2) fertilizer, and (3) light. Their science journals include the following information: (1) changes in growth, (2) changes in leaf color, and (3) the number of blooms, their size, and the number of potatoes. The comparison of the roots of a healthy potato with one that had a potato disease *(Phythophthora infestans)* using pictures from the *Illustrated London News* of August 1846 (found on the Internet) will help students understand the blight that attacked the potato, causing the famine.

STANDARDS

Social Studies Standards
III. People, Places, and Environments

Extension to Social Studies The teacher and students construct a pictorial timeline for the events they learned about Irish immigration (see Figure 1.7). First, they brainstorm the events that led to the Irish Famine and the events that happened during and after the famine. They write their ideas on large chart paper. Next, they write the year or approximate year that each event occurred. The teacher constructs a timeline of events by placing the dates in sequence on a line. Together, students and teacher write each event on the timeline under its date. Finally, they discuss each event and draw a picture under the event.

Home–School Connections Students learn the significance of first-person accounts and oral histories by listening to *Feed the Children First* and reading historical fiction

FIGURE 1.7 Timeline of Events That Led to Irish Immigration

TIMELINE OF EVENTS THAT LED TO IRISH IMMIGRATION

1800	Ireland became part of Great Britain
1803	Irish people fight the English but lose
1829	Irish were given some rights but were still poor
1845	A plant fungus caused the potato crops in Ireland to die
1846	The plant fungus attacked again
1847	Millions of Irish were sick and dying from starvation and from fever (Black '47)
	The English government took away any help for the hungry people
	The Irish received help from English businessmen and from Quakers
1847–1852	Over a million of the Irish people died
	1.5 million Irish left Ireland by boat
1852	Potato blight ended

based on stories of the Irish people, such as *Nory Ryan's Song* and *Maggie's Door.* The teacher can use these as motivation for students to discover their own histories through an oral history project focused on family immigration. They are directed to interview an older family member to gather personal histories. The teacher prepares students for this project by doing the following:

- First, the teacher works with students on developing appropriate questions, using open-ended queries to elicit more information.
- Secondly, the teacher helps students consider content, formulating a line of questioning that will provide them with useful information.
- The teacher suggests methods for writing down or recording the conversations so that important stories will not be lost.
- Students collect or draw pictures of family events and add them to their projects.

On-Your-Own Activities   Prior to independent reading, the teacher reads aloud the sophisticated picture storybook *Long March: The Choctaw's Gift to Irish Famine Relief.* This compelling piece of literature is meant to develop a disposition toward aiding others who are in need. A deeply moving story, it reveals how the Choctaw Indians suffered under the rule of the United States government; they were forced from their land, made to walk 500 miles to Indian territory, and suffered from starvation when they did not receive the promised provisions. When the call came from Europe to America to help the hungry in Ireland, it was the Choctaw who responded with help by collecting money from their meager earnings.

After hearing this story, students access information from Internet sites about hungry children living in different parts of the world today and keep notes in their journals. Three websites with appropriate information are the following:

- UNICEF: www.unicef.org
- Share Our Strength: www.strength.org
- International Famine Centre: www.ucc.ie/famine

Critical Literacy

One aspect of critical literacy is the ability to synthesize and evaluate information from the Internet and to use the process to deepen knowledge. After students have completed activities related to the Irish Famine, they brainstorm ways to help those suffering from hunger. Students form panels to review ideas and evaluate their feasibility. After each panel has presented, the class votes on which project to develop in order to help children in need around the globe.

Collaborative Literacy

The teacher provides time to share the class book *All About Irish Immigration* through a book celebration called "The Author's Tea." During the celebration of their writing, students read sections and pass the book on to other class authors. They may discuss how they found the information and why they thought it was important to include in the book. Finally, *All About Irish Immigration* receives honorable status by being placed on the bookshelf along with the literature from the text set about Ireland that they have read.

■ Middle Grades: Grades 6–8

The year is 1775 and Daniel West has a decision to make. Like Daniel, Jonathan knows he is ready to fight the British despite his father's disapproval, and Tim Meeker worries that his brother Sam's conviction that the rebel cause is worth fighting for will cause yet another argument with his father. The Revolutionary War will change their lives and personal relationships forever.

During middle school, students begin the formal study of history, because they are now cognitively able to integrate concepts of time, chronology, and multiple perspectives. As students seek to understand their historical roots and locate themselves in time, they will read fiction and nonfiction to reconstruct the past and to answer such questions as, How am I connected to the past? How has my country and the world changed and how have these changes affected my life? (National Council of Social Studies, 1994). Although history textbooks present the sequence of events that lead to political and social change, they are not effective in helping students make personally meaningful connections to the past. Unlike textbooks, narrative historical fiction brings the events of history to life by focusing on the stories of the ordinary and extraordinary people who lived through a specific period of time. The strong literary elements in this genre capture preadolescent readers and engage them in an intimate reading experience as they attempt to solve problems, achieve goals, and witness the personal growth of the main characters.

Political events provide teachers with the opportunity to help preadolescents focus not only on curricular content but on their personal concerns, increasing the possibility that students will see how school subjects relate to their lives. As young Tim Meeker in *My Brother Sam Is Dead* looks on while his rebel brother Sam and loyalist father confront each other, the students not only investigate their political views and divided loyalties but also watch how Tim changes and grows when the war engulfs his family's life. They also examine how *Johnny Tremain,* Daniel West in *Early Thunder,* and Jonathan in *The Fighting Ground* struggle with family views and personal beliefs and compare the character's conflicts to the differences in perspectives they are experiencing with their own families.

SAMPLER ■ Revolution and Personal Growth

The American Revolution not only caused many changes in the lives of the American people but also instigated political revolution in other nations around the world. Young adult literature about the American Revolution provides us with many powerful and compelling stories that will enable students to see the Loyalist and Patriot perspectives through the eyes of characters of their own age and discover that the issues in war are seldom clear.

When Tim's brother Sam bursts into the tavern with the exciting news that the Minutemen have beaten the British in Massachusetts, everyone is shocked. Most people in Redding, Connecticut, are Tories who think the colonists have some legitimate conflicts with the British government but that none are serious enough to fight over—but not 16-year-old Sam. Told through the eyes of his younger brother, Tim, *My Brother Sam Is Dead* is a moving story about the family conflicts and bitter events that grip the lives of ordinary people. Students watch Tim grow from a nervous observer of conflicts between Sam and his father to a resourceful youth who struggles to keep his family intact.

CONFLICT CAUSES PERSONAL GROWTH

Text Set

The Giver
The Language of Goldfish
Tuck Everlasting
The Secret Garden
Saying Goodbye
Night Kites

Outcomes

- Identify and describe an area of personal growth.

- Engage in simulated dialogue from the perspective of a main character from text set.

PEOPLE, POLITICS, AND CHANGE

Text Set

B. Franklin, Printer
John Adams (Presidential Leaders)
Abigail Adams: Witness to a Revolution
Paul Revere's Ride
Samuel Adams: The Father of American Independence
George Washington & The Founding of a Nation
Thomas Jefferson: The Revolutionary Aristocrat
Tom Paine: Voice of Revolution

Outcomes

- Create an organized cluster to illustrate the personal qualities, actions, and effectiveness of a specific revolutionary leader.

REVOLUTION AND PERSONAL GROWTH

Text Set

My Brother Sam Is Dead
The Fighting Ground
Johnny Tremain
Early Thunder
The Winter of Red Snow
Sarah Bishop
I'm Deborah Sampson
The Hollow Tree
Thomas in Danger
The Secret of Sarah Revere
Or Give Me Death

Outcomes

- Write double-entry journals to monitor how characters change and grow.

- Participate in literature circles to discuss the beliefs, values, and events that influence a character's change.

- Create diaries to describe events and conflicts of daily life during the American Revolution.

Growth

World Changes

UNITED STATES: AN EXPERIMENT IN GOVERNMENT

Text Set

Shh! We're Writing the Constitution
If You Were There When They Signed the Constitution
A More Perfect Union: The Story of Our Constitution
The Constitutional Convention
The Bill of Rights: How We Got It and What It Means
The American Revolutionaries: A History in Their Own Words 1750–1800
If You Were There in 1776
The Declaration of Independence
The Bill of Rights: The First Ten Amendments of the Constitution

Outcomes

- Explain how each of the documents changed political thought and practice then and how the ideas set forth influence our lives now.

CHANGE

Family Changes

DEATH AND DIVORCE

Text Set

Flip Flop Girl
Walk Two Moons
Baby
Midnight Hour Encores
Divorce Express
Thin Ice

Outcomes

- Identify events that are turning points in the story.

- Create open-mind portraits of a main character to identify their thoughts during plot.

DEFINING FAMILY AND HOME

Text Set

After the Rain
The Great Gilly Hopkins
Where the Lillies Bloom
Missing May
Dear Mr. Henshaw
Monkey Island

Outcomes

- Brainstorm definitions for *family*.

- Summarize the group's findings to reach consensus regarding definition of *family*.

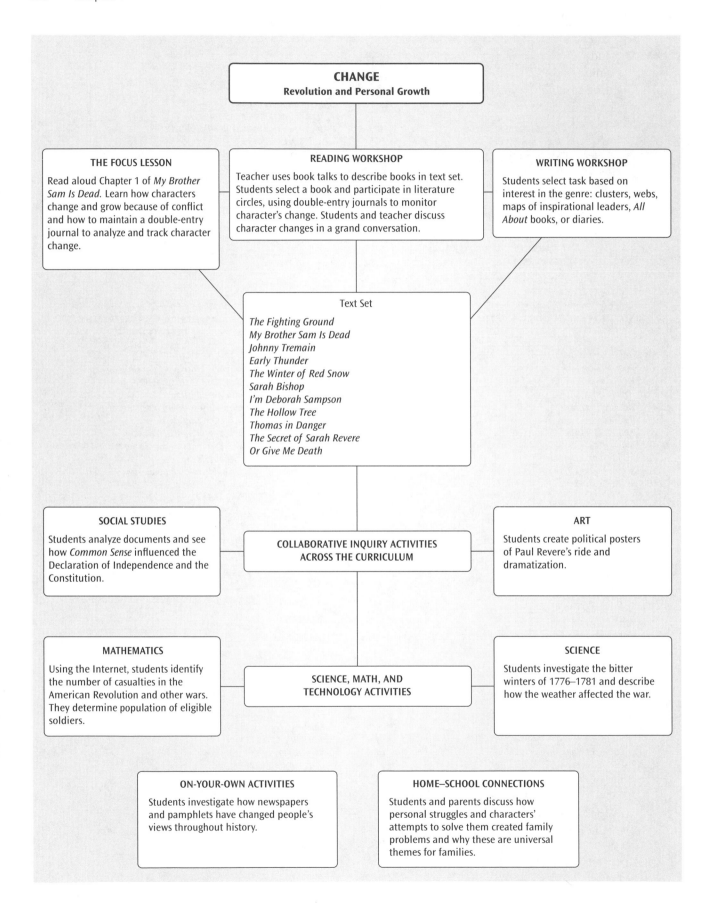

CHANGE
Revolution and Personal Growth

THE FOCUS LESSON

Read aloud Chapter 1 of *My Brother Sam Is Dead*. Learn how characters change and grow because of conflict and how to maintain a double-entry journal to analyze and track character change.

READING WORKSHOP

Teacher uses book talks to describe books in text set. Students select a book and participate in literature circles, using double-entry journals to monitor character's change. Students and teacher discuss character changes in a grand conversation.

WRITING WORKSHOP

Students select task based on interest in the genre: clusters, webs, maps of inspirational leaders, *All About* books, or diaries.

Text Set

The Fighting Ground
My Brother Sam Is Dead
Johnny Tremain
Early Thunder
The Winter of Red Snow
Sarah Bishop
I'm Deborah Sampson
The Hollow Tree
Thomas in Danger
The Secret of Sarah Revere
Or Give Me Death

SOCIAL STUDIES

Students analyze documents and see how *Common Sense* influenced the Declaration of Independence and the Constitution.

COLLABORATIVE INQUIRY ACTIVITIES ACROSS THE CURRICULUM

ART

Students create political posters of Paul Revere's ride and dramatization.

MATHEMATICS

Using the Internet, students identify the number of casualties in the American Revolution and other wars. They determine population of eligible soldiers.

SCIENCE, MATH, AND TECHNOLOGY ACTIVITIES

SCIENCE

Students investigate the bitter winters of 1776–1781 and describe how the weather affected the war.

ON-YOUR-OWN ACTIVITIES

Students investigate how newspapers and pamphlets have changed people's views throughout history.

HOME–SCHOOL CONNECTIONS

Students and parents discuss how personal struggles and characters' attempts to solve them created family problems and why these are universal themes for families.

Similarly, when *Early Thunder* roars over Massachusetts before the start of the Revolutionary War, students watch as Daniel West is forced to make a decision. This compelling story about Daniel's struggle chronicles the events in Salem in 1775 that shaped our nation. *The Fighting Ground* makes war a personal experience by vividly describing the 24 hours that help Jonathan learn what it means to be a soldier involved in fighting a war. *Johnny Tremain*, the award-winning story of Paul Revere's fictional apprentice, describes Johnny's personal growth from a bitter boy to an idealistic and courageous young man. As students read these texts, they will examine how differing viewpoints created family conflicts as well how the events of the Revolutionary War led to personal growth.

This middle grade sampler is designed to deepen students' knowledge and understanding of the causes of the American Revolution and its effects on individuals, the nation, and the world. Students are guided to think about how choosing sides created personal conflict that influenced growth. As students read and discuss the issues of war and personal and political independence, they will begin to understand the causes and the magnitude of the effects of revolution.

NCTE/IRA Standards for the English Language Arts

1. Students read a wide range of literature from many periods in many genres to build an understanding of the many dimensions (e.g., philosophical, ethical, and aesthetic) of human experience.
2. Students employ a wide range of strategies as they write and use different writing process elements appropriately to communicate with different audiences for a variety of purposes.

Learner Outcomes

Students will be able to do the following:

- Demonstrate comprehension of the reading by using evidence from biographies to define the qualities and effectiveness of specific Revolutionary leaders.
- Create an *All About* book that applies an effective organizing structure and includes appropriate facts and details.
- Create a first-person narrative that illustrates how the political and social issues and events of the American Revolution led to personal growth.
- Create tables, charts, and graphs to compare death rates during various wars.

Conduct a Focus Lesson

The text set for the sub-theme Revolution and Personal Growth includes historical fiction with a range of reading levels with a singular theme—the struggles of youth during the fight for independence from British control. For the middle school that is organized in interdisciplinary teams, the English language arts teacher uses the structured graphic organizer in Figure 1.8 to assess and activate students' social studies content knowledge and to prepare them for a shared reading of the first chapter of *My Brother Sam Is Dead.* Students are divided into groups; each group is assigned the task of adding details to one of the main ideas (leaders, causes, battles, etc.). After 10 minutes, a spokesperson from each group presents their completed section to the class, with organizers displayed on an overhead projector or chart paper. Members of the class are encouraged to add more details, if possible.

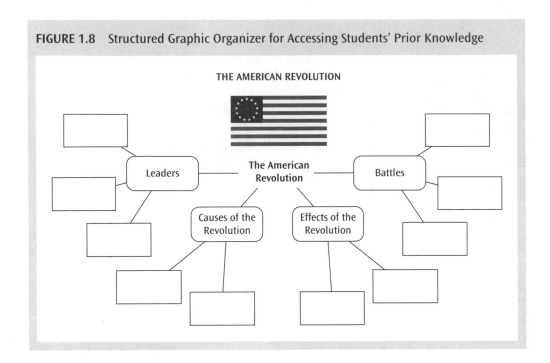

FIGURE 1.8   Structured Graphic Organizer for Accessing Students' Prior Knowledge

The teacher then explains that history is also the story of young people who, like themselves, had to make decisions that put them at odds with their family members or friends and that these personal conflicts often lead to growth.

Establish a Purpose   After the brainstorming activity, the teacher relates the purpose of the lesson to the students.

- As students and teachers read the shared or core text, *My Brother Sam Is Dead,* they analyze the issues and conflicts that bring Tim Meeker to a mature understanding of himself and the war.
- Students use a double-entry journal to reflect on the conflicts and decisions the characters made that put them in conflict with family members and friends.
- As the students attempt to make sense of the ways political change affects the characters in *My Brother Sam Is Dead,* they make connections to the independent reading text and relate the experiences to conflict and change in their own lives.

Engage in Shared Reading   The teacher distributes a copy of the core text to each student. As the teacher reads the first chapter aloud, the students see Sam Meeker burst into the family tavern in Redding, Connecticut, wearing a uniform with silver buttons. They hear him announce that the Massachusetts Minutemen have beaten the Lobsterbacks. Then they feel Tim Meeker's anxiety as Sam and their father argue about freedom, obedience, and the cost of war. The students learn that the father has a quick temper, that Sam is rebellious and often argues with the grownups, and that these quarrels frighten young Tim. As the chapter ends, the teacher asks the students the question behind their argument: "Is it worth dying to be free?"

Conduct a Mini-Lesson   The teacher explains that as the class reads *My Brother Sam Is Dead,* they will monitor the changes in Tim, the main character, by maintaining a

FIGURE 1.9   Personal Reflections

Title of Text: *My Brother Sam Is Dead*

Directions: Respond to selected quotes from the book with a personal response. Your response should show the changes that took place in the main character, Tim.

Quote	Personal Reflection

double-entry journal. The mini-lesson focuses on character traits and how to use a double-entry journal to reflect on what they are reading.

The teacher explains that a double-entry journal is a special type of reading log that enables students to use quotes to support their understanding of a text. The teacher directs students to divide the pages in a reading log into two columns, labeling the left column "Quotes" and the right column "Reflections/Assertions." The teacher clarifies that for this lesson they will focus their entries on quotes that relate to the motives, beliefs, and values that influence Tim Meeker's behavior, explaining that as they read each chapter, they will also see how events influence the character to change. After reading and listening to Chapter 1, the teacher and students select quotes and reflect on how they explain the type of boy Tim Meeker is at the start of the story, using a format like that in Figure 1.9.

The students continue reading at least three chapters per night. During class they meet in small groups to share quotes and reflections, then the teacher and students engage in a grand conversation, discussing how the events in the story change Tim's character. The teacher leads students to reflect on the pivotal events that cause Tim to grow. Finally, the students write about a pivotal event they have experienced and how it caused them to grow.

Additional Mini-Lessons

Academic Vocabulary

- Select about eight critical words required for understanding the reading.
- Guide an active discussion of each word and develop a class word wall.
- Encourage students to add new words from their readings to the class word wall as well as to their personal dictionaries.

Simulated Journals

- As students read *My Brother Sam Is Dead,* have them write a journal entry from the perspective of one of the characters.

- After they have finished their simulated journal entries, conduct a discussion from their perspectives regarding the characters they have selected.

Fishbowl Discussions

- After the students have finished reading *My Brother Sam Is Dead,* have them write responses to the following question: Is any idea worth fighting for?
- After the students have written their responses, a small group of five students will sit in a circle to discuss the question.
- The rest of the students sit outside the circle and monitor the discussion.
- After the discussion is over, the outer circle of students share their impressions of the discussion and critique their peers' arguments.

Conduct a Reading Workshop

In the focus lesson, the teacher modeled how to use a double-entry journal to track a character's personal growth. The students also learned that crises and conflicts cause individuals to make difficult decisions and that the decision-making process leads to change and growth. During the reading workshops, the students will apply these skills and understandings as they participate in literature circles.

Before Reading   The teacher explains that members of each literature circle will focus on one of the other books in the historical fiction text set. The teacher has enough copies of each book in the text set to create five main reading groups, with at least two students in each book group or literature circle. To help students make a choice, the teacher introduces each book through a short book talk highlighting the major theme and showing how the books in the text set are connected to each other and to the activities that follow the reading. For example, the teacher explains, "As you read *The Winter of Red Snow,* you will read the diary entries of Abigail Stewart and imagine what it was like to watch the soldiers of Valley Forge prepare for war. You will experience both the hardships and tragedies of that long, difficult winter as well as the excitement of meeting George and Martha Washington. Although they were often barefoot and starving, the motley Continental Army emerged from months of drill and training as a troop of trained soldiers. You will observe Abby mature from a child who sees war as an adventure to a youth who understands the sacrifices that must be made in a fight for freedom. If you read *Sarah Bishop,* you will observe that the fight for political independence was also an opportunity to find personal freedom. When the British kill Sarah's father and her brother goes off to join their cause, Sarah finds herself alone in a cruel and suspicious town. After being arrested, Sarah escapes into the Connecticut wilderness. She not only becomes involved in the struggle to survive but learns how opposing political views can affect ordinary people." The reading groups or literature circles are then formed based on the students' interests and reading proficiencies.

The teacher indicates that as students read they will again focus on the beliefs and values that influence the behavior of the main characters and how the events of the Revolutionary War cause the character to change.

During Reading   The teacher reminds students to maintain a double-entry journal as they read. Because the books are chapter books, it may take several days to complete. Middle grade students are also expected to read at home for at least a half-hour each night. Each day the students will engage in a literary discussion to share their reflections about the sections they have read and make predictions about how specific events might affect the main character. The teacher moves from group to group, facilitating the discussion when necessary. Some key questions students should consider are: What kind of person is the main character at the start of the story? What issues create conflicts between the main character and his or her family and friends? What events bring about internal conflicts? What events and decisions bring about personal change? How is the character different at the end of the story? Has the character just changed or has he or she grown?

After Reading   The teacher engages the students in a grand conversation. The purpose of the discussion is for one student from each literature group to summarize the main events in the story, for another to describe how the main character changed, and for a third to explain whether the group feels the main character has grown. The teacher will lead the class in a discussion that focuses on how the characters in the texts were similar to and different from each other and Tim Meeker.

Students write letters to one of the main characters to explain what they believe is worth fighting for and why they believe the character did or did not grow as a result of the Revolutionary War experiences.

Conduct a Writing Workshop

Students reflect on their conversations and refine their understanding of the American Revolution by engaging in one of the English/language arts extension activities. They select a writing task that is related to the genre that they enjoy reading.

Before Writing   The teacher describes each of the writing tasks and the related reading and explains the style of writing for each task, providing a model that illustrates how a completed task might look.

- *Clusters, webs, and maps.* Leaders are individuals who have the ability to inspire and move people to achieve a goal. After reading biographies from the text set about the leaders who inspired the Patriots to revolt against King George, the students brainstorm numerous words and phrases to create a cluster identifying the attributes of an effective leader. Each student selects one of the leaders and creates an organized cluster to illustrate the leader's personal qualities, what he or she did to mobilize the Patriots, and why he or she was effective. They add drawings or symbols to illustrate key ideas and understandings.
- *All About books.* Students who select biographies and other nonfiction share their information by creating a booklet with details and illustrations. They write all about the women who supported the Patriot effort, about the Constitution and other historical documents, or about the battles of the American Revolution. After selecting a topic based on interest, the students gather and organize their information and decide on illustrations for each page.
- *Diaries.* Students who prefer historical fiction use their journals to create a diary describing the events and conflicts of daily life during the American Revolution. Each student assumes the role of one of the characters and creates a first-person narrative to describe the daily routines, changing attitudes, and the effects of political and social change on personal relationships.

During Writing   As students engage in writing, the teacher meets with each group to provide direction and instruction related to the writing genre. Students are encouraged

---

FIGURE 1.10   Response Sheet for Writing Workshop: Political Change

Name: _____   Responder: _____

Date: _____   Title of Report: _____

What did you like best about this paper? _____

_____

What writing techniques were most effective? _____

_____

What did you learn from reading this paper? _____

_____

What needs to be clarified? _____

_____

Where could the writer add details, examples, and explanations to illustrate key ideas
and relationships? _____

_____

---

to extend their knowledge and elaborate their writing with details, examples, and explanations by consulting reference books and specific websites. When their drafts are completed, students conference with the teacher or peers using *The Response Sheet for Political Change* in Figure 1.10.

After Writing   Students then revise and edit as needed based on comments from the teacher and their peers. The students prepare to share completed projects with the class and/or with younger children.

Collaborative Inquiry Across the Curriculum

Extension to Mathematics and Technology   The human price of war in any time period is a difficult concept. While the specific number of deaths in a modern war may appear staggering, this number takes on meaning only when it is compared to the total population. Using the Internet and other resources, students identify the number of casualties in the American Revolution and other wars, such as the War of 1812, the Civil War, World Wars I and II, the Korean War, the Vietnam War, and so on. They also determine the population rates for eligible soldiers for each war and calculate the percent of loss, then compare the effects of war during each time period and select the most effective way to present the data. Their comparisons are made using percents, graphs, interpretation, and summary statements.

STANDARDS

Mathematics Standards
  5. Data Analysis and
     Probability
 10. Representation

Technology Standards
  5. Technology Research
     Tools

ASSESS LITERACY

The teacher assesses the students' performances in writing workshop using the rubric here. The teacher both analyzes the student's ability to apply content knowledge to the selected genre and evaluates the mechanics of writing.

Criteria	Independent	Proficient	Developing
Content Knowledge	Student is knowledgeable about content area and integrates it throughout the text. (3)	Student is somewhat knowledgeable about content area and integrates it throughout the text. (2)	Student is not knowledgeable about content area and does not integrate it throughout the text. (0–1)
Planning	Student actively participates in planning the text and discussing ideas. (3)	Student is somewhat active in planning the text and discussing ideas. (2)	Student does not actively plan the text or discuss ideas. (0–1)
Composing	Student uses planning process and writing strategies to compose text. (3)	Student somewhat uses planning process and writing strategies to compose text. (2)	Student does not use planning process and writing strategies to compose text. (0–1)
Editing	Student edits text and reviews sentence structure, vocabulary, grammar, and spelling. (3)	Student partially edits text and reviews sentence structure, vocabulary, grammar, and spelling. (2)	Students does not edit text or review sentence structure, vocabulary, grammar, and spelling. (0–1)
Independent: 9–12 Proficient: 5–8 Developing: 0–4			

Extension to Science   It has been hypothesized that the severe weather during the winter of 1777–1778 contributed as much to the loss of life and illness as the actual fighting. Students will research the weather conditions in the northeast during the winters from 1776 to 1781 and describe how the bitter cold and snow affected the course of the war. Students also investigate how wounds were treated and the types of illnesses that contributed to the death rate.

STANDARDS

Science Standards
Science in Personal and Social Perspectives, Content Standard F2

Extension to Social Studies   Students research the significant battles of the American Revolution and make a series of maps (or dioramas) to depict how geographic features such as terrain and water affected the outcome of each battle.

Students imagine that they are members of the Continental Congress and the Constitutional Convention. They explain how Thomas Paine's *Common Sense* influenced the writing of the Declaration of Independence. They then describe how the ideas in *Common Sense* and the Declaration of Independence relate to the plan for government outlined in the Constitution and the protection of freedoms guaranteed in the Bill of Rights.

STANDARDS

Social Studies Standards
II. Time, Continuity, and Change
III. People, Places, and Environments
VI. Power, Authority, and Governance

Throughout our nation's history, women have contributed to political change. When the men left to fight in the American Revolution, women took over their work. They cared for the crops and fed the army, made guns and shoes, and tended to the sick and wounded. Some, like Deborah Sampson, even fought in battle. Students read biographies and conduct research to find out about the lives of the women who supported the Patriot cause. They create a diary or memoir to highlight the specific contributions of a woman of their choice such as Handy Betsy the Blacksmith, Lydia Darragh, Phoebe Fraunces, Sybil Luddington, Molly Pitcher, Betsy Ross, Deborah Sampson, Hardy Jane Thomas, Martha Washington, or Laura Wolcott.

Home–School Connections   Informing parents of theme-based activities and creating activities that extend to the home are critical to student learning and the success of school-based projects. At the middle school level, students are encouraged to discuss the issues raised in biographies and nonfiction with parents and to connect concepts and themes to current issues and people in the news. As students read historical fiction, they are asked to discuss with parents how personal struggles and the characters' attempts to solve these problems created conflicts within families and why conflicts are universal concerns for teens and parents.

On-Your-Own Activities   Colonial printers were the first publishers of newspapers, books, and magazines in the colonies. Like the political leaders, they helped to unite the colonists against the British. Students investigate how newspapers, pamphlets, and later forms of mass communication such as radio and television helped to change people's views about specific political issues (i.e., World War II, Vietnam War, civil rights, women's rights, Iraq War). Students then select a way to share the results of their inquiry with the class.

Critical Literacy

Students in the middle grades are bombarded with factual information on a daily basis. Therefore, it is important to help them develop the necessary metacognitive skills to reflect on their own knowledge base. After completing the sub-theme, students refer back to Figure 1.8, which they completed before they began their study of the American Revolution. Working in pairs, students elaborate on their original graphic and include their new concepts about the theme. After they complete the reflective activity, they present a PowerPoint presentation to the class about their new understanding of the American Revolution and how their thinking changed as a result of their readings and research.

Collaborative Literacy

Writing projects are placed on display on bulletin boards and on library shelves to prepare for a day of celebration known as "The American Revolution Reading Fair." During the celebration authors are asked to read their projects aloud. Time is also provided for students to circulate around the room to read works from their own and other classes. Students are encouraged to respond to the work by writing sticky notes to the authors. The authors are encouraged to describe the resources they used and how the information helped to extend and refine their understanding of the American Revolution. The teacher may also work with the school librarian to hold the fair in the school library.

RESOURCE GUIDE: CHILDREN'S LITERATURE REFERENCES AND ACTIVITIES

Primary Grades

Family Changes

Changes in the Family

Flournoy, V. (1985). *The patchwork quilt.* New York: Dial Books.

Garland, S. (1993). *The lotus seed.* New York: Harcourt Brace.

Levitin, S. (1996). *A piece of home.* New York: Dial.

Oberman, S. (1994). *The always prayer shawl.* Honesdale, PA: Boyds Mills Press.

Rylant, C. (1982). *When I was young in the mountains.* New York: Puffin Books.

Rylant, C. (1985). *The relatives came.* New York: Simon & Schuster.

Woodson, J. (2004). *Coming on home soon.* New York: Putnam.

- **Family Interviews:** After reading about the many families presented in this text set, students select a grandparent or an elder friend and interview them about their childhood memories.
- **Quilt:** This collaborative activity allows students to summarize the stories presented in the text set. Working in groups, students make paper squares to represent each story and write a summary in each box. The squares are then taped together to form a quilt.
- **Personal Word Wall:** The students use file folders to create their own personal word wall. As vocabulary for the text set is introduced, students add the words to their file folders and choose an icon to represent each one.

New Family Members

dePaola, T. (2002). *A new Barker in the house.* New York: Putnam.

Girard, L. (1991). *Adoption is for always.* Illustrated by Judith Friedman. Park Ridge, IL: Albert Whitman & Company.

Hest, A. (1998). *When Jesse came across the sea.* Cambridge, MA: Candlewick Press.

Woodruff, E. (1999). *The memory coat.* Illustrated by Michael Dooling. New York: Scholastic.

- **Process Drama:** Students write a script based on a story from the text set. The script is focused on the main character and their thoughts and feelings in the text. The students then perform the play for the class.
- **Journal:** Students write in their journal about a time they were new to a class or a group and how they felt.

- **Story Board:** Students select one of the texts and create a story board to retell it. Working together, students create illustrations and a script for the text.

Growth Changes

Changing Ourselves

Brisson, P. (1998). *The summer my father was ten.* Honesdale, PA: Boyds Mills Press.

Dawson, P. R. (2001). *Human body explorer.* New York: DK Publishing.

Howard, A. (1996). *When I was five.* New York: Harcourt.

Miller, M. (1996). *Now I'm big.* New York: Greenwillow.

Milne, A. A. (1994). *Now we are six.* Illustrated by E. H. Shepard. New York: McClelland.

- **Life Size Portraits:** Students use large chart paper to outline their bodies. After they have cut out the shapes, they illustrate the front of the portrait. On the back of the illustration, the students write about themselves.
- **Data Chart:** After the students have completed the text set, they create a data chart that explores the human body. Students answer questions such as, What are some organs in my body? What does my body need to live? How can I care for my body?
- **Book Boxes:** This summation activity can be done by students working in groups. The students select a text from the set and choose three or more pictures or objects to represent the story. They put an explanation for their choices in the book box and share it with the class.

Animals Grow and Change

Arnosky, J. (1995). *I see animals hiding.* New York: Scholastic.

Collard, S. B. (2005). *A platypus probably.* New York: Charleston Publishing.

Heligman, D., & Weissman, B. (1996). *From caterpillar to butterfly.* New York: HarperTrophy.

Heller, R. (1999). *Animals born alive and well.* New York: Putnam.

Rinehart, S. (2004). *Eliza and the dragonfly.* Illustrated by Anisa Claire Heinemann. New York: Dawn Publications.

- **Diorama:** After reading about the metamorphosis of a caterpillar, students create a diorama that illustrates the changes.
- **Alphabet Book:** Students create an alphabet book focusing on the animals they studied in the text set. The students research facts about the animals and illustrate their alphabet books.

- **Interactive Message Board:** This summation activity is done by students working in pairs. The teacher saves Internet sites such as www.nationalgeographic.com that the students can use as references. The students create their own message board on a particular animal and their peers respond to their notes.

World Changes

People Who Made Changes

Cooney, B. (1996). *Eleanor*. New York: Viking.

Deedy, C. A. (2000). *The yellow star*. Atlanta, GA: Peachtree.

Giblin, J. C. (1994). *Thomas Jefferson: A picture book biography*. New York: Scholastic.

Hopkins, L. B. (1999). *Lives: Poems about famous Americans*. New York: HarperCollins.

Pinkney, A. D. (1994). *Dear Benjamin Banneker*. New York: Harcourt Brace.

Schroeder, A. (1996). *Minty: A story of young Harriet Tubman*. New York: Dial.

- **Hand Puppets:** Students select one of the characters highlighted in the text set and use a sock to create a hand puppet of the character. The students then retell the character's life story and how they changed the world.
- **Timeline:** Working in groups, students create a graphic organizer depicting the life story of one of the characters.
- **My Life:** As a culminating activity, students write their own simulated life story. In their simulated stories, students focus on changes they want to accomplish to improve our society and world.

Sudden Natural Changes

Berger, M., & Berger, G. (2000). *Do tornadoes really twist? Questions and answers about tornadoes and hurricanes*. New York: Scholastic.

Cole, J. (1996). *Magic school bus inside a hurricane*. New York: Scholastic.

Hopping, L. J. (1995). *Hurricanes!* New York: Cartwheel.

Weeks, S. (1993). *Hurricane city*. New York: HarperCollins.

- **Map It!:** Students use a map of the United States to highlight the states that are susceptible to hurricanes.
- **Cluster:** Students create a graphic organizer for either tornadoes or hurricanes, outlining major concepts and details.
- **Wall Story:** As a culminating activity, students create a wall story about either a tornado or hurricane and how to prepare for sudden storms.

Intermediate Grades

Family Changes

Changes in Families Caused by Famine and Poverty

Allan, T. (2001). *The Irish famine: The birth of Irish America*. Chicago: Heinemann.

Auch, M. (2002). *Ashes of roses*. New York: Holt.

Bartoletti, S. C. (2001). *Black potatoes: The story of the great Irish famine*. Boston: Houghton.

Branson, K. (1981). *Streets of gold*. New York: Putnam.

Conlon-McKenna, M. (1990). *Under the hawthorn tree*. Illustrated by Donald Teskey. Dublin, Ireland: O'Brien Press.

Conlon-McKenna, M. (1992). *Wildflower*. Illustrated by Donald Teskey. New York: Holiday.

Denenberg, B. (1997). *So far from home: The diary of Mary Driscoll, an Irish mill girl*. New York: Scholastic.

Fitzpatrick, M. (2001). *The long march: The Choctaw's gift to Irish famine relief*. New York: Tricycle Press.

Fontes, J., & Fontes, R. (2003). *A to Z: Ireland*. New York: Children's Press.

Giff, P. R. (2002). *Nory Ryan's song*. New York: Dell Yearling.

Giff, P. R. (2003). *Maggie's door*. New York: Dell Yearling.

Hazen, B. S. (2002). *Katie's wish*. Illustrated by Emily Arnold McCully. New York: Dial.

Holmes, A. (1974). *Plant fun: Ten easy plants to grow indoors*. Illustrated by Grambs Miller. New York: Four Winds.

Johnson, S. (1984). *Potatoes*. Illustrated by Masaharu Suzuki. Minneapolis, MN: Lerner.

Lobel, A. (2004). *Potatoes, potatoes*. (reissued edition). Illustrated by Anita Lobel. New York: Greenwillow.

Lyons, M. (2002). *Feed the children first: Irish memories of the great hunger*. New York: Atheneum.

- **Research:** Students investigate the Irish population growth in North America during the great famine with respect to the following: (1) Where the Irish settled in North America, (2) the jobs that were available for the Irish immigrants, and (3) famous Irish Americans who immigrated to North America.
- **Alphabet Book:** Students work together to create an alphabet book of facts about the Irish people.
- **Scientific Investigations:** Students grow potatoes and change the conditions for different potatoes, such as the amount of light and water or the type of soil. Students then observe the growth of the potatoes and record the differences.
- **Surveys:** Students investigate the different ways that potatoes are eaten and conduct a schoolwide survey to determine the type of potatoes that are the most popu-

lar among students. The results are presented in a bar graph.

Changes in Families Caused by Homelessness

Carlson, N. S. (1958). *The family under the bridge.* Illustrated by Garth Williams. New York: HarperCollins.

Cushman, K. (1995). *The midwife's apprentice.* New York: Clarion.

Fox, P. (1991). *Monkey Island.* New York: Orchard.

Hughes, D. (1989). *Family pose.* New York: Atheneum.

O'Connor, K. (1989). *Homeless children.* San Diego, CA: Lucent.

Sendak, M. (1993). *We are all in the dumps with Jack and Guy.* Illustrated by Maurice Sendak. New York: HarperCollins.

Tolan, S. (1992). *Sophie and the sidewalk man.* Illustrated by Susan Avishai. New York: Macmillan.

Voigt, C. (1981). *Homecoming.* New York: Atheneum.

- **Response Writing:** Several narrative texts evoke personal responses. After students have read a story, they (1) describe the emotions of the main character about being homeless and (2) describe their own feelings and emotions if they were homeless.

- **Research:** Students investigate homelessness in the United States and in their community to determine the number of people who are homeless and reasons for becoming homeless.

- **Brainstorming:** Students brainstorm different ways that children have helped those who are homeless and initiate a class or schoolwide project to help homeless families.

Changes in Families Caused by War

Amis, N. (2003). *The orphans of Normandy: A true story of World War II told through drawings by children.* New York: Atheneum.

Bergman, T. (1991). *Along the tracks.* New York: Houghton.

Giff, P. R. (1997). *Lily's crossing.* New York: Dell Yearling.

Holm, Anne. (2004). *I am David.* San Anselmo, CA: Sandpiper Press.

Lowry, L. (1989). *Number the stars.* New York: Houghton.

Vander Zee, R. (2003). *Erika's story.* Mankato, MN: Creative Editions.

- **Researching and Relating Current Events:** After reading stories of how war has changed families, students find newspaper or magazine articles on a contemporary war. They determine how the war has changed family lives or the lives of soldiers who are fighting in the war, then compare the changes of war on family life with the stories with the article on a present-day war.

- **Learning Logs:** Many texts about war describe settings and events that are new and unfamiliar to students. Through the use of learning logs, students record facts they have learned from their independent or guided reading period. They may use their learning logs during discussion of the text.

- **Word Study:** Most literature on war includes vocabulary related to the historical period. To increase students' academic vocabulary through reading of literature, direct students on how to use context clues to understand the new word.

Growth Changes

Growing-Up Changes

DiCamillo, K. (2000). *Because of Winn-Dixie.* Cambridge, MA: Candlewick.

DiCamillo, K. (2001). *The tiger rising.* Cambridge, MA: Candlewick.

Estes, E. (1974). *The hundred dresses.* Illustrated by Louis Slobodkin. New York: Harcourt.

Fleischman, S. (1986). *The whipping boy.* Illustrated by Peter Sís. New York: HarperTrophy.

Giff, P. R. (2001). *All the way home.* New York: Delacorte.

Giff, P. R. (2002). *Pictures of Hollis Woods.* New York: Dell Yearling.

Polacco, P. (2001). *Mr. Lincoln's Way.* Illustrated by Patricia Polacco. New York: Philomel.

- **Multimedia Presentation:** Students identify a character that experienced many life changes and, using a multimedia presentation, illustrate the character before and after the changes.

- **Story Board:** Direct students to use story boards to retell one of the books they have read. Using the pictures from their story boards, students engage in a storytelling event.

- **Epilogue:** Students pretend that they are the author of a story that they have read. They write the epilogue to the story, telling more about the character after the story ended or about events that the author did not know.

Becoming Courageous

Christopher, M. (1969). *Catch that pass!* Illustrated by Harvey Kidder. New York: Little, Brown.

Fox, P. (1967). *How many miles to Babylon?* Illustrated by Paul Giovanopoulos. Scarsdale, NY: Bradbury.

Hasley, D. (1983). *The scared one.* New York: Warne.

Martin, B., & Archambault, J. (1987). *Knots on a counting rope.* Illustrated by Ted Rand. New York: Holt.

Mayerson, E. (1990). *The cat who escaped from steerage.* New York: Scribner's.

Orr, W. (1996). *Peeling the onion.* New York: Holiday.

Paul, A. (1999). *All by herself: 14 girls who made a difference.* Illustrated by Michael Steinagle. New York: Harcourt.

Spinelli, J. (1997). *Wringer.* New York: HarperCollins.

- **Brainstorming:** Students tell their own personal stories that changed their attitudes about fear.
- **Storytelling:** Students bring in their picture or one of a family member or a friend to tell about a story of courage. The student identifies a character from a story that showed similar courage. Using a rope, a knot for each personal story told about courage will be made in homage to *Knots on a Counting Rope.*
- **Getting-to-Know-You Card:** After students have read a story from the text set about a character who demonstrated courage, they create a card that describes the character, including his or her actions, feelings, the hardships and happy events from the character's life, and an illustration of the character.

World Changes

Sudden Natural Changes

Berger, M., & Berger, G. (2000). *Why do volcanoes blow their tops? Questions and answers about volcanoes and earthquakes.* Illustrated by Barbara Higgins Bond. New York: Scholastic.

Byars, B. (1996). *Tornado.* Illustrated by Doron Ben-Ami. New York: HarperCollins.

Cottonwood, J. (1995). *Quake!* New York: Scholastic.

Gross, V. (1991). *The day it rained forever: A story of the Johnstown flood.* Illustrated by Ronald Himler. New York: Viking.

Harshman, M. (1995). *The storm.* Illustrated by Marc Mohr. New York: Dutton.

Kehret, P. (1996). *Earthquake terror.* New York: Cobblehill.

Markie, S. (1991). *Earth alive!* New York: Lothrop.

Martin, T. (1996). *Why does lightning strike?* New York: Dorling-Kindersley.

Milton, H. (1983). *Tornado!* Danbury, CT: Watts.

Ruckman, I. (1996). *Night of the twisters.* New York: Crowell.

Simon, S. (1997). *Lightning.* New York: Morrow.

Wood, J. (1993). *Storm.* Illustrated by Jenny Wood. New York: Thomson Learning.

- **Animated Electronic Word Walls:** After reading several informational texts on natural world changes, students work in small groups to select a set of words related to a natural change, such as an earthquake, tornado, or lightning. Using multimedia presentations, they create an animated electronic word wall to describe vocabulary words that are related to a specific natural change.
- **Quick-Lists:** Prior to reading an informational book on a natural change, students write a list of facts they know about the change. After reading the book, students revisit their quick-list to determine the accuracy of the facts and to add information to the facts they already knew. Quick-lists may be conducted as an independent, small-group, or large-group activity.
- **Venn Diagram:** In two diagrams, compare the positive and negative effects that natural changes have on the earth, people, and animals.

Inventors Who Changed the World

Adler, D. (1992). *Benjamin Franklin: Printer, inventor, statesman.* New York: Holiday.

Karnes, F., & Bean, S. M. (1995). *Girls and young women inventing.* Minneapolis, MN: Free Spirit.

Matthews, T. L. (1999). *Always inventing: A photobiography of Alexander Graham Bell.* Washington, DC: National Geographic.

McPherson, S. (1996). *TV's forgotten hero: The story of Philo Farnsworth.* Minneapolis, MN: Carolrhoda.

Rubin, S. (1998). *Toilets, toasters and telephones: The why and how of everyday objects.* San Diego, CA: Harcourt.

St. George, J. (2002). *So you want to be an inventor.* New York: Philomel.

Thimmesh, C. (2000). *Girls think of everything: Stories of ingenious inventions by women.* Boston: Houghton.

- **Problem Solving:** Students identify a problem that needs a perfect invention for its solution. They list the procedures for making the invention and the materials needed, write a set of directions for creating the invention, and finally name and draw a picture of it.
- **News Announcements:** Students choose an invention and inventor from a book that they have read. They write a news announcement of the invention, describing it and offering a biographical sketch of the inventor. News announcements should be factual information written in interesting ways to motivate the audience to listen to the announcer. News announcements may be presented in the format of a television or radio show.
- **Inventions All Around Us!** New inventions and modifications of older inventions are introduced to society daily. Have students brainstorm some new inventions or reinventions (modifications of older inventions) that are around their homes, the school, or their community.

Middle Grades

Family Changes

Defining Family and Home

Cleary, B. (1983). *Dear Mr. Henshaw.* New York: William Morrow Junior.

Cleaver, V., & Cleaver, B. (1969). *Where the lilies bloom.* New York: HarperCollins.

Fox, Paula. (1991). *Monkey Island.* New York: Orchard.

Mazer, N. F. (1987). *After the rain.* New York: Morrow.

Paterson, K. (1978). *The great Gilly Hopkins.* New York: Crowell.

Rylant, C. (1992). *Missing May.* New York: Orchard.

- **Brainstorming Web:** Before beginning the text set, students brainstorm their definition of "family."
- **Cluster Map:** When the text set is completed, students create a cluster map to define "family" based on their readings and discussions.
- **Process Drama:** Students respond to one of the texts by writing a script for a key scene and performing it for their peers. After their performance, the students defend their interpretation of the key scene.

Death and Divorce

Brooks, B. (1988). *Midnight hour encores.* New York: HarperCollins.

Creech, S. (1996). *Walk two moons.* New York: HarperCollins.

Danziger, P. (1982). *Divorce express.* New York: Delacourt.

MacLachlan, P. (1993). *Baby.* New York: Delacourt.

Paterson, K. (1994). *Flip flop girl.* New York: Dutton Juvenile.

Talbert, M. (2001). *Thin ice.* New York: Backinprint.

- **Open-Mind Portraits:** After reading the books in the text set, students select a main character, draw his or her portrait, and list character traits.
- **Plot Profile:** Students work in pairs to graph key events in the story on a plot profile chart.
- **Text-to-Self Connection:** Students respond to one of the texts by writing in their journals about a time when they experienced loss.

Growth Changes

Revolution and Personal Growth

Avi. (1984). *The fighting ground.* New York: Lippincott.

Blackwood, G. (2002). *The year of the hangman.* New York: Dutton.

Clapp, P. (1977). *I'm Deborah Sampson: A soldier in the war of the revolution.* New York: Lothrop, Lee & Shepard.

Collier, J. L., & Collier, C. (1974). *My brother Sam is dead.* New York: Simon & Schuster.

Forbes, E. (1960). *Johnny Tremain.* New York: Houghton.

Fritz, J. (1967). *Early thunder.* New York: Coward-McCann.

Gregory, K. (1996). *The winter of red snow: A revolutionary war diary of Abigail Jane Stewart.* New York: Scholastic.

Lunn, J. (1997). *The hollow tree.* New York: Penguin Putnam.

O'Dell, S. (1980). *Sarah Bishop.* Boston: Houghton.

Pryor, B. (1999). *Thomas in danger.* New York: Morrow.

Rinaldi, A. (1995). *The secret of Sarah Revere.* Orlando, FL: Harcourt.

Rinaldi, A. (2003). *Or give me death: A novel of Patrick Henry's family.* Orlando, FL: Harcourt.

- **Literature Circles:** Students form literature circles based on their story selections and discuss character changes.
- **Double-Entry Journal:** Students record character changes as they read text and respond in a double-entry journal.
- **Cluster Map:** When students have completed the text set, they create cluster maps to identify the traits of inspirational leaders.

Conflict Causes Personal Growth

Babbitt, N. (1975). *Tuck everlasting.* New York: Farrar, Straus & Giroux.

Burnett, F. H. (1911). *The secret garden.* New York: F. A. Stokes.

Kerr, M. E. (1986). *Night kites.* New York: HarperCollins.

Lee, M. (1994). *Saying goodbye.* New York: Houghton.

Lowry, L. (1993). *The giver.* New York: Houghton.

Oneal, Z. (1980). *The language of goldfish.* New York: Viking.

- **Creative Dialogue:** Students select two of the main characters in the text set and write an imaginary dialogue between them.
- **Character Matrix:** Students work in groups to create a matrix that compares and contrasts character traits of main characters.
- **Text-to-Self Connection:** Students respond to one of the texts by writing in their journals about an experience that helped them to grow.

World Changes

People, Politics, and Change

Adler, D. A. (2001). *B. Franklin, printer.* New York: Holiday.

Behrman, C. H. (2003). *John Adams (presidential leaders).* Minneapolis, MN: Lerner.

Bober, N. S. (1988). *Thomas Jefferson: Man on a mountain.* New York: Atheneum.

Bober, N. S. (1995). *Abigail Adams: Witness to a revolution.* New York: Atheneum.

Farley, K. C. (1995). *Samuel Adams: Grandfather of his country.* Austin, TX: Steck-Vaughn.

Feinberg, B. S. (2003). *John Adams: America's second president.* New York: Children's Press.

Ferris, J. C. (1998). *Thomas Jefferson: Father of liberty.* Minneapolis, MN: Carolrhoda.

Fischer, D. H. (1994). *Paul Revere's ride*. New York: Oxford University Press.

Forbes, E. (1999). *Paul Revere and the world he lived in*. New York: Houghton.

Fradin, D. B. (1998). *Samuel Adams: The father of American independence*. New York: Clarion.

Giblin, J. C. (2000). *The amazing life of Benjamin Franklin*. New York: Scholastic.

Gross, M. (2005). *John Adams: Patriot, diplomat, and statesman*. New York: PowerPlus Books.

Harness, C. (2003). *The revolutionary John Adams*. Washington, DC: National Geographic.

Harness, C. (2004). *Thomas Jefferson*. Washington, DC: National Geographic.

Irvin, B. H. (2002). *Samuel Adams: Son of liberty, father of revolution*. New York: Oxford University Press.

Marrin, A. (2001). *George Washington & the founding of a nation*. New York: Dutton.

McCullough, D. (2001). *John Adams*. New York: Simon & Schuster.

Meltzer, M. (1991). *Thomas Jefferson: The revolutionary aristocrat*. Danbury, CT: Franklin Watts.

Meltzer, M. (1996). *Tom Paine: Voice of revolution*. New York: Franklin Watts.

Redmond, S. R. (2004). *Patriots in petticoats: Heroines of the American Revolution*. New York: Random House.

Reische, D. (1987). *Patrick Henry*. New York: Franklin Watts.

Slavicek, L. C. (2003). *Women of the American Revolution*. New York: Lucent.

St. George, J. (2001). *John and Abigail Adams: An American love story*. New York: Holiday.

Vail, J. (1990). *Thomas Paine*. New York: Chelsea House.

Zall, P. M. (1993). *Becoming American: Young people in the American Revolution*. North Haven, CT: ShoeString Press.

Zeinert, K. (1996). *Those remarkable women of the American Revolution*. Minneapolis, MN: Millbrook Press.

■ **Biography Box:** After reading the books in the text set, students select a revolutionary leader and create symbols that represent traits and key events for a biography box.

■ **Slideshow:** Students work in pairs to create a multimedia presentation that focuses on revolutionary leaders.

■ **Discussion Web:** Students respond to the prompt question, How would you have reacted to the events of the American Revolution? After writing their response, they engage in a discussion.

United States: An Experiment in Government

Brenner, B. (1994). *If you were there in 1776*. New York: Bradbury.

Fink, S. (2002). *The Declaration of Independence*. New York: Scholastic.

Fritz, J. (1987). *Shh! We're writing the Constitution*. New York: Putnam.

Hudson, D. L., Jr. (2002). *The Bill of Rights: The first ten amendments of the Constitution*. Berkeley Heights, NJ: Enslow.

Levy, E. (1987). *If you were there when they signed the Constitution*. New York: Scholastic.

Maestro, B., & Muestro, G. (1987). A *more perfect union: The story of our Constitution*. New York: Lothrop, Lee & Shepard.

McPhillips, M. (1985). *The Constitutional Convention*. Saddle River, NJ: Silver Burdett.

Meltzer, M. (1987). *The American revolutionaries: A history in their own words 1750–1800*. New York: HarperCollins.

Meltzer, M. (1990). *The Bill of Rights: How we got it and what it means*. New York: Thomas Y. Crowell Junior Books.

■ **Democracy Panel:** After reading the books in the text set, students work in groups to research one of the key documents such as the Bill of Rights. They present how the document influences our lives today.

■ **Accordion Books:** Students work in pairs to create accordion books that present information on a key document and how it came to fruition.

■ **Simulated Journal:** Students respond to one of the texts by writing a simulated journal entry for a member of the Constitutional Convention.

PROFESSIONAL REFERENCES

Antonacci, P., & O'Callaghan, C. (2006). *A handbook for literacy instructional and assessment strategies, K–8*. Boston: Allyn & Bacon.

National Council of Teachers of English & International Reading Association. (1996). *Standards for the English language arts*. Newark, DE: Authors. Available at www.ncte.org/standards

National Council of Social Studies Teachers. (1994). *Expectations for excellence: Curriculum standards for social studies*, NCSS Bulletin No. 89. Baltimore: Author. Available at www.socialstudies.org/standards

Journeys

From the moment of birth, we all experience the journey of life. It is common to all humankind, yet all individuals have unique stories to tell of the hardships they overcame to reach their destination. Chapter 2 explores the theme of Journeys and shows how children's literature can be used to lead discussions on culture, courage, and equal rights.

The International Reading Association and the National Council of Teachers of English (1996) include in their standards the need for students to understand and respect diversity in language use and differences across cultures, ethnic groups, and geographic regions. The samplers illustrated in Chapter 2 implement this standard by highlighting various cultures. In the primary grade sub-theme Number Journeys Around the World, students learn how different countries count and use numbers. Intermediate grade students explore geographic regions and the language of Native Americans as they read about Lewis and Clark's historic journey westward. Chapter 2 concludes with the middle school sub-theme From Slavery to Equal Rights. Middle school students will travel back in time to the Civil War and make connections to the struggle for freedom and civil rights in modern times. The common thread running throughout all three samplers is that in order to undertake a journey, the heart must be open to the world and embrace differences.

■ Primary Grades: Kindergarten–Grade 2

Uno, dos, tres are familiar words heard on many American streets! Children often learn to count in Spanish as they hear the language around them. In *Moja Means One: A Swahili Counting Book* and *Emeka's Gift: An African Counting Story,* students will undertake a journey to Africa to discover how numbers are used there in daily life. Through children's literature, students can travel around the world as they read about different lands.

By the time children enter the primary grades they have probably undertaken many journeys with their families. These journeys might be simple, such as bus rides to school each day, or more challenging ones, such as the journey to America from another country. The universal theme of Journeys lends itself to the integration of science, mathematics, the arts, and literature across the curriculum.

In this chapter, we demonstrate how students can deepen their knowledge by reading, writing, thinking, and discussing topics such as Journey to the White House

JOURNEY AROUND MY COMMUNITY

Text Set

Wanda's Roses
On the Town: A Community Adventure
The Garden of Happiness
Tar Beach
The Trek
Abuela
An Ordinary Day

Outcomes

- Create a photo journal of key places in your community.
- Research how your community looked 100 years ago.
- Write about your imaginary places.

NUMBER JOURNEYS AROUND THE WORLD

Text Set

Moja Means One: A Swahili Counting Book
City by Numbers
Emeka's Gift: An African Counting Book
Anno's Counting House
Ten Little Dinosaurs
The Michigan Counting Book
Sunny Numbers: A Florida Counting Book
1, 2, 3 Moose: A Pacific Northwest Counting Book

Outcomes

- Create your own counting book.
- Use a flannel board to tell a math story.

JOURNEY TO THE WHITE HOUSE

Text Set

A Picture Book of Thomas Jefferson
Abraham Lincoln
Abraham Lincoln: A Man for All People
A Picture Book of Dwight David Eisenhower
Don't You Dare Shoot That Bear! A Story of Theodore Roosevelt
Abe Lincoln: The Boy Who Loved Books
Thomas Jefferson: A Picture Biography

Outcomes

- Retell the story of a president's life with a hand puppet.
- Create a symbol for the president you studied and explain its significance.

Personal Journeys

Journeys to Other Places

JOURNEYS

Journeys in Time

JOURNEY TO THE AMERICAN WEST

Text Set

Townsend's Warbler
Wagons West
Red Flower Goes West
A Picture Book of Lewis and Clark
Sacagawea
Lewis & Clark: Explorers of the American West

Outcomes

- Write a script about Sacagawea's life and perform it.
- Identify the trail westward on a map.

JOURNEY TO THE TIME OF DINOSAURS

Text Set

The Big Beast Book: Dinosaurs and How They Got That Way
Digging up Dinosaurs
Dinosaur Roar
The Dinosaurs of Waterhouse Hawkins
I Can Draw a Weeposaur and Other Dinosaurs
Time Flies
National Geographic Dinosaurs

Outcomes

- Write a poem about dinosaurs.
- Create a dinosaur mural to illustrate its habitat.
- Research one of the dinosaurs.

JOURNEY TO THE EARTH'S PAST

Text Set

Bone for Bone
Before the Sun Dies: The Story of Evolution
Shell
A Bone from a Dry Sea
Fossil Fish Found Alive
Feathered Dinosaurs

Outcomes

- Create a diorama of how the Earth looked at the time of feathered dinosaurs.
- Construct an *All About Fossils* book.
- Research on the Internet for fossil discoveries in your region.

and Journeys Around My Community. Science and mathematics will also be integrated through a Journey to the Earth's Past, where students will discover the world of fossils and Earth's history. In Journey to the Time of Dinosaurs, often a favorite among students, they learn facts about prehistoric animals.

In order to undertake a journey, the explorer must leave behind notions of home and hearth and become open to different cultures and customs. This aspect of journeying has been woven throughout the primary sampler with inclusion of multicultural songs, dances, and stories.

SAMPLER ■ Number Journeys Around the World

How many of us on those long car trips across the country spent our time in the backseat counting license plates from different states? A variation of that game is played in the book, *1, 2, 3 Moose: A Pacific Northwest Counting Book,* which takes students on a journey to the northernmost regions of our country to count native animals.

Children in the twenty-first century are increasingly mobile as they travel with their parents around the nation and the globe. As society becomes more diverse and the Internet brings the world into our own homes, it is imperative that children become aware of other languages and customs.

When the National Council of Teachers of Mathematics (2000) created standards for student performance, one goal was to introduce students to the use of mathematics around the world. The sub-theme Number Journeys Around the World is a wonderful way to introduce primary grade students to the uses of mathematics across peoples and cultures. In addition, it illustrates how the exploration of mathematics can engage young children. Too often students, especially girls, fear mathematics and do not see the subject as an area to be investigated. However, when students are given the opportunity to play with numbers at an early age, the foundation is laid for a disposition toward mathematical careers. As illustrated in the graphic organizer, children's literature can be used to explore the concept of Number Journeys Around the World.

The purpose of the sub-theme is to introduce primary grade children to the world of numbers and their myriad uses around the globe. The instructional sequence illustrates how to use picture books to motivate students to explore this sub-theme.

NCTE/IRA Standards for the English Language Arts

1. Students read a wide range of print and non-print texts to build an understanding of texts, of themselves, and of the cultures of the United States and the world.
9. Students develop an understanding of and respect for diversity in language use, patterns, and dialects across cultures, ethnic groups, geographic regions, and social roles.

Learner Outcomes

As students construct their own counting books, they use prior knowledge related to concepts of classification and sequencing. They will be able to do the following:

■ Make predictions and text-to-self connections.
■ Record journal entries about how they see numbers in everyday life.
■ Create a counting book in the style of an author they have studied.

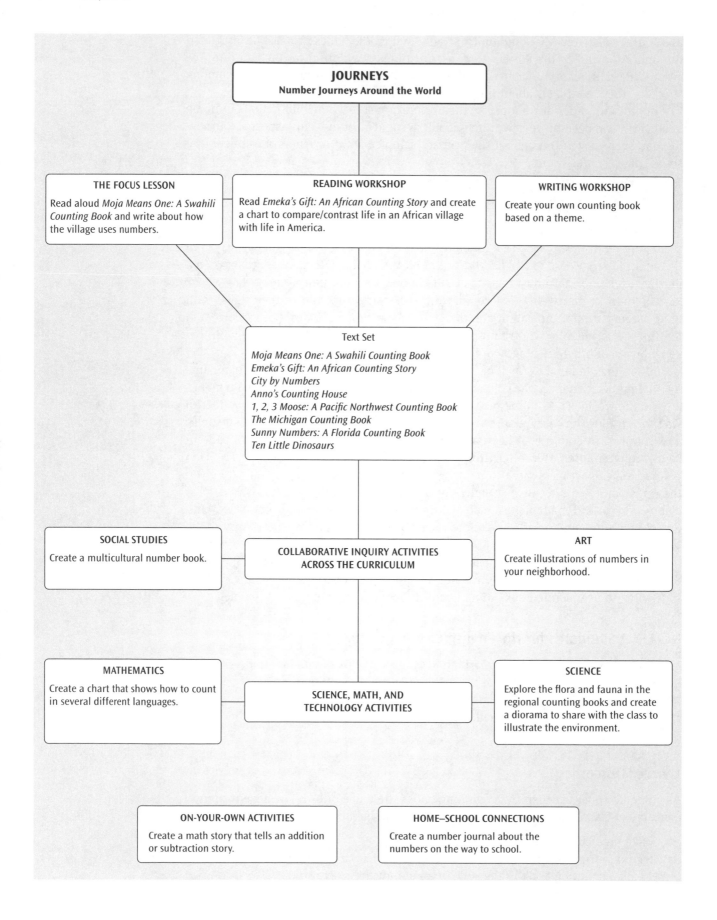

JOURNEYS
Number Journeys Around the World

THE FOCUS LESSON

Read aloud *Moja Means One: A Swahili Counting Book* and write about how the village uses numbers.

READING WORKSHOP

Read *Emeka's Gift: An African Counting Story* and create a chart to compare/contrast life in an African village with life in America.

WRITING WORKSHOP

Create your own counting book based on a theme.

Text Set

Moja Means One: A Swahili Counting Book
Emeka's Gift: An African Counting Story
City by Numbers
Anno's Counting House
1, 2, 3 Moose: A Pacific Northwest Counting Book
The Michigan Counting Book
Sunny Numbers: A Florida Counting Book
Ten Little Dinosaurs

SOCIAL STUDIES

Create a multicultural number book.

COLLABORATIVE INQUIRY ACTIVITIES ACROSS THE CURRICULUM

ART

Create illustrations of numbers in your neighborhood.

MATHEMATICS

Create a chart that shows how to count in several different languages.

SCIENCE, MATH, AND TECHNOLOGY ACTIVITIES

SCIENCE

Explore the flora and fauna in the regional counting books and create a diorama to share with the class to illustrate the environment.

ON-YOUR-OWN ACTIVITIES

Create a math story that tells an addition or subtraction story.

HOME–SCHOOL CONNECTIONS

Create a number journal about the numbers on the way to school.

Conduct a Focus Lesson

The focus lesson integrates mathematics and the language arts as students explore how numbers are used. During the focus lesson, students use colorful texts about cultures around the globe to construct background knowledge on number systems. The focus lesson concludes with a journal response activity.

Establish a Purpose   The text set for Number Journeys Around the World explores the use of numbers. As students learn how children in Vietnam or Mexico count objects in their cultures, they are exposed to other perspectives and customs. The text for this instructional sequence is *Moja Means One: A Swahili Counting Book.* As students study the illustrations of African landscapes, they are also learning how Africans count objects common in their everyday lives. The purpose of this focus lesson is to travel the world through multicultural books that explore the ways we use numbers around the globe.

Students will engage in a read aloud to discover how numbers are used in different cultures, discuss how they see numbers represented in their communities and everyday life, and then construct their own multicultural counting book.

Engage in Read Aloud   The theme begins with a preparation activity to assess the students' concept of numbers before exploring multicultural counting books. The purpose of this section of the instructional sequence is to prepare the reader with the necessary background knowledge in order to comprehend the lesson. Since the sub-theme focuses on numbers and how they are used in our lives, it is important to determine if the students have the concept of number.

The following assessment can be done in a simple, playful grab bag activity. The teacher places several number cards from 1 to 10 in a grab bag. The students are called to select a card from the grab bag and find the necessary set of objects in the classroom. As each number is selected, the teacher records the numbers on a chart and the student illustrates the set of objects on a concept chart, as depicted in Figure 2.1.

The teacher then uses the interactive read-aloud strategy for the reading of the first book in the text set, *Moja Means One: A Swahili Counting Book.* This beautifully illustrated counting book shows students how to count in Swahili and depicts scenes

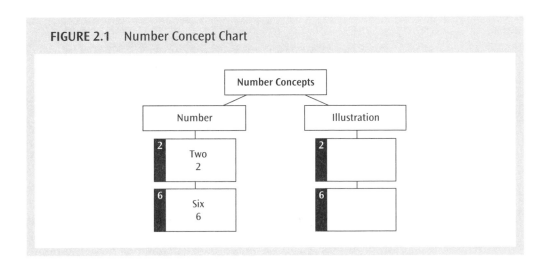

FIGURE 2.1   Number Concept Chart

FIGURE 2.2 How We Used Numbers Today

We Used Numbers For	The Numbers We Used
The date	9/9/2010
My address	81 President Street
The lunch count	14 hot lunches
The students who were absent	2 students

from African villages. The teacher reads the book once without stopping, then rereads the book and asks the students to join in on the Swahili counting words. After the read aloud, the teacher records the Swahili counting words on a chart next to their English equivalents.

When students have finished reading the selections, they use their journals to record how they used numbers during the day. If students are unable to write, they illustrate their responses in their journals. After students have finished their journal entries, the teacher records their responses on a class chart as illustrated in Figure 2.2.

Conduct a Mini-Lesson   The focus of the mini-lesson is to select objects from the classroom and create rhymes in order to write pages for a counting book. The teacher displays the first line of the counting book for the students to complete: "One is for . . ." (see Figure 2.3). Students think of a rhyme and complete the first line of each of the three pages, then illustrate each page. When the first three numbers are complete, students read the text as a choral performance.

Additional Mini-Lessons

Reading Comprehension

- The teacher directs students to retell the story after the read aloud.
- Students are given prompts or drawings to assist them.

FIGURE 2.3 Page One of *Our Counting Book*

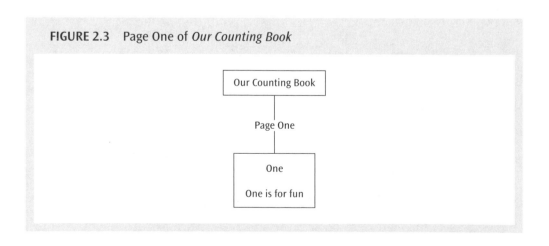

Writing

- As students learn the counting words from different languages, they write the words on the word wall.
- Students also write the words in their personal dictionaries or the word chart.
- As students construct their own multicultural counting books, they use the word wall as a reference tool.

Vocabulary

- The teacher helps the students create a semantic map for content-area words from books in the text set.
- As students create the map, the teacher leads a discussion on the concepts and connections pertaining to each word.

Conduct a Reading Workshop

Emeka's Gift: An African Counting Story complements the text used in the mini-lesson. This beautiful counting book uses photographs of a village of the Igala people of southern Nigeria to introduce children to the customs of African tribes. The main character, Emeka, is in search of a present for his grandmother. As he passes familiar objects in the village such as four new brooms, he contemplates giving them as a gift. However, in the end his grandmother says that the best gift is a hug from Emeka.

Before Reading   To prepare the students for reading the book, the teacher shows students a map of Africa and asks them to identify Nigeria on the map. The teacher asks the students to make predictions about the story based on the colorful photographs.

During Reading   As the students read the book, the teacher stops in the middle and asks the students what gift they think Emeka will give his grandmother. The teacher writes their predictions on a chart with their reasons for selecting certain objects.

After Reading   When students have finished reading the book, they discuss ways in which Emeka's life is similar or different to their own. After their discussion, they complete a chart about what they have learned about life in this small Nigerian village, as illustrated in Figure 2.4.

Conduct a Writing Workshop

The text set includes multicultural counting books; therefore, the focus of the writing workshop is on teaching students to create their own counting book.

Before Writing   The writing workshop begins with the teacher using a chart depicting characteristics of counting books, such as rich illustrations and rhyming text. The teacher shows the students counting books such as *City by Numbers,* in which the author uses everyday objects in the city landscape to represent numbers. They are shown sample pages from other books in the text set to examine. The teacher asks the students to brainstorm a theme for their counting books, such as a city counting book or one based on their own culture. The students work with a partner to plan their writing.

During Writing   The teacher reminds the students to use the books from the text set as models for their own books. They begin by developing an outline of their

FIGURE 2.4   What We Learned About Nigeria

WHAT WE LEARNED ABOUT NIGERIA

Nigeria Is a Country in Our World

We learned:

1. Water is very important to the village.

2. Loving families live in the village in Nigeria.

3. Just like our families, they have grandmothers too.

ASSESS LITERACY

The teacher uses the rubric shown here to assess students' performances after they have completed reading workshop.

Criteria	Independent	Proficient	Developing
Making Predictions	Student makes predictions using story content. (3)	Student makes predictions using story content most of the time. (2)	Student does not make predictions using story content. (0–1)
Making Connections	Student makes text-to-self connections and discusses reasoning. (3)	Student makes text-to-self connections and discusses reasoning most of the time. (2)	Student does not make text-to-self connections. (0–1)
Identifying Plot	Student identifies the main sequence of events and can plot the rising tension in the story. (3)	Student partially identifies the main sequence of events and plots the rising tension in the story. (2)	Student does not identify the main sequence of events or plot the rising tension in the story. (0–1)
Raising Questions	Student poses thoughtful and honest questions about readings. (3)	Student poses some questions about readings. (2)	Student does not initiate questions about readings. (0–1)
Independent: 9–12 Proficient: 5–8 Developing: 0–4			

ASSESS LITERACY

The teacher uses the rubric shown here to assess students' performances in the writing workshop.

Criteria	Independent	Proficient	Developing
Content Knowledge	Student is knowledgeable about content area and integrates it throughout counting book. (3)	Student is somewhat knowledgeable about content area and integrates it throughout counting book. (2)	Student is not knowledgeable about content area and does not integrate it throughout counting book. (0–1)
Planning	Student actively participates in planning the text and discussing ideas. (3)	Student is somewhat active in planning the text and discussing ideas. (2)	Students does not plan the text or discuss ideas. (0–1)
Drafting	Student uses the planning process to compose text. (3)	Student somewhat uses the planning process to compose text. (2)	Student does not use the planning process to compose text. (0–1)
Editing	Student edits text and reviews sentence structure, vocabulary, grammar, and spelling. (3)	Student partially edits text and reviews sentence structure, vocabulary, grammar, and spelling. (2)	Student does not edit text or review sentence structure, vocabulary, grammar, and spelling. (0–1)

Independent: 9–12
Proficient: 5–8
Developing: 0–4

ideas for the numbers 1 to 10, then use their ideas to write a number book. During this phase, the teacher helps students to complete their books, including appropriate illustrations.

After Writing   The students present their counting books using a choral reading performance of the rhyming text. The students compare their counting books with those in the text set.

Collaborative Inquiry Across the Curriculum

The theme Number Journeys Around the World develops concepts in science and mathematics, as well as the language arts, related to the text set that children read. This section discusses how to use literature to teach the concepts of numbers as they relate to various curricular areas.

Extension to Mathematics   In *Moja Means One: A Swahili Counting Book*, students discover how numbers are expressed in different parts of the world. In learning

STANDARDS

Mathematics Standards
1. Number and Operation
8. Communication

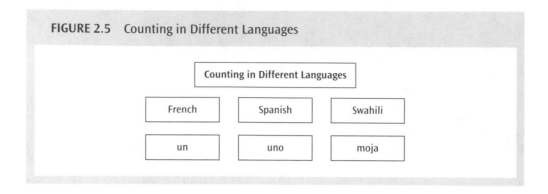

FIGURE 2.5 Counting in Different Languages

numbers that are used around the world, students complete the chart illustrated in Figure 2.5 based on the different languages already spoken in their classroom. If they do not have bilingual classmates, they can research numbers on the Internet or in the encyclopedia.

STANDARDS

Science Standards
Life Science, Content
Standard C3

Extension to Science In order to connect to the sub-theme of Numbers Around the World, students use the books *The Michigan Counting Book* and *Sunny Numbers: A Florida Counting Book* to explore flora and fauna from different regions. Students can use the Internet to extend their knowledge of plants and animals from these counting books. After gathering information, students create dioramas to present to their peers and explain the environments described in the counting books.

STANDARDS

Social Studies Standards
  I. Culture
III. People, Places, and
     Environments

Extension to Social Studies The books in this text set explore how numbers are used around the world. The two books that were highlighted are set in Africa and depict village life. Students have a choice to use the Internet to research different countries such as France or Great Britain to create their multicultural number books and illustrate them with national landmarks that emphasize numbers, such as Big Ben.

Home–School Connections Parents can help their children explore the world of numbers by recording numbers they see on their daily journeys to school. Students then have a number scavenger hunt as they try to find where numbers are displayed on this route. They share their findings with the class and discover how their school journey can take on a different perspective.

On-Your-Own Activities *Anno's Counting House* by Mitsumasa Anno completes the text set. The book uses cut-out windows to show children the process of moving into a new house while counting, adding, and subtracting. When students have completed their readings, they discuss the math stories in the text. Using the counting books they created, students compose their own stories using addition or subtraction, illustrate them, and share them with their peers.

Critical Literacy

Students in the primary grades begin to develop critical literacy skills such as researching and synthesizing information from the Internet. After completing the unit, students work in groups of three to research numbers from 1 to 10 in a different language. When they have completed their research, they synthesize their information using the graphic illustrated in Figure 2.6.

FIGURE 2.6   Numbers Around the World

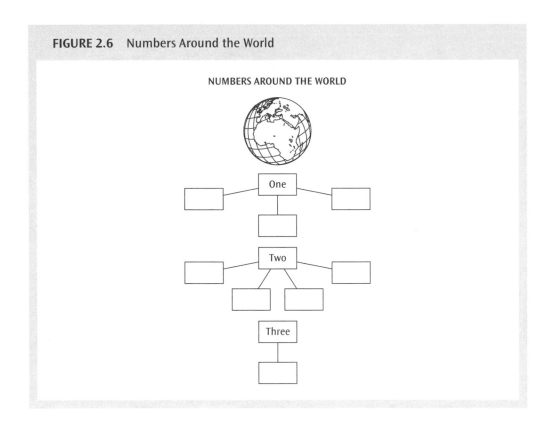

NUMBERS AROUND THE WORLD

Collaborative Literacy

As a celebration of the theme Journeys, the students can host a *Number Journeys Around the World* celebration for their peers from other classes. Students create train tracks made of butcher paper set up around the classroom. As their peers walk along the train tracks, they stop at various number stations where students present their colorful counting books and teach their peers to repeat a few numbers. As a closure to their number journey, class visitors share their own experiences of different numbers that are used around the world.

■ Intermediate Grades: Grades 3–5

Today a journey taken across the United States is rather simple: one buys a plane ticket, sits and relaxes, sometimes watches a movie, and within a few hours arrives at one's destination. Can we begin to imagine what it was like 200 years ago, exploring the uncharted territory in search of a northwest passage? In *Sacagawea* by Judith St. George, we read about the celebrated journey of Lewis and Clark with their Corps of Discovery. Unlike today's travel, the expedition from St. Louis to the Pacific Ocean was indeed a dangerous journey through unknown wilderness, including challenges of nature such as grizzly bears, impassable mountain paths, blizzards, hunger, and illness. Lewis and Clark's journals show the courageous Shoshone woman Sacagawea to be the translator of several languages, the negotiator who bargained for horses from Shoshone Indians, and the forager of food when it became scarce.

The Lewis and Clark Expedition

Text Set

Animals on the Trail with Lewis and Clark
*As Far as the Eye Can Reach: Lewis and Clark's
    Westward Quest*
Bold Journey: West with Lewis and Clark
*How We Crossed the West: The Adventures of
    Lewis and Clark*
The Incredible Journey of Lewis and Clark
*The Journal of Augustus Pelletier:
    The Lewis and Clark Expedition*
The Journey Home
*Lewis and Clark: Explorers of
    the American West*
*Lewis & Clark Expedition: Join the Corps
    of Discovery to Explore Uncharted Territory*
*Lewis and Clark: Explorers of the Louisiana
    Purchase*
Lewis and Clark and Me: A Dog's Tale
*Lewis and Clark for Kids: Their Journey
    of Discovery with 21 Activities*
Mountain Men: True Grit and Tall Tales
*My Travels with Capts. Lewis and Clark
    by George Shannon*

*New Found Land: Lewis and Clark's
    Voyage of Discovery*
Plants on the Trail with Lewis and Clark
*Seaman: The Dog Who Explored the West
    with Lewis and Clark*
*Seaman's Journal: On the Trail
    with Lewis and Clark*
Sacagawea
*Sacajawea: The Story of Bird Woman and
    the Lewis and Clark Expedition*
Sacagawea: The Journey to the West
Sacagawea: American Pathfinder
Streams to the River, River to the Sea

Outcomes

- Map the Lewis and Clark Journey.
- Create a time line.
- Create a survival kit that would be used
  by pioneers in the early 19th century.
- Write a simulated explorer's log.

Family Journeys

Text Set

Arthur for the Very First Time
Seven Kisses in a Row
What You Know First
Journey
Sarah, Plain and Tall
Skylark
Caleb's Story

Outcomes

- Conduct an author study of Patricia
  MacLachlan.
- Create a diorama for a text setting.
- Write family journals by listening to
  family stories and making entries.

Creative Journeys of Musicians

Text Set

Ella Fitzgerald: The Tale of a Vocal Virtuosa
This Land Was Made for You and Me
When Marian Sang
*Shake, Rattle, & Roll: The Founders of
    Rock & Roll*
Duke Ellington: The Piano Prince
*The Voice that Challenged a Nation: Marian
    Anderson and the Struggle for Equal
    Rights*

Outcomes

- Create a photo journal for one of the
  musicians.
- Present a slideshow on one of the
  biographies.

**Personal
Journeys**

**Journeys
in Time**

The Oregon Trail

Text Set

*Across the Wide and Lonesome
    Prairie: The Oregon Trail of
    Hattie Campbell, 1847*
The Frontier Fort on the Oregon Trail
*The Journal of Jedediah Barstow: An
    Emigrant on the Oregon Trail*
The Lost Wagon Train
*Our Journey West: Adventure
    on the Oregon Trail*
The Oregon Trail
*A Perfect Place: Joshua's Oregon
    Trail Diary, Book Two*
*The Tragic Tale of Narcissa Whitman and
    a Faithful History of the Oregon Trail*

Outcomes

- Create an accordion book of events
  that happened during the journey.
- Determine the number of miles
  covered in the journey on the Oregon
  Trail and how long it would take going
  at different rates of speed.

JOURNEYS

**Journeys to
Other Places**

Journey to the Moon

Text Set

Moon Song
Journey to the Moon
The Angry Moon
Why the Sun and Moon Live in the Sky
Moon Base: First Colony in Space
Footprints on the Moon
Moon Whales and Other Moon Poems

Outcomes

- Create a database of moon
  observations.
- Write moon poems.

Journey to the Desert

Text Set

Cactus Poems
Deserts
The Desert Is Theirs
Desert Voices
*Efrain of the Sonoran Desert: A Lizard's
    Life Among the Seri Indians*
I'm in Charge of Celebrations
One Day in the Desert
A Walk in the Desert

Outcomes

- Create *All About* books on the desert.
- Write poetry of desert life.

In addition to Journeys in Time, this section presents Journeys to Other Places such as deserts and the moon. Personal Journeys will direct readers to explore one family's journey through Patricia MacLachlan's series of books. Children will be astounded to learn about the challenges that many musicians and artists face through their creative journeys. Pam Muñoz Ryan's *When Marian Sang* allows readers a glimpse at the astonishing talent of Marian Anderson, a young African American girl with the "voice of the century," who overcame enormous challenges to sing in Constitution Hall, which only allowed white performers.

The award-winning literature included in each of the text sets will help to develop understandings around the theme and provide students with insights into broad disciplines through personal stories.

SAMPLER ▪ The Lewis and Clark Expedition

The United States had barely received its independence before its eyes were firmly planted on the West. The widely celebrated Lewis and Clark Expedition (1804–1805), commissioned by President Thomas Jefferson, is symbolic of America's westward expansion. There are numerous accounts available for young readers that detail this journey. *Girl of the Shining Mountains* by Peter and Connie Roop is one of many versions from the perspective of Sacagawea, the only woman in the expedition. When Sacagawea joined Captains Lewis and Clark, she played an integral role in the expedition as a guide, but her heartfelt goal was to return to her Shoshone people, from whom she was captured as a young girl. Within one story, *Sacajawea* by Joseph Bruchac, the journey is retold from two different perspectives, once from Sacajawea's point of view and the second from William Clark's. The journals of Captains Lewis and Clark are primary sources of this historical event, offering authors the perspectives of the explorers themselves. Such a perspective appears in *As Far as the Eye Can Reach: Lewis and Clark's Westward Quest* by Elizabeth Cody Kimmel.

Within the sub-theme The Lewis and Clark Expedition, students will learn the importance of President Thomas Jefferson's westward pursuit. Throughout their readings, they will begin to understand that, like all explorations, this commission was a perilous journey in uncharted territory. By viewing pictures of the route in *The Lewis and Clark Trail: Then and Now,* students will further develop an understanding of the concept of exploration. As students further engage in readings from the text set and discussions and projects related to the sub-theme, they will learn about the important discoveries made during the journey to the West and make critical connections with similarities in the explorations of their time.

The most interesting accounts of the Lewis and Clark Expedition are taken from journal entries written by a number of participants in the expedition, some fictitious. These varied accounts of the journey provide different viewpoints. Among a wide variety of concepts and skills related to the Lewis and Clark Expedition, the students will learn the importance of journal writing to document events or to take notes. Students will also begin to understand the concept of an author's perspective as they read different accounts of the journey.

NCTE/IRA Standards for the English Language Arts

1. Students read a wide range of print and non-print texts to build an understanding of texts, of themselves, and of the cultures of the United States and the world; to

JOURNEYS
The Lewis and Clark Expedition

THE FOCUS LESSON

Read aloud *Lewis and Clark: Explorers of the America West* and learn about the purpose for studying the Lewis and Clark Expedition and how to keep a journey journal.

READING WORKSHOP

The students will learn about the Lewis and Clark Expedition from varied perspectives by reading journal entries of different explorers. They will use a journal to record ideas and facts that they learned from reading.

WRITING WORKSHOP

After students have read several accounts of the Lewis and Clark Expedition and have heard read alouds of several tall tales, they write a tall tale integrating some of the historical events they learned from their readings.

Text Set

Animals on the Trail with Lewis and Clark
As Far as the Eye Can Reach: Lewis and Clark's Westward Quest
Bold Journey: West with Lewis and Clark
How We Crossed the West: The Adventures of Lewis and Clark
The Incredible Journey of Lewis and Clark
The Journal of Augustus Pelletier: The Lewis and Clark Expedition
The Journey Home
Lewis and Clark: Explorers of the American West

Lewis & Clark Expedition: Join the Corps of Discovery to Explore Uncharted Territory
Lewis and Clark: Explorers of the Louisiana Purchase
Lewis and Clark and Me: A Dog's Tale
Lewis and Clark for Kids: Their Journey of Discovery with 21 Activities
Mountain Men: True Grit and Tall Tales
My Travels with Capts. Lewis and Clark by George Shannon
New Found Land: Lewis and Clark's Voyage of Discovery

Plants on the Trail with Lewis and Clark
Seaman: The Dog Who Explored the West with Lewis and Clark
Seaman's Journal: On the Trail with Lewis and Clark
Sacagawea
Sacajawea: The Story of Bird Woman and the Lewis and Clark Expedition
Sacagawea: The Journey to the West
Sacagawea: American Pathfinder
Streams to the River, River to the Sea

SOCIAL STUDIES

Students compare the territory of North America in 1803 with current maps of the United States to find out what states were part of the Louisiana Purchase. They will consult *The Lewis and Clark Trail: Then and Now* to see the differences in the land and the maps that represent it. Consulting major websites on the Internet, they will study the Lewis and Clark historic places. Their project is to design a travel brochure for a sightseeing vacation.

COLLABORATIVE INQUIRY ACTIVITIES ACROSS THE CURRICULUM

ART

Students will develop an acrostic mobile of Lewis and Clark or create a boardgame for classmates, where the goal is to match the animal names with their track prints.

SCIENCE

Students will read the two books on the plants and animals along the trail of the expedition. They will create a large bulletin board of the trail using pictures and descriptions of plants and animals found along the Lewis and Clark expedition trail.

MATHEMATICS AND TECHNOLOGY

Using a variety of maps accessed from the Internet, students will calculate the distance from the beginning of the expedition at St. Louis, Missouri, to its end at Salt Camp by the Pacific Ocean. They will compare how many days it took the explorers to reach their destination with how long would it take using different modes of transportation that are available today such as car, train, and plane. The students will use a bar graph to present their calculations, comparing the first expedition to a modern day trip from St. Louis to the Pacific Ocean by different means of transportation.

SCIENCE, MATH, AND TECHNOLOGY ACTIVITIES

ON-YOUR-OWN ACTIVITIES

Using several websites, learn about the animals and plants that the Discovery Corps observed and wrote about in their journals. Identify the animals and learn about their tracks.

HOME–SCHOOL CONNECTIONS

Students read and learn the trail signs of the Native Americans. Most trail signs use materials as a code or a symbol. Students will create a set of directions from their home to school or to another place in their community by using landmarks as symbols.

acquire new information; to respond to the needs and demands of society and the workplace; and for personal fulfillment. Among these texts are fiction and nonfiction, classic and contemporary works.

4. Students adjust their use of spoken, written, and visual language (i.e., conventions, style, vocabulary) to communicate effectively with a variety of audiences and for different purposes.

12. Students use spoken, written, and visual language to accomplish their own purposes.

Learner Outcomes

Students will be able to do the following:

- Use journals to record a variety of information about the Lewis and Clark Expeditions.
- Discuss different perspectives of the retelling of the Lewis and Clark Expedition.
- Write a tall tale of an event from the Lewis and Clark Expedition and present it to the class.

Conduct a Focus Lesson

Establish a Purpose   With the map of the United States in the background, the teacher invites the students to take a journey back in time, 200 years ago, with Meriwether Lewis and William Clark. Using a map showing the explorers' expedition (included in almost every book in the text set), the teacher guides them as they trace over (1) the Louisiana Purchase, (2) the route to the Pacific, (3) Lewis's separate return route, (4) Clark's separate return route, and (5) their combined route. The teacher tells the students that they will travel with Lewis and Clark to learn about their commission from President Jefferson; meet the members of the expedition and learn the important part each played on the journey; and keep a log of all the things they learn on their journey, describing how the West was different 200 years ago than it is today.

Engage in a Read Aloud   The teacher selects the biography *Sacagawea* by Lise Erdrich to read aloud to the students. Using a book introduction, the teacher shows the beautiful illustrations as a way of introducing the students to Sacagawea and the critical role she played in the Lewis and Clark Expedition. Before the read aloud, students are introduced to the pictures of characters they would meet on the Lewis and Clark expedition and where the expedition started and ended.

As the teacher reads *Sacagawea,* he or she stops for a short explanation of words that students may not know, for example, keelboat, pirogue, and the Native American tribes of Hidatsa, Shoshone, Teton Sioux, Mandan, and Yankton Sioux.

Conduct a Mini-Lesson   After the read aloud, the teacher returns to the book and conducts a mini-lesson on using journals to record the writer's observations or learnings. The teacher explains why explorers needed to keep journals, and how Captains Lewis and Clark were commissioned to record everything they observed and learned while journeying to the West.

The teacher shows students three different books, *Plants on the Trail with Lewis and Clark, Animals on the Trail with Lewis and Clark,* and *The Journal of Augustus Pelletier,* explaining that these books, as well as many others, were written from different perspectives based on explorers' journal entries. The teacher explains that they will be reading and listening to stories about the Lewis and Clark Expedition and that they will keep a journey journal on the important ideas they learned.

Together the teacher and students brainstorm some ideas of entries that would be important to write about. The teacher models how to make a journal entry about what was learned while reading *Sacagawea*.

Additional Mini-Lessons

Grammar: Parts of Speech

- The teacher creates a chart with the headings "Proper Noun," "Noun," and "Pronoun," and helps students to understand the relationship of each.
- Then the teacher develops a list of the names of explorers that students will read about.
- The teacher uses one name, Captain Meriwether Lewis, to model to students how we can refer to him by using different parts of speech.
- The teacher writes his names, his title, and the pronoun reference for him under the proper category heading.
- Using the chart, the students work through other names from the list.

Double-Entry Learning Logs

- The teacher models how to use a double-entry learning log to the students.
- On the right side of the page, the teacher writes a sentence or two from the book that students have just read.
- Using a think aloud, the teacher demonstrates how to think through the meaning of the text recorded in the journal.
- The teacher then models how to write a meaningful response or an explanation of the text as the second journal entry.

Character Analysis

- The teacher engages students in a discussion on Sacagawea, focusing on her character traits.
- As the discussion proceeds, the teacher writes some of the character traits that were identified.
- The teacher then introduces the students to an acrostic mobile, showing the students how to match each letter in Sacagawea's name to a character trait beginning with the same letter. For example, for the first letter of her name, "S," they might choose *strong*.

Conduct a Reading Workshop

During the reading workshop, students read about the Lewis and Clark Expedition from the perspective of Sacagawea, the Native American who served as interpreter and guide to Captains Lewis and Clark. Within the suggested text set, there are a variety of books focusing on Sacagawea with a wide range of reading levels and genres, including informational, biography, historical fiction, and picture storybooks. Each book provides students with a retelling of the journey to the West from Sacagawea's perspective.

Before Reading   Students may not understand what it means "to take a perspective" or to write a story from a particular perspective. Therefore, the teacher develops this literary concept through an example, by asking the students to think of a recent occurrence at school and requesting one or two volunteers to retell the story. The teacher then follows up with his or her own retelling of the school event.

To apply the concept of "taking a perspective," the teacher presents Joseph Bruchac's *Sacajawea,* a story that offers two versions of the expedition on alternating pages. The teacher reads an excerpt of each version so that the students will further understand different perspectives.

The teacher explains that they will read Sacagawea's version of the Lewis and Clark Expedition and asks what they know about her that they expect to read about and what they learn that they do not already know. As the students respond, the teacher lists the information that the students know and think they may learn. The students are now ready to read *Sacagawea's Story: Girl of the Shining Mountains* by Peter and Connie Roop to gain Sacagawea's perspective of the expedition. Asking the students to look at the cover picture of Sacagawea and her baby Pomp, the teacher reads the first sentence, "Mama, tell me about your journey to the great salt lake, the Pacific Ocean," and tells them that Pomp is asking to hear her mother's version of the story.

During Reading   Before students read the first four chapters of their book, the teacher asks them to examine the differences in print in Chapter 1 and the other chapters. She explains that the italics indicate dialogue. The teacher directs the students to read the first page and see how Pomp, Sacagawea's baby, is asking to hear the story. The teacher then directs the students to continue to read the story independently.

After Reading   To help the students think about their reading, the teacher leads the discussion by using the following guiding questions:

1. After reading the beginning of *Girl of the Shining Mountains,* why is she called by this name?
2. We know that Sacagawea was a Shoshone. What were some of her chores and things that she learned as a Native American?
3. Why were the Shoshone attacked by the Hidatsa?
4. What happened to Sacagawea's family and friends?

Journal Writing   The students are then directed to revisit their readings and record what they have learned in a log, their Journey Journals. The teacher reminds them about the journal that Lewis and Clark kept to remember what they learned along the trail. She relates President Jefferson's letter sent to Captain Lewis on June 20, 1803, that emphasized the importance of taking great pains to write down their observations with accuracy.

To guide the students as they write in their journals, the teacher provides them with a simple graphic organizer, as shown in Figure 2.7. The teacher tells the students to draw the graphic in their journals and directs them to use it to recall what they learned about the people, land, animals, plants, big events, and customs.

Conduct a Writing Workshop

Before Writing   The teacher gathers the children and tells them that there are many legends and stories that came from the journey to the West. The mountain men who followed the trails of Lewis and Clark claim they invented "American tall tales." The teacher shares the book *Mountain Men: True Grit and Tall Tales* by Andrew Glass with the students. The teacher's read aloud of the introduction will help the students learn

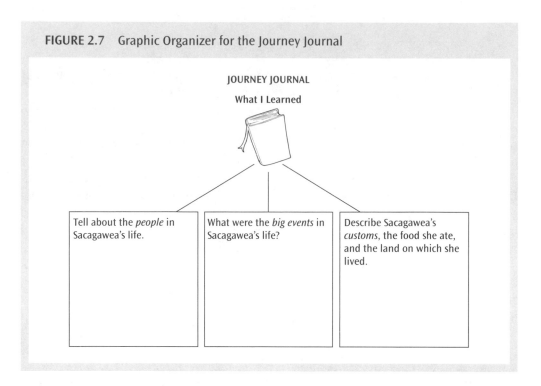

FIGURE 2.7 Graphic Organizer for the Journey Journal

JOURNEY JOURNAL

What I Learned

Tell about the *people* in Sacagawea's life.	What were the *big events* in Sacagawea's life?	Describe Sacagawea's *customs*, the food she ate, and the land on which she lived.

ASSESS LITERACY

After the students have completed the reading workshop sequence, the teacher uses the rubric here to assess their performance.

Criteria	Independent	Proficient	Developing
Analyzing Perspective	Student is able to discuss the story from a certain character's perspective. (3)	Student is able to discuss the story from a certain character's perspective most of the time. (2)	Student is not able to discuss the story from a certain character's perspective. (0–1)
Student Participation in Discussion	Student actively participates in discussions, is highly engaged in listening to group members, takes turns, and responds to others with respect at all times. (3)	Student participates in discussions, listens to group members, takes turns, and responds to others most of the time. (2)	Student participates in discussions to some degree, begins to listen to group members, takes turns, and responds to others some of the time. (0–1)
Discussion Responses	Student gives elaborate, accurate responses to teacher-led questions; frequently incorporates the language from readings; at times includes critical analysis within the response; and makes varied types of text connections. (3)	Student gives fairly accurate responses to teacher-led questions, at times incorporates the language from readings, attempts to include a critical analysis within the response, and makes some types of text connections. (2)	Student gives very brief and minimally accurate responses to teacher-led questions, rarely incorporates language from readings in responses, and does not make text connections. (0–1)

Independent: 7–9

Proficient: 4–6

Developing: 0–3

how Private John Colter received permission to leave the expedition and stay behind in the Rocky Mountains, becoming the first American mountain man. The teacher continues to read about two other mountain men in order to help students get a sense of who invented tall tales.

During Writing   The teacher directs the students to compose their own tall tales using the following procedure:

1. Pretend they are on the uncharted trails going out to the Rocky Mountains and make up a ridiculous story to entertain their friends.
2. Brainstorm unbelievable events that might happen then and select one.
3. Use what they have learned about the Lewis and Clark journey, such as the animals and plants, the conditions of the land, the weather, the food, and so on.

ASSESS LITERACY

After the students have written their tall tales, the teacher uses the rubric here to assess their writing.

Criteria	Independent	Proficient	Developing
Content Knowledge	Student integrates the content of the Lewis and Clark Expedition throughout the tale. (3)	Student integrates some content of Lewis and Clark Expedition in the tale. (2)	Student does not integrate the content from Lewis and Clark Expedition in the tale. (0–1)
Genre: Tall Tales	Student includes all the elements of a tall tale, presented creatively. (3)	Student includes the elements of a tall tale in the story. (2)	Student does not include the elements of a tall tale. (0–1)
Story Parts	All story parts are present, are well-developed, and written in a logical sequence. (3)	All story parts are present, written in a sequence that the reader can follow. (2)	Most story parts are present but do not appear in a sequential order. (0–1)
Sentence Structure	Student employs varied types of sentences in writing, using some complex structures when appropriate. (3)	Student uses sentences that are somewhat simple and lacking variety, but are accurate. (2)	Student uses sentence structure that is simple and not always accurate. (0–1)
Content Vocabulary	Student consistently uses content vocabulary throughout with a high degree of accuracy. (3)	Student uses some of the content vocabulary; may use words incorrectly. (2)	Student does not use the content vocabulary. (0–1)
Language Mechanics	No errors in language mechanics are present. (3)	Some errors in language mechanics are present but do not interfere with meaning. (2)	Many errors in language mechanics appear throughout. (0–1)

Independent: 13–18
Proficient: 7–12
Developing: 0–6

4. Work in small groups of three or four and brainstorm some ideas they have learned that can be changed to a "ridiculous" or "unbelievable" story.
5. Compose the story first by telling it to each other.
6. Write down the story after they have told it to each other.

After Writing   After they finish writing their tall tales, students learn them and practice telling them with expression. The tall tales will inspire a storytelling fest to share their stories with their friends.

Collaborative Inquiry Across the Curriculum

Extension to Mathematics and Technology   A trip from St. Louis to the Pacific Ocean today is quite different from Lewis and Clark's Expedition taken over 200 years ago. Today's sojourner to the West might travel by highways using maps, whereas the first explorers of the West rode horses through the uncharted territory of the Missouri River over the Rocky Mountains, following the Columbia River to the Pacific Ocean. Using a variety of maps from the Internet, students calculate the distance from the beginning of the expedition in St. Louis, Missouri, to its end at Salt Camp by the Pacific Ocean. How many days did it take the explorers to reach their destination? How long would it take using different modes of transportation? The students use a bar graph to present their calculations, comparing the first expedition to a modern day trip from St. Louis to the Pacific Ocean by different means of transportation.

Extension to Science   Students will use two books from the text set, *Plants on the Trail with Lewis and Clark* and *Animals on the Trail with Lewis and Clark,* to learn about the animals and plants that Lewis and Clark as well as the Corps of Discovery observed and recorded in their journals. They may also consult websites for additional information. Have each student contribute an animal and plant to the "They Were Found on the Trail" bulletin board. On large paper, the teacher and students create a map of the Lewis and Clark trail. They will draw the plant and animal they have selected, labeling and writing a brief description of each. They will then place each animal and plant along the Lewis and Clark Expedition.

Extension to Social Studies   The teacher conducts a read aloud of *The Lewis and Clark Trail: Then and Now.* Throughout the reading, the teacher shows maps and pictures comparing the land as it was 200 years ago with today. After the reading, the teacher conducts a brief mini-lesson on the following:

1. The Louisiana Purchase
2. President Jefferson's commission to Captain Meriwether Lewis to explore uncharted and unmapped land of the Louisiana Purchase
3. A comparison of the land 200 years ago with today's land, using maps found on the Internet. The teacher asks the students to (1) use the maps to determine the states that were part of the Louisiana Purchase; (2) consult the websites www.lewisandclark.org and http://lewis-clark.org to determine the present day locations and brief descriptions of historic sites of the Lewis and Clark Expedition; and (3) design a travel brochure to a favorite historic site.

Home–School Connections   Students read and learn the trail signs of the Native Americans. Most trail signs use materials or images as a code or a symbol. Students will create a set of directions from their home to school by using landmarks as symbols. They will do the following:

1. Identify each landmark as a symbol to guide them from their home to school.
2. Using the symbols, write explicit directions from home to school.
3. Draw a multimedia map from home to school that uses landmarks.
4. Use www.mapquest.com to compare their own directions and maps with the ones on the MapQuest website.

On-Your-Own Activities   Lewis and Clark kept journals of their journey westward for future generations to explore. After creating journey journals, the students will be ready to construct simulated journals of a trip they took with their parents. Students can bring in artifacts and photos from the trip to illustrate their journal entries. After creating the trip journals, the students can share them with peers and discuss the different joys and hardships they experienced.

Critical Literacy

After the students have completed the sub-theme, they synthesize their information about the Louisiana Purchase. Working in groups of three, the students pick a state that they researched in the Extension to Social Studies activity and create a podcast for their peers that recreates a journey through the state today. The podcast must describe differences in plants, animals, or other environmental changes from the time of the Lewis and Clark expedition.

Collaborative Literacy

After students have written their tall tales, they participate in a storytelling fest. They take on the persona of a fictional character and practice telling the tall tale as the character would. The fest may be elaborate or simple. The students may wear paper masks, and they may invite their parents or other classes to listen to their tall tales.

■ Middle Grades: Grades 6–8

The year is 1861, and the first shots of the Civil War have been fired. The American people are strongly divided: Southern Confederates want to uphold slavery because their economy is based on cotton and tobacco farming, whereas Northern Industrialists want to end slavery because their economy is based on wage labor and they see the institution as a violation of human rights. For President Lincoln the primary concern is to preserve the Union, but as the war continues it becomes evident that different viewpoints of slavery are at the core of the controversy. Though torn by the knowledge that abolishing slavery will severely weaken the Southern economy, the president knows that slavery is a moral injustice.

When Lincoln issued the Emancipation Proclamation on New Year's Day 1863, he called for freedom for slaves in the rebel states. Middle school students will investigate the theme of *Journeys* by reading literature illustrating that for African Americans, the Emancipation Proclamation was not an end but a beginning. As students read about the daily struggles of being a slave in *Dear Mr. President Abraham Lincoln: Letters from a Slave Girl*, Ann Maria Weems's journey along the Underground Railroad in

WARRIORS FOR EQUALITY

Text Set

Warriors Don't Cry
Through My Eyes
Growing up Black
Coming of Age in Mississippi
Bad Boy: A Memoir
Rosa Parks: My Story
Two Tickets to Freedom
Childtimes
Open Wide the Freedom Gates
Linda Brown, You Are Not Alone

Outcomes

- Compare and contrast autobiography and memoir.
- Abstract and identify the features of memoir.
- Create a memoir to tell about a critical event in your family journey.
- Retell the story of Rosa Parks.

FROM SLAVERY TO EQUAL RIGHTS

Text Set

Abraham Lincoln: Letters from a Slave Girl
Stealing Freedom
The Land
Roll of Thunder, Hear My Cry
Let the Circle Be Unbroken
The Road to Memphis

Outcomes

- Write literary letters from the perspective of Lincoln, Lettie Tucker, or Ann Maria Weems.
- Maintain learning logs to analyze life for African Americans before the Civil Rights Movement in texts by Mildred D. Taylor.
- Participate in a Socratic seminar.

OVERCOMING PHYSICAL AND EMOTIONAL CHALLENGES

Text Set

Speak
Cheat the Moon
Touch of the Clown
One Fat Summer
The Beast
Izzy, Willy Nilly
That Was Then, This Is Now
I Hadn't Meant to Tell You This

Outcomes

- Construct a plot profile to identify the pivotal events in the main character's journey to overcome a personal challenge.
- Write about your own personal challenges in a blog.

Personal Journeys

Journeys in Time

JOURNEYS

Journeys to Other Places

PAST, PRESENT, AND FUTURE

Text Set

Zoe Rising
Running Out of Time
A Wrinkle in Time
Shadows on the Wall
Vision Quest
Tanglewreck

Outcomes

- Write a postcard from a time travel perspective.
- Write predictions for life on Earth in 2108.

ALONG THE SILK ROAD

Text Set

Monkey: Journey to the West
Marco Polo: A Journey Through China
The Silk Route: 7,000 Miles of History
Empire in the East: The Story of Genghis Khan
Traveling Man: The Story of Ibn Battuta
Between the Dragon and the Eagle
Made in China: Ideas and Inventions from Ancient China

Outcomes

- Compare/contrast the Silk Road with the Oregon Trail.
- Create a mural to illustrate the Silk Road and the goods that traveled on it.

FANTASTIC REGIONS

Text Set

Peter and the Starcatchers
Inkheart
The Lion, the Witch and the Wardrobe
The Merchant of Death
Eragon
The Hobbit

Outcomes

- List the characteristics of the main character and/or hero who made the world a better place.
- Engage in a grand conversation about text set.
- Write a simulated book review on one of the texts.

Stealing Freedom, and Mildred Taylor's descriptions of the Logan family's life in the Deep South from the Civil War to the dawn of the Civil Rights Movement, they take a journey through time and come to understand the harsh realities of racism, bigotry, and segregation. Students learn that the journey from freedom to equality was filled with painful and humiliating social injustices, and they will come to admire the dignity and courage of those who persisted.

The theme of Journeys will be further explored through texts dealing with Personal Journeys, such as alcoholism and other problems.

SAMPLER ■ From Slavery to Equal Rights

In this sampler students read texts about a period in time when many experienced the injustices of slavery and discrimination. They will be expected to reconsider the concepts of freedom and equality and resolve their internal tensions about racism.

In *Abraham Lincoln: Letters from a Slave Girl,* students read an exchange of letters between Lettie Tucker, a young slave who lives on a plantation in South Carolina, and President Lincoln. Although the letters are fictional, they vividly portray the details of the life of a slave living during the Civil War and provide insights into the mind of President Lincoln. At the same time, students will read *Stealing Freedom,* a narrative based on Ann Maria Weems's dramatic journey from slavery to freedom. The students will see not only the injustice of working from dawn to dusk but the humiliation of obeying orders and living under the control of insensitive owners. Their readings will help them experience the warmth and love of Ann Maria's protective family and the despair she felt when she was sent away from them to be the housemaid of a spoiled and selfish child. Finally, students will learn about the courage of the slaves and those who helped them make the journey to freedom along the Underground Railroad.

According to Galda and Cullinan (2002), the best historical fiction comes from authors who are not only immersed in documenting facts but are good storytellers who engage well-developed characters in events consistent with historical evidence. They maintain that who the author is and how he or she understands and interprets a historical experience influences historical fiction and caution that authors should portray issues honestly and fairly when writing about periods when racism and sexism were prevalent.

In the sampler, as depicted in the graphic organizer, students will study the voice of Mildred D. Taylor, a distinguished American author who has been honored with the Newbery Medal, the Globe-Horn Book Award, the Coretta Scott King Award, the Christopher Award, the Alan Award, and the NSK Laureate. Mildred D. Taylor started writing books based on the stories told at her family gatherings, because she hoped to present an aspect of American history that was not included in the textbooks of her childhood. Although she was born in Jackson, Mississippi, Ms. Taylor grew up in the North because her father recognized the difficulties of life in the racially segregated South. However, throughout her childhood the Taylors often returned to Mississippi, where Mildred heard older members of her family tell about the struggles relatives and friends faced in the racist culture of America before the Civil Rights Movement. Ms. Taylor writes about life as she remembers it, describing the joys of growing up in a large, supportive family; her own feelings about facing segregation and bigotry; and the character and spirit of people who were treated as inferiors. As students read the Logan family stories, they learn about life in America as seen by African Americans,

JOURNEYS
From Slavery to Equal Rights

THE FOCUS LESSON

Teacher reads aloud letters from *Abraham Lincoln: Letters from a Slave Girl*. Students and teacher read *Stealing Freedom*. Learn about the daily life of a slave and how to write literary letters to reflect on and respond to ideas in a text.

READING WORKSHOP

Teacher introduces the author Mildred D. Taylor and uses book talks to describe books in text set. Students select a book and participate in book clubs, using reading logs to monitor interactions between characters. Students discuss racist beliefs and the author's craft in a Socratic seminar.

WRITING WORKSHOP

Teacher and students identify the attributes of the memoir genre. Students select a task based on the genre: *family stories, photo-memoirs, warriors for equality,* and *personal memoirs.*

Text Set

Abraham Lincoln: Letters from a Slave Girl
Stealing Freedom
The Land
Roll of Thunder, Hear My Cry
Let the Circle Be Unbroken
The Road to Memphis

SOCIAL STUDIES

Students research newspapers during school integration. Write letters to "warriors" to describe how their actions changed education. Students research the shift from cities to suburbs and create photo essays to show positive and negative effects of suburban shift.

COLLABORATIVE INQUIRY ACTIVITIES ACROSS THE CURRICULUM

ART

Collect photos of "separate but equal" conditions before 1954. Dramatize King's *I Have a Dream* speech.

MATHEMATICS

Using the Internet, students identify the number of African Americans who graduated from high school and college from 1900 to 2000. They create graph(s) to illustrate changes in levels of education for specific subgroups.

SCIENCE, MATH, AND TECHNOLOGY ACTIVITIES

SCIENCE

Students investigate planting, developing, and harvesting cotton. They investigate the soil and climate needed to raise cotton and problems that would lead to crop failure.

ON-YOUR-OWN ACTIVITIES

Students role play interviews with civil rights warriors they have researched.

HOME–SCHOOL CONNECTIONS

Students and parents discuss issues and events that led to Civil Rights Movement. They consider: Do acts of segregation and discrimination exist today?

and they experience the extraordinary journey through time of a family who remained loving, united, and strong in the face of personal indignities.

Examining how the characters respond to conflict, students will explore their own beliefs and values and come to a deeper knowledge of themselves as individuals and citizens in a diverse society. Extension activities will help students make connections to contemporary issues and events and discover that the journey to freedom and equality continues.

The middle school sampler is designed to deepen students' understanding of slavery as a violation of human rights, as well as the effects of discrimination and segregation on individuals and society. Students will be guided to explore an issue from America's past that divided society and threatened to tear the nation apart. Students will observe both the journey through time and the intense personal journeys that erupted into the Civil Rights Movement of the 1960s. As students read and discuss the issues of prejudice and segregation, they will begin to sympathize with and celebrate the pride and courage of those who attempted to live as equals in a forbidding society.

NCTE/IRA Standards for the English Language Arts

1. Students read a wide range of print and non-print texts to build an understanding of texts, of themselves, and of the cultures of the United States and the world; to acquire new information; to respond to the needs and demands of society and the workplace; and for personal fulfillment. Among these texts are fiction and nonfiction, classic and contemporary works.

3. Students apply a wide range of strategies to comprehend, interpret, evaluate, and appreciate texts. They draw on their prior experience, their interactions with other readers and writers, their knowledge of word meaning and of other texts, their word identification strategies, and their understanding of textual features (e.g., sound–letter correspondence, sentence structure, context, and graphics).

6. Students apply knowledge of language structure, language conventions (e.g., spelling and punctuation), media techniques, figurative language, and genre to create, critique, and discuss print and non-print texts.

9. Students develop an understanding of and respect for diversity in language use, patterns, and dialects across cultures, ethnic groups, geographic regions, and social roles.

Learner Outcomes

Students will be able to do the following:

- Identify and analyze examples of segregation and discrimination in texts.
- Support assertions using evidence from texts and personal experiences.
- Show how details from texts relate to the theme of Journeys.
- Use evidence from fiction and nonfiction texts to support comments during Socratic seminars.
- Gather, organize, and synthesize details and examples from a variety of texts to communicate opinions relative to Mildred D. Taylor's writing.
- Read a wide range of fiction and nonfiction to build an understanding of racism and the Civil Rights Movement in the United States.
- Create letters to respond to slavery as a human experience.
- Write a memoir to demonstrate knowledge of the distinctive features of the genre.

Conduct a Focus Lesson

The text set for From Slavery to Equal Rights includes historical fiction with a range of reading levels and a singular theme—the journey from slavery to the dawn of the Civil Rights Movement, as seen through the eyes of African Americans. The teacher prepares students for a shared reading of Chapter 1 of *Stealing Freedom* by asking them to imagine Lettie, a 12-year-old slave who lives on the Tucker plantation in South Carolina in 1861. Although it is illegal for slaves to read and write, Lettie's mistress, Katherine Potts Tucker, encourages her to write to President Lincoln, who returns letters to Lettie.

The teacher then reads the letters from *Abraham Lincoln: Letters from a Slave Girl* (part of the *Dear Mr. President* series) dated April 15, May 23, June 1, August 4, September 26, October 4, and October 19, 1861. The students are asked to reflect on what it would be like to have every movement controlled by another by writing about the details in the letters that were most upsetting to them.

Establish a Purpose   The teacher focuses students' attention on a table where the books from the text set are displayed and explains the purpose of the lesson.

The teacher introduces *Stealing Freedom,* a book based on the dramatic journey of Ann Maria Weems, who lived on a small Maryland farm in the mid nineteenth century. The teacher explains that as they read the book, they will analyze the injustices of slavery and the frustrations that led slaves to make the dangerous journey along the Underground Railroad in order to "steal freedom."

Shared reading and letter writing activities will provide the students with the background knowledge they will need to participate in an author study of Mildred E. Taylor based on independent reading of one of the other books in this text set. Then students will engage in a Socratic seminar to reflect on the saga of the Logan family and the endurance of people living in the racially segregated South. As the students attempt to understand how racism separated society and the journey of African Americans from freedom to equality, they will make connections to journeys in their own lives.

Engage in Shared Reading   The teacher provides a copy of *Stealing Freedom* to each student. As the teacher reads the first two chapters aloud, the students see Addison and Ann Maria Weems creep up a grassy slope toward the worn fence where the Prices' hounds are howling. They hear Addison's fears that Master Charles will give them a whipping if he catches them. They watch Ann Maria's smile fall because her mother thinks questions about her age and birth date are foolish whereas even the youngest white child knows the day he was born. They look on as the day's work begins and watch Ann Maria trick Richard, her owner's younger brother, into helping her figure out her age. In the evening they return to the Weems' hut and listen as Uncle Abram tells how he tried to run off to the North to be free. They hear Ann Maria ask if it's bad to try to steal freedom and her father explain that slaves have their freedom stolen the day they are born. The students learn that Ann Maria's father is free and is determined to buy his whole family's freedom. As she finishes the chapter, the teacher asks the students, "What does Papa mean when he says slaves have their freedom stolen the day they are born? What's the difference between being a slave and being free? What must it feel like not to be free?"

Conduct a Mini-Lesson   The teacher explains that as the class reads *Stealing Freedom* they will reflect on the life of a slave and the journey to freedom by writing letters. The mini-lesson focuses on using literary letters to facilitate students' reflections on their reading. Similar to the *Dear Mr. President* series, literary letters (Cohen & Cowen, 2008) is an activity based on role play that enables students to respond to texts they are reading and content they are studying. Their letters should reflect facts but are not limited only to story details.

First, the teacher reviews the form for a friendly letter and assigns roles at random by dividing the class into groups of three. Within each group, one student will assume the role of Abraham Lincoln, another the role of Lettie Tucker, and the third will be Ann Maria Weems. The teacher indicates that for the first lesson they will focus their letters on the daily life of a slave. Those playing the role of Ann Maria Weems will write to President Lincoln; students with the role of Lettie Tucker will write to Ann Maria Weems; and those playing Lincoln will respond to both slaves.

The teacher asks the students to identify some of the details they recall from Ann Maria's and Lettie's descriptions of their daily routines and tells the students to imagine what each character would write to the person assigned, providing time for reflecting and writing. As students write, the teacher moves around the room reading student letters and providing assistance as needed. When most students have a fairly complete letter, the teacher asks students to share what they have written within the small group and the class.

The teacher reads one or two letters from *Abraham Lincoln: Letters from a Slave Girl* aloud at the start of each class period. During class the students share letters with the appropriate character in the group; then group members share their letters with each other. Each group selects one letter to share with the whole class.

Students continue reading at least three chapters per night and one during class from *Stealing Freedom.* As a response to the reading, the letter they received during class, and the shared reading, students write a letter to the character assigned. In their small groups, students share reflections on the injustices that would force Ann Maria, Lettie, or any person to undertake such a dangerous journey.

Finally, the teacher and students engage in a grand conversation about the concept of a journey as passage from one place to another to discuss the issues related to the passage from slavery to freedom. The teacher asks what obstacles still lay ahead for Ann Maria and other Black Americans at the end of the nineteenth century.

Additional Mini-Lessons

Literary Sociograms

- The teacher explains that a literary sociogram (Johnson & Louis, 1987) is a diagram that depicts the relationships among the characters in a book.
- Using *Stealing Freedom* as a model, the teacher shows how the book's characters are arranged around the central character. Arrows connecting the characters illustrate the direction of the relationships while brief statements describe their nature.
- The teacher and students then identify the main characters and incidents that incite racial tensions from each book within the text set.
- Students illustrate the relationships and what the characters are thinking during these important points in the text, focusing on the interactions between characters and the beliefs and values that motivate their behaviors.

Reading Logs

- As students read one of the books by Mildred D. Taylor, they maintain a reading log. They begin by creating a cover that includes the title and author. After reading, they add a picture based on a pivotal event.

- An entry is made for each chapter. The teacher models the first entry based on a question such as What events in the first chapter illustrate the daily struggles of African Americans who live in a racist society?
- Students in the literature circle decide on the focus for each entry, such as relating the events to their lives or to *Stealing Freedom,* life for the main character at the start of the story, turning points, and so on.
- The teacher poses additional key questions such as How do the characters respond to the indignities of "Jim Crow" laws?

Writing Memoirs

- The teacher explains that recently there has been an increased interest not only in reading memoirs but in recreating individual memories on paper.
- The teacher also explains the differences between autobiographies and memoirs—autobiographies present a complete picture of an individual's life, whereas a memoir captures both the author's voice and a defining moment or series of events.
- The teacher reads aloud a section from an autobiography and a memoir from *Growing up Black.*
- The teacher guides the students in a discussion of the unique characteristics of a memoir (see Nancy Atwell's *In the Middle,* Chapter 10).
- The students then read a memoir and select one of the memoir writing activities.

Conduct a Reading Workshop

In the focus lesson, the teacher explained how to use role playing and letter writing to understand the issues that initiated African Americans' journey to freedom. Now the teacher leads students in a discussion to distinguish among the concepts: the beginning, the journey, and the destination. The teacher explains that changes in law, such as the Emancipation Proclamation and the Fourteenth Amendment, could not change people's attitudes and that there would be many more challenges African Americans would face before the journey would bring them to their destination of equality. During the reading workshops, the students will apply these understandings as they participate in book clubs focused on an author study of Mildred D. Taylor.

Before Reading   The teacher explains that Mildred D. Taylor is an award-winning author whose novels are based on stories told during family gatherings. The Logan family saga is based on Taylor's own family history, from her great-grandfather's purchase of land in Mississippi in the 1880s to their move to Ohio in the 1940s. The stories describe the humiliation and indignities many black people experienced before the Civil Rights Movement as well as the quiet determination and strength that came from family and community.

Each book club or small group focuses on one of the other books in the text set. The teacher has enough copies of each book in the text set to create four main reading groups, with at least two students in each group. To help students make a choice, the teacher introduces each book through a short book talk. The time period and main ideas are highlighted to show how the books in the text set tell a unique story while still relating to the Logan family saga.

Although not the first book written by Taylor, *The Land* is the prequel to the Logan journey. In this book we meet Paul-Edward Logan, the son of a white plantation owner and a slave. In the first part of the story we see Paul-Edward living comfortably on his father's land in Georgia, where his father and his white brothers treat him as an equal. We observe the strong bond he has with his white half-brother, Robert, and the deep love and respect he has for his father. We learn of Mitchell Thomas, the son of the plantation horse trainer who resents Paul-Edward's privileged life. When Paul-Edward offers to teach Mitchell how to read and write in exchange for mercy from regular beatings, we see the burgeoning of a lifelong friendship. As Paul-Edward becomes a teen, we watch him learn that as a boy of mixed race living in the South he is considered "colored" and will experience hurt and humiliation from the white-controlled society. We experience Paul-Edward's pain at his brother's betrayal and feel his growing resentment towards his father. We witness the broken promises that force Paul and Mitchell to run away and become aware of Paul's determination to own his own land. In the second part of the story, we learn that Paul and Mitchell have been working in turpentine and lumber camps and that Paul's dream has grown even stronger. We travel to Vicksburg, where Paul finds the land of his dreams. We wait as he works as a carpenter for a year and then makes the deal to acquire forty acres of land, but we also learn that the line dividing black and white society will fill Paul's quest with danger and complications.

Roll of Thunder, Hear My Cry is Taylor's Newbery Award–winning novel. Set in Mississippi in 1933, this story describes how the Logan family faces racial attacks and poverty during the Depression in the Deep South. Nine-year-old Cassie Logan, our narrator, has never thought of herself as inferior to a white person, but as angry night riders and acts of discrimination separate her community, Cassie and her brothers come to understand why the land means so much to their father.

Let the Circle Be Unbroken is the powerful sequel to *Roll of Thunder, Hear My Cry*. Set in a farming community during the Depression, we see how hard times fuel old racial conflicts and create new bitterness. The story begins with the trial of T. J. Avery, Stacey's trouble-seeking friend who becomes involved with the older white Simms brothers. Along with Cassie, Little Man, and Christopher John we watch from outside the courthouse as an all-white jury convicts T. J. despite evidence that points to his innocence. We learn how government programs that were designed to help farmers through hard times are manipulated by white plantation owners and of the attempts by union organizers to protect African American sharecroppers. We experience Cassie's pain and confusion as she witnesses the effects of Jim Crow laws and feel the family's strength as they unite against threats to their land.

The Road to Memphis takes us to the South in 1941. Cassie is entering her senior year in high school in Jackson, Mississippi, and Stacey has bought his first car, but discrimination and racial tensions are escalating even as the United States faces the threat of war. When Cassie and Stacey stop to repair a tire at the local garage, their friend Moe loses his temper and violently strikes out against three white harassers. Recognizing that Moe is certain to be lynched, the friends decide to drive through the night to Memphis to put Moe on a train to Chicago. The trip to Memphis is filled with a series of dangers as black youth face the hatred and injustices of the pre–Civil Rights South. This dramatic and painful story received the Coretta Scott King Award for its vivid portrayal of teenage struggles in a racist society.

The teacher may say, "Since Paul and Cassie narrate the Logan family stories, the characters speak in the natural dialect of the time. The author herself admits that some may wish to ban her books because she uses 'the n-word' and other painful language. However, Taylor uses the language spoken during the period to demonstrate how painful life was for African Americans before the Civil Rights Movement."

The reading groups or book clubs are formed based on the students' interests and reading proficiencies. The teacher indicates that as students read, they should focus on the interactions between the characters and the racist beliefs that influence their behavior. They explore the incidents that incite racial tension and the values that motivate the actions of the main characters. Finally, they will explain how, after years of enduring this painful journey, the people were ready for the Civil Rights Movement that brought African Americans closer to their destination.

During Reading The teacher indicates that the students will maintain a reading log to write about their reactions to each chapter in the book they are reading. The students are expected to read at least a chapter each night. Each day the members of each book club will engage in a discussion to share their responses to the chapter they have read and make predictions about how specific events might affect the main characters. The teacher moves from group to group and when necessary facilitates the discussion. Some key questions students should consider are the following:

■ What is life like for the main character at the start of the story?
■ What events illustrate the daily struggles of African Americans who are living in a racist society?
■ How do the main and supporting characters respond to these indignities and Jim Crow laws?
■ What feelings and values motivate their responses?
■ Have you ever had a similar experience?
■ How did/would you respond?

After Reading The teacher prepares students for participation in a Socratic seminar based on the theme A Journey Through Time: From Slavery to Equal Rights by asking each group to use the cubing activity to explore the topic with six critical thinking skills: description, comparison/contrast, association, analysis, application, and argumentation (see Figure 2.8).

FIGURE 2.8 Cubing Activity

Directions: Use this activity to reflect on the book your group has read as well as to think about the theme of African Americans' Journey from Slavery to Equal Rights. Like the six facets of a cube, you will explore this theme using six dimensions of thinking.

■ **Describe** the story you have just read, including the characters, sequence of events, and civil rights issues.
■ **Compare** the experiences of the characters in this story with the experiences of Ann Maria Weems in *Journey to Freedom.*
■ **Associate** the civil rights issues in the book you have read with your knowledge of social injustice past and present and explain why you think these are related.
■ **Analyze** the concept of civil rights and its effects on the lives of both black and white citizens.
■ **Apply** what you have learned about the journey to freedom to social issue(s) today. Explain how the lessons of the past could be used to resolve this conflict.
■ **Argue** for or against freedom and equality for all citizens.

ASSESS LITERACY

The teacher uses the rubric shown below to evaluate students' reading, thinking, and ability to participate in a discussion during Socratic seminars.

Criteria	Independent	Proficient	Developing
Planning	The student actively participates in planning for the Socratic seminar by discussing his or her ideas while completing the cubing activity. (3)	The student is somewhat active in planning for the Socratic seminar by discussing some ideas while completing the cubing activity. (2)	The student does not actively plan for the Socratic seminar. He or she does not complete the cubing activity or does not discuss ideas. (0–1)
Questioning	The student generates thought-provoking questions for discussion that illustrate insightful understanding of the theme and content. (3)	The student generates good questions for discussion that illustrate understanding of the theme and content. (2)	The student generates factual questions for discussion that illustrate minimal understanding of the theme and content. (0–1)
Content knowledge	The student demonstrates understanding of the conceptual theme and content of the text by integrating effective text references throughout the discussion. (3)	The student demonstrates some understanding of the conceptual theme and content of the text by integrating some text references throughout the discussion. (2)	The student does not demonstrate understanding of the conceptual theme and content. Few text references are made during the discussion. (0–1)
Discussion skills	The student is consistently engaged in the discussion, makes eye contact with the speaker, and uses appropriate body language. He or she asks logical questions to clarify ideas presented by a speaker or in the text. (3)	The student is generally engaged in the discussion, makes eye contact with the speaker, and uses appropriate body language. He or she asks questions to clarify ideas presented by a speaker or in the text. (2)	The student is not engaged in the discussion, does not make eye contact with the speaker, and/or uses inappropriate body language. He or she asks questions that are not related to ideas presented by a speaker or in the text. (0–1)
Critical thinking	The student's comments show insightful responses to a previous speaker's ideas in order to extend or refine understanding of the text or the theme. (3)	The student's comments are somewhat related to a previous speaker's ideas. The student attempts to extend or refine understanding of the text or the theme. (2)	The student's comments are unrelated to a previous speaker's ideas. They show minimal understanding of the text or the theme. (0–1)

Independent: 11–15
Proficient: 6–10
Developing: 0–5

To begin the seminar, the teacher divides the class into an inner circle and an outer circle, making sure that each circle has students from each book club. The students on the inside participate in the discussion while those on the outside observe and take notes. Each student on the inner circle is given two tokens used to indicate that the student wants a turn to speak.

The teacher begins the seminar by asking students in the inner circle an initiating question such as, "When Mildred Taylor accepted the Newbery Award, she indicated that one of her goals as a writer was to paint a truer picture of Black people. She wanted to tell the story of Black America that was not in textbooks. How effectively have the stories of the Logan family helped Ms. Taylor achieve her goals?"

The students integrate responses from the different books they have read. The cubing activity is used to extend and refine their understanding of the theme. The discussion lasts approximately 30 minutes. Students on the outer circle spend 10 to 15 minutes commenting on ideas from the seminar.

During the next class period, the members of the circle reverse. The second circle begins with a question from a member of the inner circle or from the teacher such as, "Why was the Emancipation Proclamation only the beginning of the journey for African Americans?"

At the end of both seminars, all students write a reflection to explain how their understanding of the theme has been extended or changed by their readings and participation in Socratic seminar discussions.

Conduct a Writing Workshop

The teacher recalls that Mildred Taylor based her books on the family stories she heard over and over at family gatherings. The teacher also explains that personal writing, especially the memoir, has recently become extremely popular. People are not only reading the memoirs of famous people, but are recreating their own memories on paper. The teacher conducts a mini-lesson to contrast memoirs and autobiographies as well as to identify the distinctive features of a memoir. Memoir writers are adept storytellers that explore a theme or aspect of the person's life in depth. They combine techniques of fiction such as plot, characters, and dialogue to describe experiences that really happened. Wilhelm (1997) emphasizes that when we tell stories it defines who we are and helps us to see who we can be (pp. 52–53).

The teacher explains that students will continue to refine their understanding of the journey to equality by reading a memoir or autobiography from the Warriors for Equality text set and engaging in one of the English/language arts extension activities.

Before Writing   The teacher describes each writing task and the related reading. The teacher begins by reading aloud a section from *Growing up Black* to provide a model that illustrates how a memoir differs from an autobiography.

- *Family Stories:* Like Mildred Taylor, all families have stories that link children to the past. The students retell a story told by their grandparents, parents, or other relatives to illustrate a critical event in the family's journey.
- *Photo Memoirs:* Gordon Parks is an African American artist who captured the lives of his people in pictures and photographs. Students select one of his photographs, or another picture that captures attention and imagination, and write a memoir to tell the story behind the picture.

- *Warriors for Equality:* After reading the memoirs of students who fought for school integration, the students pretend that they were there and assume the role of a friend, foe, or teacher. They write a memoir to describe a specific event in the journey to integration.
- *Personal Memoirs:* The students think about their own dreams and aspirations and imagine the final destination and the struggles they may encounter along the way. They write a memoir to describe their personal journey.

During Writing   Based on their writing choices, students are encouraged to sit in groups to offer each other support. The teacher meets with each group to provide direction and instruction related to writing a memoir. Students are expected to extend their knowledge of the content and skill in memoir writing by consulting resource books and specific websites. When a draft is completed, students engage in cycle writing, a strategy that enables students to give each other feedback in the form of reactions, questions, and suggestions. They then revise and edit as needed based on comments from their peers.

After Writing   Students work on revisions to prepare to share completed projects with the class. The teacher confers with individual students and analyzes their ability to apply their knowledge of the memoir genre.

Collaborative Inquiry Across the Curriculum

Extension to Mathematics and Technology   The 1954 *Brown v. Board of Education* Supreme Court ruling created educational opportunities for minorities in the United States. Using the Internet and other sources, students identify the number of African Americans who graduated from high school and college from 1940 to 2000. They create a graph to illustrate the changes in levels of education for various subgroups (white males, white females, black males, black females) for each decade from 1940 to 2000.

> **STANDARDS**
>
> **Mathematics Standards**
> 5. Data Analysis and Probability
>
> **Technology Standards**
> 5. Technology Research Tools

Extension to Science   Since the growing of the cotton plant was in many ways responsible for the increase in the need for slaves, students conduct research to learn about planting, developing, and harvesting a cotton crop. They investigate the conditions for growing cotton as well as the problems a farmer could incur that would lead to crop failure. They explain why the growth of the cotton plant was suited to the land and climate in the Southern states.

> **STANDARDS**
>
> **Science Standards**
> Science as Inquiry, Teaching Standard A1
> Life Science, Content Standard C3

Extension to Social Studies   In addition to reading their memoirs, students research articles from *The Tiger,* a student newspaper, as well as *The Arkansas Gazette* and *The Arkansas Democrat.* Students write a letter to one of the "warriors" who helped integrate the Southern schools. They describe how they think the efforts of these brave students have changed attitudes and education in America.

During the 1950s and 1960s there was a shift from cities to suburbs. Students conduct research about the growth of suburbs to major cities such as New York, Baltimore, Chicago, Detroit, and Los Angeles. They create a photo essay to show the positive and negative effects of the movement of Americans to the suburbs and draw conclusions relative to the motivations for the journey to the suburbs.

> **STANDARDS**
>
> **Social Studies Standards**
> II. Time, Continuity, and Change
> III. People, Places, and Environments
> IV. Individual Development and Identity

After the writing workshop sequence is completed, the teacher can use the rubric below to assess the student's memoirs.

Criteria	Independent	Proficient	Developing
The Writing Process			
Planning	Student carefully plans prior to writing, taking into account all of the parts. (3)	Student engages in planning throughout the writing of the memoir. (2)	Student shows little or no planning prior to constructing a draft of the memoir. (0–1)
Drafting	Student engages in the careful construction of a draft developed through planning; drafting occurs throughout writing when needed. (3)	Student develops an adequate draft that demonstrates planning for memoir was considered. (2)	Student develops a simple draft that does not demonstrate planning for memoir. (0–1)
Revising	Student makes substantial changes in the memoir. (3)	Student makes adequate changes in the memoir. (2)	Student makes no or very few changes in the memoir after being prompted. (0–1)
Editing	Student edits carefully for errors and systematically edits for a wide array of language conventions. (3)	Student edits many errors and attends to some language conventions. (2)	Student pays little attention to errors and focuses on a single error type such as spelling. (0–1)
Structure and Writing Development			
Genre	Student draws on their knowledge of the genre to develop the memoir. (3)	Student's text adequately reflects the style of memoir writing. (2)	Student's text does not reflect the style of memoir writing. (0–1)
Vocabulary	Student uses many descriptive and complex words with accuracy and incorporates the language of the literature. (3)	Student uses some descriptive words with accuracy. (2)	Student uses simple vocabulary. (0–1)
Spelling	Student's writing exhibits no or few spelling errors. (3)	Student's writing exhibits some spelling errors. (2)	Student's writing exhibits many spelling errors. (0–1)
Capitalization	Student's writing has no or few errors in capitalization. (3)	Student's writing has some errors in capitalization. (2)	Student's writing has many errors in capitalization. (0–1)
Punctuation	Student's writing has no or few punctuation errors. (3)	Student's writing has some punctuation errors. (2)	Student's writing has many punctuation errors. (0–1)
Sentence structure	Student's writing exhibits a variety of sentence structures that are used appropriately within the story. (3)	Student's writing has some errors with sentence structure and attempts at writing complex sentences. (2)	Student's writing contains incomplete and simple sentences. (0–1)
Independent: 21–30 Proficient: 11–20 Developing: 0–10			

Students create a map to illustrate the journey of the Freedom Riders as they traveled through the South to protest segregation. They describe the major events that led to desegregation regulations.

Students work in groups to collect photographs and illustrations that depict "separate but equal" conditions before the 1954 Warren Court decision. Students include excerpts from memoirs that describe the experiences of segregation. They describe their reactions to the photographs, illustrations, and stories by creating a photo essay with captions.

The teacher selects a group of volunteers to prepare a dramatic reading of Martin Luther King, Jr.'s *I Have a Dream* speech. The teacher initiates a discussion based on the question, Has Dr. King's dream come true? The other students find similar speeches for dramatic presentation. The teacher leads a discussion to explain how the speeches inspired people to action in the 1960s.

Home–School Connections Students discuss the issues and events in the fiction and memoirs they are reading with their families. They discuss the concepts of segregation, prejudice, and discrimination and the characters' struggles to live in a racist society as well as whether these concerns still exist in U.S. society.

On-Your-Own Activities The 1960s was a period marked by political and social protest. Students investigate the political and social events that created the momentum for the Civil Rights Movement. They research the Supreme Court cases beginning with *Plessy v. Ferguson* (1896) that enabled the South to build a legal and social system based on segregation. They investigate the leaders and the forms of protest that inspired their cause. To share the results of their inquiry with the class, one group will role play interviews with some civil rights leaders (Rosa Parks, Martin Luther King, Jr., Thurgood Marshall, Malcolm X, Medgar Evers, etc.). The questions will focus on how the leader's journey led to equal rights. Another group will assume the role of journalists. They will create news stories to chronicle the journey of the Civil Rights Movement.

Critical Literacy

Working in groups of five, the students synthesize their notes on civil rights to address the question, Does separate but equal still exist today? After each group has presented its findings, the class creates a chart outlining the key points that were raised by each panel and designs a webpage for the school that presents the outcome of the discussion.

Collaborative Literacy

The teacher meets with each group to organize projects to be displayed in the classroom and school library. Students prepare for sharing and celebrating their work with a publishing party. On the day of the publishing party, the teacher sets up a table with light refreshments. Students enjoy the refreshments while they listen to authors read their memoir projects. Afterward, students circulate around the classroom or library and are encouraged to read and respond to the work by writing letters to the authors.

RESOURCE GUIDE: CHILDREN'S LITERATURE REFERENCES AND ACTIVITIES

Primary Grades

Journeys in Time

Journey to the Earth's Past

Arthur, A. (1989). *Shell.* New York: Knopf.

Cosgrove, M. (1968). *Bone for bone.* New York: Dodd.

Dickinson, P. (1993). *A bone from a dry sea.* New York: Delacorte.

Gallant, R. A. (1998). *Before the sun dies: The story of evolution.* New York: Macmillan.

Sloan, C. (2000). *Feathered dinosaurs.* Washington, DC: National Geographic.

Walker, S. (2002). *Fossil fish found alive: Discovering the coelacanth.* Minneapolis, MN: Carolroda.

■ *All About* **Books:** After reading about the Earth's past, students create a book entitled *All About Fossils,* which reports the information they have learned and includes illustrations.

■ **Diorama:** The students create a diorama that illustrates how the Earth looked during the prehistoric period. They write a description of the scene and present it to the class.

■ **Digging Up:** Using the Internet, students research fossil discoveries in their region and create a poster that illustrates fossil finds from their area.

Journey to the Time of Dinosaurs

Aliki. (1988). *Digging up dinosaurs.* New York: Harper-Trophy.

Barrett, P. M. (2001). *National Geographic dinosaurs.* Washington, DC: National Geographic.

Booth, J. (1998). *The big beast book: Dinosaurs and how they got that way.* Illustrated by Martha Weston. New York: Little, Brown.

Greenfield, E. (2001). *I can draw a weeposaur and other dinosaurs.* Illustrated by Jan Spivey Gilchrist. New York: Greenwillow.

Kerley, B. (2001). *The dinosaurs of Waterhouse Hawkins.* Illustrated by Brian Selznick. New York: Scholastic.

Rohmann, E. (1997). *Time flies.* New York: Dragonfly.

Strickland, P., & Strickland, H. (2002). *Dinosaur roar.* New York: Puffin.

■ **Dinosaurama:** Working in groups of three, the students create their own poems about dinosaurs and present them to the class in a choral reading.

■ **Mural:** The students research a dinosaur they have read about and create a mural to illustrate the environment in which it lived.

■ **Timeline:** When the sub-theme is completed, the students work in groups of three to create a timeline for the prehistoric period when dinosaurs roamed the earth.

Personal Journeys

Journey Around My Community

Brisson, P. (1994). *Wanda's roses.* Illustrated by Maryann Cocca-Leffler. New York: Macmillan.

Caseley, J. (2002). *On the town: A community adventure.* New York: Greenwillow.

Dorros, A. (1991). *Abuela.* Illustrated by Elisa Kleven. New York: Dutton.

Gleeson, L. (2001). *An ordinary day.* Illustrated by Armin Gredor. New York: Scholastic.

Jonas, A. (1985). *The trek.* New York: Greenwillow.

Tamar, E., & Lambase, B. (1996). *The garden of happiness.* New York: Harcourt.

Reingold, F. (1991). *Tar beach.* New York: Crown.

■ **Photo Journal:** Students take a walk around their community and photograph key places they want to discuss. They write a caption for each photo and present it to the class.

■ **My Tar Beach:** Students make posters illustrating where they like to go to be alone and reflect. They write captions about some of the places they dream about.

■ **Journey to the Past:** Using the Internet, the students research their community and how it appeared 100 years ago. They put their findings into a book to present to the class.

Journey to the White House

Adler, D. (1990). *A picture book of Thomas Jefferson.* Illustrated by Alexandra & John Wallner. New York: Holiday.

Adler, D. (2002). *A picture book of Dwight David Eisenhower.* New York: Holiday.

Cohn, A., & Schmidt, S. (2002). *Abraham Lincoln.* Illustrated by David Johnson. New York: Scholastic.

Giblin, J. C. (1994). *Thomas Jefferson: A picture biography.* Illustrated by Michael Dooling. New York: Scholastic.

Livingston, M. (1993). *Abraham Lincoln: A man for all people.* New York: Holiday.

Quackenbush, R. M. (1984). *Don't you dare shoot that bear! A story of Theodore Roosevelt.* New York: Prentice Hall.

Winters, K. (2003). *Abe Lincoln: The boy who loved books.* Illustrated by Nancy Carpenter. New York: Simon & Schuster.

■ **Presidential Mobiles:** After completing the text set, the students create a mobile consisting of symbols that describe the life of their chosen president.

- **Slideshow:** The students create a PowerPoint slideshow that depicts one president's journey to the White House.
- **Matrix:** When the students have completed the subtheme, they create a matrix to compare and contrast two presidents' birthplaces, education, and so on.

Journeys to Other Places

Journey to the American West

Adler, D. (2003). *A picture book of Lewis and Clark.* Illustrated by Ronald Himler. New York: Holiday.

Fleischman, P. (1992). *Townsend's warbler.* New York: HarperCollins.

Gerrard, R. (1996). *Wagons west.* New York: Farrar.

Gleiter, J., & Gleiter, K. T. (1987). *Sacagawea.* New York: Raintree.

Kroll, S. (1994). *Lewis and Clark: Explorers of the American west.* Illustrated by Richard Williams. New York: Holiday.

Turner, A. W. (1991). *Red flower goes west.* Illustrated by Dennis Nolan. New York: Hyperion.

- **Reader's Theatre:** After reading about Sacagawea and the Lewis and Clark Expedition, the students write a script and perform it for their peers.
- **Map It!:** After reading *Lewis and Clark: Explorers of the American West*, students work in pairs to trace the journey of one of the Western pioneers on a map.
- **Simulated Journals:** Students use their knowledge about the westward journey to create a simulated journal for an American explorer.

Number Journeys Around the World

Anno, M. (1982). *Anno's counting house.* New York: Philomel.

Crane, C. (2004). *Sunny numbers: A Florida counting book.* Illustrated by Jane Monroe Donovan. Stamford, CT: Thomson Gale.

Feelings, M. (1971). *Moja means one: A Swahili counting book.* Illustrated by Tom Feelings. New York: Dial.

Helman, A., & Wolfe, A. (1996). *1, 2, 3 Moose: A Pacific northwest counting book.* Seattle, WA: Sasquatch Books.

Johnson, S. T. (2003). *City by numbers.* New York: Puffin.

Onyefulu, I. (1999). *Emeka's gift: An African counting story.* New York: Puffin.

Schnetzler, P. L. (1996). *Ten little dinosaurs.* Illustrated by J. Harris. Denver, CO: Accord.

Wagin, K. (2004). *The Michigan counting book.* Illustrated by Michael Glenn Monroe. Stamford, CT: Thomson Gale.

- **State Counting Books:** Using the Internet, students create a counting book that illustrates the flora and fauna found within one state.

- **My Journey with Numbers:** Students work with their parents to log the many numbers they see on their way to school in the morning, then use the log to create a book that illustrates their morning trip.
- **Stories with Numbers:** Students create addition and subtraction stories and illustrate them for their peers.

Intermediate Grades

Journeys in Time

The Lewis and Clark Expedition

Blumberg, R. (1999). *The incredible journey of Lewis and Clark.* Gloucester, MA: Peter Smith.

Blumberg, R. (2004). *York's adventures with Lewis and Clark: An African-American's part in the great expedition.* New York: HarperCollins.

Bohner, C. (2004). *Bold journey: West with Lewis and Clark.* New York: Houghton Mifflin.

Bruchac, J. (2000). *Sacajawea: The story of Bird Woman and the Lewis and Clark Expedition.* New York: Harcourt.

Erdrich, L. (2003). *Sacagawea.* Minneapolis, MN: Carolrhoda.

Eubank, P. (2002). *Seaman's journal: On the trail with Lewis and Clark.* Nashville, TN: Ideals Publications.

Fradin, D. (1997). *Sacagawea: The journey to the west.* New York: Silver Press.

Glass, A. (2001). *Mountain men: True grit and tall tales.* New York: Doubleday.

Hamilton, J. (2003). *The journey home.* Edina, MN: Abdo.

Herbert, J. (2000). *Lewis and Clark for kids: Their journey of discovery with 21 activities.* Chicago: Chicago Review Press.

Johmann, C. (2002). *Lewis & Clark Expedition: Join the Corps of Discovery to explore uncharted territory.* Illustrated by Michael Kline. Charlotte, VT: Williamson Publishing Company.

Karwoski, G. L. (1999). *Seaman: The dog who explored the west with Lewis and Clark.* Illustrated by James Watling. Atlanta, GA: Peachtree Publishers.

Kimmel, E. (2003). *As far as the eye can reach: Lewis and Clark's westward quest.* New York: Random House.

Kroll, S. (1994). *Lewis and Clark: Explorers of the American west.* New York: Holiday.

Kozar, R. (2000). *Lewis and Clark: Explorers of the Louisiana Purchase.* Philadelphia: Chelsea House.

Lasky, K. (2000). *The journal of Augustus Pelletier: The Lewis and Clark Expedition.* New York: Scholastic.

Morley, J. (1998). *Across America: The story of Lewis and Clark.* London: Franklin Watts.

Myers, L. (2002). *Lewis and Clark and me: A dog's tale.* Illustrated by Michael Dooling. New York: Henry Holt.

O'Dell, S. (1986). *Streams to the river, river to the sea: A novel of Sacagawea.* Boston: Houghton Mifflin.

Patent, D. H. (2002). *Animals on the trail with Lewis and Clark.* Illustrated by William Munoz. New York: Clarion.

Patent, D. H. (2002). *The Lewis and Clark trail: Then and now.* Illustrated by William Munoz. New York: Dutton.

Patent, D. H. (2003). *Plants on the trail with Lewis and Clark.* Illustrated by William Munoz. New York: Clarion.

Roop, P., & Roop, C. (2003). *Sacagawea: Girl of the shining mountains.* New York: Hyperion.

Schanzer, R. (1997). *How we crossed the West: The adventures of Lewis and Clark.* Washington, DC: National Geographic.

Seymour, F. (1991). *Sacagawea: American pathfinder.* New York: Aladdin.

St. George, J. (1997). *Sacagawea.* New York: Putnam.

Wolf, A. (2004). *New found land: Lewis and Clark's voyage of discovery.* Cambridge, MA: Candlewick.

Yorinks, A. (2004). *My travels with Capts. Lewis and Clark, by George Shannon.* Illustrated by Kate McMullan. New York: HarperCollins.

- **Explorer's Kit:** After completing the text set, students use a shoebox to create an explorer's kit of survival items. They use their research to defend the items that were placed in the box.
- **Map of the Exploration:** The students trace the expedition of Lewis and Clark on a map and use the map to give a performance of their journey westward.
- **Explorer's Log:** The students use their research and notes from the sub-theme to create a simulated explorer's log.

The Oregon Trail

Bly, S. (2002). *The lost wagon train.* Wheaton, IL: Crossway Books.

Fisher, L. E. (1993). *The Oregon Trail.* Illustrated by Leonard Everett Fisher. New York: Holiday.

Gregory, K. (1997). *Across the wide and lonesome prairie: The Oregon Trail of Hattie Campbell, 1847.* New York: Scholastic.

Harness, C. (2006). *The tragic tale of Narcissa Whitman and a faithful history of the Oregon Trail.* Washington, DC: National Geographic.

Hermes, P. (2002). *A perfect place: Joshua's Oregon Trail diary, book two.* New York: Scholastic.

Levine, E. (2002). *The journal of Jedediah Barstow: An emigrant on the Oregon Trail.* New York: Scholastic.

Steedman, S. (1993). *The Frontier Fort on the Oregon Trail.* Illustrated by Mark Bergin. New York: Peter Bedrick Books.

Thompson, G., & Feresten, N. (2002). *Our journey west: Adventure on the Oregon Trail.* Washington, DC: National Geographic.

- **Accordion Book:** After reading about the Oregon Trail, students work in pairs to create an accordion book that depicts a typical journey along the famous route.
- **Flannel Board:** Students create a flannel board display that shows the many items traded along the Oregon Trail that kept pioneers supplied for the journey.
- **Logging Miles:** Using the Internet, students research how many miles the journey covered and how long it took pioneers to reach their destination.

Personal Journeys

Family Journeys

MacLachlan, P. (1980). *Arthur for the very first time.* New York: HarperCollins.

MacLachlan, P. (1983). *Seven kisses in a row.* New York: HarperCollins.

MacLachlan, P. (1985). *Sarah, plain and tall.* New York: Harper and Row.

MacLachlan, P. (1991). *Journey.* New York: Delacorte.

MacLachlan, P. (1994). *Skylark.* New York: HarperCollins.

MacLachlan, P. (1995). *What you know first.* New York: HarperCollins.

MacLachlan, P. (2001). *Caleb's story.* New York: Joanna Cotler Books.

- **Author Study:** After completing the text set, students conduct an author study on Patricia MacLachlan and research how her life has inspired her fictional writings.
- **Diorama:** The students create a diorama illustrating the setting of one of MacLachlan's stories and describe how the setting affected the plot.
- **Family Journeys:** After interviewing family members, students create their own story about a memorable family journey and illustrate it.

Creative Journeys of Musicians

Freedman, R. (2004). *The voice that challenged a nation: Marian Anderson and the struggle for equal rights.* New York: Clarion.

George-Warren, H. (2001). *Shake, rattle, & roll: The founders of rock & roll.* Boston: Houghton Mifflin.

Partridge, E. (2002). *This land was made for you and me.* New York: Viking.

Pinkney, A. D. (1998). *Duke Ellington: The piano prince.* New York: Hyperion.

Pinkney, A. D. (2002). *Ella Fitzgerald: The tale of a vocal virtuosa.* New York: Hyperion.

Ryan, P. M. (2002). *When Marian sang.* New York: Scholastic.

- **Illustrate It:** After listening to the various musicians described in the text set, students illustrate a scene that depicts how the music made them feel.
- **Biography Box:** After researching one of the musicians, the students place items or illustrations that they feel

are symbolic of the artist in a shoebox and defend their choices based on research.

- **Photo Journal:** Using the Internet, students research the life of a musician and create a photo journal depicting his or her life story in a PowerPoint slideshow.

Journeys to Other Places

Journey to the Moon

Baylor, B. (1982). *Moon song.* Illustrated by Ronald Himler. New York: Scribner.

Cole, M. (1999). *Moon base: First colony in space.* Springfield, NJ: Enslow Publishers.

Daly, N. (1995). *Why the sun and moon live in the sky.* New York: Lothrop.

Ehlert, L., adapter. (1992). *Moon rope: A Peruvian folktale/ Un lazo a la luna: Una leyenda Peruana.* Illustrated by Lois Ehlert. New York: Harcourt.

Elphinstone, D. (1968). *Why the sun and moon live in the sky: An African folktale.* Illustrated by Blair Lent. New York: Houghton Mifflin.

Fuchs, E. (1969). *Journey to the moon.* New York: Delacorte.

Gibbons, G. (1997). *The moon book.* New York: Holiday.

Hughes, T. (1976). *Moon whales and other moon poems.* Illustrated by Leonard Baskin. New York: Viking.

Seymour, S. (1984). *The moon.* New York: Simon & Schuster.

Siy, A. (2001). *Footprints on the moon.* Watertown, MA: Charlesbridge.

Sleator, W. (1970). *The angry moon.* Illustrated by Blair Lent. New York: Little, Brown.

Yolen, J. (1993). *What rhymes with moon?* Illustrated by Ruth Tietjen Councell. New York: Philomel.

Young, E. (1993). *Moon mother: A Native American creation tale.* Illustrated by Ed Young. New York: HarperCollins.

- **Moon Observations:** Students observe the moon each night and keep a log on its shape, visibility, position in the sky, and surface. Students use the database to raise questions about the moon and research answers.
- **Journey to Mars:** Students use the Internet to research NASA's possible exploration of the planet Mars. Working in groups, they compare and contrast the problems with undertaking journeys to the moon and Mars.
- **Moon Poems:** Working in pairs, students create their own poems about the moon and present them to their peers in a choral reading.

Journey to the Desert

Asch, F. (1998). *Cactus poems.* New York: Harcourt.

Astorga, A., & Nabhan, G. (2001). *Efrain of the Sonoran Desert: A lizard's life among the Seri Indians.* Illustrated by Janet K. Miller. El Paso, TX: Cinco Puntos Press.

Baylor, B. (1986). *I'm in charge of celebrations.* New York: Houghton.

Baylor, B. (1987). *The desert is theirs.* Illustrated by Peter Parnall. New York: Aladdin.

Baylor, B. (1993). *Desert voices.* Illustrated by Peter Parnall. New York: Aladdin.

George, J. C. (1996). *One day in the desert.* New York: HarperTrophy.

Gibbons, G. (1996). *Deserts.* New York: Holiday.

Johnson, R. L. (2001). *A walk in the desert.* Illustrated by Phyllis Saroff. Minneapolis, MN: Carolrhoda.

- ***All About* Books:** After reading about desert life, students choose a famous desert to research and create a book that describes its habitat.
- **Climate Change:** Students use the Internet to research how climate change is affecting the world's deserts. They create a podcast of their findings to play on the class webpage.
- **Journey Through the Desert:** After completing the sub-theme, students create a simulated journal that depicts their journey through the desert, describing their battle to survive.

Middle Grades

Journeys in Time

From Slavery to Equal Rights

Carbone, E. (1998). *Stealing freedom.* New York: Dell Yearling.

Pinkney, A. (2001). *Abraham Lincoln: Letters from a slave girl.* New York: Winslow Press.

Taylor, M. D. (1976). *Roll of thunder, hear my cry.* New York: Penguin Putnam.

Taylor, M. D. (1981). *Let the circle be unbroken.* New York: Dial Books.

Taylor, M. D. (1990). *The road to Memphis.* New York: Dial Books.

Taylor, M. D. (2001). *The land.* New York: Penguin Putnam.

- **Literary Letters:** Students write letters from the perspective of Abraham Lincoln or Lettie Tucker and defend their content with research.
- **Learning Log:** Students keep a learning log as they research the journey from slavery to equal rights for African Americans.
- **Role Play:** Using the Internet, students research a civil rights leader such as Thurgood Marshall. Students role play an interview, with one acting as a journalist and the other the famous civil rights leader.

Past, Present, and Future

Conrad, P. (1996). *Zoe rising.* New York: HarperTrophy.

Haddix, M. P. (1995). *Running out of time.* New York: Simon & Schuster.

L'Engle, M. (1962). *A wrinkle in time.* New York: Farrar.

Naylor, P. R. (1980). *Shadows on the wall.* New York: Atheneum.

Service, P. (1989). *Vision quest.* New York: Atheneum.

Shackell, R. (1970). *Enchantress from the stars.* New York: Atheneum.

Winterson, J. (2006). *Tanglewreck.* New York: Bloomsbury.

■ **Predictions 2108:** After reading the sub-theme, students work in pairs to create predictions about life on Earth in 2108.

■ **Postcards from the Future:** Students create a postcard that illustrates their journey to the future and how life was different from today.

■ **Time Travel:** Using the Internet, students research a time period from the past and describe how their life would be different in a previous era.

Personal Journeys

Warriors for Equality

Beals, M. P. (1994). *Warriors don't cry: A searing memoir of the battle to integrate Little Rock's Central High.* New York: Washington Square Press.

Bridges, R. (1999). *Through my eyes.* New York: Scholastic.

David, J. (Ed.). (1992). *Growing up black.* New York: Avon Books.

Freedman, F. B. (1971). *Two tickets to freedom: The true story of William and Ellen Craft, fugitive slaves.* New York: Peter Bedrick Books.

Greenfield, E. (1979). *Childtimes: A three-generation memoir.* New York: HarperCollins.

Height, D. (2003). *Open wide the freedom gates.* New York: Public Affairs.

Moody, A. (1968). *Coming of age in Mississippi.* New York: Bantam Dell.

Myers, W. D. (2001). *Bad boy: A memoir.* New York: HarperCollins.

Parks, R., with Haskins, J. (1992). *Rosa Parks: My story.* New York: Dial Books.

Thomas, J. C. (Ed.). (2003). *Linda Brown, you are not alone: The Brown v. Board of Education decision.* New York: Jump at the Sun.

■ **Reader's Theatre:** After reading about Rosa Parks, students write a script about her life and perform it for their peers.

■ **Simulated Memoir:** When students have completed the text set, they write a simulated memoir that illustrates the life of a warrior for equality.

■ **Warriors Today:** Using the Internet, students research a warrior for equal rights today, such as Nelson Mandela. Students create a slideshow to depict the person's life story.

Overcoming Physical and Emotional Challenges

Anderson, L. H. (1999). *Speak.* New York: Farrar.

Hermes, P. (1998). *Cheat the moon.* Boston: Little, Brown.

Hinton, S. (1998). *That was then, this is now.* New York: Puffin Penguin.

Huser, G. (1999). *Touch the clown.* Toronto, Ontario: Groundwork Books.

Lipsyte, R. (1991). *One fat summer.* New York: HarperTrophy Books.

Myers, W. D. (2003). *The beast.* New York: Scholastic.

Voight, C. (1986). *Izzy, willy nilly.* New York: Atheneum.

Woodson, J. (1994). *I hadn't meant to tell you this.* New York: Delacourt.

■ **Plot Profile:** Students work in pairs and use graph paper to plot one of the stories in the text set. They describe how the main character overcame a significant challenge.

■ **Blog:** Students create a blog about a major challenge in their life. They can choose whether to share the blog with their peers or to only use it for personal reflection.

■ **Character Portraits:** Students outline the portrait of one of the main characters in the text set. On the back of the outline, they write the key character traits that led to success.

Journeys to Other Places

Along the Silk Road

Kherdian, D. (2005). *Monkey: Journey to the west.* Boston: Shambala.

MacDonald, F. (1997). *Marco Polo: A journey through China.* Danbury, CT: Franklin Watts.

Major, J. (1996). *The silk route: 7,000 miles of history.* New York: HarperTrophy.

Rice, E. (2005). *Empire in the east: The story of Genghis Khan.* Greensboro, NC: Morgan Reynolds Publishing.

Rumford, J. (2001). *Traveling man: The journey of Ibn Battuta.* Boston: Houghton Mifflin.

Schneider, M. (1997). *Between the dragon and the eagle.* Minneapolis, MN: Carolrhoda.

Williams, S. (1997). *Made in China: Ideas and inventions from ancient China.* Berkeley, CA: Pacific View.

■ **Map It!:** After reading about the Silk Road, students work in pairs to trace its outline on a map.

■ **Mural:** Students create a mural to depict a journey along the Silk Road and identify goods traded along the route.

- **Matrix:** Using a matrix graphic organizer, students compare and contrast the Silk Road with the Oregon Trail in America.

Fantastic Regions

Barry, D., & Pearson, R. (2004). *Peter and the starcatchers.* New York: Disney.

Funke, C. (2003). *Inkheart.* New York: Scholastic.

Lewis, C. S. (1994). *The lion, the witch and the wardrobe.* New York: HarperCollins.

MacHale, D. J. (2002). *The merchant of death.* New York: Aladdin.

Paolini, C. (2004). *Eragon.* New York: Knopf.

Tolkien, J. R. R. (1973). *The hobbit.* Boston: Houghton Mifflin.

- **Grand Conversation:** After completing the text set, students discuss some of the major problems facing the world today and possible ways to solve them.
- **Journeys of Heroes:** Students work in pairs to brainstorm critical character traits of the imaginary heroes depicted in the text set. After completing the list, they write their own version of hero's journey or quest.
- **Book Notes:** Students create a simulated book review show entitled "Book Notes" and share their critiques of the selections in the text set.

PROFESSIONAL REFERENCES

Cohen, V. L., & Cowen, J. E. (2008). *Literacy in an information age: Teaching reading, writing, and thinking.* Belmont, CA: Thomson.

Galda, L., & Cullinan, B. E. (2002). *Literature and the child* (5th ed.). Stamford, CT: Wadsworth Group of Thompson Learning.

Johnson, T., & Louis, D. (1987). *Literacy through literature.* London: Methuen.

National Council of Teachers of English & International Reading Association. (1996). *Standards for the English language arts.* Newark, DE: Author. Available at www.ncte.org/standards.

National Council of Teachers of Mathematics. (2000). *Principles and standards for school mathematics.* Reston, VA: Author. Available at http://standards.nctm.org

Wilhelm, J. (1997). *"You gotta BE the book": Teaching engaged and reflective reading with adolescents* (2nd ed.). New York: Teachers College Press.

3 Survival

As our world continues to experience conflicts and challenges, it becomes imperative to facilitate our students' abilities to identify and solve problems. The National Council of Teachers of Mathematics (1998) designated a separate standard to focus on problem solving and emphasize the need to help students analyze problems, apply a wide variety of strategies to solve problems, and adapt these strategies to new situations.

Our theme of Survival presents fictional and real heroes who faced challenges and developed strategies to triumph over conflict. Students in the primary grades read about Maddy Rose, a young girl living in Philadelphia during the time of the American Revolution. The intermediate grade sampler presents characters, such as Sam in *My Side of the Mountain*, who draw on their resourcefulness to survive in the wilderness. The chapter concludes with the middle grade sampler's focus on memoirs from the Holocaust. These factual accounts tell the ultimate story of good triumphing over evil and the human instinct to survive despite the odds.

As students from the primary grades through eighth grade read, discuss, and analyze text sets focusing on survival, they will explore their own determination and courage in facing the daily challenges in their lives. By reading about the resourcefulness of heroes in their text sets, students will develop the creativity to analyze and to solve the problems that are challenging them at the moment.

■ Primary Grades: Kindergarten–Grade 2

Life for primary grade students usually revolves around their families, friends, and school. Despite their young age, primary grade students often face challenges on a daily basis, whether it is determining which school bus to board or trying to figure out the math problem in class.

The theme of Survival for the primary grades will focus on problems and challenges faced by characters in the text sets or in our nation's history. As students read about families that helped slaves survive during the time of the Civil War or characters in war-torn areas, they will learn how to act toward others with compassion.

In the sub-theme Taking Care of Yourself, students will learn about nutrition and exercise and how vital it is to keep healthy. The text set presents these necessary topics in a way that is engaging and appealing for primary grade students and helps

SURVIVING POVERTY

Text Set

Barrio: Jose's Neighborhood
Mr. Bow Tie
December
Fly Away Home
I Can Hear the Sun

Outcomes

- Brainstorm ways to help those in poverty.
- Retell one of stories using a hand puppet.

OVERCOMING THE ODDS

Text Set

Twenty and Ten
So Far From the Sea
The Cello of Mr. O
The Bracelet
River Friendly, River Wild

Outcomes

- Sequence one of the texts through a story board.
- Record an interview from a character's perspective.

STORIES OF COURAGE: AMERICAN FAMILIES

Text Set

Squanto's Journey: The Story of the First Thanksgiving
Sarah Morton's Day: A Day in the Life of a Pilgrim Girl
Pioneer Girl: The Story of Laura Ingalls Wilder
Aunt Clara Brown: Official Pioneer
The Story of Thanksgiving

Outcomes

- Retell the story through process drama.
- Create a symbol for Aunt Clara Brown to illustrate her courage.

Family Survival

Surviving Tragedy

SURVIVAL

Surviving Nature

SURVIVING DIFFICULT TIMES

Text Set

Sami and the Time of the Troubles
Sweet Clara and the Freedom Quilt
The Scarlet Stockings Spy
Dad, Jackie and Me
Friend on Freedom River
The Librarian of Basra

Outcomes

- Create a quilt made from patterns.
- Discuss books that are precious and should be kept safe.

TAKING CARE OF YOURSELF

Text Set

The Vegetable Show
I Will Never Not Ever Eat a Tomato
Babar's Yoga for Elephants
My Amazing Body: A First Look at Health and Fitness
Voices of the Heart

Outcomes

- Record daily menus.
- Write an exercise journal about how you are keeping fit.

SURVIVING STORMS

Text Set

Stina
Outside, Inside
Storms
Hurricane City
Thunder Cake

Outcomes

- Compare and contrast weather patterns.
- Identify and define vocabulary related to weather.

them understand that one must take care of oneself first in order to help others. The sub-theme Surviving Storms describes natural phenomena and explores strategies for preparing for the challenges that nature often sends us.

As students engage in the text sets presented in this chapter, they learn about determination, courage, and resourcefulness. These traits help them in their daily lives as they meet the challenges of home and school.

SAMPLER ■ Surviving Difficult Times

Every day our television screens bring fresh images of violence or terror from around the globe. It is often difficult for children to discuss or comprehend these tragic events. The sub-theme Surviving Difficult Times uses children's literature to facilitate the discussion of how children and adults can cope when the world around them seems to be rapidly disintegrating.

The first book in the text set, *The Scarlet Stockings Spy,* explores the time of the American Revolution and follows Maddy Rose, a young girl in Philadelphia, as her family faces tragedy. A similar theme is explored in *Sami and the Time of the Troubles,* which presents a young Lebanese boy facing dangerous times in war-stricken Beirut. Completing the text set is *The Librarian of Basra,* a true story about Alia Muhammad Baker, a librarian in Basra, Iraq, who saves the library's collection despite the daily fires and explosions.

The main characters in all of the selections faced difficult times with courage and compassion for others. As they struggle to survive, the main characters know that the love of their family and friends will carry them through their trying times. As our children learn to live with daily news bulletins of yet another world tragedy, they can find strength in the stories of fictional and real heroes who managed to cope despite difficult times.

A recurring theme throughout the primary grade sampler is the strength of the family. In this instructional sequence, primary grade students read about children from different cultures and nations who rely on the loving support of their families and friends to withstand difficult times.

NCTE/IRA Standards for the English Language Arts

1. Students read a wide range of print and non-print texts to build an understanding of texts, of themselves, and of the cultures of the United States and the world.
2. Students read a wide range of literature from many periods in many genres to build an understanding of the many dimensions (e.g., philosophical, ethical, aesthetic) of the human experience.
9. Students develop an understanding of and respect for diversity in language use, patterns, and dialects across cultures, ethnic groups, geographic regions, and social roles.

Learner Outcomes

Students will be able to do the following:

■ Analyze the main character Maddy Rose and identify character traits
■ Sequence the main events of the story
■ Recollect, talk, and write about the story to make text-to-self connections

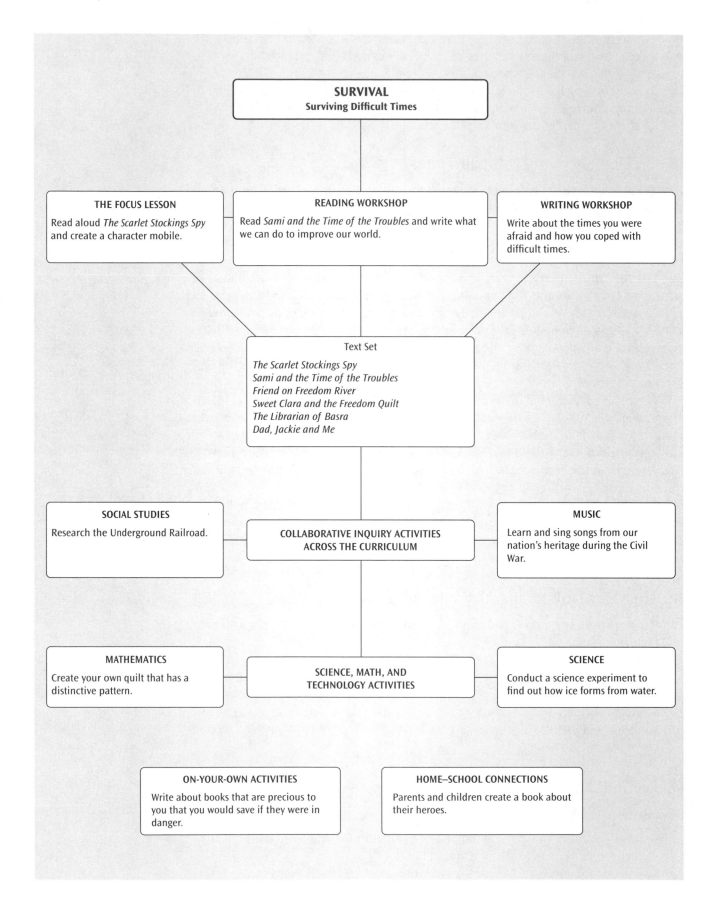

SURVIVAL
Surviving Difficult Times

THE FOCUS LESSON
Read aloud *The Scarlet Stockings Spy* and create a character mobile.

READING WORKSHOP
Read *Sami and the Time of the Troubles* and write what we can do to improve our world.

WRITING WORKSHOP
Write about the times you were afraid and how you coped with difficult times.

Text Set

The Scarlet Stockings Spy
Sami and the Time of the Troubles
Friend on Freedom River
Sweet Clara and the Freedom Quilt
The Librarian of Basra
Dad, Jackie and Me

SOCIAL STUDIES
Research the Underground Railroad.

COLLABORATIVE INQUIRY ACTIVITIES ACROSS THE CURRICULUM

MUSIC
Learn and sing songs from our nation's heritage during the Civil War.

MATHEMATICS
Create your own quilt that has a distinctive pattern.

SCIENCE, MATH, AND TECHNOLOGY ACTIVITIES

SCIENCE
Conduct a science experiment to find out how ice forms from water.

ON-YOUR-OWN ACTIVITIES
Write about books that are precious to you that you would save if they were in danger.

HOME–SCHOOL CONNECTIONS
Parents and children create a book about their heroes.

Conduct a Focus Lesson

The purpose of the sub-theme Surviving Difficult Times is to help young children discuss how fictional characters or real heroes dealt with tragedy or unsettling events. The intent of the focus lesson is to provide background knowledge of the American Revolution for primary grade students.

Establish a Purpose   The text set for Surviving Difficult Times explores how children from ages past or present have dealt with troubling events at home. The teacher uses the focus lesson to discuss Maddy Rose, the main character in *The Scarlet Stockings Spy.* The setting for the story is Philadelphia in 1777, when the British have just begun to occupy the city. Maddy Rose's brother is fighting in the Colonial Army and the family is very worried about him. The main characters in the text set illustrate what it means to be courageous in everyday events while the world is exploding around them. The lesson focuses on Maddy Rose's many acts of courage during a difficult time in American history.

Engage in Read Aloud   In order to prepare the students to discuss the story, the teacher explores the American Revolution and provides students with some background knowledge.

The teacher begins with a picture of the American flag during the Revolutionary period, asking students if they know why the stars are in a circle and why there appear to be fewer than our flag today. After discussing the 13 colonies and how our country broke away from England, the teacher can do a picture walk to give the students a sense of the time period. After the picture walk, the teacher asks this focus question: What would you have done if you lived in Philadelphia in 1777? The teacher then records their statements on chart paper, as illustrated in Figure 3.1.

Next, the teacher uses the interactive read-aloud strategy with the first book in the text set, *The Scarlet Stockings Spy.* The story opens in the autumn of 1777 and the city of Philadelphia is preparing for a British invasion. Maddy Rose has already lost her father to the war and now her 15-year-old brother Jonathan is in the rebel army. The story unfolds as Maddy and her mother cope during the invasion and learn to carry on despite the troubles around them.

When the read aloud is completed, the students can create a character mobile of Maddy Rose illustrating her courageous acts during the invasion of Philadelphia. Students present their mobiles and explain why they drew certain symbols for Maddy Rose.

FIGURE 3.1   If I Lived in Philadelphia in 1777 . . .

If I lived in Philadelphia in 1777. . .

1. I would be afraid to go out.
2. I would stay by my mom.
3. I would help if anyone asked me to.

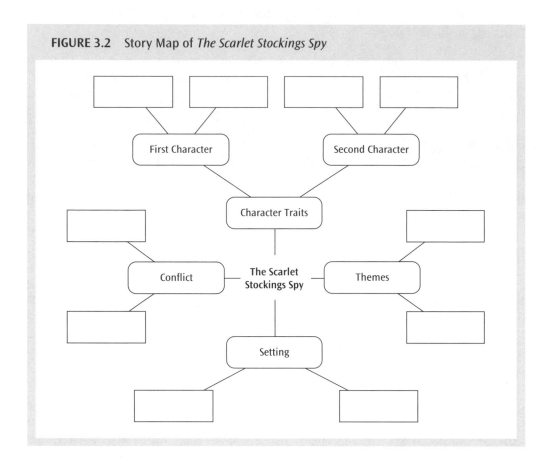

FIGURE 3.2   Story Map of *The Scarlet Stockings Spy*

Conduct a Mini-Lesson   The focus of the mini-lesson is to sequence the events in the story *The Scarlet Stockings Spy*. The teacher prepares the students to sequence the story by demonstrating the story map to the class. A sample story map is depicted in Figure 3.2. After the class has completed the story map, they can individually create a story board that illustrates the sequence of events in *The Scarlet Stockings Spy*.

Additional Mini-Lessons

Reading Comprehension

- The teacher uses the plot profile strategy.
- The teacher reads the story aloud and facilitates a discussion of the story elements that are written on chart paper.
- The teacher shows the students how to put the story events along the horizontal axis on the graph paper.
- After the story elements are charted, the numbers 1–10 are placed along the vertical axis to denote excitement or tension in the story.
- The teacher directs the students to plot the events along the plot profile.

Character Analysis

- The teacher uses the literature report card strategy.
- After students have finished reading the stories in the text set, they choose a main character to study.
- Students identify the character's traits.

ASSESS LITERACY

During the instructional sequence, the teacher uses the rubric below to evaluate the students' development of reading comprehension.

Criteria	Independent	Proficient	Developing
Main Characters	Student identifies main characters in text set and their character traits. (3)	Student identifies the main characters and some of their character traits. (2)	Student is not able to identify the main characters or their character traits. (0–1)
Setting	Student identifies setting of story and describes it using evidence from the story. (3)	Student identifies setting of story and partially describes it, using evidence from the story. (2)	Student does not identify setting of story or describe it. (0–1)
Plot	Student identifies the main sequence of events and plots the rising tension in the story. (3)	Student partially identifies the main sequence of events and plots the rising tension in the story. (2)	Student does not identify the main sequence of events or plot the rising tension in the story. (0–1)
Raising Questions	Student poses thoughtful and honest questions about the readings. (3)	Student poses some questions about the readings. (2)	Student does not initiate questions about the readings. (0–1)
Independent: 9–12 Proficient: 5–8 Developing: 0–4			

- They complete the report card by giving a grade for each trait and providing evidence from the text to support the grade.

Writing Skills
- Students respond to the text set by writing stories about heroes.
- Students write about one of the characters in the text set that they feel is a hero.
- Students include evidence from the text and illustrate their stories.

Conduct a Reading Workshop

Sami and the Time of the Troubles is set in today's Middle East and tells the story of a young boy and his family as they try to carve out a life in the midst of daily violent outbursts. The book's beautiful illustrations show how a close, loving family learns to keep on living despite difficult circumstances.

Before Reading   The teacher prepares the students for the text by conducting a picture walk and asking the students to make predictions as to where the story is located. After they have identified the setting, the teacher asks them to predict what they think are the "troubles" highlighted in the title of the story.

FIGURE 3.3   What We Can Do for the World

MAKING THE WORLD A BETTER PLACE TO LIVE

What We Can Do for the World

1. We can be nice to each other.

2. We can help the poor.

3. We can help our parents at home.

During Reading   As students reach the mid-point of the story, the teacher asks them to predict what they think Sami will find when he goes outside. The students also discuss how they would feel if they had to stay inside and couldn't go outside to play.

After Reading   The story concludes with Sami recalling the time when the children of Beirut went out into the streets with signs calling for an end to the violence. After students have completed the text, the teacher asks them what they could do to make the world a better place and writes their responses on chart paper, as illustrated in Figure 3.3.

Conduct a Writing Workshop

During the discussions about the books in the text set, the students have been focusing on how the characters maintained their courage during difficult times. The focus of the writing workshop is to help students make personal connections by writing about times they were scared and how they dealt with those feelings.

Before Writing   The writing workshop begins with a discussion of the two main characters of the text set, Maddy Rose and Sami, and how they acted while war erupted in their homelands. After a brief review, the teacher facilitates the discussion by asking the students to think about the times when they were scared. The students' responses are written on chart paper.

During Writing   After the class has discussed the various times when they were afraid, each student drafts an account of the incident. The students illustrate their stories and write about how they dealt with their fears. If students do not wish to write about a time they were afraid, they may choose another topic.

After Writing   After students have completed their final texts, they can share with the class. The teacher leads a discussion on the many strategies that students used to deal with their fears and they compare their accounts with the stories they have read in the text set.

Collaborative Inquiry Across the Curriculum

Surviving Difficult Times explores the theme of courage amid war or danger. Through the use of quality children's literature, the sub-theme is extended to several subject areas such as music, mathematics, science, and social studies.

ASSESS LITERACY

After the writing workshop is completed, the teacher uses the rubric below to assess the students' written performances.

Criteria	Independent	Proficient	Developing
Planning	Student used a planning strategy and followed it closely to write story. (3)	Student used a planning strategy and followed it somewhat to write story. (2)	Student did not use a planning strategy to write story. (0–1)
Story Sequence	Story has a logical sequence of events. (3)	Story has a somewhat logical sequence of events. (2)	Story does not have a logical sequence of events. (0–1)
Spelling	There are very few or no spelling errors. (3)	There are some spelling errors. (2)	There are many spelling errors. (0–1)
Syntax	There are very few or no grammatical errors. (3)	There are some grammatical errors. (2)	There are many grammatical errors. (0–1)
Punctuation	There are very few or no punctuation errors. (3)	There are some punctuation errors. (2)	There are many punctuation errors. (0–1)
Independent: 11–15 Proficient: 6–10 Developing: 0–5			

Extension to Mathematics   In *Sweet Clara and the Freedom Quilt,* a slave named Clara tries desperately to use the Underground Railroad to escape. Clara eventually learns to use her skills as a seamstress to create a quilt that has a secret map of the journey to Canada. As students read about Clara's courage and strength, they explore the patterns that are present on quilts and create their own geometrical patterns on paper, then tape them together to create a class quilt.

Extension to Science   In *Friend on Freedom River,* the runaway slaves must escape on the Detroit River before it freezes over for winter. Students explore how water freezes by conducting a simple experiment. After filling a plastic container with ice, they put a smaller container of water inside and keep taking the temperature to note when the ice begins to form. The activity will help students discover that water freezes at 32 degrees Fahrenheit.

Extension to Social Studies   *Sweet Clara and the Freedom Quilt* tells the story of a young slave girl who escapes on the Underground Railroad. The students can research the history of the Underground Railroad on the Internet and write about how they can help others in trouble, like those who helped slaves escape.

Home–School Connections   The sub-theme of Surviving Difficult Times is shared with the whole family through the story *Dad, Jackie and Me,* about a deaf father in Brooklyn who

STANDARDS

Mathematics Standards
2. Algebra

Technology Standards
5. Technology Research Tools

STANDARDS

Science Standards
Science as Inquiry, Teaching Standard A1

STANDARDS

Social Studies Standards
I. Culture
II. Time, Continuity, and Change
III. People, Places, and Environments

closely follows the career of Jackie Robinson as he breaks the color line in baseball. The father gains courage and inspiration by watching Jackie deal with difficult situations.

On-Your-Own Activities In *The Librarian of Basra: A True Story from Iraq,* the students learn about Alia Muhammad Baker, who managed to save the books in the library from destruction during the bombing of the city. After the students have finished reading this true account, they write about the books that are precious to them and why they are valued. After they have edited their writing, students illustrate them and share their stories with their peers.

Critical Literacy

When students have completed reading the books in the text set, they complete a critical literacy activity that requires synthesis and application of information. Working in groups of three, the students create a matrix on "Heroes for All Time" to compare and contrast the main characters and real people that they have studied in this sub-theme. When all the groups have presented their matrixes, the teacher leads a discussion on the common traits shared by the characters as well as how they differ.

Collaborative Literacy

As a culminating event, students host a session entitled Heroes for All Time. At this session, they share their character mobiles and stories about heroes that they completed as part of the instructional sequence. As they share their work with peers or family members, the group discusses heroes in today's society who have demonstrated courage and compassion despite troubling circumstances.

■ Intermediate Grades: Grades 3–5

How so many children survived the tragedy of war is harsh for adults to understand, but it is even more difficult to teach young children. Tony Johnston speaks to the hearts of his readers through the picture storybook *The Harmonica* as he addresses the question: What allowed a young child to survive Dyhernfurth concentration camp? The story is based on the life of Henryk Rosmaryn, the son of a poor coal miner, who learned a love for Schubert's music and the skill of playing the harmonica from his family. Ripped from each other by the Nazi soldiers, the young boy was doomed to the torturous life of the concentration camp, as his parents suffered death. Henryk's determination to survive was kept alive by his everlasting love for his family: "I remember their love, warm and enfolding as a song." When the commandant ordered Henryk to play the works of Schubert on his harmonica, his will to survive was strengthened as he brought hope to the other prisoners who heard his music.

Children will read different stories of challenges and survival around themes on wilderness, relationships, and tragedy. Two difficult subjects, mental illness and death, are covered in Ann M. Martin's award-winning book *A Corner of the Universe,* in which 12-year-old Hattie meets her Uncle Adam, who has been institutionalized for mental illness. Painful challenges confront Hattie as she begins to understand her uncle's illness and develop a relationship with him that serves as a lesson of love for Adam's family and neighbors.

In *The Year of Miss Agnes,* Kirkpatrick Hill illustrates the challenges that an Alaskan native village in 1948 presented to most teachers. The students expect another teacher

DEATH AND SEPARATION

Text Set

Annie and the Old One
A Corner of the Universe
Crazy Lady
Everything on a Waffle
Maniac Magee: A Novel
Missing May
Winter Holding Spring
A Place Apart
Sun and Spoon

Outcomes

• Sequence the story through illustrations.

• Retell the story from a character's perspective.

SURVIVING PREJUDICE

Text Set

All the Colors of the Race
Aunt Harriet's Underground Railroad in the Sky
Berries Goodman
Between Madison and Palmetto
Through My Eyes: The Autobiography of Ruby Bridges
Two Short and One Long
Witness
Maritcha: A Nineteenth-Century American Girl
Saturnalia
A Corner of the Universe
The Devil in Vienna
Coolies

Outcomes

• Compare and contrast character traits through a matrix.

• Interview family members to record their experiences of bias.

FAMILY DIFFICULTIES

Text Set

Abel's Island
All the Way Home
The Doll People
The Midnight Train Home
Mrs. Frisby and the Rats of NIMH
Out of the Dust
Poppy
Ramona
The Year of Miss Agnes

Outcomes

• Write a simulated journal entry from a character's perspective.

• Research the impact of drought on farmland.

Surviving Family Relationships

Surviving Tragedy

SURVIVING WAR

Text Set

Always Remember Me: How One Family Survived World War II
Daniel's Story
The Devils Arithmetic
The Flag with Fifty-Six Stars: A Gift from the Survivors of Mauthausen
The Harmonica
Terrible Things: An Allegory of the Holocaust
Wish Me Luck
I Am David
Rose Blanche
No Pretty Pictures

Outline

• Research a current conflict and write a newspaper account.

• Write a simulated journal entry from a character's perspective.

SURVIVAL

Surviving Nature

SURVIVING IN THE WILDERNESS

Text Set

Brian's Return
Brian's Winter
Frightful's Mountain
Hatchet
Incident at Hawk's Hill
Lost in the Devil's Desert
My Side of the Mountain
On the Far Side of the Mountain
The River
Tracks in the Snow
Tucket's Ride
The Sign of the Beaver

Outcomes

• Write a wall story to retell one of the texts.

• Identify items for a survival kit.

WOLVES

Text Set

Grey Wolf, Red Wolf
Journey of the Red Wolf
Julie of the Wolves
Julie's Wolf Pack
Look to the North: A Wolf Pup Diary
Return of the Wolf
To the Top of the World: Adventures with Arctic Wolves
The Wolves
The Wounded Wolf

Outcomes

• Research wolves to create a podcast.

• Write *All About Wolves* books.

to come and abruptly leave like all the rest they had, but Miss Agnes captures the hearts of these students as she learns the lessons of survival in this native village.

In the intermediate grade sampler, students learn how children their own age were forced to develop skills for surviving the wilderness when they found themselves alone in the forests.

SAMPLER ■ Surviving in the Wilderness

For many children, living in the wilderness has not just crossed their minds, it has been a dream. The reality of living and surviving in the wilderness is brought to life through the Newbery award–winning author Jean Craighead George in her classic story *My Side of the Mountain.* Unhappy with life in the city, Sam leaves his family and runs away to the wilderness in the Catskill Mountains in New York, but he discovers that living alone in the wilderness does not come easy. With courage and determination, Sam learns how to survive the elements, gather and cook food, create shelter, use nature's gifts for clothing, and train a falcon that becomes his friend.

Unlike Sam, Brian Robeson, the protagonist in Gary Paulsen's *Hatchet,* finds himself alone in the Canadian wilderness after a plane crash. With nothing but the clothes on his back and the hatchet his mother gave him as a present, Brian's courage, determination, and resourcefulness help him survive in the wilderness. Students will have "lived-through experiences" with Sam and Brian as they read and learn about how both boys developed the skills to live off the land.

Surviving in the wilderness requires learning how to live with nature, animals, land, and weather. In this sampler, students will read about how children their age survived in the wilderness of the Canadian and Catskill Mountains. Contemporary fiction that was carefully researched by the authors will help students learn about the ecosystems in the northeastern forests and the highly specialized skills that are required to survive the wilderness.

NCTE/IRA Standards for the English Language Arts

1. Students read a wide range of print and non-print texts to build an understanding of texts, of themselves, and of the cultures of the United States and the world; to acquire new information; to respond to the needs and demands of society and the workplace; and for personal fulfillment. Among texts are fiction and nonfiction, classic and contemporary works.
2. Students read a wide range of literature from many periods in many genres to build an understanding of the many dimensions (e.g., philosophical, ethical, aesthetic) of human experience.
5. Students employ a wide range of strategies as they write and use different writing process elements appropriately to communicate with different audiences for a variety of purposes.

Learner Outcomes

Students will be able to do the following:

■ Listen to a read aloud and discuss the setting of the books they will be reading
■ Read and write stories about the natural environment of the northeastern mountains and forests

SURVIVAL
Surviving in the Wilderness

THE FOCUS LESSON

Using the book *The Eastern Forest*, the teacher conducts a read aloud. To help students understand the environment of the forest that is the setting of the stories they will be reading, the teacher engages them in instructional conversations.

READING WORKSHOP

During reading workshop, the teacher uses literature circles. In the four groups, students are reading from Jean Craighead George's and Gary Paulsen's books to learn about the northeastern forests; the land, weather, and animals; and the survival skills that are required to live alone in the wilderness.

WRITING WORKSHOP

Students write survival stories. Their stories are modeled after the authors' stories that they are reading during reading workshop and independent reading.

Text Set

Brian's Return
Brian's Winter
Frightful's Mountain
Hatchet
Incident at Hawk's Hill
Lost in the Devil's Desert
My Side of the Mountain
On the Far Side of the Mountain
The River
Tracks in the Snow
Tucket's Ride
The Sign of the Beaver

SOCIAL STUDIES

Using the map of the United States, the teacher helps the students to locate the Catskill Mountains where Sam survived in its forests and the Canadian wilderness, north of New York, where Brian finds himself alone with nothing but the clothes he is wearing, a windbreaker, and the hatchet his mother gave him as a present. The students will learn about the climate, the landform and terrain, and the plants and animals. Using their descriptions, the students will create a mural of Sam's environment and of Brian's environment.

COLLABORATIVE INQUIRY ACTIVITIES ACROSS THE CURRICULUM

ART

Students identify objects that they can use in their survival kit. Working in groups, they make a multimedia presentation to advertise their survival kits.

MATHEMATICS

Working in small groups, students design and build a "survival home" for living in the northern wilderness. The teacher directs them to design a 6' × 6' room with different required necessities. Using a cardboard box, the students build the interior objects from cardboard. The box and its contents are scaled to the size of the 6' × 6' room and objects appropriate for that size, including one person. For each part of their home, students research appropriate materials found in the northern wilderness.

SCIENCE, MATH, AND TECHNOLOGY ACTIVITIES

SCIENCE

Students learn from their readings of how deer hunters used all parts of the animal for survival. They explore ways that resources are used and wasted and how they can begin to conserve nature's gifts.

ON-YOUR-OWN ACTIVITIES

Have the students examine the positive aspects of the school community as well as those that affect the environment in negative ways. Direct each student to select one way that the environment improved. To foster change that will benefit the environment, have the students do one of the following: (1) make a poster, (2) write a poem, (3) write a letter to the appropriate authority suggesting a civic action.

HOME–SCHOOL CONNECTIONS

Students discover ways they can conserve many of the natural resources that are wasted at home. They come up with ways that they can conserve on everyday resources that are found in the home.

- Read and discuss stories to learn about survival skills that were used in the wilderness
- Apply the information to create their own survival stories

Conduct a Focus Lesson

During the literature circles, each of the four groups of students selects a book from the text set about a young boy who survives in the eastern forests of North America. Because the setting is critical to the story development, the teacher develops students' background knowledge of ecosystems of North America. The concept of survival in the wilderness of the Catskill Mountains and the Canadian mountains is the second concept that needs to be discussed and developed prior to the students' reading for a deeper understanding of the story.

Establish a Purpose   The teacher conducts a book talk on *My Side of the Mountain* and *On the Far Side of the Mountain,* both by Jean Craighead George. The discussion of these books focuses on how Sam Gribley survives alone in the Catskill Mountains in the first book and continues his challenges in the wilderness with his younger sister Alice in the second.

The book talk is continued with the second book set, Gary Paulsen's *Hatchet* and *The River.* The teacher compares Sam, who yearned to leave New York City for the wilderness, with Brian, who was forced to survive in the Canadian wilderness when his plane crashed. The teacher concludes the discussion with *The River,* in which Brian returns to the place that changed him forever.

Engage in Read Aloud   Before the read aloud, the teacher emphasizes that in all four books from the text set, the main characters were in the wilderness in the northeastern part of the country. Much of the wilderness in the Catskills Mountains and in Canada consists of forests. The teacher explains that while the characters developed skills to obtain food, clothing, shelter, and protection, they learned more about the forest and how to use and protect its resources to stay alive.

The teacher introduces the book *The Eastern Forest: Ecosystems of North America* by Eileen Fielding and makes a connection to the similar story settings in each of the books they will be reading during literature circles. Using the table of contents, the teacher previews the book. Following the book introduction, the teacher reads the relevant parts of the book and stops to highlight important concepts to strengthen the students' background knowledge required for their readings. Some of the major highlights are listed here:

- Showing the map of the eastern forests, the teacher locates the Catskill Mountains in New York and the Canadian wilderness where Brian was stranded.
- Students discuss plants and animals that are part of a biological community, how all animals are hunters for food, and how plants and animals are part of a food chain.
- The teacher highlights how the rich cove forest has a greater biodiversity than most forests, evident as Sam Gribley survives in the Catskills by feasting on a number of different recipes from a variety of plants and animals.

Conduct a Mini-Lesson   The purpose of the mini-lesson is to use brainstorming and discussion techniques to learn about concepts related to Survival in the Wilderness. The teacher poses the following questions:

- How would you get food if there were no stores nearby?
- What type of clothes could you use to protect your body?
- What type of shelter would offer you protection?

Dividing the class into small groups, the teacher encourages the students to select one aspect of survival—food, clothing, or shelter. Using brainstorming and discussion techniques, each small group is directed to come up with at least four ways to survive in the wilderness of the forest by using only its resources. To demonstrate and express their ideas, the groups are directed to use a quickwrite activity to record their ideas, each accompanied by an illustration.

Additional Mini-Lessons

Vocabulary

- The teacher engages students in a brief discussion of the reading after each section of the read aloud.
- The teacher highlights the important words from the reading and writes them on the word wall.
- Students then return to the words added to the word wall to carry on an instructional conversation (Tompkins, 2009) that focuses on content information of each word.

Grammar

- The teacher selects new vocabulary words that were introduced during the read aloud and writes them on the chalkboard.
- The teacher then reviews *nouns, proper nouns, verbs,* and *adjectives.*
- The teacher engages the students in a word sort of the new vocabulary by their parts of speech.

Learning Strategies

- The teacher draws a four-by-four chart on the board.
- Returning to the read aloud, the teacher asks the students what sub-topics are related to the forest and writes them at the top of each column (for example, *Location, Plants, Animals,* and *Life in a Forest*).
- The teacher models how to organize the information that they learn around the four topics using the data chart.
- The teacher directs students to take turns writing notes on the data chart as the discussion of the read aloud progresses.

Conduct a Reading Workshop

The text set for the literature circles includes two books by Jean Craighead George and two by Gary Paulsen. Students read in four groups, with members of each group reading the same book. During literature circles, students engage in the following activities: (1) students read part of the book silently; (2) students respond to the book in a small-group discussion, pose questions about the readings, and select interesting and challenging words from the reading; (3) students engage in independent or collaborative projects; and (4) students participate in a grand conversation with the entire class at the completion of the book. The teacher works with each group for a period of time during the reading workshop, preparing them for reading by instructing them on a particular skill or concept and providing direction to the students in working on their projects. Following is an example of the teacher working with one small group of students who are reading *My Side of the Mountain.*

Before Reading   The teacher introduces the book by briefly explaining the author's preface—why she wrote the book, her editor's first response her work, and readers' questions about the main character of Sam Gibley. To help students understand the literary style and the context of the story, the teacher reads the first chapter that begins with the main character in a snowstorm, six months after he began his life in the Catskill Mountains. The teacher asks the students questions: What did Sam need to know to survive the December snowstorm? How did he acquire these survival skills?

ASSESS LITERACY

After the reading workshop, the teacher uses the rubric below to evaluate student performance.

Criteria	Independent	Proficient	Developing
Silent Reading	Student is highly engaged during silent reading, remaining on task throughout the allotted time. (3)	Student is engaged during silent reading, remaining on task for most of the allotted time. (2)	Student is somewhat engaged during silent reading, remaining on task for some of the allotted time. (0–1)
Participation in Discussion	Student actively participates in discussions, is highly engaged in listening to group members, takes turns, and responds to others with respect at all times. (3)	Student participates in discussions, listens to group members, takes turns, and responds to others most of the time. (2)	Student participates in discussions to some degree, begins to listen to group members, and takes turns and responds to others some of the time. (0–1)
Discussion Responses	Student gives elaborate and accurate responses to teacher-led questions, frequently incorporates language from the readings, at times includes critical analysis within the response, and makes varied types of text connections. (3)	Student gives fairly accurate responses to teacher-led questions, at times incorporates language from the readings, attempts to include a critical analysis within the response, and makes some types of text connections. (2)	Student gives very brief and minimally accurate responses to teacher-led questions, rarely incorporates language from the readings in responses, and does not make text connections. (0–1)
Raising Questions	Student poses thoughtful and honest questions about the readings. (3)	Student poses some questions about the readings. (2)	Student does not initiate questions about the readings. (0–1)
Independent: 9–12 Proficient: 5–8 Developing: 0–4			

During Reading   As the students begin to read silently, they are reminded to think about the location of the wilderness, where the story takes place, and the plants and animals that are part of Sam's new environment. While the students are reading, they use their learning logs to write all the new things that Sam learned and the skills he developed to survive in the Catskill Mountains.

After Reading   First, the teacher leads the student discussion on what Sam learned during his survival in the Catskill Mountains, then turns the discussion over to the students, who continue to talk about the survival skills that Sam needed to develop in order to stay alive. Using their learning logs, the students discuss the resources in the forest and how Sam used them to survive. Finally, students make a chart of what Sam learned and the survival skills he developed.

After students from the four literature circles read their books, the teacher conducts a grand conversation with the entire class. Within the discussion, the students compare and contrast the ideas that the main character learned during survival, the skills they developed to help them survive, and the characters' traits and attitudes that helped them to survive the wilderness.

Conduct a Writing Workshop

Before Writing   The students use the information from the books that they read to write an adventure story. Although they are given latitude with respect to the content, the teacher directs them to follow a story pattern. The teacher explains that in each book that they read during literature circles, both authors followed a similar sequence: (1) how the main character got there, (2) a description of the wilderness, (3) how the main character was placed in danger and used the resources to survive, and (4) how the story ends, with the main character either staying or going home.

The teacher directs the students to begin with a discussion on ways they could write the first part of their story. Small groups of students propose different ideas, respond to each other, and share their ideas with the group.

During Writing   The students work on their ideas for the first part of the story. As they are engaged in writing, the teacher works with individual students. In cases when a student does not know where to begin, the teacher brings him or her back to the brainstorming session to get ideas. The student then rehearses or talks through their draft to the teacher. The teacher continues individual conferencing on students' drafts.

After Writing   After writing their first part, students share their story introductions. The students save their drafts and continue their stories during writing workshop for the duration of the sub-theme, Survival in the Wilderness, until all parts are complete.

Collaborative Inquiry Across the Curriculum

Extension to Mathematics and Technology   Working in small groups, students design and build a "survival home" for living in the northern wilderness. The teacher directs them to design a 6' × 6' room with required necessities. Students construct the interior objects from cardboard. The box and its contents are scaled to the size of the 6' × 6' room, including room for one person. For each part of their home, students research appropriate materials found in the northern wilderness that they would need to build their survival home.

STANDARDS

Mathematics Standards
3. Geometry
4. Measurement

Technology Standards
5. Technology Research Tools

ASSESS LITERACY

When the students have finished their drafts and have revised and edited their stories for publication, the teacher assesses their writing using the rubric below.

Criteria	Independent	Proficient	Developing
The Writing Process			
Planning	Student carefully plans prior to writing, taking into account all of the story parts. (3)	Student engages in planning throughout the writing of the story. (2)	Student shows little or no planning prior to constructing a draft of the story. (0–1)
Drafting	Student engages in the careful construction of a draft developed through planning; drafting occurs throughout as needed. (3)	Student develops an adequate draft that demonstrates planning for story parts was considered. (2)	Student develops a simple draft that does not account for planning for story parts. (0–1)
Revising	Student makes substantial changes to the story. (3)	Student makes adequate changes to the story. (2)	Student makes no or very few changes to the story after being prompted. (0–1)
Editing	Student edits the story carefully for errors and systematically edits for a wide array of language conventions. (3)	Student edits many errors in the story and attends to some language conventions. (2)	Student pays little attention to errors in the story and focuses on a single error type, such as spelling. (0–1)
Story Structure and Writing Development			
Main Character	Student develops the character and begins to show an analysis of character traits. (3)	Student adequately describes the character. (2)	Student simply describes the character. (0–1)
Setting	Student carefully describes the setting, showing its relation to the story problem and events. (3)	Student adequately describes the story setting. (2)	Student alludes to the story setting with no description. (0–1)
Problem	Student clearly describes the story problem and makes connections to the story events. (3)	Student briefly states the story problem. (2)	Student does not state the problem. (0–1)
Story Events	Student clearly writes about the story events. (3)	Student mentions a few story events. (2)	Student mentions one or no story events. (0–1)

Solution	Student provides a story solution and makes connections to the story problem and events. (3)	Student provides an adequate solution to the story problem. (2)	Student does not offer a solution to the story problem. (0–1)
Vocabulary	Student uses many descriptive and complex words with accuracy and incorporates the language of the literature. (3)	Student uses some descriptive words with accuracy. (2)	Student uses simple vocabulary. (0–1)
Spelling	Student's writing exhibits no or few spelling errors. (3)	Student's writing exhibit some spelling errors. (2)	Student's writing exhibits many spelling errors. (0–1)
Capitalization	Student's writing has no or few errors in capitalization. (3)	Student's writing has some errors in capitalization. (2)	Student's writing has many errors in capitalization. (0–1)
Punctuation	Student's writing has no or few punctuation errors. (3)	Student's writing has some punctuation errors. (2)	Student's writing has many punctuation errors. (0–1)
Sentence Structure	Student's writing exhibits a variety of sentence structures that are used appropriately within the story. (3)	Student's writing has some errors with sentence structure and attempts at writing complex sentences. (2)	Student's writing contains incomplete and simple sentences. (0–1)

Independent: 29–42
Proficient: 15–28
Developing: 0–14

Extension to Science   The teacher directs the discussion on how each of the main characters uses resources within the environment to survive. As an example, the teacher reads a selection from *My Side of the Mountain* where Sam uses all of the parts of a deer that was killed by hunters. The students list what parts of the deer were used and how Sam used each part. Returning to their books, students identify other ways in which the two main characters used the resources within the environment. As a follow-up, extend the discussion to different products we buy, the resources that are needed to manufacture them, and how we waste and may conserve our resources. The focus of the discussion turns to energy, where it comes from, how it is used, and ways to conserve it.

> **STANDARDS**
> **Science Standards**
> Science in Personal and Social Perspectives, Content Standards F2 and F3

Extension to Social Studies   Using a map, the teacher helps the students locate the Catskill Mountains, where Sam survives in the forest, and the Canadian wilderness, where Brian finds himself alone with nothing but the clothes he is wearing, a windbreaker, and the hatchet his mother gave him as a present. Students learn about the climate, the landform and terrain, and the plants and animals. Using their descriptions, the students will create a mural of Brian's environment.

> **STANDARDS**
> **Social Studies Standards**
> III. People, Places, and Environments

Home–School Connections Students are directed to discover ways they can conserve many of the natural resources that are wasted, identifying one food that is eaten in their homes, a piece of clothing that they wear, and furniture in their room. The teacher then directs their assignment to the study of energy. They work with someone at home to determine: (1) how they use energy, (2) the source of energy, (3) the ways energy is wasted, and (4) the ways they can conserve it (see Figure 3.4).

On-Your-Own Activities The teacher has the students examine the positive aspects of the school community as well as those that affect the environment in negative ways. Each student is directed to select one way that the environment can be improved. To foster change that will benefit the environment, the students do one of the following: (1) make a poster, (2) write a poem, or (3) write a letter to the appropriate authority suggesting a civic action.

Critical Literacy

When students have completed the study of survival, they work in pairs to research on the Internet how climate change influences mountain ranges such as the Catskills. After researching the effects of global warming on the flora and fauna of the moun-

FIGURE 3.4 Ways to Conserve Our Natural Resources

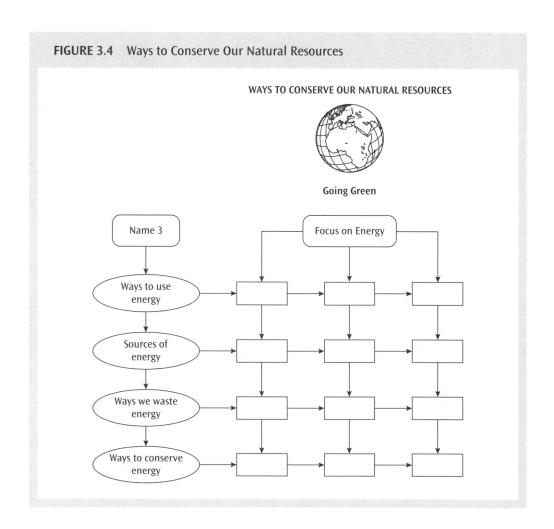

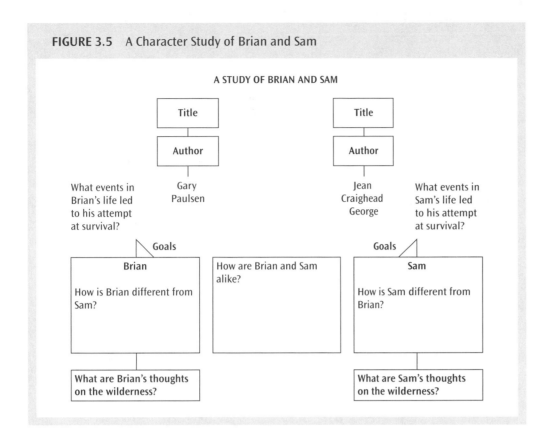

FIGURE 3.5 A Character Study of Brian and Sam

tains, the students present a slideshow that synthesizes the information and suggests possible ways to help the habitats survive.

Collaborative Literacy

The teacher directs the students to select a book by Jean Craighead George or Gary Paulsen that they have not read in literature circles to read independently. After they have completed their books during independent reading, they will be able to work together to compare how two characters, Brian and Sam, survived the wilderness.

Students are directed to use the graphic organizer in Figure 3.5 to work together to compare the characters from the two different authors. During their small-group discussions of the protagonists, students decide on the similarities and differences between Brian and Sam, what brought them to the wilderness, how they developed survival skills, and what they learned. To guide their discussions, students use the graphic organizer to direct their attention to different aspects of the characters. Upon completion, each small group will share the group's ideas with the whole class.

■ Middle Grades: Grades 6–8

The year is 1933, and the most powerful person in the German government is Adolf Hitler. He is expected to lead his country out of serious economic and political crisis. Instead, he moves quickly to implement his radical ideology of the Nazi Party and end German democracy.

HOMELESSNESS

Text Set

The Double Life of Zoe Flynn
Street Child
Monkey Island
Where's Home?
Can't Get There from Here
The Loner

Outcomes

- Identify causes and effects of homelessness.

- Write a simulated interview from a character's perspective.

- Research homelessness in the community.

SURVIVING THE HOLOCAUST

Text Set

No Pretty Pictures: A Child of War
Surviving Hitler: A Boy in the Nazi Death Camps
Lonek's Journey: The True Story of a Boy's
    Escape to Freedom
Maus: A Survivor's Tale: My Father Bleeds History
The Seamstress: A Memoir of Survival
In My Hands: Memories of a Holocaust Rescuer
Child of the Warsaw Ghetto
Luba: The Angel of Bergen-Belsen

Outcomes

- Analyze behaviors and traits of main characters to create a Portrait of a Survivor.

- Create and use plot profiles to engage in grand conversations about the growth of a survivor.

RUNAWAYS

Text Set

Breakout
Hold Fast
North
Secrets of the Shopping Mall
Runaway
Chu Ju's House
Kathleen, Please Come Home

Outcomes

- Engage in a grand conversation about the text set.

- Identify character traits and compare/contrast them.

- Identify reasons for running away.

Family Survival

Surviving Tragedy

SURVIVING WAR

Text Set

After the Dancing Days
Lisa's War
The Boys from St. Petri
Under the Blood Red Sun
The Year of Impossible Goodbyes
Fallen Angels

Outcomes

- Investigate the war that is the setting for each text to create a graphic that illustrates political and economic causes of the war.

- Using the discussion web strategy, students discuss: Is war ever justified?

SURVIVAL

DISASTER

Text Set

Shipwreck at the Bottom of the World: The
    Extraordinary True Adventure of Shackleton
    and the Endurance
Quake: A Novel!
Into Thin Air: A Personal Account of the Mount
    Everest Disaster
The Great Fire
Blizzard's Wake
Catastrophe in Southern Asia: The Tsunami
    of 2004

Outcomes

- Create a three-level cluster map to identify disasters in recent world events that could occur in their communities (cities or states) and the texts read about them.

- Brainstorm necessary items for a Go Kit.

Surviving Nature

HOSTILE ENVIRONMENTS

Text Set

Hatchet
Julie of the Wolves
Call It Courage
The Girl in the Box
Frozen Fire
A Boat to Nowhere

Outcomes

- Identify and describe difficulties of survival in a hostile environment.

- Identify character traits and plot actions of the character in the story.

Hitler and the Nazis identify the Jews as a race and through a hate-filled propaganda program make the Jewish people the scapegoat for Germany's defeat in World War I and the country's economic problems. Jews are prevented from attending public schools, theaters, and vacation resorts. Synagogues, stores, and homes are destroyed and Jewish possessions are stolen. In 1939, Germany invades Poland and World War II begins. As the German army invades European countries, large numbers of Jews, gypsies, the handicapped, and political opponents are imprisoned in ghettos, transit camps, forced-labor camps, and death camps. By the time the war ends in 1945, the Nazis will have killed more than six million Jewish men, women, and children in the systematic mass destruction known as the Holocaust.

Middle school students will investigate the theme of Survival by reading literature that describes the physical and emotional atrocities Holocaust victims were forced to endure. They discover that it was the determination and strength of character that enabled some to survive the human tragedy caused by starvation, exposure to cold, and contagious diseases. As students read the inspiring stories of Holocaust survivors such as Jack Mandelbaum, Lonek, and Anita Lobel, they hear the haunting descriptions of being captured and marched from camp to camp in the voices of children whose youth was spent surviving a nightmare world of dehumanizing conditions. Students' readings of the gripping tales of Sara Tuvel Bernstein, Irene Gut Opdyke, and Vladek Spiegelman will help them experience the extraordinary horror that results from abuse of power and recognize the danger of remaining indifferent to the oppression of others. They learn that love, determination, and human dignity help make survival possible in a world filled with moral depravity and evil.

Middle school students are often interested in studying survival, because it is so close to their personal experiences. Trying to survive issues such as peer pressure, social cliques, and the insecurity of living in an ever-changing body is a daily struggle. Middle school students want to know about the world and its conflicts and social issues. They want to discuss violence, discrimination, and racism. By examining the skills required to survive the Holocaust through the eyes of youth who lived through years of physical and emotional turmoil, middle school students will realize that teens have the power to survive and control any hostile environment.

Though the memoirs graphically describe Hitler's reign of terror, students will also be encouraged to read historical fiction about the human costs of war. Stories such as *The Boys from St. Petri* and *Lisa's War* not only provide a context for the effects of the war on all people, but they also emphasize that in the midst of inhumanity there is goodness. These are the stories of young people who chose to make a difference. They describe characters who joined resistance efforts to fight back and provide hope in the face of an unbearable future. These stories emphasize that war is always tragic and that survival is also based on the extraordinary bravery of ordinary people. Text sets based on realistic fiction also help students explore contemporary issues of family survival, such as running away from home or homelessness, in addition to surviving natural disasters or hostile environments.

SAMPLER ■ Surviving the Holocaust

The events of World War II and the Holocaust make us keenly aware of man's potential for inhumanity. The horrors of this period were so unimaginable that the survivors kept silence for decades, believing they could detach themselves from the burden of their memories and the nightmares of a shameful past. However, since truth can be

SURVIVAL
Surviving the Holocaust

THE FOCUS LESSON

Students use list-group-label to analyze the concept of survival. The teacher reads *Child of the Warsaw Ghetto* and compares the main character's actions with students' ideas about survival and implements mini-lesson relative to character analysis and inferring traits.

READING WORKSHOP

The teacher describes memoir genre and presents the text set that are memoirs. Students use book pass to preview texts, work in literature discussion groups to analyze survivors' behavior and traits, and use plot profiles to evaluate tension.

WRITING WORKSHOP

Teacher implements mini-lesson(s) on newspaper writing. Students assume roles of different types of reporters to write and publish *Holocaust Newspapers*.

Text Set

No Pretty Pictures: A Child of War
Surviving Hitler: A Boy in the Nazi Death Camps
Lonek's Journey: The True Story of a Boy's Escape to Freedom
Maus: A Survivor's Tale: My Father Bleeds History
The Seamstress: A Memoir of Survival
In My Hands: Memories of a Holocaust Rescuer
Child of the Warsaw Ghetto
Luba: The Angel of Bergen-Belsen

SOCIAL STUDIES

Students research beliefs and events in European history to create process–cause graphs that show how anti-Semitism, rise of dictators, economic depression, etc., led to the Holocaust and create a timeline and map to illustrate the Nazi march across Europe.

COLLABORATIVE INQUIRY ACTIVITIES ACROSS THE CURRICULUM

ART

Find examples of victims' paintings, diaries, poems, and stories.

MATHEMATICS

Using print and electronic resources, calculate distances survivors traveled. Calculate distance for each time interval.

SCIENCE, MATH, AND TECHNOLOGY ACTIVITIES

SCIENCE

Students identify physical and emotional illnesses victims experienced in camps. Research causes, treatments available then and now, and long-term effects. Discuss how the human spirit and will to live helped survivors.

ON-YOUR-OWN ACTIVITIES

Students find propaganda posters and paintings of the Nazis. They explain how symbols were used to reinforce the Nazi message.

HOME–SCHOOL CONNECTIONS

Students and parents discuss issues and events from the memoirs. They identify current examples of oppression in the news. They discuss what victims would need to survive a modern holocaust.

healing, many survivors are now revealing their stories, as evidenced by the overwhelming number of survivor memoirs published in the last decade.

In this sampler, students read Holocaust memoirs not only to enable them to understand the will of the survivor, but to ensure that a tragedy of this enormity will never be repeated. This is an important topic for middle grade students, who are beginning to develop the concept of empathy. As they enter the world of the Holocaust victim, they will not only explore the terrifying experiences of the author but will develop their own beliefs about the physical and emotional damages of racial persecution and war. As a literary genre, memoir has the advantage of presenting both an eyewitness account and the intimacy of a personal perspective of a historic period. The tone of these texts will provide students with insight into the character of a survivor while placing the events of World War II into a frame of human feeling.

As students read *No Pretty Pictures: A Child of War, Surviving Hitler: A Boy in the Nazi Death Camps,* and *Lonek's Journey: The True Story of a Boy's Escape to Freedom,* they develop enduring images of the harrowing experiences children endured in Nazi prison camps. Each story helps the reader discover how intelligence, luck, and the compassion of others helped young people survive in a dangerous and unpredictable world.

Students who read *The Seamstress* experience the compelling story of Sara Tuvel, an extraordinary woman caught in the Nazi web of terror. After a series of dramatic escapes, they will enter Ravensbruck, a concentration camp for women, and observe how Sara's personal strength and fiery determination lead to survival for herself, her sister Ellen, and two friends. Students who select *Maus,* the Pulitzer Prize–winning survivor story told in cartoon form, read two stories. The main text describes how the author's father and mother survived confinement, betrayal, and narrow escapes from death while the subtext reveals the strained relationship typical of a child and a parent who survived the tragedy of human despair.

If students read *In My Hands: Memories of a Holocaust Rescuer,* they will witness the growth of a heroine. When the war begins, Irene Gut is a 17-year-old student nurse and a Catholic, but when the war separates her from her family, her friends, and her innocence, she becomes determined to fight back. Irene starts by passing food and information to Jews in a ghetto and later hides Jews in the basement of a Nazi major's house.

As students experience these inspiring memoirs of survivors and rescuers, they will discover that the actions of teens and the choice between good and evil have the power to make a difference. Extension activities will help students explore the Holocaust and its effects from a variety of perspectives and will deepen their appreciation of the human spirit.

In this sampler, students will read several texts about young survivors of concentration camps and how they overcame extreme challenges in order to live.

NCTE/IRA Standards for the English Language Arts

3. Students apply a wide range of strategies to comprehend, interpret, evaluate, and appreciate texts. They draw on their prior experience, their interactions with other readers and writers, their knowledge of word meaning and of other texts, their word identification strategies, and their understanding of textual features (e.g., sound-letter correspondence, sentence structure, context, graphics).

5. Students employ a wide range of strategies as they write and use different writing process elements appropriately to communicate with a variety of audiences for different purposes.

7. Students conduct research on issues and events by generating ideas and questions and by posing problems. They gather, evaluate, and synthesize data from a variety of sources (e.g., print and non-print texts, artifacts, people) to communicate their discoveries in ways that suit their purpose and audience.

Learner Outcomes

Students will be able to do the following:

- Demonstrate comprehension of their reading by inferring character traits of a survivor based on abstract evidence describing a character's actions, words, thoughts, and feelings
- Make text-to-text connections to create a portrait of a survivor concept web
- Abstract and sequence events from the texts to create a plot profile
- Support assertions relative to story tension using evidence from the texts
- Create analogies to demonstrate understanding of euphemisms

Conduct a Focus Lesson

The English language arts teacher initiates the investigation by tapping the students' prior knowledge of the concept of survival. The list-group-label strategy (Taba, 1967) is an effective tool for reviewing words, concepts, and information. The teacher asks each student to list at least seven words, phrases, and ideas he or she associates with the topic of Survival. After 10 minutes the students are placed in groups of three or four and asked to combine their lists. They create categories that include all the words on their lists. Next, they select or create labels for the categories. Each group shares their work and places the list-group-label chart on a word wall to support unit activities for reading and writing. The teacher helps students clarify their understanding of the concept by asking: How is surviving different from living?

Establish a Purpose The teacher introduces *Child of the Warsaw Ghetto,* a picture storybook that describes life in the Warsaw Ghetto of 1940 through the eyes of Froim Baum. The teacher explains that as students read, they will learn about the painful experiences of Jews who were transported to the Warsaw Ghetto and how Froim managed to survive after Germany invaded Poland in 1939. The shared reading and character analysis activities provide the students with the background knowledge and skills they will need to engage in independent reading of one of the memoirs.

The students select texts and participate in literature discussion groups to reflect on the actions the main character took in response to the terrors imposed by the Nazis as well as the personal traits that enabled the character to survive in an environment of moral depravity and human suffering. As the students begin to understand the events of the Holocaust and the extent of Nazi control, they will make connections to discrimination and terrorism and the problems of survival in their own times.

Engage in Shared Reading The teacher begins by asking students to listen carefully while she reads *Child of the Warsaw Ghetto* aloud, directing them to focus on how Froim Baum survives the physical and emotional strains of living under Nazi control. The teacher also asks them to compare the events in this story with the ideas they generated in the list-group-label activity. As the teacher reads, the students learn that

Froim is the youngest son of a poor Jewish tailor who lives in a one-room house. They see Froim playing with homemade toys and witness how he tries to help his family after his father's death. At this time, students begin to learn about Hitler's invasion of Austria and then Poland. They experience not only the bombing of the city of Warsaw but also how young Jewish men are forced to work for the Germans. They watch as Jews have their possessions stolen and are transported behind barbed wire walls. Students see how thousands of people struggle to survive in overcrowded spaces and create secret schools and libraries. They travel with Froim in and out of this ghetto, observe how the Nazis trick the people into moving to death camps, and how Froim and some of his brothers survive a series of these camps. After finishing the book, the teacher asks the students, "What are some of the tragedies Froim and his family experienced? What did Froim do to survive? What was he thinking and feeling? How do the events and actions of this story compare with your ideas about survival?"

Conduct a Mini-Lesson   The teacher explains to students that as they read one of the memoirs, they will come to know not only the discrimination and pain the Nazis imposed during the Holocaust but also the character traits and actions that enabled each author to survive. The mini-lesson focuses on the use of graphic organizers and a character web to help students reflect on their reading.

The teacher explains that those who survived the devastating events and experiences of the Holocaust did so because they possessed extraordinary personal qualities. The teacher models how to analyze a character's attributes by using the graphic organizer in Figure 3.6 (Antonacci & O'Callaghan, 2006). After reading *Child of the Warsaw Ghetto* the teacher distributes the graphic organizers, directing students to work in pairs to complete the charts and to find evidence in the story to support their responses. The teacher provides sufficient time for each student to provide at least one response in each column, and then asks students to share their ideas while recording them on a class chart.

The teacher explains that a character's behavior, words, thoughts, and feelings reveal his or her personality traits. For example, when Froim takes a job sweeping the barbershop to earn a few *zlotys* for food, his actions show that he is responsible. The teacher asks each pair of students to create a group of four. Using their graphic organizers, the groups create a character web (Antonacci & O'Callaghan, 2006), illustrated in Figure 3.7, to identify the traits they believe helped Froim survive. When the groups have completed their webs, the teacher asks one person from each group to share their analysis with the class.

The teacher then asks students to create a personal response to the story and include any questions that were raised by the story about to how people survived the painful experiences of the Holocaust (see Figure 3.8 on page 111). Finally, the teacher and students engage in a dialogue about the concept of survival and what they think it takes to be a survivor.

Additional Mini-Lessons

Analogies to Extend Vocabulary

■ The teacher explains that analogies are tools to help students extend their understanding of words by determining the relationships among a set of four terms: A is to B as X is to Y.

FIGURE 3.6   Graphic Organizer for Character Analysis

Title: _____   Author: _____   Chapter: ___

Character: _____

Identify the difficult situations or events within the story.	What actions did the character take in response to each situation?	What was the character thinking during each response?	What did the character say?	What emotions was the character feeling?

FIGURE 3.7   The Character Web

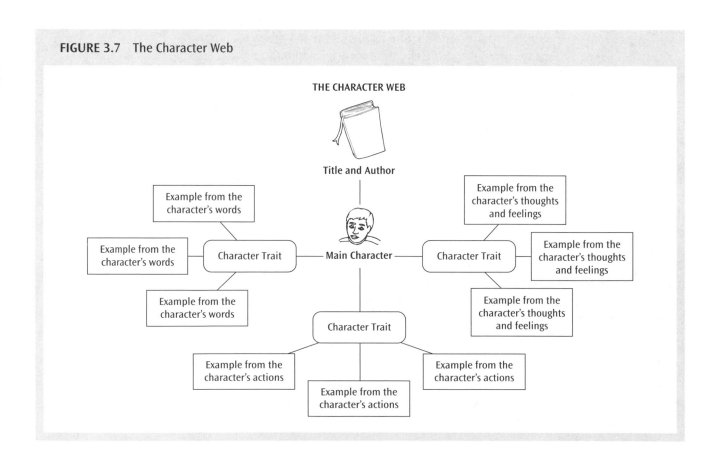

FIGURE 3.8   Surviving the Holocaust: Personal Responses

Title	Chapter	Response	Questions	What Does It Take to Be a Survivor?

- The teacher uses specific examples to model types of relationships: part to whole, synonym/antonym, people to place, cause and effect, characteristic or attribute, action/object.
- The teacher explains that *euphemisms* are terms used to manipulate the real meanings of words.
- Students provide examples of euphemisms from experience and discuss how speakers and writers use euphemisms to conceal meanings.
- Students and teachers identify terminology the Nazis used to mask their evil intent, such as *emigration* for *expulsion, evacuation* for *deportation, Final Solution* for *annihilation.* The teacher selects words for literary analysis, such as *victim, survivor, bystander, oppressor.*
- After reading memoirs students discuss the meanings of key terms selected by the book group and teacher to create analogies. Each group shares their analogies and explains the relationships and reasons behind their responses.

Plot Profiles

- The teacher reads *Luba: The Angel of Bergen-Belsen* (or another Holocaust picture storybook).

- After a "grand conversation," the students identify key events in the story and number them in correct sequence.
- Using a prepared plot profile graph, the teacher explains how to place the story events along the horizontal *(x)* axis using the event number.
- The teacher demonstrates how to rate the degree of excitement or tension along the vertical *(y)* axis, with 1 representing little excitement and 10 a high degree of tension.
- Teacher and students engage in discussion to evaluate and plot the events in the shared text.
- Students in each memoir book group collaborate to create a plot profile of the text and share it with the class.

Writing Newspaper Articles

- The teacher guides students in examining a newspaper to identify the types of articles: news, editorials, feature stories, profiles, sports, entertainment, and so on.
- Teacher helps students analyze and identify the features of journalistic writing in a sample news article. They abstract the "lead" and explain that it is the opening sentence that should hook the reader. They discuss the five Ws (Who? What? Where? When? Why? And sometimes How?). The teacher describes the inverted pyramid, explaining that the most important information comes first, followed by less important details.
- Using sample articles, students discuss the importance of supporting statements with facts and statistics. They identify ways reporters gather information, such as research and interviews.
- Students brainstorm ideas for articles for a Holocaust Newspaper based on the memoirs and knowledge of the period.
- Students use a word-processing application to create a newspaper with column formatting and graphics to support each article. They may also include a cross-word puzzle based on unit vocabulary.

Conduct a Reading Workshop

In the focus lesson, the teacher described how to use a graphic organizer to gather data about a character and how to use that information to understand the traits that a survivor might possess. The teacher explains that during the reading workshops, students will apply these techniques as they read one of the memoirs written by a Holocaust survivor.

Before Reading   The teacher explains that the six books in the text set are memoirs written by or about people who were either children or teenagers when Hitler unleashed his power. The teacher indicates that the stories are compelling because they give eyewitness testimony not only to the evils imposed at the hands of the oppressors but to the courage and will of the survivors. The teacher comments that many of the Holocaust memoirs were written almost 50 years after the liberation and asks the students why they think the survivors waited so long to write their stories.

Each literature discussion group focuses on one of the memoirs in the text set. The teacher has enough copies of each book in the text set to create six groups of at least two students each. To help students make a choice, the teacher implements the book pass strategy (Allen, 2004). The teacher divides the class into groups of six; each

FIGURE 3.9 Book Pass Chart

Title	Author	Award(s)	Comments	Questions

group is given a basket with one copy of each title. Each student takes a book and a book pass chart (illustrated in Figure 3.9) from the basket.

Students indicate the title and author and begin to "sample" the book by examining illustrations and other graphics and by reading the flaps, front and back covers, and a few pages from the story. In the comment column, the students highlight information about the author, topic, or story. They then add questions the book instigates. After five minutes, the teacher says "Book pass," and the students pass the book to the student sitting next to them. The process continues until each student has reviewed all six books.

No Pretty Pictures: A Child of War is the piercing memoir of the Caldecott-winning illustrator Anita Lobel. This book, a finalist for the 1998 National Book Award, describes how Lobel spent five years on a turbulent course that included assumed identities, hiding in a ghetto attic and convent, and capture and confinement in a concentration camp, all the while protecting her younger brother, who was often disguised as a girl. Focused on survival, Lobel narrates the story in the voice of a child with the eyes of an artist who creates vivid and enduring images of the Holocaust and its tragic consequences.

Surviving Hitler: A Boy in the Nazi Death Camps by Andrea Warren received the William Allen White Children's Book Award and was named as a Robert F. Sibert

Honor Book. Jack Mandelbaum and his family live a comfortable life in Poland until the German invasion forces them to flee. In 1939 Jack and his mother seek safety in a small village in the one-room home of his uncle. For two years he supports his mother and brother by working on a forced-labor crew. When the orders are given to send the Jews to concentration camps, Jack's desperate attempt to save them all backfires; he is jerked away from his family and sent to the nightmarish world of a male concentration camp. As a 15-year-old boy caught up in Hitler's plan to annihilate the Jews, Jack learns to "play the life and death game" with his captors. Despite the intolerable conditions, Jack survives day to day by forging friendships and believing that he would see his family again.

The astonishing story of an 11-year-old boy's survival is told in *Lonek's Journey: The True Story of a Boy's Escape to Freedom*. When the German army marches into their small town in Poland, Lonek's family tries to avoid being captured by hiding under a barn; eventually they are caught and sent to a labor camp in Siberia. Although only a boy, Lonek helps his family survive by supplementing their meager food supply with fish and berries. When the Russians release the Poles, Lonek's mother is so poor she places him in an orphanage. With 1,000 other Jewish children, Lonek begins a dangerous and amazing journey by land and sea across Europe to Palestine. Lonek's childlike optimism and resourcefulness help him survive a two-year odyssey that reunites him with his family.

Sara Tuvel Bernstein narrates her riveting story of wartime survival in *The Seamstress*. Sara is the smartest girl in her Romanian village, but rather than ignore her teacher's anti-Semitic remarks, she leaves the school and begins a new life in Bucharest as a seamstress, using her blonde hair and skill with a needle to survive the early days of Nazi invasion. However, after several dangerous escapes from prison, Sara, her sister, and two friends are sent to the Ravensbruck concentration camp in Germany. Sara's extraordinary street smarts and her determination help them survive the horrors of Nazi oppression. This is a memoir of courage and the will to survive as told by a woman with an independent spirit who will do everything in her power to keep herself and her loved ones alive.

Maus: A Survivor's Tale: My Father Bleeds History is a captivating story that examines the Holocaust through the eyes of Vladek and his young wife, Anna, as they attempt to survive the early days of war in Poland, life in the ghetto, and a flight into hiding to escape the Final Solution. This is the story not only of the struggle to survive but of the effects of the events on the survivor's later life and on the following generation.

In My Hands: Memories of a Holocaust Rescuer, written by Irene Gut Opdyke with Jennifer Armstrong, was named one of the ALA Best Books for Young Adults. Irene Gutnowa is just a girl when World War II begins, but as the war progresses, German and Russian soldiers deprive her of her family and strip her of her innocence. After hiding out in the forest and tending to the surviving Polish soldiers, the student nurse is captured by the Russians and forced to work in their military hospital. Told in the first person, the readers come to know of Irene's pains, fears, and determination to sacrifice herself to save her friends.

The information and questions from each student are synthesized into a group chart and used to help students select the book they will read. The charts are saved and hung on bulletin boards for future reference. The teacher indicates that as students read, each book group will focus on the personality traits and strategies that enabled the main characters to survive. They will examine the extent of the Nazis' treatment of their victims as well as the deeds of heroism in the ghettos and concentration camps. They explore the idea of resistance in terms of overt opposition as well as the spiritual resistance found in secret writings, diaries, poetry, and works of art. They identify the roles of victim, oppressor, bystander, and rescuer and examine the moral choices thrust on people during times of war.

During Reading   The teacher indicates that as they read the selected memoir, the students will apply the graphic organizer strategy from the focus lesson to analyze the development of each character from victim to survivor. The students are expected to read one to two chapters each night and to complete a graphic organizer form to document their understanding of the survivor's actions, words, thoughts, and feelings. At the start of each class period, the members of each book club bring their graphic organizers to the group and engage in a discussion to share their analysis of the reading. They use the organizers and text evidence to develop a character web and to identify the main character's traits that help them become a survivor. The teacher moves to each group to facilitate the discussion. Some key questions students should consider are: What was life like for the main character at the start of World War II? What cruelties did the main character and his or her family experience at the hands of the Nazis? What acts of heroism and/or resistance illustrate the evolution of the main character from victim to survivor? What moral choices did the main character face? How did the main character's decisions help him/her emerge as a survivor? Faced with a similar decision, how would you respond? What characters would you classify as oppressors, victims, bystanders, or rescuers?

After Reading   The teacher directs students to the questions they generated before reading and engages them in a discussion that uses text evidence to answer the questions they raised.

The teacher then asks, "In what ways was the memoir you read stranger than and/or more exciting than fiction about the same period?" After book groups share their ideas, the teacher explains that they will use the plot profile strategy (Antonacci & O'Callaghan, 2006) to identify the most exciting parts of the story and to explain how specific incidents and events created various levels of tension within the story and eventually resulted in a dramatic resolution. The students in each book group (1) select the events in the beginning of the memoir that describe the main character's life, (2) identify the incidents and events under Nazi control affecting the main character, and (3) abstract the events and actions that led to resolution. Students engage in a grand conversation in order to rate the degree of excitement attached to each element relative to the theme and share their completed graphs with the class.

Based on each group's character web and plot profile, the class creates a "portrait of a survivor" web that synthesizes the traits needed to be a survivor. They write a reflection to explain whether or not they could have survived the atrocities of the Holocaust.

Conduct a Writing Workshop

The teacher asks, "Why do you think freedom of the press is a central right in a democratic society?" After students respond, the teacher explains that Hitler and the Nazis were able to continue their oppression of the Jews and others because they controlled the media. They discuss how propaganda and the use of language in the form

ASSESS LITERACY

When the reading workshop sequence is completed, the teacher uses the rubric below to evaluate students' performances.

Criteria	Independent	Proficient	Developing
Making Text-to-Self Connections	Student makes text-to-self connections demonstrating comprehension of text. (3)	Student begins to develops text-to-self connections demonstrating comprehension of text. (2)	Student needs assistance to develop text-to-self connections demonstrating comprehension of text. (0–1)
Locating Information in Text	Student is proficient at locating information in the text. (3)	Student is beginning to locate information in the text. (2)	Student needs assistance to locate information in the text. (0–1)
Summarizing Information	Student is proficient at paraphrasing information from the text. (3)	Student is beginning to paraphrase information from the text. (2)	Student needs assistance to paraphrase the information from the text. (0–1)
Using Information from Text in Discussions	Student is proficient at using information during discussions. (3)	Student is beginning to use information during discussions. (2)	Student needs assistance to use information during discussions. (0–1)

Independent: 9–12
Proficient: 5–8
Developing: 0–4

of euphemisms kept the truth of the Holocaust from the world. Students continue to extend their understanding of surviving the Holocaust by creating newspaper stories that should have been written.

Before Writing   The teacher conducts a mini-lesson on newspaper writing that begins with brainstorming a list of articles that could be included in a Holocaust newspaper based on the memoirs they read as well as their interest in and knowledge of the period. The teacher organizes students into newspaper groups that may be the same as the book group or may include students from each of the book clubs. If the writing groups and book groups are the same, each newspaper will focus on the issues, events, and people from the text. If the group is mixed, the articles will address the range of events. Members of each group take on roles associated with a newspaper staff, such as editor, reporter, feature writer, and so on.

During Writing   Students within each group select specific types of articles: news, feature stories, editorials, puzzles, and so on. They may conduct further research in nonfiction texts and the Internet or role play interviews to add details to their articles.

Using the rubric below to assess students' performances during the writing workshop, the teacher analyzes the students' ability to apply content knowledge from the texts and research as well as to write in the genre of a newspaper article. The teacher may assess each student's piece or the newspaper as a whole.

Criteria	Independent	Proficient	Developing
The Writing Process			
Planning	Student carefully plans prior to writing, taking into account all of the parts. (3)	Student engages in planning throughout the writing of the newspaper component. (2)	Student shows little or no planning prior to constructing a draft of the newspaper component. (0–1)
Drafting	Student engages in the careful construction of a draft developed through planning; drafting occurs throughout writing as needed. (3)	Student develops an adequate draft that demonstrates planning for newspaper component was considered. (2)	Student develops a simple draft that does not account for planning for newspaper component. (0–1)
Revising	Student makes substantial changes to the newspaper component. (3)	Student makes adequate changes to the newspaper component. (2)	Student makes no or very few changes to the newspaper component after being prompted. (0–1)
Editing	Student edits carefully for errors and systematically edits for a wide array of language conventions. (3)	Student edits many errors and attends to some language conventions. (2)	Student pays little attention to errors and focuses on a single error type, such as spelling. (0–1)
Writing Mechanics			
Vocabulary	Student uses many descriptive and complex words with accuracy and incorporates the language of the literature. (3)	Student uses some descriptive words with accuracy. (2)	Student uses simple vocabulary. (0–1)
Spelling	Student's writing exhibits no or few spelling errors. (3)	Student's writing exhibits some spelling errors. (2)	Student's writing exhibits many spelling errors. (0–1)
Capitalization	Student's writing has no or few errors in capitalization. (3)	Student's writing has some errors in capitalization. (2)	Student's writing has many errors in capitalization. (0–1)
Punctuation	Student's writing has no or few punctuation errors. (3)	Student's writing has some punctuation errors. (2)	Student's writing has many punctuation errors. (0–1)
Sentence Structure	Student's writing exhibits a variety of sentence structures that are used appropriately within the story. (3)	Student's writing has some errors in sentence structure and attempts at writing complex sentences. (2)	Student's writing contains incomplete and simple sentences. (0–1)
Independent: 19–27 Proficient: 10–18 Developing: 0–9			

The teacher meets with each group to provide direction and instruction in writing a newspaper story. When a draft is completed, the students take on the role of editors and assess each other's stories based on the type of article, accuracy of facts, inverted pyramid model, and so on.

After Writing Student "reporters" revise and edit as needed based on comments from the teacher and peers. Completed newspapers are displayed in the classroom. Students from other classes are encouraged to read and respond to the work by writing sticky notes to the editor-in-chief of each newspaper.

Collaborative Inquiry Across the Curriculum

Extension to Mathematics and Technology The main characters in each memoir traveled over long distances and struggled for survival for years. The students use print and electronic resources to determine the distance in miles each main character traveled. Using details from the texts, they determine how far each character traveled within each time interval from home to camp to liberation to rebuilding their lives.

Students use a word-processing application to create a newspaper with headlines, two-column format, graphics, puzzles, and so on.

Extension to Science Holocaust victims who were forced into labor and death camps were subjected to horrifying conditions that resulted in physical and emotional illnesses. The students list the diseases and emotional problems described in each text. They research the causes, treatments available then and now, and long-term effects of each illness. They also discuss how the human spirit and will to live helped survivors to overcome isolation, starvation, disease, and near-death experiences.

Extension to Social Studies The teacher and students investigate beliefs and events in European history that led to the Holocaust, such as anti-Semitism, the rise of dictators between two world wars, the rise of nationalism in Germany, Germany's defeat in World War I, the development of "race science," and economic depression. Students create process–cause graphics to illustrate the relationships among the factors.

Students construct a timeline and map that illustrates the Nazi march across Europe and explains how the Jews and other victims were transported from their homes to ghettos and camps in Germany, Russia, and Poland. Details about life in the ghettos and specific camps should also be included.

Home–School Connections Students are encouraged to discuss the issues and events in the memoirs they are reading with parents. They identify current issues of oppression and/or discrimination and reflect on the traits victims will need to survive modern-day genocides.

On-Your-Own Activities Both victims and oppressors used art to further their cause. Victims created works of art as a form of resistance as well as therapy. Students find examples of paintings and drawings, diaries, poems, and stories written by victims and survivors and share the works to explain how art was used to document the victims' experiences. Other students investigate the propaganda posters, paintings, and drawings of the Nazis, explaining how they used symbols to reinforce their message.

STANDARDS

Mathematics Standards
1. Number and Operations

Technology Standards
3. Technology Productivity Tools
5. Technology Research Tools

STANDARDS

Science Standards
Life Science, Content Standard C5

Science in Personal and Social Perspectives, Content Standard F1

STANDARDS

Social Studies Standards
I. Culture
II. Time, Continuity, and Change
III. People, Places, and Environments
IV. Individual Development and Identity
V. Individuals, Groups, and Institutions

Critical Literacy

As a closure activity, students use their research on current issues of oppression and/or discrimination to create a podcast that presents their findings and offers possible ways for their classmates to get involved. Students can integrate their podcast with news videos or songs that illustrate the plight of modern-day holocaust victims.

Collaborative Literacy

Students prepare for a day of sharing called "Radio Free" School Name. The teacher explains that during World War II people in occupied countries tried to keep informed by tuning in to radio broadcasts from the free world. The student reporters from each newspaper group will share their articles by working as a radio or television news team.

RESOURCE GUIDE: CHILDREN'S LITERATURE REFERENCES AND ACTIVITIES

Primary Grades

Family Survival

Stories of Courage: American Families

Anderson, W. (1998). *Pioneer girl: The story of Laura Ingalls Wilder.* Illustrated by Dan Anderson. New York: HarperCollins.

Bartlett, R. M. (2001). *The story of Thanksgiving.* Illustrated by Sally Wern Compart. New York: HarperCollins.

Bruchac, J. (2000). *Squanto's journey: The story of the first Thanksgiving.* Illustrated by Greg Shed. New York: Harcourt.

Lowery, L. (1999). *Aunt Clara Brown: Official pioneer.* Illustrated by Janice Lee Porter. Minneapolis, MN: Carolrhoda.

Waters, K. (1989). *Sarah Morton's day: A day in the life of a pilgrim girl.* New York: Scholastic.

- **Process Drama:** Students select a story from the text set and write a script focused on the main character and their thoughts and feelings in the text. The students then perform their play for the class.
- **Symbol:** Students create a symbol for Aunt Clara Brown and explain how it represents her character.
- **Story Board:** Students select one of the texts and create a story board to retell it. Working together, students create illustrations and a script for the text.

Surviving Poverty

Ancona, G. (1998). *Barrio: Jose's neighborhood.* New York: Harcourt.

Barbour, K. (1991). *Mr. Bow Tie.* New York: Harcourt.

Bunting, E. (1991). *Fly away home.* Illustrated by Ronald Himler. New York: Clarion.

Bunting, E. (1995). *December.* Illustrated by David Diaz. New York: Harcourt.

Polacco, P. (1996). *I can hear the sun.* New York: Philomel.

- **Puppets:** Students create puppets to retell the story of *Fly Away Home.*
- **Book Buddies:** Students work in pairs to write a response to the story *I Can Hear the Sun* and share their response with the class.
- **Brainstorming Web:** The teacher leads a discussion on poverty and possible ways that students can help others in need. Students brainstorm possible projects to help those in poverty and the teacher records the responses.

Surviving Nature

Surviving Storms

Anderson, L. (1989). *Stina.* New York: Greenwillow.

Crimi, C. (1995). *Outside, inside.* Illustrated by Linnea A. Riley. New York: Simon & Schuster.

Polacco, P. (1990). *Thunder cake.* Illustrated by P. Polacco. New York: Philomel.

Seymour, S. (1989). *Storms.* New York: Morrow.

Weeks, S. (1993). *Hurricane city.* Illustrated by James Warhola. New York: HarperCollins.

- **Word Wall:** Students select vocabulary words from the word wall that relate to the sub-theme. Students create a vocabulary book that illustrates and defines the terms.

- **Weather Chart:** The class keeps a weather chart for two weeks to log storms and their duration. After the two weeks, students formulate questions about weather to use as a basis for a research project.
- **Newspaper:** Using the Internet, students recreate a newspaper account of a storm in their region with photos and text.

Taking Care of Yourself

Brown, L. K. (1995). *The vegetable show.* New York: Little, Brown.

Child, L. (2000). *I will never not ever eat a tomato.* Cambridge, MA: Candlewick Press.

deBrunhoff, L. (2002). *Babar's yoga for elephants.* New York: Abrams.

Thomas, P. (2001) *My amazing body: A first look at health and fitness.* New York: Barron's Educational Series.

Young, E. (1997). *Voices of the heart.* New York: Scholastic.

- **Food Chart:** With help from their parents, students keep a food chart at home of what they eat for breakfast, lunch, and dinner for one week. Afterward, students note patterns in eating patterns and how they can improve their diet.
- **Menu:** Working in pairs, students look through magazines to find pictures of food and plan a healthy menu for one day.
- **Exercise Log:** Students record their daily exercise for one week and note how it made them feel. Afterward the teacher leads a discussion on patterns of exercise and ways to improve.

Surviving Tragedy

Surviving Difficult Times

Heide, F. P., & Gilliland, J. H. (1992). *Sami and the time of the troubles.* Illustrated by Ted Lewin. New York: Clarion.

Hopkinson, D. (1993). *Sweet Clara and the freedom quilt.* Illustrated by James Ransome. New York: Scholastic.

Noble, T. H. (2004). *The scarlet stockings spy.* Illustrated by Robert Papp. Chelsea, MI: Thomson Gale.

Uhlberg, M. (2005). *Dad, Jackie and me.* Illustrated by Colin Bootman. Atlanta, GA: Peachtree.

Whelan, G. (2004). *Friend on freedom river.* Illustrated by Gijsbert van Frankenhuyzen. Chelsea, MI: Thomson Gale.

Winter, J. (2004). *The librarian of Basra: A true story from Iraq.* New York: Harcourt.

- **Quilt:** After reading *Sweet Clara and the Freedom Quilt,* students create their own quilts with geometrical patterns and symbols.

- **Water Experiment:** When students have completed *Friend on Freedom River,* they keep an observation log as they attempt to freeze water.
- **Book Box:** After reading *The Librarian of Basra,* students create a book box that contains cover illustrations for the books that are most precious to them. Students present the box to the class and explain their selections.

Overcoming the Odds

Bishop, C. (1990). *Twenty and ten.* Illustrated by W. DuBois. New York: Scholastic.

Bunting, E. (1998). *So far from the sea.* Illustrated by C. K. Soentpiet. New York: Clarion.

Cutler, J. (1999). *The cello of Mr. O.* Illustrated by Greg Couch. New York: Dutton.

Kurtz, J. (2000). *River friendly, river wild.* Illustrated by Neil Brennan. New York: Simon & Schuster.

Uchida, Y. (1996). *The bracelet.* New York: Putnam.

- **Interview:** Students interview a family member or friend and ask them about a time when they overcame a difficult problem. Students write up their interviews to be placed in a class book, *Overcoming the Odds.*
- **Character Mobile:** After completing the text set, students select one of the main characters and create a mobile with symbols that represent their character traits.
- **Story Board:** Students select one of the texts and create a story board to retell it. Working together, students create illustrations and a script for the text.

Intermediate Grades

Surviving Nature

Surviving in the Wilderness

Bledsoe, L. (1997). *Tracks in the snow.* New York: Holiday.

Eckert, A. (1971). *Incident at Hawk's Hill.* Illustrated by John Schoenherr. New York: Little, Brown.

Fielding, E. (1998). *The eastern forest: Ecosystems of North America.* New York: Benchmark Books.

George, J. (1990). *My side of the mountain.* New York: Viking.

George, J. (1990). *On the far side of the mountain.* New York: Dutton.

George, J. (1999). *Frightful's mountain.* New York: Dutton.

Paulsen, G. (1987). *Hatchet.* New York: Simon & Schuster.

Paulsen, G. (1991). *The river.* New York: Random House.

Paulsen, G. (1997). *Tucket's ride.* New York: Delacorte.

Paulsen, G. (1998). *Brian's winter.* New York: Bantam Doubleday Dell.

Paulsen, G. (1999). *Brian's return.* New York: Dell Laurel Leaf.

Skurznyski, G. (1982). *Lost in the devil's desert.* New York: Lothrop.

Speare, E. (1983). *The sign of the beaver.* Boston: Houghton Mifflin.

- **Survival Box:** Students research what items are necessary to survive in the wilderness and create a box containing illustrations of each item.
- **Diorama:** Working in groups, students select one of the texts from the set and create a diorama illustrating the wilderness setting of the story.
- **Wall Story:** After completing *Hatchet,* the teacher leads the class in retelling the plot and writing a wall story, which is written on chart paper and displayed.

Wolves

Brandenburg, J. (1993). *To the top of the world: Adventures with arctic wolves.* New York: Walker.

Fuchs, B. (1996). *The wolves.* New York: Dial.

George, J. C. (1972). *Julie of the wolves.* New York: HarperCollins.

George, J. C. (1978). *The wounded wolf.* Illustrated by John Schoenherr. New York: Harper & Row.

George, J. C. (1997). *Julie's wolf pack.* New York: Scholastic.

George, J. C. (1997). *Look to the north: A wolf pup diary.* New York: HarperCollins.

Patent, D. (1990). *Grey wolf, red wolf.* Photographs by William Nunoz. New York: Clarion.

Patent, D. (1995). *Return of the wolf.* Illustrated by Jaret Tay Williams. New York: Clarion.

Smith, R. (1996). *Journey of the red wolf.* New York: Cobblehill.

- ***All About* Books:** Working in pairs, students research wolves on the Internet and create an *All About* book that provides facts about wolves and their habitats.
- **Poster Board:** When the text set is completed, students create poster boards about wolves that explain their eating habits, habitats, and role in the food chain.
- **Podcast:** As a concluding activity, students record their information about wolves as a podcast to be shared with students in the primary grades.

Surviving Tragedy

Surviving War

Bunting, E. (1989). *Terrible things: An allegory of the Holocaust.* Illustrated by Stephen Gammell. Philadelphia: Jewish Publication Society of America.

Heneghan, J. (1998). *Wish me luck.* New York: Laurel Leaf.

Holm, A. (1993). *I am David.* Translated from the Danish by L. W. Kinsland. Orlando, FL: Harcourt.

Innocenti, R., Gallaz, C., Coventry, M., & Graglia, R. (2003). *Rose Blanche.* San Diego, CA: Creative Editions.

Johnston, T. (2004). *The harmonica.* Illustrated by Ron Mazzellan. Watertown, MA: Charlesbridge.

Lobel, A. (2008). *No pretty pictures.* New York: Greenwillow Books.

Matos, C. (1993). *Daniel's story.* New York: Scholastic.

Rubin, S. (2005). *The flag with fifty-six stars: A gift from the survivors of Mauthausen.* Illustrated by Bill Farnsworth. New York: Holiday.

Russo, M. (2005). *Always remember me: How one family survived World War II.* New York: Atheneum.

Yolen, J. (1990). *The devil's arithmetic.* New York: Puffin.

- **Reader's Theatre:** Students select a story from the text set and write a script focused on the main character's thoughts and feelings. The students then perform their play for the class.
- **Simulated Journal:** Students write a simulated journal from the perspective of one of the characters in the text set.
- **Newspaper Article:** Working in pairs, students research a conflict in the world today and write a newspaper article about the event.

Surviving Prejudice

Aamundsen, M. (1990). *Two short and one long.* New York: Houghton Mifflin.

Adoff, A. (1982). *All the colors of the race.* Illustrated by John Steptoe. New York: Lothrop.

Bolden, T. (2005). *Maritcha: A nineteenth-century American girl.* New York: Abrams.

Bridges, R. (1999). *Through my eyes: The autobiography of Ruby Bridges.* New York: Scholastic.

Fleischman, P. (1990). *Saturnalia.* New York: HarperCollins.

Hesse, K. (2001). *Witness.* New York: Scholastic.

Martin, A. (2002). *A corner of the universe.* New York: Scholastic.

Neville, E. (1965). *Berries Goodman.* New York: HarperCollins.

Orgel, D. (2004). *The devil in Vienna.* New York: Dial.

Ringgold, F. (1995). *Aunt Harriet's underground railroad in the sky.* Edmond, OK: Dragonfly Books.

Woodson, J. (2002). *Between Madison and Palmetto.* New York: Putnam.

Yin. (2001). *Coolies.* New York: Philomel.

- **Family Stories:** Students interview their parents or family members about times they experienced bias or prejudice and how they overcame it.
- **Wall of Heroes:** Students research Ruby Bridges or others who fought against prejudice and create a portrait to place on the Wall of Heroes.

- **Matrix:** When the text set is completed, the teacher leads a discussion of the main characters and students list their common elements on a matrix graphic organizer.

Surviving Family Relationships

Death and Separation

Conly, J. (1993). *Crazy lady.* New York: HarperCollins.

Dragonwagon, C. (1990). *Winter holding spring.* Illustrated by Ronald Himler. New York: Macmillan.

Fox, P. (1980). *A place apart.* New York: Farrar, Straus & Giroux.

Henkes, K. (1998). *Sun and spoon.* New York: Puffin.

Horvath, P. (2001). *Everything on a waffle.* New York: Farrar, Straus & Giroux.

Martin, A. (2002). *A corner of the universe.* New York: Scholastic.

Miles, M. (1985). *Annie and the old one.* Illustrated by Peter Parnall. New York: Little, Brown.

Rylant, C. (2004). *Missing May.* New York: Scholastic.

Spinelli, J. (1990). *Maniac Magee: A novel.* New York: Little, Brown.

- **Role Play:** Students select a character from one of the texts and retell the story from the character's perspective.
- **Mural:** Working in groups of three, students create a mural illustration for a key scene from one text.
- **Rolled Story:** After the text set is completed, students select one of the texts and create a rolled story, by displaying story frames on cardboard tubes, and illustrate key events in the narrative.

Family Difficulties

Avi. (1995). *Poppy.* Illustrated by Brian Floca. New York: Orchard.

Cleary, B. (1984). *Ramona.* Illustrated by Alan Tiegreen. New York: Morrow.

Giff, P. (2001). *All the way home.* New York: Dell.

Hesse, K. (1997). *Out of the dust.* New York: Scholastic.

Hill, K. (2000). *The year of Miss Agnes.* New York: Aladdin.

Martin, A., & Godwin, L. (2000). *The doll people.* Illustrated by Brian Selznick. New York: Hyperion.

O'Brien, R. (1971). *Mrs. Frisby and the rats of NIMH.* Illustrated by Edward S. Gazi. New York: Atheneum.

Steig, W. (1976). *Abel's island.* New York: Farrar.

Tamar, E. (2000). *The midnight train home.* New York: Alfred A. Knopf.

Whelan, G. (2002). *The wanigan: A life on the river.* Illustrated by Emily Martindale. New York: Alfred A. Knopf.

- **Slideshow:** Working in groups of three, students research the impact of drought on farmland and create a PowerPoint slideshow to present to the class.
- **Simulated Journal:** Students write a simulated journal entry from the perspective of a main character from one of the texts.
- **Plot Profile:** Working in pairs, students use graph paper to track the action in one of the texts in the set.

Middle Grades

Family Survival

Runaways

Fleischman, P. (2005). *Breakout.* New York: Simon Pulse.

Major, K. (2003). *Hold fast.* Toronto, Canada: Groundwood Books.

Napoli, D. J. (2004). *North.* New York: HarperCollins.

O'Dell, S. (1985). *Kathleen, please come home.* New York: Dell.

Peck, R. (1980). *Secrets of the shopping mall.* New York: Laurel Leaf.

Van Draanen, W. (2006). *Runaway.* New York: Alfred A. Knopf.

Whelan, G. (2004). *Chu Ju's House.* New York: HarperCollins.

- **Grand Conversation:** Students form literature circles based on their favorite text and discuss characters and their actions.
- **Quilts:** Students create a quilt to represent the feelings of one of the main characters in the text set.
- **Simulated Blog:** Working in pairs, students select one of the main characters from the text set and create a blog entry explaining their reasons for running away.

Homelessness

Carey, J. L. (2004). *The double life of Zoe Flynn.* New York: Atheneum.

Doherty, B. (1994). *Street child.* New York: Orchard.

Fox, P. (1991). *Monkey Island.* New York: Dell.

London, J. (1995). *Where's home?* New York: Viking.

Strasser, T. (2004). *Can't get there from here.* New York: Simon & Schuster.

Wier, E. (1963). *The loner.* New York: McKay.

- **Cause–Effect:** The teacher leads a class discussion using a cause–effect graphic organizer to highlight the causes of homelessness.
- **Action Research:** Working in groups, students research homelessness in their region as well as its causes and brainstorm ways to get involved.
- **Simulated Interviews:** Students role play interviewing one of the main characters in the text set.

Surviving Nature

Disaster

Armstrong, J. (1998). *Shipwreck at the bottom of the world: The extraordinary true adventure of the Shackleton and the Endurance.* New York: Crown.

Cottonwood, J. (1995). *Quake! A novel.* New York: Scholastic.

Krakauer, J. (1997). *Into thin air: A personal account of the Mount Everest disaster.* New York: Villard.

Murphy, J. (1995). *The great fire.* New York: Scholastic.

Naylor, P. R. (2002). *Blizzard's wake.* New York: Atheneum.

Stewart, G. B. (2005). *Catastrophe in southern Asia: The tsunami of 2004.* Detroit, MI: Lucent Books.

- ■ **Cluster Map:** Working in pairs, students create a cluster map that outlines the causes and effects of each disaster in the text set.
- ■ **Go Kit:** Students use a shoebox to create a "Go Kit" that contains necessary supplies for emergencies.
- ■ **Photo Journal:** Using the Internet, students research a natural disaster in their region and create a photo journal account of the event.

Hostile Environments

George, J. C. (1972). *Julie of the wolves.* New York: Harper & Row.

Houston, J. (1977). *Frozen fire.* New York: Atheneum.

Paulsen, G. (1987). *Hatchet.* New York: Bradbury.

Sebestyen, O. (1988). *The girl in the box.* Boston: Joy Street.

Sperry, A. (1968). *Call it courage.* New York: Macmillan.

Wartski, M. C. (1980). *A boat to nowhere.* New York: Signet.

- ■ **Process Drama:** Students select a story from the text set and write a script focused on the main character's thoughts and feelings. The students then perform their play for the class.
- ■ **Survival Guide:** Working in groups, students use information gleaned from the text set and their own research to create a survival guide for the wilderness.
- ■ **Pictograph:** Students select one of the main characters in the text set and graph out their traits and actions in the story.

Surviving Tragedy

Surviving the Holocaust

Adler, D. A. (1995). *Child of the Warsaw ghetto.* New York: Holiday.

Bernstein, S. T., with M. B. Samuels. (1997). *The seamstress: A memoir of survival.* New York: Berkley Books.

Lobel, A. (2008). *No pretty pictures: A child of war.* New York: Greenwillow Books.

Opdyke, I. G., with Armstrong, J. (1999). *In my hands: Memories of a Holocaust rescuer.* New York: Alfred A. Knopf.

Spiegelman, A. (1986). *Maus: A survivor's tale: My father bleeds history.* New York: Pantheon Books.

Trypzynska-Frederick, L., with McCann, M. R. (2003). *Luba: The angel of Bergen-Belsen.* Berkeley, CA: Tricycle Press.

Warren, A. (2001). *Surviving Hitler: A boy in the Nazi death camps.* New York: HarperCollins.

Whiteman, D. B. (2005). *Lonek's journey: The true story of a boy's escape to freedom.* New York: Sea Bright Books.

- ■ **Literature Circles:** Students form literature circles based on their selection from the text set and discuss their responses to the story.
- ■ **Simulated Account:** Working in pairs, students create a simulated newspaper account of the Holocaust.
- ■ **Action Research:** When the text set is completed, students work in groups to research accounts from survivors of the Holocaust and present their stories to their peers in a slideshow.

Surviving War

Choi, S. N. (1991). *The year of impossible goodbyes.* New York: Houghton Mifflin.

Matas, C. (1987). *Lisa's war.* New York: Scribner's.

Myers, W. D. (1988). *Fallen angels.* New York: Scholastic.

Reuter, B. (1994). *The boys from St. Petri.* Translated by A. Bell. New York: Dutton.

Rostkowski, M. I. (1986). *After the dancing days.* New York: Harper & Row.

Salisbury, G. (1994). *Under the blood red sun.* New York: Delacorte.

- ■ **Discussion Web:** The teacher leads the students in discussing the question, Is war ever justified?
- ■ **Cause–Effect:** Working in pairs, students select one of the texts and create a cause–effect graphic organizer for the war depicted in the story.
- ■ **Slideshow:** Students research a present day global conflict and create a PowerPoint slideshow to present to their peers.

PROFESSIONAL REFERENCES

Allen, J. (2004). *Tools for teaching content literacy.* Portland, ME: Stenhouse Publishers.

Antonacci, P. A., & O'Callaghan, C. M. (2006). *A handbook for literacy instructional & assessment strategies, K–8.* Boston: Allyn & Bacon.

National Council of Teachers of English & International Reading Association. (1996). *Standards for the English language arts.* Newark, DE: Authors. Available at www.ncte.org/standards

National Council of Teachers of Mathematics. (1998). *Principles and standards for school mathematics:* Reston, VA: Author. Available at http://standards.nctm.org

Taba, H. (1967). *Teacher's handbook for elementary social studies.* Reading, MA: Addison-Wesley.

Tompkins, G. (2009). *Literacy for the 21st century: A balanced approach.* New York: Prentice Hall.

Discovery

As the twenty-first century unfolds, the impact of science and technology on our daily lives continues to develop at a rapid pace. At the forefront of this global change is humankind's quest for discovery. Since the beginning of time, we have sought out new frontiers and concepts to expand our horizons and to better our lives. Chapter 4 will elaborate on this theme of Discovery, which is listed in the *National Science Education Standards* (2000). The *National Science Education Standards* require K–8 students to explore how science has been a human endeavor throughout time as men and women further their knowledge of nature using observations and experiments.

In this chapter, primary grade students will read about Intrepid Explorers who defied the conventions of the day to learn more about the world around them. Intermediate grade students will Discover the Frozen World of Antarctica by reading and discussing text sets about the explorers who broadened our knowledge about the planet. Middle school students will read about Great Minds of Medical Science and learn about scientific innovators who broke through the accepted ideas of their time to bring us the medicine and methods we use today (*National Science Education Standards,* 2000). As K–8 students explore the world of Discovery, they will learn that part of scientific inquiry is to evaluate the work of other explorers and innovators so that they can bring knowledge forward in our world today.

■ Primary Grades: Kindergarten–Grade 2

Primary grade students begin each school day with a natural curiosity to discover how things work and to explore the world around them. In this chapter, text sets revolve around the theme of Discovery and activities demonstrate how to use students' natural sense of wonder to learn about science, math, and social studies.

The sampler begins the thematic cycle with the sub-theme Intrepid Explorers. In this sampler, students hear about heroes such as Mary Kingsley, who broke through social conventions of the time to discover more about Africa. The theme is elaborated further in Discoveries in Science, in which biographies of scientists illustrate how new medicines or inventions were often born from questions and puzzles about daily life or events. The sub-theme Discovering the Silk Road uses picture books about the Silk Road in China to broaden students' knowledge about trade and the infusion of

DISCOVERIES IN SCIENCE

Text Set

A Picture Book of George Washington Carver
Starry Messenger
A Picture Book of Benjamin Franklin
Marie Curie
Odd Boy Out: Young Albert Einstein
Marvelous Mattie: How Margaret E. Knight Became an Inventor
How Ben Franklin Stole the Lightning

Outcomes

- Analyze and use information from print and electronic sources.
- Sequence story events.
- Make a text-to-text connection.
- Infer themes from biographies of scientists.

DISCOVERING OUR PAST

Text Set

Rare Treasure: Mary Anning and her Remarkable Discoveries
Archaeologists Dig for Clues
The Magic School Bus Shows & Tells: A Book About Archaeology
Eyewitness: Archaeology
Magic Tree House Research Guide: Ancient Greece and the Olympics

Outcomes

- Compare/contrast Ancient Egypt and Ancient Greece.
- Use print and electronic sources to research archaeology.
- Collect data and analyze facts about local artifacts.

INTREPID EXPLORERS

Text Set

Uncommon Traveler: Mary Kingsley in Africa
Ruth Law Thrills a Nation
Reaching for the Moon
The Lamp, the Ice and the Boat Called Fish
Matthew Henson
Dragon Bones and Dinosaur Eggs: A Photo-biography of Explorer Roy Chapman
If You Decide to Go to the Moon

Outcomes

- Analyze character traits.
- Sequence the events of the story.
- Respond to the story through a text-to-text connection.
- Analyze and use information from print and electronic sources.

Discovery by People

Discovery in Time

DISCOVERY

Discovery of Places

DISCOVERING ANCIENT EGYPT

Text Set

Valley of the Golden Mummies
Hatshepsut, His Majesty, Herself
Ms. Frizzle's Adventures: Ancient Egypt
The Ancient Egypt Pop-Up Book
If I Were a Kid in Ancient Egypt

Outcomes

- Collect data and analyze facts about Ancient Egypt.
- Locate Egypt and the Nile River on a map.
- Discuss values and practices of Ancient Egyptians.
- Make a text-to-self connection.

DISCOVERY OF THE NEW WORLD

Text Set

Encounter
Follow the Dream
Where Do You Think You're Going, Christopher Columbus?
A Picture Book of Christopher Columbus in 1492

Outcomes

- Sequence events of Columbus's journey.
- Infer Columbus's character traits.
- Use electronic and print sources to research the journey.
- Analyze texts to discover why Columbus is a hero to some groups and not to others.

DISCOVERING THE SILK ROAD

Text Set

The Silk Road: 7,000 Miles of History
Marco Polo for Kids
Stories from the Silk Road
Marco Polo: A Journey Through China

Outcomes

- Use text to discover relationships and concepts.
- Compare/contrast different cultures along the Silk Road.
- Discuss why some people are heroes to certain groups and not to others.
- Make a text-to-text connection.

cultures along this famous trade route. The theme also includes Discovering Our Past to investigate how archaeologists, such as Mary Anning, hunt for fossils to unravel the Earth's history. Exploration of ancient cultures is included in the sub-theme Discovering Ancient Egypt. The text set illustrates how many of our ideas and tools were formed in antiquity.

As students read about intrepid explorers or great scientists, they start to question the world around them and use their natural curiosity to expand their knowledge. After studying the theme of Discovery, primary grade students begin to conceptualize the process of collecting data and analyzing facts to solve the puzzles that daily life presents.

SAMPLER ■ Intrepid Explorers

Imagine standing on the surface of the moon and looking back at Earth and knowing that you are one of the few humans ever to leave the planet! It takes a special courage to travel to the unknown despite dangers and fears of unexplored territories. Yet throughout the history of humankind, men and women have been driven to overcome their fears and to face many dangers to venture abroad in search of new lands or discoveries. This sampler illustrates how a group of intrepid explorers undertook perilous journeys to investigate new lands or to expand knowledge through scientific experiments.

The first book in the text set, *Uncommon Traveler: Mary Kingsley in Africa,* tells the story of an English woman in 1893 who defied the norms of the day to explore Africa alone. She had many adventures with crocodiles and animal traps but returned safely home to entertain others with her tales of the jungle and the different cultures she visited.

Ruth Law Thrills a Nation, the second book in the text set, tells the story of an unsung heroine who became the first woman to fly cross-country in 1916. Ruth's bravery and determination provide students with yet another example of how to obtain goals in life.

The final book in the text set, *Reaching for the Moon,* recounts the Apollo 11 trip to the moon in 1969. The story is told through the eyes of Buzz Aldrin, one of the Apollo 11 astronauts. Students sense the danger as well as the thrill of the rocket blast as the astronauts defy Earth's gravity and fly off into the final frontier.

The sampler illustrates how the text set may be implemented during the literacy block. Teachers use the text set to scaffold students' abilities to sequence events and to analyze character traits.

In the sub-theme Intrepid Explorers, students discuss how famous figures faced their fears and overcame severe odds to attain their goals of discovery and adventure.

NCTE/IRA Standards for the English Language Arts

1. Students read a wide range of print and non-print texts to build an understanding of texts, of themselves, and of the cultures of the United States and the world.

Learner Outcomes

Students will be able to do the following:

■ Analyze character traits of explorers to identify similarities and differences between people
■ Sequence the events of a story
■ Respond to a story through a text-to-text connection

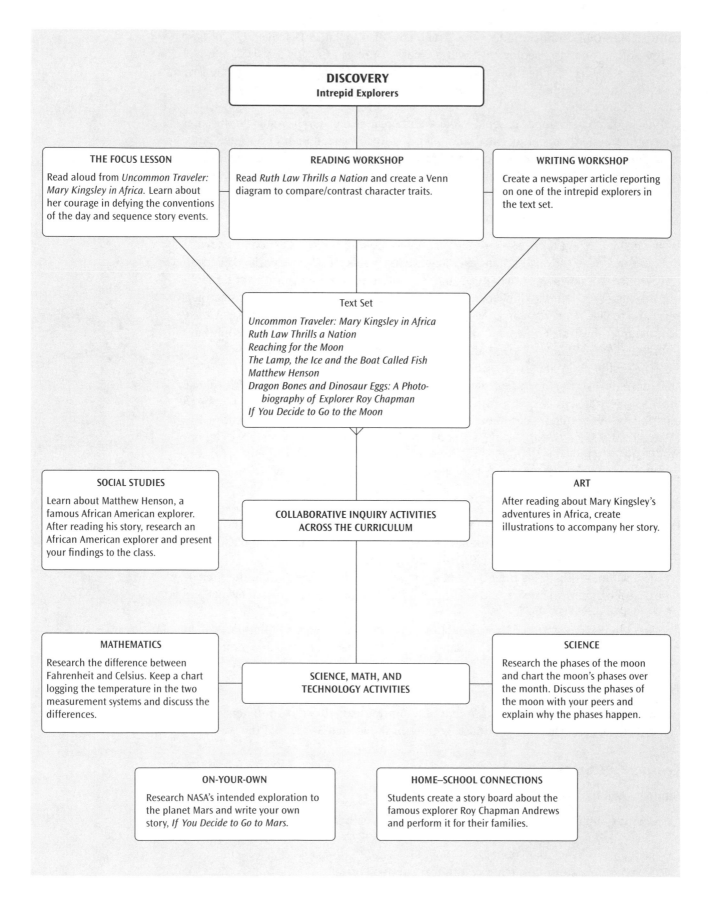

DISCOVERY
Intrepid Explorers

THE FOCUS LESSON

Read aloud from *Uncommon Traveler: Mary Kingsley in Africa.* Learn about her courage in defying the conventions of the day and sequence story events.

READING WORKSHOP

Read *Ruth Law Thrills a Nation* and create a Venn diagram to compare/contrast character traits.

WRITING WORKSHOP

Create a newspaper article reporting on one of the intrepid explorers in the text set.

Text Set

Uncommon Traveler: Mary Kingsley in Africa
Ruth Law Thrills a Nation
Reaching for the Moon
The Lamp, the Ice and the Boat Called Fish
Matthew Henson
*Dragon Bones and Dinosaur Eggs: A Photo-
    biography of Explorer Roy Chapman*
If You Decide to Go to the Moon

SOCIAL STUDIES

Learn about Matthew Henson, a famous African American explorer. After reading his story, research an African American explorer and present your findings to the class.

COLLABORATIVE INQUIRY ACTIVITIES ACROSS THE CURRICULUM

ART

After reading about Mary Kingsley's adventures in Africa, create illustrations to accompany her story.

MATHEMATICS

Research the difference between Fahrenheit and Celsius. Keep a chart logging the temperature in the two measurement systems and discuss the differences.

SCIENCE, MATH, AND TECHNOLOGY ACTIVITIES

SCIENCE

Research the phases of the moon and chart the moon's phases over the month. Discuss the phases of the moon with your peers and explain why the phases happen.

ON-YOUR-OWN

Research NASA's intended exploration to the planet Mars and write your own story, *If You Decide to Go to Mars.*

HOME–SCHOOL CONNECTIONS

Students create a story board about the famous explorer Roy Chapman Andrews and perform it for their families.

Conduct a Focus Lesson

In the focus lesson, the teacher uses an interactive read aloud to study expository text structure. Students use the text set to deepen their knowledge about exploration and discovery. As students read about these courageous explorers, they also learn how to attain their own personal goals through determination and perseverance.

Establish a Purpose   The books in the text set for Intrepid Explorers illustrate how famous heroes and heroines ventured abroad or to outer space in order to discover new frontiers or broaden their personal horizons. The first text in the set, *Uncommon Traveler: Mary Kingsley in Africa,* recounts the true story of a Victorian woman in England who defied the conventions of the day to realize her dream of exploring the African continent. The teacher discusses the following purposes of the focus lesson with the students:

- Engage in an interactive read aloud.
- Brainstorm character traits that describe the explorer Mary Kingsley.
- Create rolled stories to retell the story.

Engage in Read Aloud   Since the setting of the story is Africa during the 1800s, the teacher prepares the students by assessing their background knowledge about the continent. The teacher begins with a map of Africa and asks the students if they know anything about the continent. As the students respond, the teacher writes their comments on a chart marked "What We Know About Africa." In order to supplement their knowledge, the teacher shows pictures of African landscapes for the students to compare to their own local climate and region.

The teacher uses the interactive read-aloud strategy for the reading of the first book in the text set. Before beginning the interactive read aloud, the teacher conducts a picture walk and asks the students to predict why the title is *Uncommon Traveler.* The vocabulary word, *uncommon,* is written on chart paper and the students brainstorm its definition. In order to focus the interactive read aloud, the teacher asks the question, "What is uncommon in this story?"

When the read aloud is completed, the students complete a character map for Mary Kingsley. The discussion begins with their answers to the focus question. The students explain their choices for character traits by discussing parts of the story that support their decisions. A sample character map is illustrated in Figure 4.1.

Conduct a Mini-Lesson   The focus of the mini-lesson is to sequence the events in the story *Uncommon Traveler: Mary Kingsley in Africa.* Students first discuss the events of the story by completing a story chain depicting the plot in sequence. After the class has completed the story chain, they break up into groups to create rolled stories. The students create story frames for the different events of the story and provide narration as they unroll their events.

Additional Mini-Lessons

Academic Vocabulary

- The teacher uses the strategy of interactive word walls to introduce content-area vocabulary from the text set.
- First, the teacher selects 8 to 10 unfamiliar words and introduces them to the students.

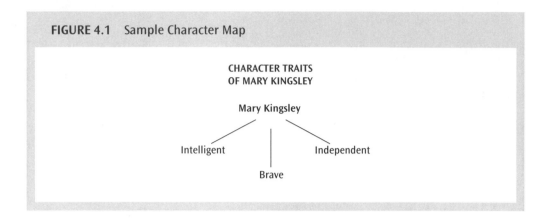

FIGURE 4.1   Sample Character Map

CHARACTER TRAITS
OF MARY KINGSLEY

Mary Kingsley

Intelligent   Independent

Brave

- The words are placed on the class word wall, and students write sentences with the words.
- The students use the word wall vocabulary to engage in several games such as word sorts or Guess My Word.

Academic Discourse

- The teacher uses a simple biography box strategy to begin the discussion.
- The students bring in a box containing symbols or pictures that refer to their favorite explorer.
- After explaining the items in their biography box, their peers write down three questions to ask about the explorer.
- The students discuss the explorer and follow up any unanswered questions with research on the Internet.

Expository Text

- Students use a graphic organizer to review famous scientific discoveries.
- The students choose one of the discoveries and write in their journals how their lives have changed as a result.

Conduct a Reading Workshop

Ruth Law Thrills a Nation is the true story of a young heroine who fascinated America in 1916. Ruth was determined to fly solo from New York City to Chicago to discover the world of aviation. Ruth faced many obstacles in her path; for example, she had to fly a tiny old plane because manufacturers wouldn't sell her a new one. She also had to use old maps taped together to navigate her flight. Despite the odds, Ruth Law reached her destination and became an inspiration to women across the country.

Before Reading   Before beginning the story, the students discuss the title *Ruth Law Thrills a Nation* and predict what they think Ruth did to cause such a stir. The teacher charts their responses on a brainstorming web.

During Reading   As students reach the midpoint of the story, the teacher asks them to share some of the adjectives they have selected to describe Ruth Law. The teacher also

ASSESS LITERACY

The teacher uses the rubric below to monitor students' progress during the focus lesson. As students discuss the story and identify character traits, the teacher records their performance on the learner outcomes and adjusts instruction accordingly.

Criteria	Independent	Proficient	Developing
Description of Character Traits	Student identifies several character traits and supports them with evidence from the text. (3)	Student identifies some character traits and supports them with evidence from the text. (2)	Student does not identify character traits and cannot cite evidence from the text. (0–1)
Response to Story	Student retells the story in full and gives details about the plot and characters. (3)	Student retells the story partially and gives a few details about the plot and characters. (2)	Student does not retell the story or provide details about the plot and characters. (0–1)
Analysis of Characters	Student compares and contrasts the character traits of the main characters in the text set. (3)	Student partially compares and contrasts the character traits of the main characters in the text set. (2)	Student does not compare or contrast the character traits of the main characters in the text set. (0–1)
Sequencing of Story	Student sequences story events in proper order and retells story with details. (3)	Student sequences story events in proper order and retells story with some details. (2)	Student cannot sequence story events or retell the story in detail. (0–1)
Student Participation	Student participates in discussion of character traits and focuses on the story. (3)	Student partially participates in discussion of character traits and focuses on the story. (2)	Student does not participate in discussion of character traits or focuses on the story. (0–1)
Independent: 11–15 Proficient: 6–10 Developing: 0–5			

leads a discussion on how Ruth's courage and determination helped her to achieve her goals.

After Reading When students have finished the text, the teacher discusses the book title and their predictions. After they have finished discussing Ruth Law, students compare her to Mary Kingsley and discuss what they had in common and how they differed, completing the Venn diagram illustrated in Figure 4.2.

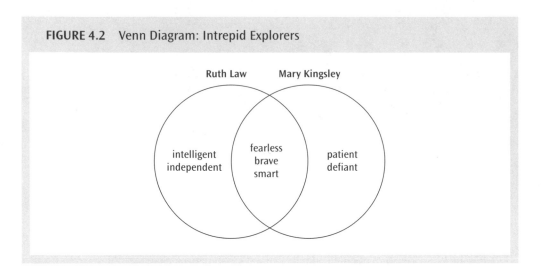

FIGURE 4.2   Venn Diagram: Intrepid Explorers

Conduct a Writing Workshop

The text set for Intrepid Explorers exposes children to men and women across generations and cultures who have answered the call for discovery and exploration. Since
this text set deals with biographical and factual material, it provides the opportunity to
address the genre of newspaper reporting. The teacher assigns students to groups and
asks them to select one of the explorers they have read about and write an eyewitness
account of their adventures.

Before Writing   Before students begin their eyewitness accounts, the teacher distributes an article and leads the discussion on what constitutes a good newspaper article,
writing questions on chart paper, such as Who, What, When, Where, and How?

During Writing   After the class has discussed the characteristics of a newspaper article,
students brainstorm on the graphic organizer illustrated in Figure 4.3. Once their think
sheet is completed, they work collaboratively to draft their eyewitness account. Students use the text to check for information or for content vocabulary words.

After Writing   When students have completed their eyewitness accounts, they type
them on the computer and create a newspaper for their classmates to read. The newspaper can also be distributed for parents to enjoy at home.

Collaborative Inquiry Across the Curriculum

The sub-theme Intrepid Explorers investigates courage and tenacity in the face of
inestimable odds. This sub-theme is extended to several subject areas, including
mathematics, science, and social studies, through quality children's literature, as discussed in the following section.

Extension to Mathematics   In *The Lamp, the Ice and the Boat Called Fish,* the Canadian
Arctic exploration of 1913 is retold, with description of the many hardships the team
endured in their quest to discover the northern territories. As part of the discussion of
the text, the teacher introduces the different ways to measure freezing temperatures

STANDARDS

Mathematics Standards
4. Measurement

FIGURE 4.3 Brainstorming Activity

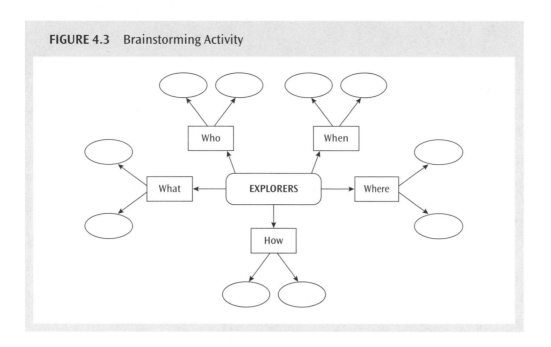

When students have completed their eyewitness accounts, the teacher uses the rubric below to evaluate the students' writing samples and ability to accurately describe an event.

Criteria	Independent	Proficient	Developing
Content Knowledge	Student knows the content and integrates it throughout newspaper account. (3)	Student knows the content somewhat and attempts to integrate it in newspaper account. (2)	Student does not know the content and does not integrate it throughout newspaper account. (0–1)
Planning	Student actively participates in planning text and discussing ideas. (3)	Student is somewhat active in planning text and discussing ideas. (2)	Student does not actively plan text or discuss ideas. (0–1)
Drafting	Student uses the planning process to compose text. (3)	Student somewhat uses the planning process to compose text. (2)	Student does not use the planning process to compose text. (0–1)
Editing	Student edits text and reviews sentence structure, vocabulary, grammar, and spelling. (3)	Student partially edits text and reviews sentence structure, vocabulary, grammar, and spelling. (2)	Student does not edit text or review sentence structure, vocabulary, grammar, and spelling. (0–1)
Independent: 9–12 Proficient: 5–8 Developing: 0–4			

using the Fahrenheit and Celsius scales. Students use the daily weather chart in the newspaper to record the temperature in a cold climate of their choice in both Fahrenheit and Celsius. After a week of charting the two temperature scales, students record what they observed about the two types of measurement and how they differ.

Extension to Science   *Reaching for the Moon* recounts the famous Apollo 11 trip to the moon as told by Buzz Aldrin, one of its astronauts. Students learn more about the moon by researching its phases and using a monthly calendar to record the phases of the moon each day. They also check their accuracy with the phases of the moon chart published in their local paper.

STANDARDS

Science Standards
Earth and Space Science, Content Standard D2

Extension to Social Studies   *Matthew Henson* by Maryann Weidt tells the story of the African American explorer who traveled with Robert Peary to the North Pole in 1891. After reading about his story, students use the Internet to research other African American explorers and create an *All About* book to describe their adventures. The books are then placed in the classroom library for peers to enjoy.

STANDARDS

Social Studies Standards
III. People, Places, and Environments

Home–School Connections   *Dragon Bones and Dinosaur Eggs: Explorer Roy Chapman Andrews* is the fifth photobiography released by the National Geographic Society. It tells the story of one of the great explorers of the century, who is best known for his discoveries of dinosaur bones and fossil eggs. The famous movie character Indiana Jones is based on the adventures and personality of Roy Chapman Andrews. Since this is a challenging text it would be advisable to have it read aloud by a parent or an older sibling. As students read about Roy Chapman Andrews's discoveries and adventures, they create a story board of the "Incredible Adventures of Roy Chapman Andrews." Students then narrate it for their parents and also share it with the class when they return to school.

On-Your-Own Activities   *If You Decide to Go to the Moon* by Faith McNulty is an excellent text to use for individual study. The text includes facts about the moon and describes what it would be like to experience weightlessness and landing in a rocket. The text supplements *Reaching for the Moon* because it is another retelling of the first lunar landing. After the students have completed the activity, they research the current exploration of Mars on the NASA website (www.nasa.org) and create their own *If You Decide to Go to Mars* book that includes facts about the red planet.

Critical Literacy

As a summative activity, primary grade students synthesize and evaluate their new concepts about explorers by completing a cluster map that compares and contrasts those who traveled on land, sea, or space. Teachers may use the graphic organizer illustrated in Figure 4.4 with students for this activity.

Collaborative Literacy

As a conclusion to the instructional sequence, students present their favorite explorer during a celebration entitled "Intrepid Explorers" for their parents. Students use poster boards to briefly write about their favorite explorer. In the middle partition of the board, students share a graphic organizer outlining the explorer's character traits. On the third panel of the poster board, students explain why they admire this particular

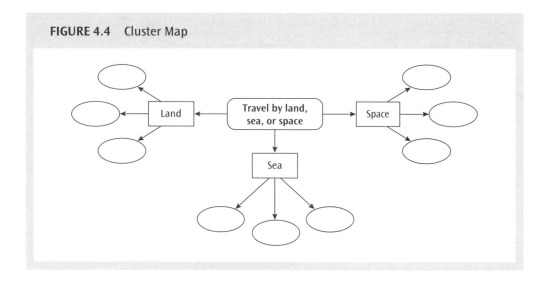

FIGURE 4.4   Cluster Map

explorer. The students may also choose to come dressed as their favorite explorer for the presentation.

Primary grade students are not alone in their quest for exploration and natural curiosity about the world. The next section of this chapter will discuss how the theme of Discovery is implemented in the intermediate grades through the sampler Discover the Frozen World of Antarctica.

■ Intermediate Grades: Grades 3–5

Students in the intermediate grades delight in discovering their past, witnessing the present, and wondering about the future. Discovery will take them to the ancient civilizations of the Aztecs, Mayans, and Incans, some of whom lived on the same continent where students live. Through the voices and illustrations of authors and illustrators such as Leonard Everett Fisher, students will discover the mysteries of the ancient times. In *Pyramid of the Sun, Pyramid of the Moon,* students will read about two mighty structures, the adobe pyramids built by farmers to symbolize the people's commitment to religion. They will learn how the pyramids were part of the history of the Mexican civilization and remain the only monuments to stand after the terrible devastation of Tenochtitlan, the sparkling Aztec capital, in 1521.

Students will be given the opportunity to discover the frozen worlds of Antarctica and the Arctic. In the sampler Discover the Frozen World of Antarctica, there are numerous opportunities for students to use literature to learn about the ecosystem of the mysterious, ice cold desert of Antarctica. For example, they will read *Antarctic Journal: Four Months at the Bottom of the World* and learn how scientists study the world of Antarctica and what they do to survive the ravaging storms as they study penguins, observe a "red tide," observe one-celled animals called zooplankton, or watch the fairy Morgana, ice hanging suspended in the sky for 10 or 15 minutes. In *My Season with Penguins: An Antarctic Journal* they will discover how artist Sophie Webb spent two months in Polar Haven to paint penguins.

Finally, students discover the lives of authors and poets through biographies. They will make connections between the lives of authors and poets and their works by reading books such as *Henry David's House: Henry David Thoreau, Walt Whitman: Words for America,* and *On the Bus with Joanna Cole.*

DISCOVER THE ANCIENT MAYA

Text Set

Ancient Civilizations: Maya
Children of the Maya: A Guatemalan Indian Odyssey
People of Corn: A Mayan Story
People of the Ancient World: The Ancient Maya
Rain Player
Technology in the Time of Maya
The Maya
The Mystery of the Maya: Uncovering the
  Lost City of Palenque
Your Travel Guide to Ancient Mayan Civilization
Understanding the People of the Past: The Maya
World History Series: Maya Civilization

Learner Outcomes

• Students use the Maya number system to solve simple math problems.

• Students use glyphs (hieroglyphics) to tell a story about an event in the Maya people's lives.

• Assuming the role of archaeologists, students will use a picture of an artifact to develop questions that would lead to information about the Maya culture.

• Students map the Maya cities and settlements that existed throughout the civilization.

DISCOVER THE ANCIENT INCAS

Text Set

Aztecs and Incas: A Guide to Precolonized Americas in 1504
The Grandchildren of the Incas
Inca & Spaniard (Pizarro & the Conquest of Peru)
The Incas
Macchu Picchu: The Story of the Amazing Inkas and Their
  City in the Clouds
Miro in the Kingdom of the Sun
Step Into the...Inca World
The Incas

Learner Outcomes

• Students create a timeline of the Inca civilization and record historic events on the timeline as they learn about them.

• Students use the Inca number system to represent their age, birth, and weight.

• Students keep academic journals in which they record new words and meanings they have learned.

Discovery in Time — **DISCOVERY** — **Discovery by People**

DISCOVER THE ANCIENT AZTECS

Text Set

The Aztec News
Journey into Civilization: The Aztecs
Lost Temple of the Aztecs
Musicians of the Sun
People of the Ancient World: The Ancient Aztecs
Pyramid of the Sun, Pyramid of the Moon
The Aztecs
The Ancient World: The Aztecs
The Aztecs
The Fifth and Final Sun: An Ancient Aztec Myth
Technology in the Time of the Aztecs
Two Mountains: An Aztec Legend

Learner Outcomes

• Students compare their own culture with the Aztec culture.

• Students show how the Aztec gods were related to the people's way of life.

• Students compare the Tlatelolco market place activities with their shopping mall activities.

• Students will construct a pyramid similar to the Pyramid of the Sun or Pyramid of the Moon.

DISCOVER THE AUTHORS' WORLDS

Text Set

A Biography: Laura Ingalls Wilder
Charles Dickens: The Man Who Had Great Expectations
Dickens: His Work and His World
The Man Who Created Narnia
Mark Twain and Huckleberry Finn
Mark Twain: Great American Fiction Writer
On the Bus with Joanna Cole
Shakespeare: His Work and His World
Through the Tempests Dark and Wild: A Story of Mary
  Shelley: Frankenstein's Creator
26 Fairmount Avenue
What Do Authors Do?

Learner Outcomes

• Students identify characteristics of their favorite author.

• Students write their autobiographies, viewing themselves as writers.

• Students read the works of an author.

• Students conduct a five-minute book talk on the biography of their favorite author.

DISCOVER THE FROZEN WORLD OF THE ARCTIC

Text Set

Animal Survivors of the Arctic
Arctic Foxes
Arctic Lights, Arctic Nights
Arctic Tundra
The Bear Says North: Tales from Northern Lands
Buried in Ice: The Mystery of a Lost Arctic Expedition
The Girl Who Dreamed Only Geese
Into the Ice: The Story of Arctic Exploration
Life in the Arctic: Ecosystems
Life in the Polar Lands
Little Cliff and Cold Place
Pipaluk and the Whales
Polar Bear Patrol
The Polar Bear Sun: An Inuit Tale
Step into the Arctic World

Learner Outcomes

- Students are able to write about what they have learned about the Arctic regions.

- Students write postcards to friends about their imaginary trip to the Arctic regions.

- Students produce a commercial on how pollution and other human activities are creating serious threats to the environment.

- Students develop a set of trading cards of the polar bears and other Arctic animals.

**Discovery
of Place**

DISCOVER THE FROZEN WORLD OF ANTARCTICA

Text Set

Antarctica: Journeys to the South Pole
A Mother's Journey
After the Last Dog Died: The True-Life, Hair-Raising Adventure of Douglas Mawson and His 1911–1914 Antarctic Expedition
Antarctica: The Last Unspoiled Continent
Antarctic Antics: A Book of Penguin Poems
Antarctic Journal: Four Months at the Bottom of the World
Antarctica's Land, People, and Wildlife: A myreportlinks.com Book
Desert of Ice: Life and Work in Antarctica
The Emperor Lays an Egg
The Endurance: Shackleton's Perilous Expedition in Antarctica
Explorers of New Worlds: Sir Ernest Shackleton and the Struggle Against Antarctica
Eyes on Nature: Penguins
Geography of the World: Antarctica
Ice Story: Shackleton's Lost Expedition
Life Under Ice
My Season with Penguins: An Antarctic Journal
Penguin Parade
Penguins
Penguins: A Portrait of the Animal World
Pioneering Frozen Worlds
Polar Exploration: Journeys to the Arctic and Antarctic
Under the Ice
Science on the Ice: An Antarctic Journal
Trapped by the Ice! Shackleton's Amazing Antarctic Adventure

Learner Outcomes

- Students compare and contrast the first explorations to Antarctica with current ones.

- Students use one book they have read about Antarctica to create the ecosystem through the "book box" strategy.

- Students use word webs to demonstrate meanings of vocabulary related to Antarctica.

- Students will show how animals such as the penguins survive the frigid waters of Antarctica.

DISCOVER POETS' WORLDS

Text Set

Been to Yesterdays: Poems of a Life
Carl Sandburg: Adventures of a Poet
Cool Melons—Turn to Frogs! The Life and Poems of Issa
Emily Dickinson's Letters to the World
Henry David's House: Henry David Thoreau
Let Freedom Ring! Phillips Wheatley
Love to Langston
Maya Angelou: Journey of the Heart
New Suns Will Arise: From the Journals of Henry David Thoreau
Phillis Wheatley: Young Revolutionary Poet
Poetry for Young People: Rudyard Kipling
Poetry for Young People: Walt Whitman
Walt Whitman: A Biography
Walt Whitman: Words for America

Learner Outcomes

- Students use choral reading to present a poem.

- Students respond to a poem using drawings.

- Students read with fluency and expression.

- Students write poems and create a class book of poems.

SAMPLER ■ Discover the Frozen World of Antarctica

This mysterious desert of ice—who lives here and what do they do? Since the discovery of the Antarctic region by Captain James Cook in the 1770s, many explorers dreamed of encounters with the South Pole. *Trapped by the Ice! Shackleton's Amazing Antarctic Adventure* introduces students to one of the first expeditions to Antarctica. When Ernest Shackleton's ship, *Endurance*, was trapped in the Antarctic ice, his fortitude that led the expedition did not diminish. Indeed, it strengthened as Schackleton's goal turned from exploration to survival. A similar story of the perils of the first expeditions to Antarctica is found in Bredson's biography of Douglas Mawson, *After the Last Dog Died*.

The early explorers laid the groundwork for the scientists who continue to visit Antarctica to study the geography, climate, and the wildlife, especially the most popular animal living in Antarctica, the penguin. *A Mother's Journey, The Emperor Lays an Egg*, and *My Season with Penguins: An Antarctic Journal* introduce emperor penguins and their living conditions. The readings will open up the world of Antarctica to students as they enjoy the mysterious behaviors of this much-loved animal.

The purpose of the instructional sequence is to teach students how to read and write informational text with an emphasis on reading to learn and writing to convey information. Included in this section are demonstrations of teaching students to (1) learn to select their topics of study, (2) develop questions to guide their collection of information from multiple sources, and (3) create data charts to record information that will be used to write on selected topics. For example, as part of the focus lesson, the teacher conducts book talks and models how to find a variety of topics related to Antarctica and how to search for information on their selected topics.

NCTE/IRA Standards for the English Language Arts

1. Students read a wide range of print and non-print texts to build an understanding of texts, of themselves, and of the cultures of the United States and the world; to acquire new information; to respond to the needs and demands of society and the workplace; and for personal fulfillment. Among these texts are fiction and nonfiction, classic and contemporary works.
2. Students conduct research on issues and interests by generating ideas and questions, and by posing problems. They gather, evaluate, and synthesize data from a variety of sources (e.g., print and non-print texts, artifacts, people) to communicate their discoveries in ways that suit their purpose and audience.

Learner Outcomes

Students will be able to do the following:

- Generate questions related to their selected topic of research
- Read informational literature for meaning
- Learn to answer questions and gather data related to their selected topic of research
- Create a group multimedia presentation on their selected topic of research using text, maps, and visuals that support the information being presented

THE FOCUS LESSON

Students are engaged in a book talk on several books in the text set, the teacher uses one book for shared reading that introduces the essential concepts of the theme, and within the mini-lesson, students learn how to organize the information they learn from reading through the use of data charts.

DISCOVERY
Discover the Frozen World of Antarctica

READING WORKSHOP

Students engage in reading informational books on Antarctica during reading workshop. To guide their reading and organize information on selected topics, they use data charts.

WRITING WORKSHOP

In small groups, students use information from their data charts to create multimedia presentations on their topics of interest related to Antarctica.

Text Set

Antarctica: Journeys to the South Pole
A Mother's Journey
After the Last Dog Died: The True-Life, Hair-Raising Adventure of Douglas Mawson and His 1911–1914 Antarctic Expedition
Antarctica: The Last Unspoiled Continent
Antarctic Antics: A Book of Penguin Poems
Antarctic Journal: Four Months at the Bottom of the World
Antarctica's Land, People, and Wildlife: A myreportlinks.com Book

Desert of Ice: Life and Work in Antarctica
The Emperor Lays an Egg
The Endurance: Shackleton's Perilous Expedition in Antarctica
Explorers of New Worlds: Sir Ernest Shackleton and the Struggle Against Antarctica
Eyes on Nature: Penguins
Geography of the World: Antarctica
Ice Story: Shackleton's Lost Expedition
Life Under Ice
My Season with Penguins: An Antarctic Journal
Penguin Parade

Penguins
Penguins: A Portrait of the Animal World
Pioneering Frozen Worlds
Polar Exploration: Journeys to the Arctic and Antarctic
Under the Ice
Science on the Ice: An Antarctic Journal
Trapped by the Ice! Shackleton's Amazing Antarctic Adventure

SOCIAL STUDIES

Students will locate Antarctica and compare it to their own country, the United States, with respect to size, climate, government, people, language, and land formation. After reading about the first expeditions to Antarctica and the modern scientific expeditions, students will create a Venn Diagram to compare and contrast the early expeditions with 21st-century expeditions.

COLLABORATIVE INQUIRY ACTIVITIES ACROSS THE CURRICULUM

ART

There are different species of penguins in Antarctica that can be distinguished by their markings. After students know the distinguishing features of the species, they may make hand or paper bag puppets of a species of interest.

MATHEMATICS AND TECHNOLOGY

Explorers used longitude and latitude to locate the frozen world of Antarctica. Students will learn how the numbers of longitude and latitude were used to represent points on the earth and distance. Students will use the Internet to see how current technology is used to help find places, and they will see satellite maps of Antarctica.

SCIENCE, MATH, AND TECHNOLOGY ACTIVITIES

SCIENCE

Students learn the role of an Antarctic animal's blubber in staying warm in ice-cold water. Students engage in an experiment showing the effects of fat as an insulator of ice-cold water. Students may engage in several different experiments involving ice: (1) interaction of sea ice and water, (2) the effects of sugar on freezing, (3) creation of a glacier.

ON-YOUR-OWN ACTIVITIES

Penguins are very interesting animals that live on Antarctica. Create a book of penguin facts. Read and write about different penguin behaviors with accompanying illustrations. Draw the different types of penguins or draw the hatching of a penguin chick from an egg.

HOME–SCHOOL CONNECTIONS

After learning the effects of human activity on the environment, students will discuss global warming. They will talk with family members about things that they may do to prevent global warming.

Conduct a Focus Lesson

Through book talks, a shared reading, and a mini-lesson on student-generated questions for conducting research around a selected topic, the teacher helps students to learn about Antarctica, its land, and its ecosystem.

Establish a Purpose   The teacher conducts short book talks on selected books from the text set to provide the students with an overview of what they will be reading and to stimulate their interest in topics related to Antarctica. The teacher holds up Walter Dean Myers's *Antarctica: Journeys to the South Pole* and reads the table of contents, showing them the photographs of different journeys to the South Pole, from the earliest to the ones conducted today. With the question, Why do people continue to travel to this frozen land? the teacher continues the book talk with Jennifer Owings Dewey's *Antarctic Journal: Four Months at the Bottom of the World* and Laurence Pringle's *Antarctica: The Last Unspoiled Continent.* The brief introductions to the text set provide students with a preview of their readings, preparing them for what they will be learning.

Engage in Shared Reading   Throughout the unit on Antarctica, the teacher engages students in a shared reading from *Antarctic Journal: Four Months at the Bottom of the World.* The book was written by Jennifer Dewey, a scientist who spent four months studying Antarctica and making journal entries and sketches in her diary. The daily read aloud provides students with the opportunity to navigate topics of interest about the frozen desert continent. For example, when students hear about the trip to Antarctica, the gear that the scientists need to sustain themselves in frigid temperatures, their lodgings and food, and the animals that are part of the ecosystem in Antarctica, they begin to identify topics that they wish to study further.

Conduct a Mini-Lesson   The teacher conducts a mini-lesson on developing questions for students' selected topics related to Antarctica. To organize the questions and the information gathered from their readings, the teacher uses the data chart strategy, "a graphic organizer to help students sort information from different text sources into categories" (Antonacci & O'Callaghan, 2006, p. 17). (See Figure 4.5.)

The teacher demonstrates to students the importance of asking questions and using the right type of questions to guide their gathering of information from various books for their research. The teacher refers to *Antarctic Journal: Four Months at the Bottom of the World* to model how to select a topic for research and writes it on the prepared data chart. To demonstrate how to develop questions around the selected topic, animals of Antarctica, the teacher uses a think aloud. The teacher says aloud, "I would like to know about some of the animals that live in Antarctica and how they survive the cold. The question that I will ask is, 'How do different types of animals live in Antarctica?' This question is better than 'What are the names of the animals that live in Antarctica?' because it asks for more information." The teacher directs the students to think about what they learned from the shared reading, to record their ideas, and to change their ideas or topics into questions that will help them gather more research. The teacher and students work together to complete a sample data chart.

FIGURE 4.5 Data Chart

TOPIC: THE FIRST EXPEDITIONS TO ANTARCTICA					
Source	Who were some of the first explorers? Why did they want to explore Antarctica?	When did they explore Antarctica? How long did it take them to travel to Antarctica?	What were the ships like during the first expeditions?	What were some of the discoveries made by the first explorers?	How did they eat and keep warm? Where did they sleep?	What were some of the main problems and obstacles that faced the first explorers?
After the Last Dog Died					
The Endurance: Shackleton's Perilous Expedition in Antarctica					
Trapped by the Ice!					
Ice Story: Shackleton's Lost Expedition					

Additional Mini-Lessons

Personal Word Walls

■ The teacher helps the students to build vocabulary in the content areas that they are reading by using personal word walls.

■ Using an oaktag folder, each student creates six boxes on each side of the folder and labels each with a letter of the alphabet, with the letters *x, y,* and *z* sharing the last box.

■ As students read, they record words that represent concepts related to their topics, such as *expedition, equator,* and *peninsula.*

■ The teacher directs the students to record each new word under the appropriate letter.

■ The teacher provides time for children to share and discuss the words from their personal word walls.

Learning Logs

■ The teacher uses learning logs to help students record new information that they have learned while reading.

■ The teacher demonstrates to students how to use a journal to record new information.

■ The teacher then helps the students to use the information in writing their reports.

Venn Diagrams

■ The teacher models the use of the Venn Diagram as a structured approach to compare and contrast a concept.

■ The teacher selects a concept that students discussed during the shared reading, such as wildlife in Antarctica.

■ The teacher assists the students with comparing the wildlife in another region that was studied with that of Antarctica.

Conduct a Reading Workshop

During reading workshop, students read informational books that target their reading level. The purpose is to provide a structured experience for students in reading informational text, to develop specific comprehension strategies in reading nonfiction books, and to expand students' concepts of learning from reading as they develop strategies on reading to learn. Briefly, students select a topic related to Antarctica to study and choose a book from the appropriate text set related to their selected topic and reading level. During reading workshop, students work in groups to read their books and gather information about their topic using the data chart strategy.

Before Reading The teacher introduces books from the text sets and offers an overview of each text set. The overview is a guided discussion, using the table of contents to predict the kinds of information found in the book. As the students choose books, the teacher guides them toward selecting texts with the appropriate interest and reading levels.

Students in each reading group examine their books by looking at the table of contents and the index, and the teacher directs them to make predictions about what they will be reading. The teacher engages students in developing at least three questions that may be answered by reading their books. Using the blank data chart, the students record their questions in the appropriate box and use them to find information in their texts.

During Reading   The teacher works with students while they are reading, assessing and providing assistance to students in the following areas:

- *Developing questions.* The teacher may need to help some students reframe questions so that they facilitate the reader in garnering information. Students should be encouraged to develop additional questions or revise original questions based on their readings.
- *Reading for meaning.* Understanding informational books may be difficult for some students; therefore, assistance in comprehending text may be needed by those with reading difficulties.
- *Finding the main idea or gist.* Students need to know how to summarize or find the main idea(s) when taking notes on their data charts. Some students will need instruction and guidance in summarizing a paragraph or two into one sentence.

Reading for learning and writing to recall information are important skills that students are developing during reading workshop. Therefore, students should be given time to learn the process of questioning, reading for information, and recording ideas. Their books should be divided into sections, and each section may be completed within one sitting. It is important for teachers to provide feedback to the students at the end of each reading workshop session.

After Reading   After each reading workshop session, the teacher guides the students within their small groups to engage in a think-pair-share. With their partners, they share the information that they have collected from their reading and recorded on their data charts and offer a brief explanation.

When students have completed their books and their data charts, the teacher engages them in a whole-class discussion. Using a large data chart with a list of books the students have read recorded in the left column and the topics related to their readings in the right, the students share their information. As each group discusses their books, they use their data charts to jog their memories. They may add their information to the whole-class data chart.

Conduct a Writing Workshop

The teacher brings the students back to their individual data charts and the large data chart on Antarctica created by the whole class. During writing workshop, students engage in developing a multimedia presentation on the specific topics about which they have read and gathered information. Multimedia presentations involve all aspects of language as well as visual and audio demonstrations. Depending on whether the students have had experience with multimedia presentations, the teacher directs the students on how to incorporate different media forms to communicate their ideas.

Before Writing   The teacher begins by discussing the purpose of a multimedia presentation. Prior to writing, the teacher works with the students to focus on the topics that they will present and to organize the ideas that will be part of the discussion.

ASSESS LITERACY

The teacher assesses students' skills in the following areas: (1) developing questions, (2) reading for information, (3) summarizing and finding the gist or main idea from the text, and (4) recording the information accurately. As students engage in reading workshop, the teacher works with individual groups and observes students' performances in each of these skill areas. Using the rubric below, the teacher documents each student's performance.

Criteria	Independent	Proficient	Developing
Developing appropriate questions	Student demonstrates proficient skills in developing questions that help the reader to garner information from the text on a specific topic. (3)	Student demonstrates adequate skills in developing questions that help the reader to garner information from the text on a specific topic. (2)	Student demonstrates little or no skills in developing questions that help the reader to garner information from the text on a specific topic. (0–1)
Locating information	Student locates information from the text at all times. (3)	Student locates information from the text most of the time. (2)	Student needs assistance in locating information from the text. (0–1)
Reading for meaning and understanding	Student demonstrates proficient skills in reading for meaning and understanding. (3)	Student demonstrates adequate skills in reading for meaning and understanding. (2)	Student demonstrates little or no skills in reading for meaning and understanding. (0–1)
Recording information accurately	Student records information from the text with a high degree of accuracy. (3)	Student records information from the text with some degree of accuracy. (2)	Student records information from the text with a low or no degree of accuracy. (0–1)
Summarizing information	Student demonstrates proficient skills in summarizing information or recording the main idea(s) of what was read. (3)	Student demonstrates adequate skill in summarizing information or recording the main idea(s) of what was read. (2)	Student demonstrates little or no skill in summarizing information or recording the main idea(s) of what was read. (0–1)

Independent: 11–15
Proficient: 6–10
Developing: 0–5

Students in the same reading group may work together to present different aspects of the same topic.

To prepare for the presentation, the teacher asks the students to write a list of important ideas that will be presented and briefly discuss the ideas within the small group. Depending on the technology resources or lack thereof, the teacher may ask the children how they would use Microsoft PowerPoint, ClarisWorks, Inspiration, Kid Pix, or HyperStudio to present their information. Students may incorporate visuals from different websites or use audio clips that enhance the meaning and motivate their audience.

During Writing   The small groups work together to write about their topics. During their writing, the teacher conferences with the groups to help students develop their ideas. This aspect of writing may take several blocks of time. As the students write, they may continue to further research their ideas. In addition to working on their writing, the discussion among group members will include the use of media in their presentation. Often, students will work on incorporating different forms of media into their presentations as they write. The teacher works with the group to ensure that group presentations utilize similar forms of multimedia so that their group production is consistent.

After Writing   To bring closure to the multimedia project, small groups present their work in "An Antarctica Celebration." Presentations are made in a roundtable format so that they can view one another's work. At the closure of the celebration, students discuss how their thinking has changed regarding Antarctica.

Collaborative Inquiry Across the Curriculum

Extension to Mathematics and Technology   Geographers often use numbers to describe locations. The explorers of the frozen worlds of the Arctic and the Antarctic regions relied on these number locations. Their discoveries have given us the location and distances of the two polar regions represented through longitude and latitude. Students learn that the Arctic Circle is an imaginary line drawn at latitude 66" 32' North and the Antarctic Circle at 66" 32' South. Why were numbers used to represent points on Earth? What do these numbers of latitude mean with respect to distance? How are numbers of longitude and latitude used to determine exact points through points of intersection? Using the numerous maps from the text set, the classroom wall map of the world, and the atlas, the teacher directs the students to explore the two polar regions using lines of latitude and longitude. Students can also compare the technology that was used by the explorers of the first expeditions to Antarctica and those used by scientists and tourists today.

As the students research their topics for writing, they are directed to websites such as www.usap.gov. A wide range of topics and activities are offered, including information about the U.S. Antarctic Program, the continent of Antarctica, the Antarctic Treaty, researchers and science projects, science discoveries, vessel science and operations, and the technology that is used to support scientific discoveries in Antarctica.

STANDARDS

Mathematics Standards
4. Measurement

Technology Standards
5. Technology Research Tools

Extension to Science   Reading informational books on Antarctica provides many opportunities for extensions to science lessons. Students will read about the bone-chilling water that surrounds Antarctic and wonder, "How do Antarctic animals survive in such freezing water?" The following lesson will provide firsthand information they can use to answer their questions.

STANDARDS

Science Standards
Life Science, Content Standards C1 and C2

How Do Penguins and Other Antarctic Animals Stay Warm?

- Begin the discussion with how our own bodies react to very cold weather. What do we do to keep warm in the winter?

- Animals must stay warm on very cold days. How do animals stay warm? How do animals in Antarctica that live in frigid water stay warm? Show and tell how animals use blubber to stay warm. Discuss what blubber is and show students solid fat or shortening that is a form of blubber.
- Prepare a large bucket filled with ice cubes and water. Have students put one hand in an empty plastic bag the other in a second plastic bag that contains a generous amount of shortening. Both bags are secured with tape to waterproof each bag.
- Students place both hands in the bucket of ice water. Monitoring students, have them keep both hands in the water for an equal amount of time and describe how each hand feels.
- Students will state the effects of blubber on keeping the body warm in cold water and how the bodies of penguins have blubber to insulate them from the freezing cold water.

> **STANDARDS**
>
> **Social Studies Standards**
> III. People, Places, and Environments

Extension to Social Studies   Students will learn that Antarctica has an unusual ecosystem; as the driest continent in the world, it is considered an ice-cold desert. As they read *Antarctic Journal: Four Months at the Bottom of the World,* students learn about Antarctica's ecosystem from a scientist's perspective, developing their concept of a desert and how ecosystems affect all aspects of life. They may create wall charts using visuals and text to represent the land of Antarctica, including glaciers and ice as well as its location, animal life, climate, and plant life. Students will also learn the important and critical role that Australia has played in scientific explorations to Antarctica by visiting www.aad .gov.au. They will view maps of Antarctica and see its geographic relation to Australia; read about the Australian explorations to Antarctica; read and learn about Antarctica's different ice forms, the animals, and the effects of pollution on its environment; and understand why the Antarctic Treaty was formed by a number of countries.

Home–School Connections   Students read about and discuss the effects of humans on the environment, including the results of global warming and the ozone layer on an environment that supports healthy living. They talk with family members about things that people can do to prevent global warming and the destruction of the ozone layer. Students generate a list of what their families will do to preserve the environment.

On-Your-Own Activities   Students read *Antarctic Antics: A Book of Penguin Poems* and learn about penguin behaviors and habitats that appear in the poems. *My Season with Penguins: An Antarctic Journal* by Sophie Webb will give students a glimpse into the lives of penguins through an artist's four-month experience painting penguins. Students are directed to use their readings on Antarctica to develop a senses poem similar to the penguin poem shown in Figure 4.6.

Sensory poems are developed using the five senses to describe a person, place, or thing. The poem follows the specific pattern outlined below, and in the sixth line, the name of the person, place, or thing is given.

Line 1: _____   look _____

Line 2: _____   smell_____

Line 3: _____   sound _____

Line 4: _____   taste _____

Line 5: _____   feel _____

Line 6: _____   are _____

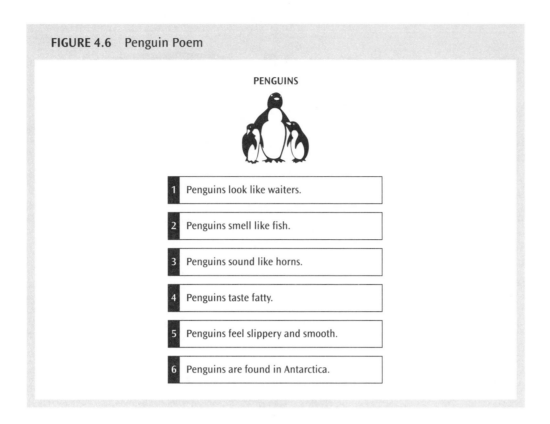

FIGURE 4.6 Penguin Poem

PENGUINS

1 Penguins look like waiters.

2 Penguins smell like fish.

3 Penguins sound like horns.

4 Penguins taste fatty.

5 Penguins feel slippery and smooth.

6 Penguins are found in Antarctica.

Critical Literacy

As a closure activity, students will work in groups to synthesize and apply their information about Antarctica and create a podcast that presents the information they have accumulated from the instructional sequence. The podcast can be incorporated into their multimedia presentation for the collaborative literacy activity.

Collaborative Literacy

When students have finished their multimedia presentations, they will share their production with the class. The class may develop a program of presentations that lists each topic and its presenters. If technology is used, a suitable program would take the form of a slide.

The theme of Discovery is extended to the middle school grades as students explore medical discoveries in the sampler, *Medical Discoveries: Great Minds of Science.*

■ Middle Grades: Grades 6–8

Twentieth-century scientific and technological discoveries have revolutionized almost every domain of human experience. These discoveries and related inventions have changed not only the way we travel, communicate, and learn, but even the length of our lives.

Changes in transportation systems from horse-drawn carriages to cars, airplanes, and even spaceships have created a shrinking globe and the need for cross-cultural interaction based on mutual respect and understanding. Changes in communication

GREAT MINDS OF MEDICAL SCIENCE

Text Set

All About Great Medical Discoveries
The History News: Medicine
Wilhelm Roentgen and the Discovery of X-Rays
Louis Pasteur: Fighter Against Contagious Disease
Marie Curie: A Brilliant Life
Dr. Jenner and the Speckled Monster: The Search for the Smallpox Vaccine
Jonas Salk: Conquering Polio
Alexander Fleming: The Man Who Discovered Penicillin
William Harvey: Discoverer of How Blood Circulates
Great Inventions: Medicine
The Head Bone's Connected to the Neck Bone
Marie Curie: Discoverer of Radiation
Ancient Medicine: From Sorcery to Surgery

Outcomes

- Analyze and interpret information from print and electronic resources.
- Support claims with facts, details, and illustrative materials.
- Collaborate and develop authoritative stance relative to a topic and establish validity of sources.
- Use writing process to develop a persuasive argument.

EXPLORERS DISCOVER NEW LANDS

Text Set

Sir Walter Ralegh and the Quest for Eldorado
The Remarkable Voyages of Captain Cook
A Long and Uncertain Journey: The 27,000 Mile Voyage of Vasco daGama
The Sea King: Sir Francis Drake and His Times
Ferdinand Magellan: First to Sail Around the World
Henry Hudson: Ill-Fated Explorer of North America's Coast

Outcomes

- Abstract information relative to objects, ideas, and customs explorers discovered.
- Read a biography and maintain an explorer's journal.
- Use information from print and electronic resources to develop a proposal for exploring new frontiers.
- Create a web to analyze etymology and meaning of new words.

DISCOVERING THE MIDDLE EAST

Text Set

Three Wishes: Palestinian and Israeli Children Speak
Figs and Fate: Stories About Growing Up in the Arab World Today
Habibi
Alia's Mission: Saving the Books of Iraq
Thura's Diary
The Persian Gulf and Iraqi Wars

Outcomes

- Analyze and explain a character's thinking at pivotal points in story.
- Abstract details to compare and contrast life in Middle East with life in the U.S.
- Use text-to-text, text-to-self, and text-to-world connections to participate in discussion.

DISCOVERING PREHISTORIC PEOPLE

Text Set

Stone Age Farmers Beside the Sea: Scotland's Village of Skara Brae
Prehistoric Peoples: Discover the Long-Ago World of the First Humans
The Art and Civilization of Prehistory
Exploring the Ice Age
Eyewitness Books: Early Humans
Time of the Bison

Outcomes

- Create process–cause graphic organizers to explain how climatic change affected prehistoric societies.
- Create pictographs to explain changes in technology during the Stone Ages.
- Generate research questions, gather information from print and electronic resources to design and write *All About* books.

DISCOVERING ANCIENT CIVILIZATIONS

Text Set

The Ancient Persians
Ancient Romans
Bodies from the Ash: Life and Death in Ancient Pompeii
Ancient Greece
Mesopotamia
Outside and Inside Mummies
Egyptian Mummies: People from the Past

Outcomes

- Draw inferences from illustrations to support an opinion.
- Abstract information from print and electronic resources to support opinions.
- Use information from texts to describe contributions of specific ancient civilizations to the modern world.

DISCOVERING AFRICA

Text Set

The Middle of Somewhere: A Story of South Africa
African Princesses: The Amazing Lives of Africa's Royal Women
Facing the Lion: Growing Up Maasi on the African Savanna
Dream Freedom
Journey to Jo'berg: A South African Story
Chain of Fire
Out of Bounds: Seven Stories of Conflict and Hope

Outcomes

- Abstract details to explain the cause–effect relationship between geography and culture.
- Use text references to explain a character's viewpoint relative to apartheid.
- Pose questions and gather information from print and electronic resources to plan and organize a collaborative report.

Discovery by People

Discovery in Time

DISCOVERY

Discovery of Place

systems such as radios, telephones, television, and computers have made worldwide information sharing not only possible but instantaneous. In addition, advances in medical science have increased the average lifespan from 47 to 80 years. Medical discoveries have resulted in the development of vaccines and antibiotics as well as technologies for the diagnosis and treatment of disease and improved health care.

Middle grade students will examine the theme of Discovery by reading the biographies of men and women such as William Harvey, Edward Jenner, Louis Pasteur, Wilhelm Roentgen, Marie Curie, Alexander Fleming, and Jonas Salk, who worked to conquer disease and add new knowledge to the science of improving health. They will also learn about the determination and personal qualities that enabled each researcher to pursue his or her goal despite public scrutiny and criticism.

Multicultural literature that focuses on the Middle East and Africa will open students' minds to knowledge that will help them discover more about themselves and the young people living in other parts of the world. These text sets emphasize that Earth is a global village. Discovery is an appropriate topic for today's middle grade students because they are living in the most technologically advanced society in history.

SAMPLER ■ Great Minds of Medical Science

Through the miracles of modern medicine, more people live to a healthy old age today than in any other period in history. As a result of the pioneering research of scientists who pursued their hypotheses despite early failures and criticism, today's doctors know more about how the human body works and about germs, viruses, and other causes of disease and have better, more powerful drugs and procedures for keeping people healthy than ever before.

According to Galda and Cunningham (2002), biographies can help students develop their understanding of historical events while discovering ideas about the basic needs and desires of all people. Students who read biographies begin to see connections between modern life and the past. They learn that even heroes and heroines made mistakes and had false starts. In this sampler students read biographies about the scientists who made significant discoveries in medical science. As they read the stories of William Harvey, Edward Jenner, Louis Pasteur, Wilhelm Roentgen, Marie Curie, Alexander Fleming, and Jonas Salk, the students will discover that their contributions to medical science came as a result of many years of painstaking work. Students will learn that these true science biographies are filled with as much suspense and adventure as science fiction.

As students experience the stories of medical pioneers, they will place each discovery in its historical perspective while examining the life and personality of the individual. These stories will enable students to understand not only that people from many different cultures made and continue to make contributions to science and technology but also how difficult it was for scientific innovators to break through the accepted ideas of their time to reach the conclusions that we take for granted. Extension activities will help students explore the effects of each discovery on health care through time and throughout the world as well as to design and conduct a scientific investigation. They will communicate and defend a scientific argument based on a contemporary issue in health science.

Most great scientific and medical discoveries evolved slowly from the determination and hard work of generations of scientists. Working tirelessly, often without the support of their contemporaries, researchers pursue a goal such as a cure for smallpox

DISCOVERY
Great Minds of Medical Science

THE FOCUS LESSON

Create a Venn diagram to compare and contrast discovery and invention.

Read aloud from *The History News: Medicine* and *All About Great Medical Discoveries*.

Use REAP strategy to abstract and recode main ideas in own words.

READING WORKSHOP

Select a biography of one of the scientists who made a great medical discovery.

Participate in a cooperative jigsaw group to abstract details about the qualities of a research scientist.

Trace the sequence of events that led to the discovery.

Explain the impact of the discovery.

WRITING WORKSHOP

Using persuasive writing techniques, write a letter to nominate a medical discoverer to a Scientists Hall of Fame.

Text Set

All About Great Medical Discoveries
The History News: Medicine
Wilhelm Roentgen and the Discovery of X-Rays
Louis Pasteur: Fighter Against Contagious Disease
Marie Curie: A Brilliant Life
Dr. Jenner and the Speckled Monster: The Search for the Smallpox Vaccine
Jonas Salk: Conquering Polio
Alexander Fleming: The Man Who Discovered Penicillin
William Harvey: Discoverer of How Blood Circulates
Great Inventions: Medicine
The Head Bone's Connected to the Neck Bone
Marie Curie: Discoverer of Radiation
Ancient Medicine: From Sorcery to Surgery

SOCIAL STUDIES

Investigate the changes in health care and medicine from prehistoric to modern times. Create a timeline to show how changes in inventions, medicine, or practices, etc., have contributed to quality of health care.

COLLABORATIVE INQUIRY ACTIVITIES ACROSS THE CURRICULUM

ART

Create illustrations to accompany a timeline of medical changes.

MATHEMATICS

Investigate and use statistics to explain how specific discoveries changed health science.

Participate in a simulation to illustrate the exponential spread of infectious diseases.

SCIENCE, MATH, AND TECHNOLOGY ACTIVITIES

SCIENCE

Conduct experiments based on the work of biographies read. For example, learn about the work of the heart or how bacterial cells grow, etc.

ON-YOUR-OWN

Investigate current medical controversies such as: stem cell research, universal health care, bioterrorism, etc. Participate in a debate.

HOME–SCHOOL CONNECTIONS

Discuss current medical issues such as care for the aged, etc., with parents. Discuss the impact of various solutions on the family and/or community.

or polio. Sometimes a scientist's keen observation skills enable him or her to make a discovery by accident. This sampler will help middle grade students explore the lives of innovators whose discoveries changed medical practice.

NCTE/IRA Standards for the English Language Arts

1. Students read a wide range of print and non-print texts to build an understanding of texts, of themselves, and of the cultures of the United States and the world; [and] to acquire new information.
7. Students conduct research on issues and interests by generating ideas and questions, and by posing problems. They gather, evaluate, and synthesize data from a variety of sources (e.g., print and non-print texts, artifacts, people) to communicate their discoveries in ways that suit their purpose and audience.

Learner Outcomes

Students will be able to do the following:

- Use facts to support assertions relative to distinctions between discoveries and inventions
- Abstract information from listening to and reading biographies to identify the important details about a medical scientist
- Take and use notes from listening and reading to describe and explain the impact of a medical discovery

Conduct a Focus Lesson

The English language arts teacher begins the exploration by asking students to consider the relationship between discovery and invention. Using a Venn diagram, the teacher asks students to think about how a discovery and an invention are alike and different. After at least 10 minutes, students share their ideas while the teacher encourages students to extend their thinking by giving an example to support their ideas. The teacher or a student records ideas on a large graphic to be posted in the classroom for reference during the study. The teacher helps students clarify their understanding of the concepts by asking: How are discoveries and inventions related? Do discoveries lead to inventions? Do inventions lead to discoveries?

Establish a Purpose The teacher introduces *The History News: Medicine*, a picture book that describes the struggles and triumphs of the people who made medical discoveries and inventions. The teacher explains that this is a special collection of newspaper articles that could have been written to represent the history of man's battle against disease. As the teacher does a picture walk and reads selections from this shared text, students discover that prehistoric people believed demons and spirits invaded the human body to make people sick and that magic was often the treatment. They learn about the medical ideas of Hippocrates, the great Greek healer and how superstition influenced European medicine for hundreds of years after the fall of the Roman Empire. They see that although many discoveries were made between the 1500s and 1700s, they had little effect on treatment until 1796, when William Jenner discovered a technique for treating smallpox that inspired scientists and doctors from that time on to find new methods to treat and prevent illness.

The shared reading and research/reporting activities provide students with the curiosity and skills they will need for independent reading of one of the biographies. Students select a biography and participate in cooperative jigsaw groups to reflect on the life and times of a person who made a medical discovery. They discuss the series of events that led to the discovery and its effects. Students then examine how the discovery was received in its time and make connections to contemporary medical controversies.

Engage in Read Aloud   The teacher begins by explaining that records of Egyptian history show that around 3500 B.C. there were many physicians and surgeons as well as eye specialists, skin specialists, and dentists. Imhotep was the first doctor who came to be worshiped as a god of medicine. Many temples were built in his honor that later became centers for healing. Like Imhotep, the first Greek doctor, Asclepios, was worshiped as a god. The Greek centers of healing were also in temples, but they were the first to explain health and disease in natural terms. The Greeks not only introduced the concept of medical science but created medical schools. Hippocrates, the father of modern medicine, expected doctors in his time to take an oath promising to be faithful to the ideals of their profession. Doctors today continue to take the Hippocratic oath.

The teacher indicates that little was known about the structure of the human body during the Middle Ages until the work of a young doctor, Andreas Vesalius. The teacher reads Chapter 3, The Human Body, from *All About Great Medical Discoveries,* and asks students to focus on his discoveries, the steps leading up to the discoveries, how the people in Vesalius's time received his discoveries, and the effects of Vesalius's discoveries. After finishing the book, the teacher asks, "Why do you think Vesalius's discovery represents a turning point in medical science?"

Conduct a Mini-Lesson   The teacher explains that as students read one of the biographies they will become experts on the scientist, his or her life and times, and the effects of the scientist's discovery. The mini-lesson focuses on using REAP (Allen, 2004), a strategy for improving students' understanding of a text by revisiting it in order to think about ways to represent the main ideas and author's message in their own words.

The teacher indicates that each discoverer made an extraordinary contribution to science because he or she questioned the ideas and practices of the time. The teacher models how to gather information and reprocess it by using the REAP strategy and data-gathering graphic in Figure 4.7. After reading about Andreas Vesalius, the teacher distributes the graphic organizers. Students use their notes from listening to contribute to a class chart. The teacher provides sufficient time for each student to provide at least one response. Students then generate questions about the topic of medical discoveries, which are added to the chart that will be placed on display. The teacher asks students to use a quickwrite (Tompkins, 2009) to connect these ideas to the previous discussion about discovery and invention.

Additional Mini-Lessons
Semantic and Concept Definition Mapping

- The teacher explains that concepts are mental images or structures that help us organize our understanding of a topic. Because our world is so complex, people use concepts or categories to help reduce the complexity of the environment, and in the process discover how ideas are related. The ideas in science are very com-

FIGURE 4.7   REAP: Graphic Organizer for Analyzing Medical Discoveries

Directions: You will use this graphic organizer to reflect on the biography your group has read as well as to think about the work of medical scientists who have made discoveries that have changed our understanding of human health and our ability to fight disease. Work collaboratively to discuss your views and reach consensus.

R	**Read** the title and author of the biography you are reading. Write a question about the person and his or her discovery you hope the book will answer.
E	**Encode** the text by abstracting the key events that led to the discovery.
A	**Annotate** the text by identifying the discovery, summarizing how the discovery was made, and explaining its importance.
P	**Ponder** the text by discussing the effects of the discovery on science and medicine. Explain the benefits to medical science today.

REAP	
R	E
A	P

plex, but students can use semantic maps or webs to help organize experiences and background knowledge.

■ Students begin by selecting words from their readings that are technical and/or unfamiliar.

■ The teacher explains that students will create a conceptual network or semantic map to illustrate how the words are related. In this conceptual network, the terms will be organized in a hierarchy consisting of superordinate and subordinate concepts.

■ Students in expert groups create semantic maps based on words selected from their reading of a specific biography.

■ Finally, each group shares their semantic maps and explains the relationships and reasons behind their responses.

Instructional Conversations

■ After the students complete the REAP activity, the teacher arranges the classroom into a circle for a discussion.

- The teacher initiates the discussion by posing the focus question: Do you think a person who makes a medical or scientific discovery must possess specific qualities? Students refer to their notes and may write a brief response before the discussion begins.
- During the discussion, the teacher notes the main ideas and opinions on a chart while students add information to extend or refine each point.
- The students defend their positions with information from their reading and consider additional questions such as, Do all scientists face obstacles and opposition to new ideas?
- Students are encouraged to note ideas and information provided by their peers that they wish to investigate further.
- After the discussion, students use the information to select the scientist they will nominate for the Hall of Fame and explain how the conversation helped them make their decision.

Writing to Persuade

- The teacher explains that a persuasive essay is used to influence or change a reader's ideas on a specific topic. Successful persuasive writing requires careful planning and specific techniques.
- The teacher and students collect examples of effective persuasive writing such as newspaper articles, editorials, movie and/or book reviews, advertisements, and so on.
- Together the teacher and students identify the strategies the authors used to persuade the audience: appeal to reason by using facts, statistics, data from research, and logical arguments; appeal to credibility by quoting reliable sources and respected people; or appeal to emotion by evoking beliefs and values.
- The teacher leads students through the steps for developing a persuasive essay. Students select the scientist they want to nominate for the Science Hall of Fame.
- Based on notes from the cooperative learning experiences, students develop the content they will use to support their opinions. They are encouraged to use information about all the candidates as well as to use print and Internet resources to find additional information.
- Using the facts from their research, students develop the arguments for their candidate and predict the arguments that may be used for the other side. They brainstorm several examples to support each claim. The teacher explains that a good persuasive writer understands the other perspectives in order to develop the strongest case.
- Finally, students plan the structure of the argument with following steps: (1) Develop an introduction that will hook the reader into wanting to read more; (2) provide background information and state the position clearly and definitively; (3) create a paragraph for each argument that includes compelling evidence (details, examples, explanations, statistics, etc.) to support each claim; (4) include information about the other side (other scientists) that illustrates why this position (nominee) is better; (5) write a closing paragraph that restates the viewpoint and summarizes the main arguments to illustrate the strength of this position; and (6) develop a powerful closing statement to convince the audience.

Conduct a Reading Workshop

In the focus lesson, the teacher described how to use the REAP strategy to improve comprehension and internalize the content from their reading. The teacher explains that during the reading workshops, they will apply this technique as they read a biography of a person who made a significant medical discovery.

Before Reading   The teacher explains that the six books in the text set are biographies that profile the achievements of men and women who worked to conquer a disease or add to our understanding of the mysteries of the human body. The teacher explains that although they are based on fact, the stories are compelling because each scientist was charting an unknown course. As they read their stories, students experience the agony of unsuccessful results, the thrill of discovery, and the hurt of critical reviews.

Each cooperative jigsaw base team will have a member who focuses on one of the biographies. The teacher has enough copies of each book in the text set to create six to seven expert groups of at least two students in each. To help students to make a choice, the teacher does a brief book talk.

The teacher places the books on a display table and describes that *William Harvey, Discoverer of How Blood Circulates* is the story of the man whose discovery challenged Galen's ideas about how the heart works. Harvey was born in a small coastal town in England in 1578. In 1600 he went to the University at Padua in Italy, where his anatomy teacher, Fabricius, encouraged him to use dissections to learn more about the bodies of living things. Curious about how blood moves through the body, Harvey noticed something Galen and Fabricius missed. Students who read this book discover why a person who receives a heart transplant today owes more to William Harvey than his surgeon.

Before the late eighteenth century, people believed disease and death were inevitable. *Dr. Jenner and the Speckled Monster: The Search for the Smallpox Vaccine* is a spellbinding history that tracks the deadly virus through time and around the world. It describes how the observations and experiments of an unknown country doctor proved that people are not helpless in battling disease. Students who read this story learn how one man's curiosity about a disease that caused untold fear and human loss turned the tide in scientific knowledge and experimentation.

The Life of Louis Pasteur is the biography of the teacher who encouraged his students to challenge ideas that were not based on the standards of the scientific method. Pasteur's desire to uncover the secrets of nature led him to a series of incredible discoveries that resulted in the germ theory of disease. Students who select his biography learn how Pasteur's persistence, carefully designed experiments, and detailed explanations helped him illustrate the link between microbes and disease and to develop pasteurization and immunization.

In 1895, Wilhelm Roentgen was in his laboratory experimenting with electricity when he accidentally discovered x-rays. Students who read *Wilhelm Roentgen and the Discovery of X-Rays* learn how the discovery affected the life of this humble scientist, who refused to profit from his discovery, claiming that discoveries and inventions belong to humanity.

Marie Curie: Discoverer of Radium tells the story of one of the most famous women in science. Born in Poland in 1867, she was forced to move to France to get an education. Madame Curie was one of the first women to receive a doctorate from the Sorbonne, where she met and married Pierre Curie. Students who select this book learn how together Marie and Pierre pursued their interest in radiation and discovered two new elements, radium and polonium.

Alexander Fleming had been looking for a medicine to kill dangerous bacteria for many years. However, his actual discovery occurred by accident, as recounted in

Alexander Fleming: The Man Who Discovered Penicillin. In the summer of 1928, Fleming, a research doctor in London, left the glass dishes filled with bacteria samples in the laboratory while he went on a two-week vacation. On his return he observed something strange: mold had formed on one of the dishes and the bacteria at the edges of the mold had died! After several painstaking experiments, Fleming discovered that the mold, which he called *penicillium notatum,* could destroy some of the strongest bacteria, including those that cause diseases such as diphtheria, scarlet fever, and pneumonia. This book illustrates how Howard Florey and Ernst Chain used Fleming's discovery to create penicillin, the medicine that today is used routinely to cure infection.

In the 1950s many feared being attacked by the polio virus. Each summer this disease that attacked the nerve cells of the brain and spinal cord crippled thousands of children and adults. *Jonas Salk: Conquering Polio* is the biography of the young medical scientist from the University of Pittsburgh who undertook the challenge of finding a vaccine to conquer this dreaded disease.

Expert groups are formed based on students' interests. The teacher asks, "What qualities do you think a research scientist needs? What are some obstacles they might experience?" Student responses are recorded and saved for future reference.

During Reading   The teacher explains that as students read the selected biography they will apply the REAP technique to trace the events that led to the discovery and its effects on medical science. Students are expected to read at least two chapters each night and to use information from the reading to discuss key questions: What was the problem the scientist wanted to solve? What inventions and or other discoveries helped him or her make the discovery? How was the discovery received by the public? How does the discovery affect our lives today? The teacher moves from group to group facilitating the discussions.

After Reading   When they finish the book, students collaborate to complete the REAP form (Figure 4.7). According to Allen (2004), the REAP strategy will help students extend their comprehension of the text by engaging them in representing the main ideas and author's message in their own words as well as encouraging them to connect the text with their knowledge of science. On an agreed-on date, the members of each expert group return to the base team and use their REAP materials to share information about the subject of their biography.

The teacher brings the class together for an instructional conversation (Antonacci & O'Callaghan, 2006) to help them use the information to form an opinion. The teacher begins the conversation with the questions raised before reading: What qualities did the scientists you read about possess? What obstacles did they experience? What did each person feel was his or her greatest success? Students use text evidence to answer the questions they raised before reading.

The teacher continues, "The State Council of Arts and Science is establishing a Hall of Fame to honor the contributions of people who have made important contributions to medical science. If you could nominate one person for the Medical Discovery Hall of Fame, who would it be?" Each student writes a brief reflection in support of his or her candidate.

Conduct a Writing Workshop

The teacher asks students to share their nominations and explains that they will expand their understanding of medical discoveries by using persuasive writing techniques to

ASSESS LITERACY

The teacher uses the rubric below to assess students' performances during the reading and writing workshops. The teacher analyzes the students' ability to work collaboratively, abstract content from the texts, and share the information developed by the expert groups with the base teams. Students are assessed relative to reading comprehension and cooperative interaction skills.

Criteria	Independent	Proficient	Developing
Contributes to Gathering Information	The student actively participates in gathering information from a variety of resources during reading workshops. (3)	The student is somewhat active in gathering information from a variety of resources during reading workshops. (2)	The student does not actively participate in gathering information from a variety of resources during reading workshops. (0–1)
Contributes Accurate Information	The student provides accurate information and examples and explanations that illustrate insightful understanding of the content. (3)	The student provides basic information with some examples and explanations that illustrate good understanding of content. (2)	The student provides very little information with few examples and explanations, indicating minimal understanding of the content. (0–1)
Discussion Skills and Respect for Teammates	The student consistently and actively contributes information, opinions, and support; values the knowledge and opinions of others; and works hard to help the group reach consensus. (3)	The student generally contributes information, opinions, and support, but may need prompting; shows some sensitivity to the knowledge and opinions of others; and usually considers all views but may argue. (2)	The student either does not contribute or does not allow others to contribute; is insensitive to others and often argues with teammates; does not consider teammates' ideas and opinions; and may impede group's effort. (0–1)
Contributes to the Development of the Group Report	Student uses effective summarizing skills that take into account audience, tone and style, and use of technical vocabulary. (3)	Student uses good summarizing skills that generally account for audience, tone and style, and use of technical vocabulary. (2)	Student does not apply good summarizing skills; may not consider audience, tone and style; or uses technical vocabulary inappropriately. (0–1)
Technology Skills	Student effectively uses PowerPoint to design and implement a report to present information about a biome and integrates graphics that enhance the oral presentation. (3)	Student demonstrates good use of PowerPoint to design and implement a report to present information about a biome and integrates some graphics that enhance the oral presentation. (2)	Student does not use PowerPoint to design and implement a report to present information about a biome; may read all the slides verbatim or not use technology appropriately; or does not integrate graphics to enhance the oral presentation. (0–1)
Oral Presentation Skills	Student effectively presents information orally by making eye contact, speaking loud enough for all to hear, and using a tone and style that engages the audience. (3)	Student generally presents information well by making some eye contact, speaking loud enough for all to hear, and using a tone and style that engages most of the audience. (2)	Student does not present information well; may not make eye contact or speak loud enough for all to hear; or uses a tone and style that does not engage most of the audience. (0–1)

Independent: 13–18

Proficient: 7–12

Developing: 0–6

support their opinions relative to the scientist that they nominated for the Hall of Fame.

Before Writing   The teacher conducts a mini-lesson on persuasive writing. Students share their initial reflections and form writing groups based on their nominations. They use ideas from their reflections to begin to develop a case. Students may use library and Internet resources to find additional information to support their candidate as well as to identify the arguments that could be used to support the other scientists.

During Writing   Students within each group plan the structure for their argument and select the persuasive writing techniques they will employ. They may write one nomination letter as a group, or each student may compose his or her own. The teacher meets with each group to facilitate discussion about logic of the arguments and the content of the supporting evidence. When a draft is completed, students collaborate to assess the strength of the opening and closing statements, the evidence that supports each argument, and the grammar and mechanics.

After Writing   Students revise and edit based on comments from the teacher and peers. They prepare for a panel presentation by creating visuals (pictures, charts, graphs, etc.) to support their nomination letters.

Collaborative Inquiry Across the Curriculum

> **STANDARDS**
>
> **Mathematics Standards**
> 5. Data Analysis and
>   Probability
> 10. Representation

Extension to Mathematics and Technology   Students use print and electronic resources to determine the impact each discovery had on improved health care and increased lifespan. Using statistics from the texts and Internet research, they create graphics to show how each discovery changed health science. Students participate in a simulation activity on how infectious diseases spread. They use a mathematical model to explain the exponential spread of disease in a population.

> **STANDARDS**
>
> **Science Standards**
> Science in Personal and
> Social Perspectives,
> Content Standard F

Extension to Science   Students conduct experiments based on the work of the scientists they read about in the biographies. For example, like William Harvey, they conduct experiments to learn more about the work of the heart. Students feel inside the wrist or throat to find a pulse. Using a watch that can measure seconds, they count the number of heartbeats in one minute before and after physical exercise and explain why the number changes. Students examine the heart of an animal outside and inside, creating diagrams and labeling the parts. They explain how the blood flows and compare the parts and flow of blood to the human heart.

Like Louis Pasteur, students can study microorganisms by growing them in the laboratory on plates containing a solid, nutrient-rich medium (agar plates). After several days, a single bacterial cell will grow into a population of bacterial cells that will be visible to the naked eye. Using this microbial colony, the students test for the presence of microorganisms on their hands and on objects they select.

Like Alexander Fleming, students can examine the way antibiotics work by streaking bacteria onto solid media (agar plates). Each student will have two agar plates—one plate will contain agar medium that has an antibiotic (ampicillin) added to it, and the other plate consists of agar medium without the antibiotic. Students observe whether the addition of an antibiotic to the medium inhibits the growth of microorganisms by

ASSESS LITERACY

When students have completed their nomination letters, the teacher may use the rubric below to evaluate their performance.

Criteria	Independent	Proficient	Developing
Planning	Student carefully plans prior to writing, taking into account all of the components. (3)	Student engages in some planning throughout the writing. (2)	Student shows little or no planning prior to constructing a draft. (0–1)
Drafting	Student engages in the careful construction of a draft developed through planning. (3)	Student develops an adequate draft that demonstrates planning was considered. (2)	Student develops a simple draft that does not account for planning. (0–1)
Revising	Student makes substantial changes in persuasive argument. (3)	Student makes adequate changes in their argument. (2)	Student makes no or very few changes after being prompted. (0–1)
Editing	Student edits carefully for errors a wide array of language conventions. (3)	Student edits many errors and attends to some language conventions. (2)	Student pays little attention to errors and focuses on a single error type, such as spelling. (0–1)
Vocabulary	Student uses many descriptive and complex words from the readings with accuracy. (3)	Student uses some descriptive words with accuracy. (2)	Student uses simple vocabulary and some words are used incorrectly. (0–1)
Spelling	Student's writing exhibits no or few spelling errors. (3)	Student's writing exhibits some spelling errors. (2)	Student's writing exhibits many spelling errors. (0–1)
Capitalization	Student's writing has no or few errors in capitalization. (3)	Student's writing has some errors in capitalization. (2)	Student's writing has many errors in capitalization. (0–1)
Punctuation	Student's writing has no or few punctuation errors. (3)	Student's writing has some punctuation errors. (2)	Student's writing has many punctuation errors. (0–1)
Sentence Structure	Student's writing exhibits a variety of sentence structures used appropriately. (3)	Student's writing has some errors with sentence structure. (2)	Student' writing contains incomplete and simple sentences. (0–1)

Independent: 19–27
Proficient: 10–18
Developing: 0–9

comparing the organisms grown in the presence and absence of the antibiotic. The science teacher finds or creates additional laboratory experiences based on the medical discoveries.

STANDARDS

Social Studies Standards
II. Time, Continuity, and Change
III. People, Places, and Environments

Extension to Social Studies   Students investigate the changes in health care and medicine from prehistoric to modern times. They may focus on medical discoveries, medical inventions, medicines, medical practices, Nobel Prize winners, and so on. They create a timeline that illustrates the changes and how each contributes to the quality of health care today. They discuss the cause–effect relationship between scientific discoveries and medical inventions as well as how religion and politics may have influenced the thinking in a specific time period.

Home–School Connections   Students are encouraged to discuss the issues they are debating with parents. They identify the various views on the issues and how they affect their family and community.

On-Your-Own Activities   Just as in the past, there are many controversies within medicine today, such as stem-cell research, universal health care, bioterrorism, care for the aged, and so on. Students select a controversial topic, research both sides of the issue, and engage in debate.

Critical Literacy

When students have completed the sub-theme, they work in groups of five to create a PowerPoint slideshow for their peers that presents innovations in medical science. Students glean information from their readings in the text set and from other activities in the instructional sequence in order to create presentations.

Collaborative Literacy

Students prepare for a panel presentation that will enable the members of the State Council for Arts and Science to select the candidate(s) that will be admitted to the Hall of Fame. The teacher explains that each group will share their nomination letter and visuals to provide the rationale for recommending the scientist. The teacher may ask high school students and/or science teachers to serve as the panel of judges.

RESOURCE GUIDE: CHILDREN'S LITERATURE REFERENCES AND ACTIVITIES

Primary Grades

Discovery by People

Intrepid Explorers

Aldrin, B. (2005). *Reaching for the moon.* New York: HarperCollins.

Baumsum, A. (2000). *Dragon bones and dinosaur eggs: A photobiography of explorer Roy Chapman Andrews.* Washington, DC: National Geographic Society.

Brown, D. (1995). *Ruth Law thrills a nation.* Boston: Houghton Mifflin.

Brown, D. (2000). *Uncommon traveler: Mary Kingsley in Africa.* Boston: Houghton Mifflin.

Martin, J. B. (2001). *The lamp, the ice, and the boat called Fish.* Illustrated by B. Krommes. New York: Houghton Mifflin.

McNulty, F. (2005). *If you decide to go to the moon.* Illustrated by Steven Kellogg. New York: Scholastic.

Weidt, M. (2002). *Matthew Henson* (History Makers Bio). Minneapolis, MN: Lerner Publications.

■ **Moon Exploration:** Students chart the phases of the moon as they change during the month.

- **Rolled Story:** Students create a rolled story about Mary Kingsley's adventures in Africa and narrate it as a class presentation.
- **Story Boards:** Students illustrate a story board about Roy Chapman Andrews's explorations and discoveries of fossils and dinosaur bones.
- *All About* **Books:** Students write an *All About* book to describe the African American explorer Matthew Henson.
- **Weather Charts:** Students chart the temperature in both Fahrenheit and Celsius scales and compare the two measurements to explain how temperature affected the explorers in *The Lamp, the Ice and the Boat Called Fish.*
- **Creative Writing:** Students research the planned exploration of Mars and write *If You Decide to Go to Mars.*
- **Venn Diagram:** Students compare the character traits of Ruth Law and Mary Kingsley in a Venn diagram.
- **Reporter Stance:** Students write an eyewitness account of one of the explorers from this text set and create a class newspaper.

Discoveries in Science

Adler, D. (1996). *A picture book of Benjamin Franklin.* Illustrated by J. and A. Wallner. New York: Holiday.

Adler, D. (2000). *A picture book of George Washington Carver.* Illustrated by D. Brown. New York: Holiday.

Brown, D. (2004). *Odd boy out: Young Albert Einstein.* New York: Houghton Mifflin.

Fisher, L. (1994). *Marie Curie.* New York: Macmillan.

McCully, E. (2006). *Marvelous Mattie: How Margaret E. Knight became an inventor.* New York: Farrar, Straus & Giroux.

Schanzer, R. (2002). *How Ben Franklin stole the lightning.* New York: HarperCollins.

Sís, P. (1996). *Starry messenger.* New York: Farrar, Straus & Giroux.

- **Role Playing:** Dress as your favorite scientist and have a classmate interview you.
- **Writing:** Research one of the scientists in the text set and create a picture book about them.
- **Creating Icons:** Create a symbol for each scientist and explain your choices.
- **Simulated Journals:** Write a journal entry about things you are curious about and how you might study them.
- **Research:** Research Marie Curie on the Internet and create a poster board that explains her contributions to science.
- **Story Boards:** Create a story board based on the text *Starry Messenger* and narrate the story.
- **Invention:** Write down ways you could improve a tool you use at home or school.

Discovery of Places

Discovering the Silk Road

Gilchrist, C., & Mistry, N. (2005). *Stories from the Silk Road.* Cambridge, MA: Barefoot Books.

Herbert, J. (2001). *Marco Polo for kids.* Chicago: Chicago Review Press.

MacDonald, F. (1998). *Marco Polo: A journey through China.* New York: Franklin Watts.

Majer, J. S., & Fieser, S. (1996). *The Silk Road: 7,000 miles of history.* New York: HarperTrophy.

- **Map Skills:** Students outline the Silk Road on a map of China.
- **Puppets:** Students create a Marco Polo puppet and then tell his story.
- **The Market Place:** Students draw a symbol for some of the goods traded on the Silk Road.
- **Diorama:** Students create a diorama that illustrates the people of the Silk Road and the goods traded.
- **Trade Today:** Students list some of the goods in their homes that came from other countries.

Discovering the New World

Adler, D., & Wallner, J. (1992). *A picture book of Christopher Columbus.* New York: Holiday.

Fritz, J. (1997). *Where do you think you're going, Christopher Columbus?* New York: Putnam.

Marzollo, J. (1991). *In 1492.* New York: Scholastic.

Sís, P. (1996). *Follow the dream.* New York: Dragonfly Books.

Yolen, J. (1996). *Encounter.* Illustrated by David Shannon. New York: Voyager Books.

- **My Book:** Students create a picture book illustrating the life of Christopher Columbus.
- **Reader's Theatre:** Students write a script for reader's theatre and reenact the story *Encounter.*
- **Simulated Journal:** Students write a diary entry as a native of the land Columbus discovered.
- **Timeline:** Students create a timeline to chart Columbus's voyage.
- **Making News:** Students present a newscast reporting Columbus's voyage and include voices of the native people as written in *Encounter.*

Discovery in Time

Discovering Ancient Egypt

Andronik, C. (2001). *Hatshepshut, his majesty, herself.* Illustrated by J. D. Fiedler. New York: Antheneum.

Cobblestone. (2007). *If I were a kid in ancient Egypt.* Peru, IL: Cricket Publishers.

Cole, J., & Degen, B. (2003). *Ms. Frizzle's adventures: Ancient Egypt*. Illustrated by B. Degen. New York: Scholastic.

Holub, J. (2002). *Valley of the golden mummies*. New York: Grosset Publishers.

Putnam, J. (2003). *The ancient Egypt pop-up book: In association with the British Museum*. New York: Universe Publishers.

- **Diorama:** Students create a diorama that depicts life in ancient Egypt.
- **Famous Pharaohs:** Students create a poster about famous Egyptian pharaohs.
- **Simulated Journals:** Students write about daily life in ancient Egypt.
- **Creative Writing:** Students illustrate their own *If I Were a Kid in Ancient Egypt* books and present them to the class.
- **Geography:** Students outline Egypt on a map and highlight the Nile River.

Discovering Our Past

Brown, D. (2003). *Rare treasure: Mary Anning and her remarkable discoveries*. Boston: Houghton Mifflin.

Cole, J. (1997). *The Magic School Bus shows and tells: A book about archaeology*. New York: Scholastic.

Duke, K. (1997). *Archaeologists dig for clues*. New York: HarperCollins.

McIntosh, J. (2000). *Eyewitness: Archaeology*. New York: DK Publishing.

Osborne, M., Boyce, N., & Murdocca, S. (2004). *Magic tree house research guide: Ancient Greece and the Olympics*. New York: DK Publishing.

- **Exploring:** Students create a poster that shows the tools of an archaeologist.
- **Diorama:** Students construct a diorama of ancient Greece or Rome.
- **Report Writing:** Students write about the Olympics in ancient Greece.
- **Story Boards:** Students illustrate the story of Mary Anning in a story board and narrate it for the class.
- **Fact Finding:** Students research the ichthyosaur, discovered by Mary Anning, and make a drawing of it.

Intermediate Grades

Discovery in Time

Discover the Ancient Aztecs

Fisher, L. (1988). *Pyramid of the sun, pyramid of the moon*. New York: Macmillan.

Gregor, C. (1994). *The fifth and final sun: An ancient Aztec myth of the sun's origin*. Boston: Houghton Mifflin.

Hull, R. (1998). *The ancient world: The Aztecs*. Austin, TX: Raintree Steck-Vaughn.

Kimmel, E. (2000). *Two mountains: An Aztec legend*. Illustrated by Leonard Everett Fisher. New York: Holiday.

McDermott, G. (1997). *Musicians of the sun*. New York: Simon & Schuster.

Morgan, N. (1998). *Technology in the time of the Aztecs*. Austin, TX: Raintree Steck-Vaughn.

Nicholson, R., & Watts, C. (1994). *Journey into civilization: The Aztecs*. New York: Chelsea Juniors.

Odijk, P. (1989). *The Aztecs*. Englewood Cliffs, NJ: Silver Burdett.

Sonneborn, L. (2005). *People of the ancient world: The ancient Aztecs*. New York: Franklin Watts.

Steele, P. (2000). *The Aztec news*. Cambridge, MA: Candlewick Press.

Tanaka, S. (1998). *Lost temple of the Aztecs*. Illustrated by Greg Ruhl. Toronto, ON: Madison Press.

Wood, T. (1992). *The Aztecs*. New York: Viking.

- **Daily Activities—Theirs and Ours:** The culture and daily lives of the Aztec people are similar to ours. Have small groups of children take one cultural activity (language, music and dance, houses, occupations, education, games, food and cooking, religion and worship, health and healing, and weapons and warriors) and compare the Aztec culture and way of living to their own.
- **The Ancient Aztec Gods:** An important part of the Aztec culture was religion, which included many different gods that were related to the Aztec way of life. Have children select one god and describe the role that it played in the lives of the Aztec people.
- **The Market Place Is a Mall:** The market place, central to the lives of the Aztec people, involved more than just buying and selling by 60,000 people. Students draw a map of the Tlatelolco Market indicating the daily activities, and they draw a map of their own mall that includes activities. Compare the maps and show how daily activities from both cultures are important to people's lives.
- **A Pyramid for the Aztec:** After reading *Pyramid of the Sun, Pyramid of the Moon* by Leonard Everett Fisher, students construct a pyramid that might be used by the Aztec people.
- **An Aztec Newspaper:** Students read *The Aztec News* by Phillip Steele and submit an article for publication. The article may represent a piece of news such as an invasion by another civilization, a religious ceremony, games or other events, an event in the market, and so on. Put the articles together to create a new version of an Aztec newspaper.
- **Picture It:** The Aztec people used pictures to tell their stories. With a similar art style, students use pictures to tell their news stories.

- **Map It:** Students draw a map of North America, Central America, and South America and indicate the Aztec Empire. They may show where they live as well.
- **Timeline:** Create a timeline of the history of the Valley of Mexico (150 B.C.–A.D. 1521) and place the Aztec Empire and its important events on the timeline.

Discover the Ancient Incas

Kurtz, J. (1996). *Miro in the kingdom of the sun.* Illustrated by David Framton. Boston: Houghton Mifflin.

Mann, E. (2000). *Macchu Picchu: The story of the amazing Inkas and their city in the clouds.* Illustrated by Amy Crehore. New York: Mikaya Press.

Marrin, A. (1986). *Inca & Spaniard (Pizarro & the conquest of Peru).* New York: Atheneum.

Nicholson, R. (2000). *Aztecs and Incas: A guide to precolonized Americas in 1504.* New York: Kingfisher.

Odijk, P. (1989). *The Incas.* Englewood Cliffs, NJ: Silver Burdett.

Pitkänen, M., Lehtinen, R., & Nurmi, K. E. (1991). *The grandchildren of the Incas.* Minneapolis, MN: Carolrhoda.

Steele, P. (2000). *Step into the . . . Inca world.* London: Lorenz Books.

Wood, T. (1996). *The Incas.* New York: Viking.

- **An Inca Timeline:** Before reading the related literature, the teacher creates a timeline of the Inca Empire. As the students read books on the Inca people and civilization, they write the facts and dates that they have learned on their timelines.
- **Record Keeping:** Students have read that the Incas had developed a way to record numerical information. *Quip,* which means *knot* in Quechua, their native language, was used to keep track of numbers. The different colors of string stood for different products, the knots indicated numbers, and numbers of string that were used corresponded to the place value in a number. Students may use the Mayan system to represent their age, birth year, weight, or other numbers.
- **Academic Journals:** Academic journals provide students with a way to develop their academic vocabulary. As students read, they are directed to take notes on new words that relate to the study of the Inca culture. They use their readings to define the word, including a picture.
- **Possible Sentences:** Using the key words from their academic vocabulary, students create sentences that represent the meaning of the word.
- **Word Sorts:** Students record vocabulary words related to their study of the Inca civilization on small index cards. They may sort them into groups and explain how words in each set are related.

Discover the Ancient Maya

Ashabranner, B. (1986). *Children of the Maya: A Guatamalan Indian odyssey.* Photographs by Paul Conklin. New York: Dodd.

Crosher, J. (1998). *Technology in the time of Maya.* Austin, TX: Raintree Steck-Vaughn.

Day, N. (2001). *Your travel guide to ancient Mayan civilization.* Minneapolis, MN: Runestone.

Deedrick, T. (2001). *Ancient civilizations: Maya.* Austin, TX: Raintree Steck-Vaughn.

Gerson, M. (1995). *People of corn: A Mayan story.* Illustrated by Carla Golembe. New York: Little, Brown.

Greene, J. (1992). *The Maya.* New York: Franklin Watts.

Kirkpatrick, N. (2003). *Understanding the people of the past: The Maya.* Chicago: Heinemann.

Lourie, P. (2001). *The mystery of the Maya: Uncovering the lost city of Palenque.* Honesdale, PA: Boyds Mills Press.

Netzley, P. (2002). *World history series: Maya civilization.* San Diego, CA: Lucent.

Perl, L. (2005). *People of the ancient world: The ancient Maya.* New York: Scholastic.

Wisniewski, D. (1991). *Rain player.* New York: Clarion.

- **Numbers and Keeping Time:** From their readings, students will learn about number systems and calendars of the ancient world. Maya as well as Aztec peoples developed sophisticated number systems that were different from ours. First, direct students to look at the ancient Maya number system and try a few math problems. Then demonstrate how the Maya counted days and years and explore the Aztec calendar system with its special symbols for particular days, months, and years. Finally, students study different images from the Sun Stone, a famous Aztec artifact, and reproduce their own.
- **Tell Me a Story:** Students have learned how the ancient civilizations that did not have an alphabetic system to write and record their stories used pictures or hieroglyphics to represent events. The Maya recorded their stories in manuscripts called *codices* using a series of pictures called *glyphs* rather than words. Students are directed to write a story about the Maya people, using their knowledge of the culture, history, and geography of the Mayan civilization. They then translate their stories by using glyphs or sets of pictures that tell their story. Students may share their stories using their codices and then add them to the set of artifacts that they have created.
- **Asking Questions, Finding Answers:** Students assume the role of archaeologists, working together to explore the ancient cultures and to understand how archaeologists learned about an ancient culture. Each small group of two or three students receives a picture of an artifact

from the Mayan culture. They brainstorm as many as 10 questions about the artifact. Using what they already know about the culture, they begin to answer the questions using pictures as artifacts.

- **Mapping Maya Cities and Settlements:** Students create a map that represents the cities and settlements throughout the ancient Maya civilization.
- **Land of the Ancient Maya:** Students compare and contrast the three landforms where the Maya settled: lowlands, highlands, and Pacific coastal plains. Using a diagram, they show the similarities and differences of the three regions.

Discovery of Place

Discover the Frozen World of the Arctic

Barton, B. (2003). *The bear says north: Tales from northern lands.* Illustrated by Mirnia Marton. Toronto: Groundwood Books.

Beattie, O., & Geiger, J. (1992). *Buried in ice: The mystery of a lost Arctic expedition.* New York: Scholastic.

Byles, M. (2000). *Life in the polar lands.* Lanham, MD: Two-Can Publishers.

Curlee, L. (1998). *Into the ice: The story of Arctic exploration.* Boston: Houghton Mifflin.

Dobcovich, L. (1999). *The polar bear sun: An Inuit tale.* New York: Clarion.

Green, J. (2000). *Step into the Arctic world.* Lanham, MD: Lorenz Books.

Himmelman, J. (2003). *Pipaluk and the whales.* Washington, DC: National Geographic Books for Children.

Matthews, D., & Ovsyanikov, N. (1995). *Arctic foxes.* Illustrated by Dan Guravich. New York: Simon & Schuster.

Miller, D. (2003). *Arctic lights, Arctic nights.* Illustrated by Jon Van Zyle. New York: Walker Books for Young Readers.

Norman, H. (1997). *The girl who dreamed only geese.* Illustrated by Leo and Diane Dillon. San Diego, CA: Gulliver Books.

Orr, T. (2004). *Life in the Arctic: Ecosystems.* Farmington Hills, MI: Kid Haven Press.

Silver, D. (1997). *Arctic tundra.* Illustrated by Patricia Wynne. New York: McGraw Hill.

Somervill, B. (2004*). Animal survivors of the Arctic.* Danbury, CT: Franklin Watts.

Stamper, J. (2003). *Polar bear patrol.* Illustrated by Steve Haefele. New York: Scholastic.

Taulbert, C. (2002). *Little cliff and cold place.* New York: Penguin Putnam.

- **Postcards from the Arctic:** Students take an imaginary trip to the Arctic and create postcards to send to their classmates and friends. Their postcards describe the Arctic region, its climate, the people, the animals, and so on.
- **Exit Slips:** Exit slips provide students with the opportunity to think and write about what they have learned and offer the teacher a way to assess student learning. Students simply respond to the teacher's prompt, taking three to four minutes to write their ideas on a slip of paper. One prompt may be for students to write five new facts they have learned about the people who live in the Arctic region.
- **Double-Entry Journal:** This activity is designed to help students process and think about the information they have learned. Students' journals are divided into two columns. In the first column they write notes on their reading, and in the second they reflect on the information, respond to it, or ask a question.
- **Trading Cards:** Students make a set of polar bear trading cards that include the picture of a polar bear on one side and interesting facts about the animal, such as their habitat, how their bodies are more suited for swimming in cold water than walking, or the importance of ice to polar bears.
- **Commercial:** Students produce a commercial for the classroom that emphasizes how polar bears are threatened by the changing environment and what they can do to help.
- **Study Boards:** Study boards are similar to story boards that students use to tell a story through drawing and writing. Students select one aspect of the Arctic lands, such as the people and their language, occupations, the climate, and so on. Students present their information on large sheets of paper through drawings and writings that are displayed around the room.

Discover the Frozen World of Antarctica

Bramwell, M. (1998). *Polar exploration: Journeys to the Arctic and Antarctic.* Illustrated by Marje Crosby-Fairall and Ann Winterbotham. New York: DK Publishing.

Bredeson, C. (2003). *After the last dog died: The true-life, hair-raising adventure of Douglas Mawson and his 1911–1914 Antarctic expedition.* Washington, DC: National Geographic.

Cerullo, M. (2005). *Life under ice.* Illustrated by B. Curtainger. Toronto: Tillsbury House.

Conlan, K. E., & Conlan, K. (2002). *Under the ice.* Toronto: Kids Can Press.

Dewey, J. (2001). *Antarctic journal: Four months at the bottom of the world.* New York: HarperCollins.

Gibbons, G. (1998). *Penguins.* New York: Holiday.

Graham, A. (2004). *Antarctica's land, people, and wildlife: A myreportlinks.com book.* Berkeley Heights, NJ: Enslow.

Guiberson, B. (2001). *The emperor lays an egg.* Illustrated by Joan Paley. New York: Henry Holt.

Hackwell, W. (1991). *Desert of ice: Life and work in Antarctica.* New York: Scribner's.

Hastings, D. (1997). *Penguins: A portrait of the animal world.* New York: Smithmark.

Hooper, M., & Robertson, M. P. (2001). *The endurance: Shackleton's perilous expedition in Antarctica.* New York: Abbevile Kids.

Johnson, R. (1995). *Science on the ice: An Antarctic journal.* Minneapolis, MN: Lerner.

Kaehler, W. (1989). *Penguins.* San Francisco: Chronicle.

Kimmel, E. C. (1999). *Ice story: Shackleton's lost expedition.* New York: Clarion.

Marcovitz, H. (2002). *Explorers of new worlds: Sir Ernest Shackleton and the struggle against Antarctica.* Philadelphia: Chelsea House Publishers.

Markle, S. (1996). *Pioneering frozen worlds.* New York: Atheneum.

Markle, S. (2005). *A mother's journey.* Illustrated by Alan Marks. Watertown, MA: Charlesbridge.

McCurdy, M. (2002). *Trapped by the ice! Shackleton's amazing Antarctic adventure.* New York: Walker Books for Young Readers.

Myers, W. D. (2004). *Antarctica: Journeys to the South Pole.* New York: Scholastic.

Ollason, R. (1995). *Penguin parade.* Minneapolis, MN: Lerner.

Pringle, Laurence. (1992). *Antarctica: The last unspoiled continent.* New York: Simon & Schuster.

Rau, D. M. (2004). *Geography of the world: Antarctica.* Chanhassen, MN: The Child's World.

Resnick, J. (1997). *Eyes on nature: Penguins.* Chicago: Kidsbooks.

Sierra, J. (1998). *Antarctic antics: A book of penguin poems.* Illustrated by Jose Aruego and Ariane Dewey. New York: Gulliver.

Stone, L. (1998). *Penguins.* Minneapolis, MN: Lerner.

Webb, S. (2000). *My season with penguins: An Antarctic journal.* Boston: Houghton Mifflin.

■ **Wonder Journals:** Students keep wonder journals, or nonfiction notebooks where they write about their thinking, record ideas and thoughts they have learned, ask questions about information, develop ideas for projects, draw diagrams and pictures, and list interests on a specific aspect of a topic to explore.

■ **Travel Agents:** Students develop brochures for vacationing or joining a team of scientists traveling to Antarctica. Their brochures provide information on Antarctica in the form of persuasive writing, intended to convince their classmates to take a trip to Antarctica.

■ **Word Walls:** Students keep a word wall on academic vocabulary that that they have learned from reading about Antarctica.

■ **Word Webs:** Students engage in making word clusters on vocabulary related to their study of Antarctica.

■ **Venn Diagrams:** Using Venn diagrams, students compare and contrast the first explorations to Antarctica with the current ones.

■ *All About* **Books:** As a culmination of studying Antarctica, students work in small groups and create an *All About* book. They consider their readership and may create a picture storybook for students in kindergarten or first grade and have a shared reading session, author talk, or book talk with their audience. They may also write the book for their own classroom library.

■ **Book Boxes:** Students learn about the ecosystem of the polar desert Antarctica. Using one of the books they have read such as *Desert of Ice: Life and Work in Antarctica* by W. John Hackwell, students create a book box. They decorate the outside of the box so that it represents the ecosystem of the ice-cold desert and place objects inside to represent the various aspects of the environment and its effects on life in Antarctica.

Discover by People

Discover Poets' Worlds

Borland, K., & Speicher, H. (2005). *Phillis Wheatley: Young revolutionary poet.* Carmel, IN: Patria Press.

Crocitto, F. (Ed.). (2000). *New suns will arise: From the journals of Henry David Thoreau.* Photographs by John Dugdale. New York: Hyperion.

Gillooly, E. (Ed.). (2000). *Poetry for young people: Rudyard Kipling.* Illustrated by Jim Sharpe. New York: Sterling.

Gollub, M. (1998). *Cool melons—turn to frogs! The life and poems of Issa.* Illustrated by Kazuko G. Stone. New York: Lee and Low.

Gregson, S. (2002). *Let freedom ring! Phillis Wheatley.* Mankato, MN: Bridgestone Books.

Hopkins, L. (1995). *Been to yesterdays: Poems of a life.* Illustrated by Charlene Rendeiro. Honesdale, PA: Wordsong.

Kerley, B. (2004). *Walt Whitman: Words for America.* Illustrated by Brian Selznick. New York: Scholastic.

Levin, J. (Ed.). (1997). *Poetry for young people: Walt Whitman.* Illustrated by Jim Burke. New York: Sterling.

Media, T. (2002). *Love to Langston.* Illustrated by Christie R. Gregory. New York: Lee and Low.

Meltzer, M. (2002). *Walt Whitman: A biography.* Brookfield, CT: Twenty-First Century Books.

Niven, P. (2003). *Carl Sandburg: Adventures of a poet.* Illustrated by Marc Nadel. New York: Harcourt.

Pettit, J. (1996). *Maya Angelou: Journey of the heart.* New York: Lodestar.

Schnur, S. (2002). *Henry David's House: Henry David Thoreau.* Illustrated by Peter Fiore. Watertown, MA: Charlesbridge.

Winter, J. (2002). *Emily Dickinson's letters to the world.* New York: Farrar, Straus & Giroux.

- **Choral Reading:** Small groups of students select a favorite poem to present to the class through choral reading.

- **Sketch to Stretch:** After the teacher reads aloud the works of a poet, students respond to one poem through sketch to stretch activity by drawing their responses to the poem and sharing them with the class.

- **Tea Party:** After the students select their favorite poems, the teacher reproduces them, places them on heavy paper, and laminates them. Students practice reading their poem to themselves several times, then pair and share, and finally read their poem to the class. Their favorite poems are then displayed around the room so that other students may read them.

- **Story Theater:** A small group of students present a poem using the story theater activity. As the narrator reads the poem, a group of students dramatize it by pantomiming the selection.

- **Class Book of Poems:** Students write a poem and contribute it to the class book of poems. Poems may be themed around a topic of study.

- **Research on Poets:** Students research their favorite poets and read as many poems from their works as they can. They share their research and their favorite poems with the class.

Discover the Authors' Worlds

Anderson, W. (1992). *A biography: Laura Ingalls Wilder.* New York: HarperCollins.

Carew-Miller, A. (2003). *Mark Twain: Great American fiction writer.* Illustrated by Andrea Di Gennaro. Philadelphia: Mason Crest.

Christelow, E. (1995). *What do authors do?* New York: Clarion.

Cole, J. (1996). *On the bus with Joanna Cole.* Illustrated by Wendy Saul. Portsmouth, NH: Heinemann.

Coren, M. (1999). *The man who created Narnia.* Grand Rapids, MI: Eerdmans.

Darrow, S. (2003). *Through the tempests dark and wild: A story of Mary Shelley, creator of Frankenstein.* Illustrated by Angela Barrett. Cambridge, MA: Candlewick.

de Paola, T. (1999). *26 Fairmount Avenue.* New York: Putnam.

Rosen, M. (2001). *Shakespeare: His work and his world.* Illustrated by Robert Ingpen. Cambridge, MA: Candlewick.

Rosen, M. (2005). *Dickens: His work and his world.* Illustrated by Robert Ingpen. Cambridge, MA: Candlewick.

Ross, S. (1999). *Mark Twain and Huckleberry Finn.* Illustrated by Ronald Himler. New York: Viking.

Stanley, D., & Vennema, P. (1993). *Charles Dickens: The man who had great expectations.* Illustrated by Diane Stanley. New York: Morrow Junior Books.

- **Autobiographies—My Life as an Author:** Students read biographies of authors and learn the relationship between a writer's life and his or her work. Students will write about their own lives as writers, including their families, experiences, interests, and the stories they have written and plan to write.

- **Cubing:** Students use the cubing activity to represent the six dimensions of their favorite authors' lives.

- **Author Study:** After reading about the lives of a number of authors, students engage in an author study by reading several of the writer's works. Students respond to the author's stories through discussions as well as journal reflections.

- **Book Talks:** Students present a five-minute book talk on their favorite author.

- **Open-Mind Portraits:** Students select an author and create an open-mind portrait. They draw a portrait of their author on one side and create pictures to represent their author's life, works, interests, and feelings, on the side of the portrait.

- **Author Interview:** Students develop questions and set up interviews for their favorite authors. Within pairs, one student becomes the interviewer, the other is the author being interviewed. After the interview, the students switch roles.

- **Book Collage:** After reading several books by one author, students collect pictures from magazines, headlines from newspapers, and other forms of visuals that represent the author's works. Using the pictures and headlines, students create a collage of the books written by the selected author and present it to the class.

Middle Grades

Discovery by People

Great Minds of Medical Science

Dietz, D. (1960). *All about great medical discoveries.* New York: Random House.

Dowswell, P. (2002). *Great inventions: Medicine.* Chicago: Heinemann.

Garcia, K. (2002). *Wilhelm Roentgen and the discovery of x-rays.* Hockessin, DE: Mitchell Lane Publishers.

Gates, P. (1998). *The history news: Medicine.* Cambridge, MA: Candlewick.

Kjelle, M. M. (2005). *Louis Pasteur: Fighter against contagious disease.* Hockessin, DE: Mitchell Lane Publishers.

MacLeod, E. (2004). *Marie Curie: A brilliant life.* Tonawanda, NY: Kids Can Press.

Marrin, A. (2002). *Dr. Jenner and the speckled monster: The search for the smallpox vaccine.* New York: Dutton.

McClafferty, C. K. (2001). *The head bone's connected to the neck bone: The weird, wacky and wonderful x-ray.* New York: Farrar, Straus & Giroux.

McPherson, S. S. (2001). *Jonas Salk: Conquering polio.* Minneapolis, MN: Lerner Publications.

Newfield, M. (1991). *The life of Louis Pasteur.* Minneapolis, MN: Twenty-First Century Books.

Poynter, M. (1994). *Marie Curie: Discoverer of radium.* Hillside, NJ: Enslow Publishers.

Tocci, S. (2002). *Alexander Fleming: The man who discovered penicillin.* Springfield, NJ: Enslow Publishers.

Woods, M., & Woods, M. B. (2000). *Ancient medicine: From sorcery to surgery.* Minneapolis, MN: Lerner Publishing.

Yount, L. (1994). *William Harvey: Discoverer of how blood circulates.* Springfield, NJ: Enslow Publishers.

- **Cooperative Learning Jigsaw:** Students work in cooperative learning jigsaw groups to learn about the work of a medical scientist who made an important discovery, using the REAP strategy to trace the events that led to the discovery and its impact on medical science.
- **Instructional Conversation:** Students participate in an instructional conversation to share ideas about the great minds of medical science.
- **Hall of Fame:** Students select a scientist to nominate for a Hall of Fame and use persuasive writing techniques to write a nomination letter.

Explorers Discover New Lands

Aronson, M. (2000). *Sir Walter Raleigh and the quest for El Dorado.* New York: Clarion.

Blumberg, R. (1991). *The remarkable voyages of Captain Cook.* New York: Bradbury Press.

Goodman, J. E. (2001). *A long and uncertain journey: The 27,000 mile voyage of Vasco daGama.* New York: Mikaya Press.

Marrin, A. (1995). *The sea king: Sir Francis Drake and his times.* New York: Atheneum.

Meltzer, M. (2001). *Ferdinand Magellan: First to sail around the world.* New York: Benchmark Books.

Saffer, B. (2001). *Henry Hudson: Ill-fated explorer of North America's coast.* Philadelphia: Chelsea House.

- **Exploration:** Students create a graphic to illustrate the new and unusual objects, customs, and ideas the explorers learned from the inhabitants of new lands and brought back to their homelands.
- **Reporting Theatre:** Students dress as fifteenth-century explorers and tell why they should be on the cover of a magazine entitled *Explorer of the Century.* They describe the geography, politics, and culture of the time that led to each discovery and its impact on world geography and history.
- **Navigation:** Students investigate the concept of latitude and how it influenced fifteenth century navigation and map making, using the website www.ruf.rice.edu.

Discovery of Place

Discovering the Middle East

Ellis, D. (2004). *Three wishes: Palestinian and Israeli children speak.* Toronto: Groundwood Books.

Marston, E. (2005). *Figs and fate: Stories about growing up in the Arab world today.* New York: George Braziller.

Nye, N. S. (1997). *Habibi.* New York: Simon & Schuster.

Stamaty, M. A. (2004). *Alia's mission: Saving the books of Iraq.* New York: Knopf.

Tal-Windawi. (2004). *Thura's diary.* New York: Viking.

Zwier, L. J., & Weltig, M. S. (2004). *The Persian Gulf and Iraqi Wars.* Minneapolis, MN: Lerner Publishing.

- **Open-Mind Portrait:** After reading one of the short stories or novels, students create an open-mind portrait (Tompkins, 2009) of the main character to explain the character's thinking at pivotal points in the story. They then write a reflection to describe what was discovered about life in the Middle East.
- **Venn Diagram:** Students create a Venn diagram to show how a middle school student's life in the United States is similar to and different from life in the Middle East.
- **Instructional Conversation:** Students engage in an instructional conversation (Antonacci & O'Callaghan, 2006) that begins with the focus question: If so many people living in the Middle East wish to see an end to the fighting, why is a peaceful solution so difficult to attain?

Discovering Africa

Gordon, S. (1990). *The middle of somewhere: A story of South Africa.* New York: Orchard Books.

Hansen, J. (2005). *African princesses: The amazing lives of Africa's royal women.* New York: Hyperion.

Lekuton, J. L., & Viola, H. (2004). *Facing the lion: Growing up Maasi on the African savanna.* Washington, DC: National Geographic Society.

Levitin, S. (2001). *Dream freedom.* New York: Harcourt Brace.

Naidoo, B. (1986). *Journey to Jo'berg: A south African story.* New York: Lippincott.

Naidoo, B. (1989). *Chain of fire*. New York: Lippincott.

Naidoo, B. (2004). *Out of bounds: Seven stories of conflict and hope*. New York: HarperCollins.

- **Map It!** Students draw a map of Africa, designing a key to illustrate the geographic and cultural features, and explain how and why geography may have contributed to the variety of cultures.
- **Role play:** Students role play a conversation between two characters in one of the novels they have read—for example, Nelson Mandela and a political leader. They express each person's views on apartheid.
- **Journal Reflection:** After reading one of the novels or short stories, students write a reflection about how the story led to discoveries about life in an African country.
- **I-Charts:** Using I-charts (Allen, 2004), students pose research questions and collect information about a country in Africa. Students use the information to plan and organize a collaborative report.

Discovery in Time

Discovering Prehistoric People

Arnold, C. (1997). *Stone age farmers beside the sea: Scotland's village of Skara Brae*. New York: Houghton Mifflin.

Brooks, P. (2000). *Prehistoric peoples: Discover the long-ago world of the first humans*. London: Anness Publishing.

Carvalho De Magalhaes, R., & Carvalho, R. (2000). *The art and civilization of prehistory*. New York: Peter Bedrick Books.

Cooper, M. (2001). *Exploring the ice age*. New York: Simon & Schuster.

King, D. (2005). *Eyewitness Books: Early Humans*. London: Dorling Kindersley.

Turner, A. W. (1987). *Time of the bison*. New York: Macmillan.

- **Process–Cause Organizer:** Students create a series of process–cause graphic organizers to illustrate how changes in climate led to changes in food production

from hunting and gathering (Old Stone Age) to fishing (Middle Stone Age) to farming (New Stone Age) societies.

- **Pictographs:** Students create pictographs to illustrate the changes in technology from the Old to the New Stone Age.
- **Data Chart:** Students generate a set of questions to guide investigation of the prehistoric period. Students and teacher develop the structure for a data chart (Antonacci & O'Callaghan, 2006) based on sub-topics students are interested in exploring and the sources of information they will use.

Discovering Ancient Civilizations

Barter, J. (2005). *The ancient Persians*. San Diego, CA: Lucent.

Bingham, J. (2006). *Ancient Romans*. Milwaukee, WI: World Almanac Library.

Deem, J. M. (2005). *Bodies from the ash: Life and death in ancient Pompeii*. New York: Houghton Mifflin.

Hynson, C. (2006). *Ancient Greece*. Milwaukee, WI: World Almanac Library.

Hynson, C. (2006). *Mesopotamia*. Milwaukee, WI: World Almanac Library.

Markle, S. (2005). *Outside and inside mummies*. New York: Walker & Co.

Pemberton, D. (2001). *Egyptian mummies: People from the past*. New York: Harcourt Children's Books.

- **Archaeology Panel:** Pretending to be archaeologists, students use a book that contains pictures of the artifacts from a specific group of ancient people and indicate to a panel of historians their opinion about whether the people who produced these artifacts were civilized.
- **Touring Ancient Worlds:** Students dress in the clothing of a specific group of ancient people, create an audiovisual tour of their city, and tell why they are proud to be a citizen.
- **Pictograph:** Students create a pictograph to illustrate the contributions of a specific civilization to world culture.

PROFESSIONAL REFERENCES

Allen, J. (2004). *Tools for teaching content literacy*. Portland, ME: Stenhouse.

Antonacci, P. A., & O'Callaghan, C. M. (2006). *A handbook for literacy instructional & assessment strategies, K–8*. Boston: Allyn & Bacon.

Galda, L., & Cullinan, B. E. (2002). *Literature and the child*. Belmont, CA: Wadsworth Thomson Learning.

National Council of Teachers of English & International Reading Association. (1996). *Standards for the English language arts*. Newark, DE: Authors. Available at www.ncte.org/standards

National Committee on Science Education Standards and Assessment & National Research Council. (1995). *National science education standards*. Washington, DC: National Academies Press. Available at www.nap.edu/catalog.php?record_id=4962

Tompkins, G. E. (2009). *Literacy strategies: Step by step* (3rd ed.). Boston: Allyn & Bacon.

Connections

5

I is estimated that the coming decades will bring increasing changes to our climate as Earth adjusts to global warming (BBC News, 2007). It is already apparent that our country is no longer isolated environmentally from carbon gases emitted on other continents. People worldwide have Connections to one another in searching for solutions to this global problem. To save our planet, we must be aware of our carbon footprint and endeavor to provide good stewardship of our environment for the next generation.

The National Commission on Science Education Standards and Assessment, along with the National Research Council, highlighted the importance of studying the environment in the *National Science Education Standards* (1995). Content Standard C: Life Science requires students to investigate organisms and ecosystems as they use the scientific method to generate solutions to our environmental problems. The instructional samplers in this chapter revolve around the idea of stewardship of planet Earth. Students in the primary and middle school grades will explore the concept of Ecosystems and how changes in the fragile cycle of producers and consumers can affect all of us. Intermediate grade students will also focus on Natural Connections as they read and discover the world of monarch butterflies and research how humankind can preserve their delicate life cycle. As students across the grades study the fragile balance that sustains life

on Earth, they will also acquire the skills necessary to preserve it.

In Historical Connections, primary grade students will explore texts that discuss the quest for democracy that crosses the boundaries of time and culture. Intermediate grade students will focus on the Underground Railroad and how compassionate citizens from the North and South united to help slaves escape. Middle grade students will examine human rights issues as they read texts that highlight how we are connected in our quest for justice.

The final sub-theme, Global Connections, attempts to illustrate how our similarities often outnumber our differences across the planet. Primary grade students will examine Cinderella stories from different cultures and discuss their similar features. Intermediate grade students will explore immigration and how recent immigrants connect to their new homeland. The theme of immigration is continued in the middle school grades as students discuss texts that focus on the immigrant experience.

As students across the grades explore the theme of Connections, they will read, write, and discuss the myriad ways we are linked to one another and our environment. The fragile thread that binds us all is increasingly strained as cultures and countries clash due to misunderstandings. As students focus on the text sets in these sub-themes, they will reflect on their connections to their families, neighborhoods, country, and the world.

FROM SEED TO PLANT

Text Set

The Tiny Seed
The Reason for a Flower
From Seed to Plant
Tree for All Seasons
How Do Apples Grow?

Outcomes

• Dissect a flower and label its parts.

• Chart plant growth from seed.

• Sequence growth from flower to fruit.

CINDERELLA STORIES AROUND THE WORLD

Text Set

Mufaro's Beautiful Daughters
The Rough-Face Girl
Fair, Brown & Trembling: An Irish
 Cinderella Story
The Persian Cinderella

Outcomes

• Compare and contrast elements of Cinderella stories from around the globe.

• Write a version of the Cinderella story to fit your culture.

• Share responses to text set through a tea party.

ECOSYSTEMS

Text Set

The Great Kapok Tree
The Lorax
Brilliant Bees
On the Way to the Beach
Antarctic Ice
Will We Miss Them? Endangered Species
Horseshoe Crabs and Shorebirds
Guide to the Oceans
Panda Bear, Panda Bear, What Do You See?

Outcomes

• Research waterways and outline them on map of the region.

• Create a photo journal of how community changes through the seasons.

• Log recycling for one week.

Natural Connections

Global Connections

MYTHS FROM AROUND THE WORLD

Text Set

The Origin of Life on Earth: An African
 Creation Myth
The Woman Who Fell from the Sky: The
 Iroquois Story of Creation
The Star Bearer: A Creation Myth from
 Ancient Egypt
How the Whale Became and Other Stories

Outcomes

• Create a matrix depicting the characteristics of creation myths.

• Illustrate one of the creation myths in a rolled story format.

• Role play and write the script for one of the creation myths.

CONNECTIONS

Historical Connections

TRADING AROUND THE WORLD

Text Set

We're Riding on a Caravan
Ghenghis Khan
Stories from the Silk Road
Supermarket
Caravan to America
Life in a Greek Trading Post
The Silk Route: 7,000 Miles of History

Outcomes

• Retell the story *We're Riding on a Caravan* through Reader's Theatre.

• Research goods the U.S. trades with other nations and create a wall chart.

• Record food log and where items came from.

THE QUEST FOR DEMOCRACY

Text Set

Gandhi
A Picture Book of Martin Luther King, Jr.
If a Bus Could Talk: The Story of Rosa Parks
Susan B. Anthony
Harriet Tubman
Harvesting Hope: The Story of Cesar Chavez

Outcomes

• Compare and contrast lives of two historical figures.

• Write and illustrate a picture biography of one of the historical figures.

• Create a class experience story about democracy in our lives.

■ Primary Grades: Kindergarten–Grade 2

As technology continues to shrink our planet, events that happen a world away are brought simultaneously into our living rooms. The Internet, television, cell phones, and iPods have transformed our lives and our world by illustrating how we connect to each other and to the environment. This sampler explores the theme of Natural Connections as evidenced in Ecosystems. Ecosystems are defined as biological communities of interacting organisms and their physical environments (Oxford American Desk Dictionary, 2001). As children learn about ecosystems of the rainforest, the ocean, and our fragile world, their understanding of good stewardship of Earth will be expanded.

The sampler begins with *The Great Kapok Tree* by Lynne Cherry. This simple yet classic tale of the fragility of the rain forest illustrates for children the interdependence of the world around us. As children listen to the story unfold, they wonder about the trees in their own neighborhoods and animals dependent on them.

As students learn about their stewardship of planet Earth, they discover that they are responsible for one another as well. Primary grade students investigate Historical Connections as they read about courageous men and women such as Gandhi, who never tired in the fight for freedom and human rights.

The final sub-theme, Global Connections, explores the power of the myth as students read narratives from around the world. As they compare similar themes and plots from differing nations and people, students gain the understanding that we are all united in our quest for meaning.

SAMPLER ■ Ecosystems

Imagine visiting the rainforest and exploring all of its myriad flora and fauna! The sub-theme, Ecosystems, explores the interdependence of organisms in the rainforest and other environments. As students read, discuss, and critically think about their stewardship of planet Earth, their understanding of their role in maintaining life's delicate balance will be deepened.

Primary grade students are very observant of the world around them. As they read and write about the environment, the students will be able to see how our actions are connected to all living things in our world.

NCTE/IRA Standards for the English Language Arts

1. Students read a wide range of print and non-print texts to build an understanding of texts, of themselves, and of the cultures of the United States and the world.

Learner Outcomes

Students will be able to do the following:

- Preview the selection by using pictures, diagrams, titles, and headings
- Set a purpose for reading
- Demonstrate comprehension of information in reference materials

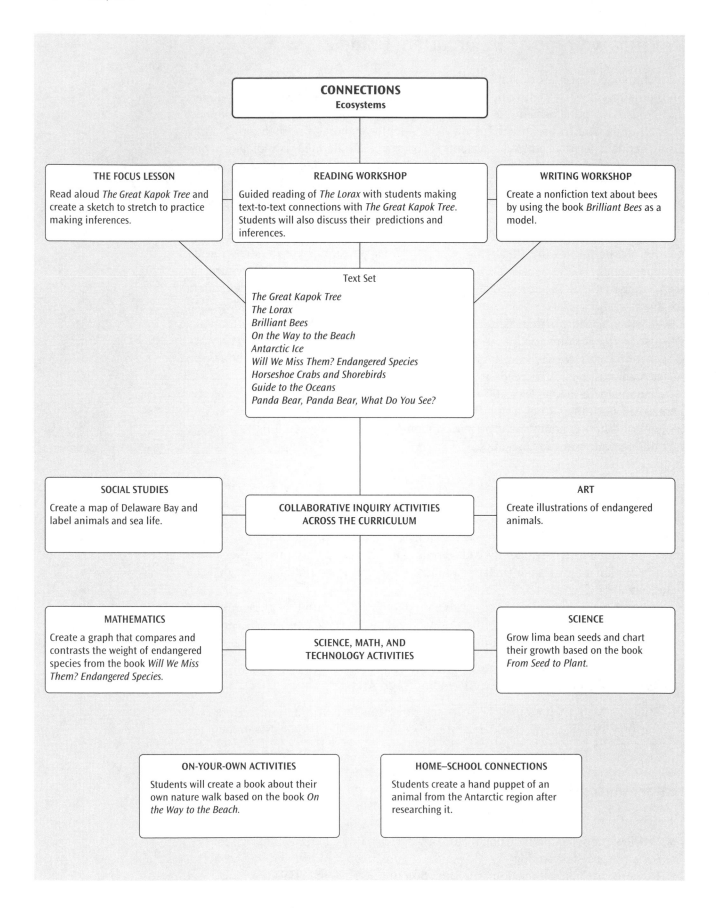

CONNECTIONS
Ecosystems

THE FOCUS LESSON

Read aloud *The Great Kapok Tree* and create a sketch to stretch to practice making inferences.

READING WORKSHOP

Guided reading of *The Lorax* with students making text-to-text connections with *The Great Kapok Tree*. Students will also discuss their predictions and inferences.

WRITING WORKSHOP

Create a nonfiction text about bees by using the book *Brilliant Bees* as a model.

Text Set

The Great Kapok Tree
The Lorax
Brilliant Bees
On the Way to the Beach
Antarctic Ice
Will We Miss Them? Endangered Species
Horseshoe Crabs and Shorebirds
Guide to the Oceans
Panda Bear, Panda Bear, What Do You See?

SOCIAL STUDIES

Create a map of Delaware Bay and label animals and sea life.

COLLABORATIVE INQUIRY ACTIVITIES ACROSS THE CURRICULUM

ART

Create illustrations of endangered animals.

MATHEMATICS

Create a graph that compares and contrasts the weight of endangered species from the book *Will We Miss Them? Endangered Species*.

SCIENCE, MATH, AND TECHNOLOGY ACTIVITIES

SCIENCE

Grow lima bean seeds and chart their growth based on the book *From Seed to Plant*.

ON-YOUR-OWN ACTIVITIES

Students will create a book about their own nature walk based on the book *On the Way to the Beach*.

HOME–SCHOOL CONNECTIONS

Students create a hand puppet of an animal from the Antarctic region after researching it.

Conduct a Focus Lesson

The sub-theme Ecosystems describes how organisms are codependent and rely on each other for life itself. Students summarize information about ecosystems and then apply it to their own neighborhood environments.

Establish a Purpose   The text set for Ecosystems illustrates fragile ecosystems struggling to survive as man increasingly encroaches on the natural world. The teacher prepares the students for the first text with the nonfiction book *Here Is the Tropical Rain Forest*. This beautifully illustrated text is perfect for introducing students to the concept of a rainforest. The teacher highlights important vocabulary words such as *canopy* and shows students the illustrations.

The first text in the set, *The Great Kapok Tree*, presents the story of a man entering the rainforest determined to cut down the Great Kapok Tree. As he is engaged in his task, the many animals that depend on the tree come out of hiding to plead with him. One by one they relay the importance of this one tree to their world. Eventually the man walks away and the tree and its inhabitants are saved for the time being. The focus lesson will analyze the author's meaning and scaffold students' text-to-self connections. The teacher introduces the book to students and relays the purpose of the lesson. Students will participate in a guided reading of *The Great Kapok Tree*, make predictions based on a picture walk, and complete a wall story activity (Antonacci & O'Callaghan, 2006) to respond to the text.

Engage in Guided Reading   In order to prepare the students for the story, the teacher begins by discussing the rainforest environment and assessing students' prior knowledge. First, the teacher presents students with pictures of the animals depicted in *The Great Kapok Tree* and asks them to identify each one. If students cannot identify the animals, the teacher provides the vocabulary words. After students have identified the animals, the teacher will show them pictures of rainforests and ask them to describe the environment. Student responses are recorded on chart paper. The teacher also shows students where some rainforests are located on a map.

Next, the teacher uses the guided reading strategy for the reading of the first book in the text set, *The Great Kapok Tree*. Before beginning the book, the teacher guides the students through the text by conducting a picture walk and then asks students to make predictions based on the illustrations and the title of the story.

As students read the text, they use Post-it notes to write down questions or jot down new vocabulary words while they read. When students have finished reading the text, they discuss how their predictions changed as they delved into the story. The teacher also reviews any new vocabulary words chosen by the students or questions raised during the guided reading session.

Conduct a Mini-Lesson   The focus of the mini-lesson will be to facilitate students' writing of expository text (Antonacci & O'Callaghan, 2006). The teacher discusses the facts about the rainforest that were presented in the two texts, and students decide what important information about the rainforest they want to convey to their readers.

The teacher tapes five large squares of paper to the board with a space provided for information. The teacher begins by modeling writing an expository sentence, then students continue by providing the factual information for each page. After the wall story is completed, the class does a choral reading of the text to edit their work. Students work in groups to illustrate their stories.

Additional Mini-Lessons

Sketch to Stretch

- During the read aloud of *The Great Kapok Tree*, students illustrate their inferences about the story.
- After the reading, they repeat the process and write about their interpretations of the story.

Content-Area Vocabulary

- As students learn about ecosystems they are also introduced to content vocabulary words.
- Students learn new words such as *ecosystems* and *food chain* and record them in their own picture dictionaries and write a definition for each one.
- After they add words to their picture dictionaries, they play a word sort game with a peer and categorize the words such as by parts of speech or beginning and ending sounds.

Making Connections

- After students have finished reading books in the text set for the Ecosystem sampler, they create a descriptive graphic organizer.
- The organizer outlines the definition of ecosystems, types of ecosystems, animals and their habitats, ways ecosystems can be harmed, and ways humans can help to keep ecosystems thriving.

Conduct a Reading Workshop

The Lorax is Dr. Seuss's (Theodore Geisel) imaginative tale of a greedy character who pollutes his environment to the brink of destruction before a few seeds save the day and restore green to the planet. Although it was written in 1971, children today will relate to the serious tale of our stewardship of the Earth. As students explore the concept of ecosystems and the interdependence of organisms, *The Lorax* discusses the damage done to our fragile world through carelessness.

Before Reading   Before beginning the story, the teacher shows students Dr. Seuss's imaginative illustrations and characters. After a picture walk of the text, the teacher solicits from students characteristics of Dr. Seuss's other books. The students' comments, such as silly rhymes or nonsense words, can be recorded on chart paper.

During Reading   As students are reading, the teacher can stop at the midpoint to ask if they notice any similarities between *The Lorax* and *The Great Kapok Tree*. Students make text-to-text connections regarding the possible destruction of both environments.

After Reading   When students have finished the text, the teacher discusses how the environment was saved in *The Lorax*. After students have finished their discussion, they can create a double bubble map showing the comparisons between *The Great Kapok Tree* and *The Lorax*. A sample is shown in Figure 5.1. The double bubble map is completed by the whole class with descriptions of how the environments were portrayed in both stories.

Conduct a Writing Workshop

As students read nonfiction and fictional text, they begin to understand the differences in text structure. In the primary grades, students are often engaged in producing fic-

FIGURE 5.1   Double Bubble Map

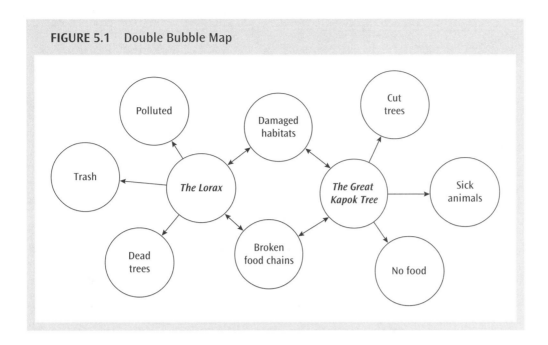

tional text but rarely write nonfiction. The objective of this writing workshop will be to immerse students in the elements of nonfiction.

Before Writing   As preparation for their writing of nonfiction text, the teacher reads the text *Brilliant Bees* and asks students to describe how bees are crucial to keeping our planet green. After the read aloud, students work in pairs to research more facts about bees on the Internet.

During Writing   After students have discussed the research with their peers, they begin to outline the information with their partners. The teacher guides students in their outlines by placing the following questions on chart paper:

How do bees help us?

How do bees live and work together?

What products come from bees?

When students have answered these questions, they write their research report by creating an informational book entitled *Our Brilliant Bees.*

After Writing   When students have completed their informational books about bees, they illustrate their texts with pictures from the computer or their own drawings. When the texts are completed and edited, they are placed in the classroom library or science center for everyone to enjoy.

Collaborative Inquiry Across the Curriculum

The sub-theme Ecosystems explores how our world is interconnected and how we are dependent on the Earth's fragile balance. This sub-theme can be extended to several subject areas, including mathematics, science, and social studies, through quality children's literature.

ASSESS LITERACY

The rubric presented below may be used to conduct progress monitoring as the teacher observes student performance in the reading workshop. The rubric may be used to look at the student's developmental progress on skills that were presented in previous samplers, such as making inferences.

Criteria	Independent	Proficient	Developing
Interpretation of the Author's Meaning	The student interprets author's meaning by using clues from the text and illustrations. (3)	The student partially interprets author's meaning by using clues from the text and illustrations. (2)	The student does not interpret author's meaning by using clues from the text and illustrations. (0–1)
Response to Story	The student responds to the story through a text-to-self connection. (3)	The student partially responds to the story through a text-to-self connection. (2)	The student does not respond to the story through a text-to-self connection. (0–1)
Analysis of Story	The student compares and contrasts the plots of both stories in the text set through a double bubble map. (3)	The student partially compares and contrasts the plots of both stories in the text set through a double bubble map. (2)	The student does not compare and contrast the plots of both stories in the text set through a double bubble map. (0–1)
Written Response	The student interprets the author's meaning in a written response. (3)	The student partially interprets the author's meaning in a written response. (2)	The student does not interpret the author's meaning in a written response. (0–1)
Student Participation	The student participates in discussion of both stories and activities. (3)	The student partially participates in discussion of both stories and activities. (2)	The student does not participate in discussion of both stories and activities. (0–1)
Independent: 11–15 Proficient: 6–10 Developing: 0–5			

STANDARDS

Mathematics Standards
4. Measurement

Extension to Mathematics   *Will We Miss Them? Endangered Species* explores animals from around he globe that are in danger of extinction. As each animal is presented, children learn its location on Earth and why it is presently hunted or in danger of losing its environment. Readers also learn facts about each species such as the animal's weight or how many teeth it has. As an activity to deepen their knowledge of endangered species, the students create a bar graph depicting the weight of each animal. After they have completed the bar graph, they compare and contrast the species by answering several questions such as: *Which animal is the biggest? Which animal is the smallest?* After students have completed the activity, they write and illustrate their new understandings in an *All About Endangered Species* book.

ASSESS LITERACY

The teacher uses the following rubric to assess students' work.

Criteria	Independent	Proficient	Developing
Content	Student integrates the content of bees throughout the text. (3)	Student integrates some content in writing. (2)	Student does not integrate the content in writing. (0–1)
Planning	All parts are present, well-developed, and written in a logical sequence. (3)	All parts are present and written in a sequence that the reader can follow. (2)	Text does not have a logical order and parts are not easy for the reader to follow. (0–1)
Sentence Structure	Student employs varied types of sentences in writing, using some complex structures when appropriate. (3)	Student uses sentences that are somewhat simple, but accurate. (2)	Student uses sentences that are simple and not always accurate. (0–1)
Vocabulary	Student consistently uses vocabulary content throughout with a high-degree of accuracy. (3)	Student uses some of the content vocabulary and may use words incorrectly. (2)	Student does not use the content vocabulary from study of bees. (0–1)
Language Mechanics	No errors in language mechanics are present. (3)	Some errors in language mechanics are present, but they do not interfere with meaning. (2)	Many errors in language mechanics appear throughout. (0–1)
	Independent: 11–15 Proficient: 6–10 Developing: 0–5		

Extension to Science   In *Guide to the Oceans: A Thrilling Journey into a Watery World,* students explore the mysteries of the ocean and learn how its fragile ecosystems are under the constant threat of hunting and oil spills. In this activity, students focus on two sections of the book: "Perfect Balance" and "Partners and Parasites." These sections discuss the food chain and the interdependence of different species that inhabit the ocean. After reading, students create a diorama that explores either the ocean's food chain or partners and parasites. Students then present their dioramas to the class and discuss new concepts they have learned about the delicate coexistence of the ocean's inhabitants and how man can disturb the fragile balance of life.

> **STANDARDS**
>
> **Science Standards**
> Life Science, Content
> Standards C2 and C3

Extension to Social Studies   In the story *Horseshoe Crabs and Shorebirds: The Story of a Food Web,* students learn about Delaware Bay and the food chain that surrounds the eggs of the horseshoe crab. The beautiful illustrations depict the migrating shorebirds

> **STANDARDS**
>
> **Social Studies Standards**
> III. People, Places, and
> Environments

from South America that devour some of the horseshoe crabs as well as the predatory falcons that eat the shorebirds. The text gently introduces the reader to the concept of a food web and the renewable cycle. The book ends with the horseshoe crab laying eggs again to continue the food chain. As students read about Delaware Bay, they create a map of the area and illustrate it with the animals and sea life depicted in the text. After students have shared their maps, they research rivers or bays in their own area and study their geography.

Home–School Connections   *Antarctic Ice* contains beautiful photographs of the wildlife on, around, and under the ice. There are four primary animals in the text: weddell seal, orca whale, adelie penguin, and emperor penguin. The text depicts the delicate ecosystem as baby seals are born, adelie penguins lay eggs, and the algae provide food for several animals. After the family has discussed the text, the parents help their child research one of the animals from the region. After exploring facts about it, the child creates a hand puppet of the animal and presents their own *Antarctic Ice* show to discuss their research. If students choose to do so, they may bring the puppets into the class to share with their peers.

On-Your-Own Activities   *On the Way to the Beach* is narrated by a little girl as she takes an early morning walk to the beach. As she passes woods, salt marshes, and dunes the students are introduced to the animals and foliage along the way. The descriptive text and beautiful illustrations, with depictions of snowy egrets and other wildlife, draw the reader in. After students have completed the book, they create their own text entitled "On the Way to the _____." Students choose a local park, beach, or neighborhood region and recreate the style of the book by depicting a nature walk through the area. As they describe the animals and foliage, they illustrate the text. After the texts are completed, students present their work to the class and answer further questions about the ecosystem they chose to write about.

Critical Literacy

When students have completed the Ecosystems sub-theme, the teacher leads the class in a discussion regarding the fragile ecosystems of Earth. Working in groups of three, students complete the cluster map illustrated in Figure 5.2 to synthesize and apply their new information regarding ecosystems. After the cluster map is completed, each student summarizes their knowledge regarding ecosystems.

Collaborative Literacy

In order to share their new concepts about ecosystems, students host "Celebrating Our Planet Earth" for other primary grade classrooms. During this celebration, students read from their *Brilliant Bees* books and use their double bubble maps to explain how fragile Earth has become. Students from other primary grades can pose questions about the environment for their hosts to answer. Any questions that the students are unable to answer will go in a "research box" and become projects for the students to explore.

The theme of Connections is continued in the intermediate grades as students learn about the fragile ecosystem of the monarch butterfly in the sampler, Connecting to Nature: The Flight of the Monarch Butterfly.

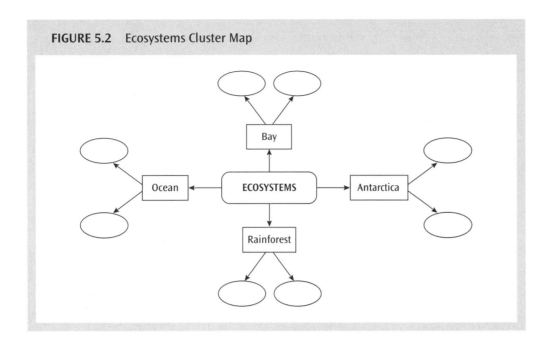

FIGURE 5.2   Ecosystems Cluster Map

■ Intermediate Grades: Grades 3–5

Connections will offer students opportunities to read and learn about concepts that are often difficult for children in the intermediate grades to grasp. Historical connections will offer students the opportunity to connect to their past by reading about Haillie, a young Quaker, who encounters neighbors, Aunt Katy and Mr. Levi Coffin, who are helping slaves escape to freedom through the Underground Railroad. Suddenly, Haillie finds herself making a choice between protecting her family from the slave catchers or helping two young girls who are seeking their freedom.

For Global Connections students read literature such as *My Name Is Jorge: On Both Sides of the River* or *Coolies* to learn the difficulties that Mexican Americans and Asian Americans had in making connections to their newly adopted country of the United States, and they will begin to make connections to the cultures of others. There are many folktales from around the world that offer students occasions to understand the cultures of others, but they will find *The Legend of Hong Kil Dong: The Robin Hood of Korea* an exceptional delight. Author and illustrator Anne Sibley O'Brien uses the graphics of a comic strip and the experiences of twenty-first-century children to tell a classic tale from the early seventeenth-century Korean Chosun dynasty.

Students develop an understanding of Natural Connections by reading about how manmade structures connect natural divides. For example, in the book *The Brooklyn Bridge: A Wonders of the World Book,* students read about the exciting challenge that faced John Roebling and his family in connecting the land separated by a great river. Another example of Natural Connections occurs as animals respond to nature. The mysterious monarch butterfly's migration is a wonderful example of animals connecting with nature. For this unit, we have selected the flight of the monarch butterfly as the intermediate grade sampler.

BRIDGES THAT CONNECT NATURAL DIVIDES

Text Set

Bridges
Bridges: Amazing Structures to Design, Build, and Test
Bridges Are to Cross
Brooklyn Bridge
Extreme Places: The Longest Bridge
From My Side to Yours
The Brooklyn Bridge: A Wonders of the World Book
The Brooklyn Bridge: They Said it Couldn't Be Built
The Golden Gate Bridge: Symbols, Landmarks, and Monuments
Twenty-One Elephants and Still Standing

Outcomes

- Students identify different types of bridges.
- Students discuss the history and location of bridges.
- Students build bridges from a variety of materials.
- Students locate the major bridges in the United States.

MEXICAN AMERICANS CROSS BORDERS TO MAKE CONNECTIONS

Text Set

Calling the Doves/El Canto de las Palamas
Breaking Through
Any Small Goodness: A Novel of the Barrio
My Name Is Jorge:
    On Both Sides of the River
My Diary from Here to There/Mi Diario de Aqui Hasta Alla
Horse Hooves and Chicken Feet:
    Mexican Folktales
Esperanza Rising

Outcomes

- Students create a word wall of Spanish words and their translations.
- Students engage in a grand conversation on their readings from the text set.

THE FLIGHT OF THE MONARCH BUTTERFLY

Text Set

The Butterfly
Butterfly Fever
An Extraordinary Life: The Story of a Monarch Butterfly
The Great Butterfly Hunt
Hurry and the Monarch
La Mariposa Monarca: Life Cycle
Melody's Mystery: El Misterio de Melodia
Mexico or Bust! Migration Patterns
Monarch Butterflies: Mysterious Travelers
Monarch Butterfly
Monarchs
Monarch Magic! Butterfly Activities and Nature Discoveries
My Monarch Journal
The Prince of Butterflies
Spring Moon

Outcomes

- Students track the migration routes of the monarch butterfly.
- Students plant a garden that contains plants to attract the monarch butterfly.
- Students create a story board that contains the life cycle and the migration routes of the monarch butterfly.

ASIAN AMERICANS CROSS BORDERS TO MAKE CONNECTIONS

Text Set

Shanghai Messenger
I.M. Pei
A Grain of Rice
Apple Pie Fourth of July
The Earth Dragon Awakes: The San Francisco Earthquake of 1906
Coolies
Voices of the Heart
The Legend of Hong Kil Dong

Outcomes

- Students discuss the contributions that Asian people have made to the world.
- Students research one Asian contribution and share it with the class.

Global Connections

Natural Connections

CONNECTIONS

Historical Connections

CONNECTING WITH OUR PAST: ELLIS ISLAND

Text Set

Ellis Island: Gateway to the New World
Ellis Island: A Primary Source History of an Immigrant's Arrival in America
Ellis Island: New Hope in a New Land
My America: Hope in My Heart: Sofia's Ellis Island
At Ellis Island: A History in Many Voices
Island of Hope: The Journey to America
Orphan of Ellis Island: A Time-Travel Adventure

Outcomes

- Students read and write about the diverse stories of immigrants who came through Ellis Island.
- Students research their own families to determine if they had a relative who entered the country through Ellis Island.

CONNECTING TO FREEDOM: THE UNDERGROUND RAILROAD

Text Set

The Underground Railroad
Many Thousands Gone: African Americans from Slavery to Freedom
If You Traveled on the Underground Railroad
Who Was Harriet Tubman?
Wanted Dead or Alive: The True Story of Harriet Tubman
The Patchwork Path: A Quilt Map to Freedom
When Harriet Tubman Led Her People to Freedom

Outcomes

- Students read and respond to their stories through pictures, words, and symbols.
- Students read a biography of Harriet Tubman and retell the important events in her life.

SAMPLER ■ The Flight of the Monarch Butterfly

Have you ever wondered how animals know when to migrate or hibernate? The intermediate grade sampler will help begin to unravel the mysteries of the flight of monarch butterflies as they connect to nature in the late summer and early spring.

Using a variety of informational books for third graders, students will read about the life cycle of a butterfly, the kinds of environments and plants that support their growth, why and how such fragile animals can travel the long distances, the importance of the butterfly to our planet, and how we can preserve the monarch butterfly.

NCTE/IRA Standards for the English Language Arts

1. Students read a wide range of print and non-print texts to build an understanding of texts, of themselves, and of the cultures of the United States and the world; to acquire new information; to respond to the needs and demands of society and the workplace; and for personal fulfillment. Among texts are fiction and nonfiction, classic and contemporary works.

Learner Outcomes

Students will be able to do the following:

- Make connections between previous experiences and reading selections
- Organize information and events logically
- Summarize major points found in nonfiction materials

Conduct a Focus Lesson

The teacher engages students in a read aloud to focus students' attention on the concept of animal migration and its importance to their survival. During this part of the lesson, the teacher helps students focus on the mystery of the flight of the monarch butterfly at the end of summer.

Establish a Purpose   Prior to the read aloud, the teacher begins by helping students make a connection between animals' self-preservation from weather changes and their migratory habits. The teacher engages students in a guided discussion on animal migration, and the students share their ideas about why animals move from their habitats, different animals that migrate, and when migration takes place.

Engage in a Read Aloud   The teacher introduces Cynthia Rylant's picture storybook *The Journey: Stories of Migration* to the students through a picture walk. During the walk, students discuss Lambert Davis's illustrations of six migratory animals in their habitats. The teacher focuses on the monarch butterfly and tells the students how the delicate-winged animal travels south to escape the cold winter. At this time, students listen to the story about the wonders of the flight of the monarch. After the story is read aloud, the teacher poses the following questions for a guided discussion intended to activate and further develop students' prior knowledge on migration and the flight of the monarch butterfly.

- Why do monarch butterflies migrate?
- If monarch butterflies lived in the northwestern part of the United States, where would they migrate?

CONNECTIONS
The Flight of the Monarch Butterfly

THE FOCUS LESSON

Conduct a read aloud to help students develop the purpose of the migration of the monarch butterfly and how to ask questions to understand what is being read.

READING WORKSHOP

Prepare the students for reading through the use of previewing techniques and helping students to develop questions for reading around the five "W"s. Direct the students to use their questions in reflecting on their reading and taking notes of important ideas related to their readings.

WRITING WORKSHOP

Guide students in using their notes from reading workshop, independent reading, and scientific observations and investigations to transform their notes into scientific summaries.

Text Set

The Butterfly
Butterfly Fever
An Extraordinary Life: The Story of a
    Monarch Butterfly
The Great Butterfly Hunt
Hurry and the Monarch
La Mariposa Monarca: Life Cycle
Melody's Mystery: El Misterio de Melodia
Mexico or Bust! Migration Patterns
Monarch Butterflies: Mysterious Travelers
Monarch Butterfly
Monarchs
Monarch Magic! Butterfly Activities and
    Nature Discoveries
My Monarch Journal
The Prince of Butterflies
Spring Moon

SOCIAL STUDIES

Guide students in studying the flight patterns used by migrating monarch butterflies. Students locate their home state and determine the flight of the monarch butterflies to their wintering stations. They learn why monarchs migrate by studying the relationship between the monarchs' summer and winter environments.

COLLABORATIVE INQUIRY ACTIVITIES ACROSS THE CURRICULUM

ART

Students make a paper garden of a variety of nectar plants that attract butterflies. They decorate one large wall and post their research summaries on the large flowers.

MATHEMATICS

Guide students in understanding the distance of the monarch butterflies' flight to their wintering station through a study of their flight patterns.

SCIENCE, MATH, AND TECHNOLOGY ACTIVITIES

SCIENCE

Students learn the role of way stations in the migration of the monarch butterfly, they learn how to create one, and may make a waystation. Students may make a butterfly garden and conduct a butterfly watch, learning about the variety of butterflies.

ON-YOUR-OWN ACTIVITIES

Engage students in creative writing of a point-of-view conversation poem on an animal, plant, or object that is related to their study of the migration of the monarch butterfly.

HOME–SCHOOL CONNECTIONS

Students engage in a book talk with their families. They include parts of the book and ideas that they may have learned about the migration of monarch butterflies. For each idea, students select a brief selection and read it to their families.

- If they lived in the northeastern part of the United States, where would they migrate?
- What kinds of dangers does the butterfly encounter on its flight?

Conduct a Mini-Lesson   The teacher conducts a mini-lesson to teach students to take notes that are accurate and complete. The simple strategy that the teacher uses is called "The Five Ws." Briefly, the teacher shows students how to organize ideas from their reading by creating five questions using *who, what, when, where,* and *why* that are related to what they have read, they record their answers to their questions.

After the discussion of the read aloud, the teacher reminds students that they know several facts about the flight of the monarch butterfly from listening to the story and that they can keep a record about what they know by taking notes as they read. Prior to the lesson on note-taking, the teacher crafts five "W" questions related to the reading (see Figure 5.3). With the students, the teacher models how to ask each of the five "W" questions, writes them on the chalkboard or on large paper, and leaves space to write a sentence or two to answer each question. The teacher asks students to recall the reading on the butterflies' migration and once again conducts a guided discussion around the five questions. The teacher and the students work together to develop responses to each question, writing the response to each question in the appropriate space.

Additional Mini-Lessons

Spelling

- The teacher teaches and reviews the spelling rules as they apply to vocabulary across the curriculum.
- Suffixes *(tion, ment): migration, development*
- Compound words: *milkweed, overwintering, offspring, featherweight*
- Drop -*y* and *add -ies: butterflies, identifies, cities*

Interesting Words

- The teacher directs students to collect interesting words related to butterfly migration as they read.

FIGURE 5.3 Notes on the Migration of the Monarch Butterfly

Notes on the Migration of Monarch Butterflies

WHO is the monarch butterfly?

WHAT is the monarch migration?

WHEN do monarch butterflies migrate?

WHERE do monarch butterflies go when they migrate?

WHY do monarch butterflies migrate?

- The teacher demonstrates words that are interesting: long words, words with different sounds, new words, words from other languages, words that are difficult to pronounce, and words that students may use in their writing.
- The teacher directs students to record their words and their meanings.
- The teacher selects a time for sharing interesting words, such as at the end of the reading block.
- Students add one word to the "Interesting Word Chart" under the appropriate category, explaining what the word means and why they have selected the word for the interesting word category.

Self-Monitoring Comprehension

- The teacher demonstrates how to paraphrase or retell the main ideas after reading a selection, explaining to students that when they stop after reading a portion of the text, think about it, and put it into their own words, they will be able to determine whether they understand what they are reading.
- After modeling to students how to paraphrase text, the teacher checks their skills during independent reading.

Conduct a Reading Workshop

During Reading workshop, students read different informational books that they select from the text set on the migration of monarch butterflies. The teacher guides students in selecting books that target their different reading levels.

Before Reading   Because each student may be reading a different book, the teacher takes time to prepare students for reading by introducing previewing techniques.

The teacher directs students to preview their books before reading. During this session, the previewing techniques that the teacher uses will focus on the book titles. Asking students to look at the titles of their books, the teacher says, "Does the title give you a clue about what you will read?" Students share their titles and ideas about what they think the book will be about. The teacher redirects their attention to "The Five Ws" and asks them to answer one "W" question using the title of their book.

Not all informational books have subtitles, tables of contents, or indexes to use for previewing a book and making predictions. The teacher directs students to look at their books to determine if they have a table of contents as in *An Extraordinary Life: The Story of a Monarch Butterfly;* a variety of titles, chapter titles, and subtitles, as in *The Life Cycle of a Butterfly;* or only pictures, as in *Monarch Butterflies: Mysterious Travelers.* The students preview their books and, using the clues that are provided, they make predictions about what they will be reading.

During Reading   As students begin to read their books, the teacher monitors their reading by conducting two-minute individual conferences with students, asking them what they have learned from their readings, determining if their reading confirmed their initial predictions, or working with students who need help with specific skills while reading their selected books.

After Reading   After each 25-minute reading workshop session, the teacher guides students to use the graphic organizer in Figure 5.3 to develop questions and find and record information on what they have read about monarch butterflies. Students are

---

ASSESS LITERACY

The teacher will assess students' skill in the following areas: (1) developing questions on their reading based on "The Five Ws", (2) locating information in text after reading, (3) paraphrasing information, summarizing and finding the gist or main idea from the text to answer questions, and (4) recording information accurately.

Criteria	Independent	Proficient	Developing
Development of Questions	After reading the book, the student develops valuable questions that lead to the retrieval of appropriate information from the text. (3)	After reading the book, student begins to develop questions that lead to the retrieval of appropriate information from the text. (2)	After reading the book, student needs assistance to develop questions to retrieve appropriate information. (0–1)
Using Questions for Finding Information	Student is proficient at using questions to find information from books. (3)	Student is beginning to use questions to find information from books. (2)	Student needs assistance in using questions to find information from books. (0–1)
Paraphrase Information	Student is proficient at paraphrasing information from the text to answer questions. (3)	Student is beginning to paraphrase information from the text to answer questions. (2)	Student needs assistance to paraphrase information from the text to answer questions. (0–1)
Accuracy of Information	Student's notes contain information that is complete and accurate. (3)	Student's notes contain information that is somewhat complete and accurate. (2)	Student's notes contain information that is not complete and/or accurate. (0–1)
Independent: 9–12 Proficient: 5–8 Developing: 0–4			

---

directed to review what they have read and to take notes. As students take notes, the teacher monitors them and helps students locate information and paraphrase what they have read.

Conduct a Writing Workshop

During writing workshop, the teacher will engage students in a genre known as scientific writing. Students will select a specific topic related to the monarch butterfly. During reading workshop and independent reading as well as science activities, students were actively engaged in taking notes on what they read and observed. The purpose of writing workshop is to teach them how to transform their scientific notes into research summaries. The instructional sequence will include learning the difference between a collection of notes, story writing, and scientific summaries. Thus, students will be engaged in writing a coherent paragraph on a specific topic using a collection of notes from readings and observations.

Before Writing   Before they engage in writing, students will learn the difference between *research notes* and *research summaries*. The teacher will demonstrate the difference between notes and summaries through the following procedures.

■ *Step 1.* The teacher reminds the students that during their reading workshop block and independent reading, they read books on the monarch butterfly and took notes. Additionally, the teacher helps students recall how they took research notes during science investigations and observations of the monarch butterfly, during their discussions about butterfly behaviors, and while studying the flight patterns of the monarch.

■ *Step 2.* The teacher demonstrates how research notes are a collection of facts about a specific topic or topics related to the monarch butterfly. The teacher then displays several sample sets of research notes, and uses a guided discussion to show how the notes are separate sets of facts. The students examine their own notes to understand how some statements are isolated observations or words that they used in their notes.

■ *Step 3.* The teacher displays a research summary consisting of a coherent paragraph constructed around a topic statement to show students how the research notes were organized and rewritten into a paragraph. The teacher then (1) displays all the notes related to a specific topic, (2) conducts a think aloud while organizing the notes, (3) shows students how to write an introductory or lead sentence for the research summary, and (4) demonstrates how to use notes as details to support the introductory sentence.

During Writing   As students begin to write their scientific summaries, the teacher helps individual students in planning for writing. The teacher reminds students to read their notes, organize them, write a lead sentence that will identify the topic, and use their notes to write a paragraph that will summarize and support the topic.

After Writing   When students have completed the writing task, the teacher introduces them to a rubric that will facilitate a self-assessment of their writing.

Collaborative Inquiry Across the Curriculum

STANDARDS

Mathematics Standards
2. Algebra

Technology Standards
5. Technology Research Tools

Extension to Mathematics and Technology   Students measure the migration routes that the monarch butterfly takes to determine the approximate distance butterflies cover to reach their wintering stations. Using the scale on the map legend, students study the relationship between the lines on the map that represent the migration routes of the monarch butterflies from different points in the United States and the approximate distance that the lines represent.

The teacher introduces students to websites on the migration of the monarch butterfly, guiding them in locating information on their topic. Students may read about the life cycle of the butterfly, study maps that show the monarch's flight patterns during migration from various points in the United States, develop a waystation and a butterfly garden, and study various nectar plants that support the life of the monarch butterfly.

ASSESS LITERACY

When the writing workshop is completed, the teacher may use the rubric below to help students evaluate their own writing.

Criteria	Independent	Proficient	Developing
Planning	My writing shows that I used a planning strategy and followed it while I was writing. (3)	My writing shows that I used a planning strategy but did not always follow it. (2)	My writing does not show that I used a planning strategy. (0–1)
Central Idea	My writing includes a lead sentence that contains a clearly stated central idea. (3)	My writing includes a central idea, but it is not clearly stated. (2)	My writing does not have a central idea. (0–1)
Related and Supporting Details	All of the details clearly support the central idea. (3)	Many (three or four) of the details support the central idea. (2)	Few (one or two) of the details support the central idea. (0–1)
Clarity of Ideas	All of the ideas are clearly stated. (3)	Some of the ideas are clearly stated (2)	Ideas are not clearly stated. (0–1)
Use of Scientific Vocabulary	In my writing, I used many vocabulary words from my science research. (3)	In my writing, I used some vocabulary words from my science research. (2)	In my writing, I did not use any vocabulary words from my science research. (0–1)
Language Skills			
Sentence Sense	All sentences make sense. (3)	Most sentences make sense. (2)	Some sentences make sense. (0–1)
Spelling	There are very few or no spelling errors. (3)	There are some spelling errors. (2)	There are many spelling errors. (0–1)
Punctuation	There are very few or no punctuation errors. (3)	There are some punctuation errors. (2)	There are many punctuation errors. (0–1)
Legible Writing	My writing is very legible. (3)	My writing is somewhat legible. (2)	My writing is not legible. (0–1)

Independent: 19–27
Proficient: 10–18
Developing: 0–9

Extension to Science

■ *Create a butterfly garden.* The teacher directs the students to create a butterfly garden. The teacher begins with a guided discussion on the role of the garden—to preserve and restore the butterfly population. The creation of the garden begins with research on the kinds of butterflies that are part of the geographic area. Students begin to engage in a "butterfly watch" to determine what butterflies frequent the area. Students research their literature and may visit the website www.monarch watch.org to learn about the variety of plants that butterflies need to sustain them.

■ *Create a waystation for monarch butterflies.*   More advanced students may develop a waystation for butterflies. The waystation provides monarch butterflies with sustenance as they migrate to their wintering sites, as in their journey from the northeast United States or Canada to Mexico. As students participate in the monarch waystation program, they will learn about: (1) the life cycle of the monarch butterfly, (2) the role of migration in preserving the monarch butterflies, (3) why resources for the monarch are declining, (4) the importance of supporting the monarch butterflies during their flight, and (5) what a monarch waystation is and how to develop one.

Extension to Social Studies   Students read and learn about the migration patterns of monarch butterflies. For example, at the end of August, monarch butterflies in the northeast regions will connect to the beginning of the climate change. They know they must leave the northeast and migrate to Florida.

Students use a map to follow the migration route of the monarch butterflies to Florida, California, and Mexico, calculate the miles between the monarch's summer and wintering sites, and estimate how long the journey will take from their home to each site. Such maps are found on a variety of websites.

To understand why the monarch migrates from the northeast regions to Florida or the northwest regions to southern California and Mexico for a winter stay, students compare the following:

■ The patterns of annual temperature in each area
■ Forms of precipitation—humidity, rainfall, snow, ice, and sleet—in each area
■ Water, vegetation, and animal life in each area

Students read about different types of butterflies and learn that different species of butterflies live in different places in the United States. In *The Butterfly Book,* North America is divided into seven zones. Students find the zone they live in and identify the species of butterflies that live there.

Home–School Connections   Encourage students to engage in a book talk of their selections from reading workshop with their families. Demonstrate one model of a book talk that includes the following:

■ Reading the title, author, and illustrator or photographer
■ Providing a brief overview of the book using the table of contents
■ Showing and explaining some interesting illustrations or photographs
■ Sharing at least three important concepts or ideas about the migration of monarch butterflies and reading brief excerpts that highlight the ideas.

On-Your-Own Activities   Students write a point-of-view conversation poem about the flight of a monarch butterfly, the life cycle of the butterfly, the butterfly garden, or the waystation. Such poems give life to objects or animals, are written in the form of a conversation, and use language and thoughts to express the butterfly's point of view. One example is shown in Figure 5.4.

FIGURE 5.4   Monica Monarch

MONICA MONARCH

Summer is leaving and I must go.

I will travel so far far away.

First I'll stop for some nectar sweet.

I must not forget to say, "Goodbye to you

my friends!" My friends who stay behind

Do I need a map so I can find Mexico?

Now I'm ready, I'm on my way.

Critical Literacy

As a closure activity, students synthesize and evaluate their information about the monarch butterfly. Working in groups of four, they create a wall chart that illustrates the life cycle of the butterfly, its habitat, and threats to the environment that affect the species. After students have completed the wall charts, they present them to their peers.

Collaborative Literacy

Students share their scientific summaries through a collaborative classroom display. One possibility is a large milkweed plant that students decorate with their scientific writings and visuals or drawings that further explain the writings. Students explain what they have learned through their readings and answer teacher and student questions about their work.

Stewardship of Earth is continued in the middle grade sampler, Food Chains, Webs, and Pyramids—The Web of Life. Through text sets, middle grade students learn about our fragile environment and its preservation.

■ Middle Grades: Grades 6–8

Scientific advances such as space exploration indicate that planets like Earth are rare. Despite climatic and other environmental changes, our planet has sustained life for almost four billion years. From ice ages to agricultural, industrial, and technological changes one species has emerged that dominates the Earth—humankind.

As citizens of an ever-shrinking globe, students should understand that the environmental, cultural, and social future of Earth is in their hands. Middle school students will examine the theme of Natural Connections by reading nonfiction texts that enable

EXPLORING BIOMES

Text Set

Biomes of the Earth series
Biomes of the World series
Water Ecology (Activity series)
An American Safari: Adventures on the North American Prairie
Looking for Seabirds: Journal from an Alaskan Voyage
My Season with the Penguins

Outcomes

- Construct and use data charts to abstract information about specific biomes.
- Work in cooperative learning groups to prepare an oral or written report.
- Use text evidence to support an opinion relative to an environmental issue.
- Use journal writing techniques to create a scientist's journal.

BUILDING BRIDGES TO UNDERSTANDING

Text Set

The Breadwinner
Parvana's Journey
Haveli
Shabanu, Daughter of the Wind
Under the Persimmon Tree
Homeless Bird

Outcomes

- Abstract and research the political and social issues that are affecting the life of the main character.
- Create a double-entry journal to reflect on how political and social conflict affects the life of youth living through turbulent times.

FOOD CHAINS, WEBS, AND PYRAMIDS—THE WEB OF LIFE

Text Set

Endangered Planet
What Is a Biome?
Our Environment
Endangered Environments
Food Chains
Food Chains & Webs
Chains, Webs, & Pyramids: The Flow of Energy in Nature

Outcomes

- Create process–cause graphic organizers to explain how threats to one level in a food chain, web, or pyramid affect other organisms.
- Create a model to explain connections among organisms at different levels in a food chain, biomass, and/or numbers of organisms.
- Investigate a current environmental issue and use a discussion web to examine it from different perspectives.

EAST MEETS WEST: UNDERSTANDING THE IMMIGRANT EXPERIENCE

Text Set

Maya Running
The Trouble Begins
A Step from Heaven
The Not-So-Star-Spangled Summer of Sunita Sun
Blue Jasmine
Child of the Owl
Thief of Hearts

Outcomes

- Abstract information relative to values and customs of the homeland that create tensions for immigrants.
- Create a first-person narrative to describe an immigrant's journey.

Global Connections

Natural Connections

CONNECTIONS

Historical Connections

EXAMINING HUMAN RIGHTS ISSUES

Text Set

Purely Rosie Pearl
Iqbal
Radical Red
Iqbal Masih and the Crusaders Against Child Slavery
Out of Bounds: Seven Stories of Conflict and Hope
Counting on Grace
Freedom of Religion

Outcomes

- Analyze the human rights issues in the text. Research the work of an organization that is working to resolve this issue.
- Use text-to-text, text-to-self, and text-to-world connections to participate in discussion.
- Write a position paper relative to a human rights issue.

INVESTIGATING TECHNOLOGICAL ADVANCES

Text Set

Before Hollywood: From Shadow Play to Silver Screen
Computers: Processing the Data
The Internet: The Impact on Our Lives
The Printing Press
Weapons: Designing the Tools of War
The Lightbulb

Outcomes

- Use a data chart to research a specific technological advance. Explain the effects of the new technology in the past, present, and future.
- Write a narrative to describe daily life from the perspective of a person living before a specific technological advance.

them to discover how every living thing is connected through a complex set of food chains, webs, and pyramids. They will learn how each member of a community is interconnected by a natural flow of energy from the sun to their food and how every living thing plays a part in the web of life.

In the sub-theme Historical Connections, students examine the global tensions created by technological change and predict how future generations might use technology to promote the welfare of all people.

The sub-theme Global Connections uses literature that focuses on the struggles of contemporary immigrants from Asia to help middle school students see that adjustment to a new country and culture is more difficult than they might imagine. They will learn the importance of making connections with classmates from other lands and discover the best in both cultures. The books in these text sets illustrate that the Earth is our home and that the study of global connections will promote understanding and facilitate peaceful coexistence.

SAMPLER ■ Food Chains, Webs, and Pyramids—The Web of Life

Planet Earth is the home to life. While the outer atmosphere is too cold and the inner crust is too hot, it is the biosphere, a relatively thin layer between, that sustains all living things. In this sampler students read nonfiction texts to study the relationships among living things within specific ecosystems such as forests, deserts, and oceans. They learn how a single change can upset the balance of nature and affect all the organisms within an environment or biome.

In this sampler middle school students explore the delicate web of the natural cycles that connect living things in an ever-increasing demand for food, fuel, and space.

NCTE/IRA Standards for the English Language Arts

1. Students read a wide range of print and non-print texts to acquire new information and to respond to the demands of society.
4. Students adjust their use of spoken, written, and visual language (e.g., conventions, style, and vocabulary) to communicate effectively with a variety of audiences and for different purposes.
7. Students conduct research on issues and interests by generating ideas and questions, and by posing problems. They gather, evaluate, and synthesize data from a variety of sources (e.g., print and non-print texts, artifacts, people) to communicate their discoveries in ways that suit their purpose and audience.

Learner Outcomes

Students will be able to do the following:

- Use knowledge of text structures to aid comprehension
- Distinguish fact from opinion in newspapers, magazines, and other print media
- Identify the source, viewpoint, and purpose of texts
- Organize and synthesize information for use in written and oral presentations

Conduct a Focus Lesson

The English language arts teacher begins the investigation by implementing the list-group-label (LGL) strategy (Taba, 1967) to activate students' background knowledge

CONNECTIONS
Food Chains, Webs, and Pyramids—The Web of Life

THE FOCUS LESSON

Use LGL strategy to activate prior knowledge about ecology.

Read aloud *Food Chains and Webs*. Discuss concepts: food chains, webs, pyramids, producers, consumers, etc.

Use process–cause maps to trace sequence of events when a toxic substance invades a biome.

READING WORKSHOP

Read: *What Is a Biome?*

Select a biome. Participate in a cooperative learning group to abstract details about the biome from a variety of resources using a data chart.

Prepare an oral (PowerPoint) or written report to describe the relationships in the biome.

WRITING WORKSHOP

Using journal writing techniques create an illustrated scientist's journal that describes a specific biome.

Text Set

Endangered Planet
What Is a Biome?
Our Environment
Endangered Environments
Food Chains
Food Chains and Webs
Chains, Webs, & Pyramids: The Flow of Energy in Nature

SOCIAL STUDIES

Investigate a current environmental issue. Examine the issue from the perspective of environmentalists, industrialists, governmental agencies, etc. Prepare a debate and/or write an opinion-persuasion essay.

COLLABORATIVE INQUIRY ACTIVITIES ACROSS THE CURRICULUM

ART

Use the techniques of scientific illustrators to enhance journals.

MATHEMATICS

Create a mathematical model to explain relationships among organisms at different trophic levels in the food chain for a specific biome. Consider biomass and/or number of organisms.

SCIENCE, MATH, AND TECHNOLOGY ACTIVITIES

SCIENCE

Conduct experiments to explain how living things affect and are affected by the environment.

ON-YOUR-OWN

Investigate the work of scientific and medical illustrators. Learn about the tools and techniques used to illustrate plants, animals, fossils and/or medical subjects. Investigate the work of a specific artist/illustrator.

HOME–SCHOOL CONNECTIONS

Discuss current environmental issues such as pollution with parents. Discuss the various views on the issues and the impact on local, regional, and global communities.

FIGURE 5.5   List-Group-Label Activity

Directions: You will use the list-group-label strategy to analyze vocabulary related to ecology. As you explore the meanings of these words and terms you will increase your understanding of science vocabulary.

Step 1—LIST: Examine this list of words and brainstorm other words you associate with them.

food chain	ecology	decomposers
producers	photosynthesis	prey
predators	consumers	energy
ecosystem	food web	pyramid

Step 2—GROUP: Work with your partner or group to organize the words into categories.

Step 3—LABEL: Find a label that fits each category. You may choose a word from the list or create a heading of your own. Be ready to share your categories with the class. Explain the reasons for your category groups.

about ecology. Students may brainstorm a list of words they associate with ecology or they may be provided with a list of words developed by the teacher (see Figure 5.5). Students work in small groups to combine the list into groups or categories. As they consider the relationships among the words, they create labels for the categories. After at least 10 minutes each group of students shares their web by explaining the categories they have created and places the graphic on a word wall. The teacher helps students clarify their understanding of the topic by doing a picture walk and guided discussion of the key concepts in the first chapter of *Endangered Planet.* Together they discuss their understanding of the biosphere, the need for energy, natural cycles such as water, carbon, and nitrogen, evolution and adaptation, habitats and biomes, and the conditions that contribute to change. To arouse their interest, the teacher asks students to generate questions that will guide their study of the conditions that sustain life, the patterns of life in each biome, and the natural and unnatural events that endanger life.

Establish a Purpose   The teacher introduces *Chains, Webs, & Pyramids: The Flow of Energy in Nature,* a concept book that explains how the sun's energy is changed into the food energy that flows from one living thing to another and how plants and animals in a particular place, such as the rainforest or ocean, are linked by what they eat. The teacher indicates that as they read this book, students will discover how scientists use models such as webs, chains, and pyramids to show how living things are connected. The teacher explains that understanding these relationships may help us to appreciate not only the complexity of nature but also our responsibility for acting as stewards of the planet. The shared reading and research/reporting activities provide students with the concepts and skills they will need for independent investigations of one of the biomes.

Students select a biome and participate in cooperative learning groups to investigate the connections among the climate, plants, and animals living in a specific biome. They identify the threats to each level in the food web/pyramid and offer solutions that will meet human wants and environmental needs. Finally, students examine how political and economic interests create tensions between economic development and environmental quality.

Engage in a Read Aloud   The teacher begins by explaining that an ecosystem is made up of a habitat that supplies all the resources the community of plants and animals that live in it need, as well as the plants and animals themselves. Except for humans, most of the world's living things have adapted to survival in only one habitat. Many types of habitats are scattered across the globe. Some species, such as the barn owl, are global while others are specific. For example, giant tortoises live on volcanic slopes in the Galapagos Islands but not on the volcanic slopes in South America or Europe. The teacher introduces the book *What Is a Biome?* by asking students to think about how a biome is different from a habitat and to identify some of the biomes of earth. After finishing the book, the teacher returns to the focus question: What are some threats that are endangering the balance of nature in each biome?

The teacher may expand on the topic by reading Chapter 6 "Invaders in the Food Chain," from *Food Chains* to illustrate what happens when a toxic substance or foreign species invades an ecosystem. The teacher guides students' understanding by using process–cause maps to trace the sequence of events that lead to imbalances caused by chemical pollutants such as DDT, hormone pollutants such as PCBs, and radioactive substances such as dangerous isotopes of iodine.

Conduct a Mini-Lesson   The teacher explains that students will work collaboratively to learn how the climate of a specific region influences the pattern of plants and animals that live together in a complex community or biome. The mini-lesson focuses on using data charts (Antonacci & O'Callaghan, 2006), a strategy that helps students abstract and organize information from a variety of text sources in order to facilitate comprehension and expository writing.

The teacher works with students to design a class data chart. The teacher begins by asking students to identify the categories of information about each biome that they wish to explore. These may be listed across the top of the data chart in the form of a phrase or question. Down the left side of the chart, they list the sources they will use to gather their information, such as texts, reference books, and electronic resources (see Figure 5.6). Since students may want to compare and contrast information about each biome, the class will reach consensus about the categories on the chart. The teacher may then assign students to cooperative learning groups or allow students to select topics (deserts, grasslands, taiga, tundra, temperate forests, tropical forests, wetlands, lakes and rivers, oceans) based on interest.

Additional Mini-Lessons

Use a Discussion Web

- The teacher explains that a discussion web (Muth & Alvermann, 1992) is a graphic aid that helps to structure a conversation about a controversial issue that allows students to explore two points of view.
- The teacher prepares a graphic that places the question or issue in the center with spaces on either side where students can list evidence to support or oppose the question.
- The teacher explains that after reading about a controversial ecological issue such as whether Alaskan oil resources should be further developed, students will work

FIGURE 5.6 Data Chart for Analyzing the Biome

Biome: _____

Sources	What is the geography of the biome (location, soil, water)?	What is the climate? How does climate affect the biome?	What are the living things in the biome? How do they interact?	What are the resources of the biome? Why are the resources important to people?	What are the dangers to the biome? How can people preserve the ecology of the biome?
Book 1: Title					
Book 2: Title					
Website 1					
Website 2					
Encyclopedia					
Other resources					

in pairs to identify reasons for and against further development. Pairs of students are encouraged to identify an equal number of reasons for each column.

■ Each pair of students joins with another pair to share their ideas. To enable all students to share information, each member of the group of four presents a reason for and against further development.

■ The group of four tries to reach a group conclusion and prepare a three-minute presentation. If the group cannot reach consensus they may present both the majority and minority view.

■ After each group has presented, the topic is opened up for a class discussion.

Create a Scientific Journal

■ After giving students time to examine several scientific journals, the teacher asks the students: "How are a diary and journal alike and different?"

■ The teacher then explains that the first step in scientific writing is to organize and order the information the scientist wants to include. Since they will be pretending to be field observers, students may want to create an outline or a list of the points they expect to include. If the students are going to work with a partner or group, this step may require negotiation to ensure that all the topics the group members want are included.

■ The teacher explains the importance of writing clearly and concisely and using examples from the literature, and emphasizes the importance of using scientific terminology to say a lot with few words as well as the need to use terms and acronyms suited to the intended audience.

■ The teacher and students then examine the texts to find examples that demonstrate the effectiveness of active voice and first-person construction.

■ Finally, the teacher and students discuss how illustrations, photographs, and diagrams enhance the text.

Use GIST Strategy to Write a Summary

■ After the students have completed their data charts, the teacher explains that they will learn how to use the GIST (Generating Interactions between Schemata and Texts) strategy developed by Cunningham (1982; Allen, 2004) to organize and summarize their information.

■ The teacher begins by providing the students with a short article or section from a nonfiction text relative to one of the concepts, such as food chains and webs, biodiversity in a temperate forest, and so on.

■ The teacher reads the first sentence aloud and asks students to work in groups to summarize the main idea(s) in 15 words or less. The students share their suggestions while the teacher writes a group summary on the board.

■ They then read the second sentence and write a summary of the first two sentences in 15 words or less. They share ideas and the teacher writes the group summary on the board.

■ Students and teacher continue reading and summarizing one or two sentences until the entire paragraph is read and students have written a summary of the entire paragraph in fifteen words or less.

■ After modeling the strategy, the students apply the summarizing skills to create a research report and/or PowerPoint presentation about a specific biome. Students are also encouraged to find models of scientific report writing to guide the development of their presentation.

Conduct a Reading Workshop

In the focus lesson, the teacher explained how to use data charts to improve comprehension and internalize the content from the reading. The teacher explains that during the reading workshops, students will apply this technique as they research a specific biome.

Before Reading   The teacher explains that each series includes individual texts that outline the main features of Earth's biomes. As students research specific biomes such as deserts, grasslands, or oceans, they use these books and other resources to find the information they will need to complete the data charts. After gathering the facts, they organize the information to create a comprehensive report describing the landforms, climate, and living things in each biome as well as the conditions that threaten its future.

Each cooperative learning group will have enough books about the specific biome and access to electronic resources to enable each student to find information to be added to the data chart. To help groups of students make a choice about the biome they will investigate, the teacher gives a brief description of the features that make it fascinating.

After the learning groups are formed, the teacher reminds students that as they gather and organize information about their specific biome they should consider the ways in which its biodiversity and rich resources will help to improve the quality of human life.

During Reading   The teacher explains that as students read about their biome, they will synthesize information from a variety of print and electronic resources to complete the data charts. Students are expected to collaborate on finding details and reach consensus if they find conflicting information in different resources. Each student may find details relative to each data category, or students within a group may focus on one or two categories.

After Reading   When students finish gathering information, the teacher brings the class together to consider the formats they may use to organize and present their findings. The teacher explains that they may use the details in the data charts to inform, to evaluate or critique, to persuade, and/or to show relationships such as cause and effect or comparison and contrast. Students and teacher discuss the importance of thinking about audience, tone, and style as well as the distinctions between oral and written reports. Students may decide that they will synthesize their information in a PowerPoint presentation that informs their classmates about the relationship among the geography, geology, and climate of the biome; how the living things in the biome are connected by food chains, webs, and pyramids; and how people have influenced the history and resources in the biome. They may also agree that part of the presentation will focus on persuading the audience to preserve the resources of the biome.

Conduct a Writing Workshop

The teacher explains that scientists often present a great deal of scientific information by creating illustrated journals of their field experiences. Two good books for a read aloud are *Looking for Seabirds: Journal from an Alaskan Voyage* and *My Season with*

The teacher uses the rubric below to assess students' performances during the reading and writing workshops. The teacher analyzes students' ability to work collaboratively to abstract information from nonfiction texts as well as to create a report and present information to the class. Students are assessed relative to reading comprehension, data gathering, and oral presentation skills.

Criteria	Independent	Proficient	Developing
Contributes to Gathering Information	The student actively participates in gathering information from a variety of resources during reading workshops. (3)	The student is somewhat active in gathering information from a variety of resources during reading workshops. (2)	The student does not actively participate in gathering information from a variety of resources during reading workshops. (0–1)
Contributes Accurate Information	The student provides accurate information and provides examples and explanations that illustrate insightful understanding of the content. (3)	The student provides basic information with some examples and explanations that illustrate good understanding of content. (2)	The student provides very little information with few examples and explanations, indicating minimal understanding of the content. (0–1)
Discussion Skills and Respect for Teammates	The student consistently and actively contributes information, opinions, and support; values the knowledge and opinions of others; and works hard to help the group reach consensus. (3)	The student generally contributes information, opinions, and support but may need prompting; shows some sensitivity to the knowledge and opinions of others; and usually considers all views but may argue. (2)	The student either does not contribute or does not allow others to contribute; is insensitive to others and often argues with teammates; does not consider teammates' ideas and opinions; and may impede group's effort. (0–1)
Contributes to the Development of the Group Report	The student uses effective summarizing skills that take into account audience, tone and style, and use of technical vocabulary. (3)	The student uses good summarizing skills that generally account for audience, tone and style, and use of technical vocabulary. (2)	The student does not apply good summarizing skills; may not consider audience, tone, and style; and uses technical vocabulary inappropriately. (0–1)
Technology Skills	The student effectively uses PowerPoint to design and implement a report to present information about a biome, integrating graphics that enhance the oral presentation. (3)	The student demonstrates good use of PowerPoint to design and implement a report to present information about a biome, integrating some graphics that enhance the oral presentation. (2)	The student does not use PowerPoint to design and implement a report to present information about a biome, may read all the slides verbatim or not use technology appropriately, and does not integrate graphics to enhance the oral presentation. (0–1)
Oral Presentation Skills	The student effectively presents information orally by making eye contact, speaking loud enough for all to hear, and using a tone and style that engage the audience. (3)	The student generally presents information well by making some eye contact, speaking loud enough for all to hear, and using a tone and style that engage most of the audience. (2)	The student does not present information well, may not make eye contact or speak loud enough for all to hear, or uses a tone and style that does not engage most of the audience. (0–1)

Independent: 13–18

Proficient: 7–12

Developing: 0–6

the Penguins: An Antarctic Journal. These and other scientists' journals should be available to students during writing because they are effective models.

Before Writing   The teacher conducts a mini-lesson on scientific journal writing. Students examine the texts and form writing groups based on their interests. Students create a journal to describe the experiences of a scientist exploring the biome they researched during the reading workshop, or they may choose another biome.

During Writing   Students within each group consult each other about the details they will include and the illustrative techniques they will employ. Students may create individual journals or they may work with a partner or group. The teacher meets with each group to facilitate the discussions about the organization of the journal, the content, and the illustrations, diagrams, and/or photographs.

After Writing   Students revise and edit based on comments from the teacher and peers. They prepare for a day of sharing both the journals and oral presentations.

ASSESS LITERACY

The teacher uses the rubric below to help the students self-reflect on their scientific journal writing. After the students have completed the assessment, the teacher leads a discussion on how to use the information to improve their performance.

Criteria	Reflective Notes
Content Knowledge	Did I use my content knowledge in my journal writing?
Central Idea	Did I focus on a central idea in my journal writing?
Related and Supporting Details	Have I used related and supporting details in my journal writing?
Research Process	Did I use my journal to aid my research?
Use of Scientific Vocabulary	Have I used scientific vocabulary in my journal?
Editing	Did I edit my journal for spelling, grammar, and punctuation?

Collaborative Inquiry Across the Curriculum

Extension to Mathematics and Technology Students use print and electronic resources to find information for the data charts. Using statistics from the texts and Internet research, they create a mathematical model to explain the relationships among the organisms at different trophic levels in the food chain(s) for a specific biome. The students may illustrate the relationship between producers and consumers, the number of organisms, and/or the biomass.

Extension to Science Students work in cooperative groups to conduct experiments to explore urban ecology and global warming. Students may choose to investigate the food chains in their neighborhood or the impact of carbon emissions on their local climate. After keeping a scientific journal of their experiments, students present their findings in a panel discussion before their peers.

Extension to Social Studies Students investigate current environmental issues such as developing Arctic oil and mineral resources, animals on the endangered species list, destroying and managing the rainforests, or pollution. They examine the issue from a variety of perspectives, including environmentalists, industrialists, and governmental and nongovernmental agencies. They work in teams to prepare a debate or write a persuasive essay.

Home–School Connections Students are encouraged to discuss the environmental issues they are investigating with parents. They identify the various views on the issues and talk about how the issues affect their local, regional, and global communities.

On-Your-Own Activities Students investigate the work of scientific and medical illustrators. They identify the skills, techniques, and digital drawing tools illustrators in this unique field use. They learn about 3D modeling, the care and handling of specimens, and the anatomy of taxonomic groups as well as how to illustrate and diagram plants, animals, fossils, and medical subjects. They may choose to examine the work of a specific illustrator.

Critical Literacy

When students have completed the Connections sub-theme, they synthesize and apply their new concepts by creating a podcast entitled "Our Fragile Earth." Using information gathered from their readings of the text set as well as research, students create a report about our fragile environment and what they and their fellow students can do to help the planet. The podcast is posted on the class website for other students and parents in the school community to download.

Collaborative Literacy

Students share their PowerPoint presentations to help classmates learn about the web of life in each biome as well as how human interaction is threatening the balance of life in each ecosystem. Students enhance the oral presentations by placing their journals on display and encouraging classmates to examine them. Students may respond to journal authors by writing sticky notes.

RESOURCE GUIDE: CHILDREN'S LITERATURE REFERENCES AND ACTIVITIES

Primary Grades

Natural Connections

Ecosystems

Cherry, L. (1990). *The great Kapok tree: A tale of the Amazon rain forest.* New York: Harcourt.

Cole, H. (2004). *On the way to the beach.* New York: Greenwillow.

Crension, V. (2003). *Horseshoe crabs and shorebirds: The story of a food web.* Illustrated by Anne Cannon. New York: Marshall Cavendish.

Dipper, F. (2002). *Guide to the oceans: A thrilling journey into a watery world.* New York: DK Publishing.

Dunphy, M. (2006). *Here is the tropical rainforest.* Berkeley, CA: Web of Life Children's Books.

Geisel, T. S. (1971). *The Lorax.* New York: Random House.

Glaser, L. (2004). *Brilliant bees.* Wallingford, CT: Millbrook.

Martin, B. (2003). *Panda bear, panda bear what do you see?* Illustrated by Eric Carle. New York: Henry Holt.

Mastro, J., & Wu, N. (2004). *Antarctic ice.* New York: Henry Holt.

Wright, A. (1992). *Will we miss them? Endangered species.* Illustrated by Marshall Peck III. Watertown, MA: Charlesbridge.

- **Greening Our Planet:** Students collect recycled items at home and chart how they have helped to keep the planet green for one week.
- **Photo Journal:** Students adopt a tree in their own neighborhood and keep a photo journal of how it changes over a season. The journal will also record the animals who keep their habitat there.
- **Keeping Our Waterways Clean:** Using Google, students find maps of their local waterways and research the species that depend on them. Students create a chart outlining ways they can help to keep the waterway clean.
- **My World:** Using index cards, students create a word card for each new vocabulary word from the Ecosystems sampler. The students define the word on the card and provide an illustration. After the students have placed their word cards on a ring, they can play Guess My Word with a peer.

From Seed to Plant

Bernard, R. (2003). *Tree for all seasons.* Salt Lake City, UT: Sagebrush.

Carle, E. (2005). *The tiny seed.* New York: Little Simon.

Fowler, A. (2001). *From seed to plant.* Danbury, CT: Children's Press.

Heller, R. (1992). *The reason for a flower.* New York: Grosset & Dunlap.

Maestro, B. (1992). *How do apples grow?* New York: HarperCollins.

- **Making Our Gardens Grow:** Students plant marigold seeds and chart their plant's growth, noting when the stem, leaves, and flower appear.
- **From Flower to Seed:** Students select their favorite fruit and research it on the Internet. After the students have researched their selected fruit, they draw a sequence chart illustrating how the flower is transformed into fruit.
- **Dissecting a Flower:** Using tulips, the students take apart a flower and label its parts on chart paper. After the students have dissected the flower, they can research the function of each component on the Internet.

Historical Connections

The Quest for Democracy

Adler, D. (1989). *A picture book of Martin Luther King, Jr.* New York: Holiday.

Demi. (2001). *Gandhi.* New York: Margaret K. McElderry.

Krull, K. (2003). *Harvesting hope: The story of Cesar Chavez.* New York: Harcourt.

Ringgold, F. (1999). *If a bus could talk: The story of Rosa Parks.* New York: Simon & Schuster.

Rustad, M. E. (2001). *Harriet Tubman (first biographies).* Mankato, MN: Capstone Press.

Rustad, M. E. (2006). *Susan B. Anthony (first biographies).* Mankato, MN: Capstone Press.

- **Struggling to Be Free:** Students select two biographical figures they have read about in the text set and create a double bubble map to compare and contrast their lives. After the students have completed the task, they can discuss how the heroes were alike and different.
- **Democracy in Our Lives:** After the unit is completed, students discuss what they do every day that is the result of the struggle for democracy, such as riding on a bus, reading the newspaper, or watching the news on television.
- ***All About* Books:** Students create an *All About* book focusing on their favorite hero for democracy. The students illustrate their biographies and then present them to the class.

Trading Around the World

Demi. (2009). *Genghis Khan.* Tarrytown, NY: Marshall Cavendish.

Gilchrist, C. (2004). *Stories from the Silk Road.* New York: Barefoot Books.

Krebs, L. (2005). *We're riding on a caravan.* New York: Barefoot Books.

Krull, K. (2001). *Supermarket.* Illustrated by Melanie Hope Greenburg. New York: Holiday.

Major, J. S., & Belamus, B. J. (2002). *Caravan to America: Living arts of the Silk Road.* New York: Cricket Books.

Major, J. S., & Fieser, S. (1996). *The Silk Route: 7,000 miles of history.* New York: HarperTrophy.

Shuter, J. (2005). *Life in a Greek trading post.* Portsmouth, NH: Heinemann.

- **Where Did That Come From?** Students log their dinners for one month and then try to chart the state or country the food items came from.
- **Reader's Theatre:** After students have read *We're Riding on a Caravan,* they write a script for the text and perform it for their peers.
- **Trading USA:** Students use the Internet to research the top 10 items that the United States exports to other nations. After their research, the class creates a wall chart with the top ten exports illustrated.

Global Connections

Cinderella Stories Around the World

Climo, S. (1999). *The Persian Cinderella.* Illustrated by R. Florczak. New York: HarperCollins.

Daly, J. (2000). *Fair, brown and trembling: An Irish Cinderella story.* New York: Farrar, Straus & Giroux.

Martin, R. (1992). *The rough-face girl.* Illustrated by David Shannon. New York: Putnam.

Steptoe, J. (1987). *Mufaro's beautiful daughters.* Illustrated by John Steptoe. New York: Lothrop.

- **Our Cinderella Story:** As students read books in the text set, the class charts story ideas for an American version of the classic story. The students then work in groups of three to create their own version.
- **Tea Party:** The teacher selects excerpts from a book for students to practice until they reach fluency in reading. The students participate in the tea party by forming pairs and taking turns reading the excerpt and discussing it. The tea party continues as students move into small groups to read and discuss their parts.
- **Cinderella Matrix:** After the whole class has completed the text set, they complete a matrix depicting the main characteristics of a Cinderella story and discuss whether each version embodied the classic elements of the tale.

Myths from Around the World

Anderson, D. (1991). *The origin of life on Earth: An African creation myth.* Mt. Airy, MD: Sights Productions.

Bierhorst, J. (1993). *The woman who fell from the sky: The Iroquois story of creation.* Illustrated by Robert Andrew Parker. New York: Morrow.

Hofmeyr, D. (2001). *The star bearer: A creation myth from ancient Egypt.* New York: Farrar, Straus & Giroux.

Hughes, T. (2000). *How the whale became and other stories.* Illustrated by Jackie Morris. London: Orchard Publishers.

- **Rolled Story:** A small group of students create a story sequence by illustrating each part of the myth on paper. The students then roll the sequenced story on cardboard rolls and perform it for the class.
- **Myth Matrix:** Similarly to the Cinderella stories, there are classic elements of a myth. After the students have completed the text set, they can create a matrix of the elements of a myth and use it to compare and contrast the different stories.
- **How the ____ Came to Be:** As the students read mythical versions of how animals were created, they work in pairs to create their own myth about their favorite animal. After they have edited and illustrated their version, they can perform it for the class.

Intermediate Grades

Natural Connections

Bridges That Connect Natural Divides

Adkins, J. (2002). *From my side to yours.* New York: Roaring Brook.

Britton, T. (2005). *The Golden Gate Bridge: Symbols, landmarks, and monuments.* Edina, MI: Checkerboard Books.

Corbett, S. (1978). *Bridges.* Illustrated by Richard Rosenblum. New York: Scholastic.

Curlee, L. (2001). *Brooklyn Bridge.* New York: Atheneum.

Johmann, C., & Reith E. (1999). *Bridges: Amazing structures to design, build, and test.* Illustrated by Michael P. Kline. Charlotte, VT: Williamson.

Johnson, D. (2002). *Extreme places: The longest bridge.* San Diego, CA: Kidhaven Press.

Kaner, E. (1995). *Bridges.* Illustrated by Pat Cupples. Toronto: Kids Can Press.

Landau, E. (2001). *Bridges.* New York: Children's Press.

Mann, E. (1996). *The Brooklyn Bridge: A wonders of the world book.* Illustrated by Alan Witschonke. New York: Mikaya Press.

Prince, A. (2005). *Twenty-one elephants and still standing.* New York: Houghton Mifflin.

Ricciuti, E. (1997). *Bridges.* Woodbridge, CT: Blackbirtch Press.

Robbins, K. (1991). *Bridges.* New York: Scholastic.

St. George, J. (1982). *The Brooklyn Bridge: They said it couldn't be built.* New York: Putnam.

Sturges, P. (1998). *Bridges are to cross.* Illustrated by Giles Laroche. New York: Putnam.

Willard, K. (1999). *Bridges.* Mankato, MN: Creative Education.

- **Classifying:** After reading about different bridges, students match specific characteristics with types of bridges.
- **Bridge Cards:** Students learn about various bridges, their history, location, size, and so on. Using index cards, they draw the bridge on one side of the card and write its facts on the reverse side.
- **Bridge Building Contest:** Using miniature marshmallows, toothpicks, uncooked spaghetti and other types of pasta, cardboard, rubber bands, and string, students build a bridge. After the contest, they name it, classify what type of bridge it is, name its various parts, and tell what natural divide it would be appropriate for connecting.
- **My Bridge:** Students draw or take a picture of a bridge in their community, then write about its history, the type of bridge it is, and what areas it connects.
- **Visual Word Connections:** As students read about different types of bridges, they learn new words related to bridge characteristics. They are directed to use their learning logs to draw the meaning of each word, providing a visual description. For example, when reading *The Brooklyn Bridge,* the students examine the labeled parts of a suspension bridge, then draw and identify the bridge parts with labels.

The Flight of the Monarch Butterfly

Coville, B. (2002). *The prince of butterflies.* Illustrated by John Clapp. New York: Harcourt.

Crew, S. (1997). *The butterfly.* New York: Steck-Vaughn.

Flatharta, A. (2005). *Hurry and the monarch.* Illustrated by Meilo So. New York: Knopf.

George, J. C. (2002). *Spring moon.* New York: HarperTrophy.

Gibbons, G. (1991). *Monarch butterfly.* New York: Holiday.

Harvey, D. (1991). *Melody's mystery: El misterio de melodia.* Woodburn, OR: Beautiful America Publishing Company.

Haskins, L. (2004). *Butterfly fever: Science solves it.* Illustrated by Jerry Smath. Kane Press.

Herberman, E. (1990). *The great butterfly hunt.* New York: Houghton Mifflin.

Holland, W. (2010). *The butterfly book: A popular guide to the butterflies of North America.* Berlin: NABU Press.

Kalman, B. (2006). *The life cycle of a butterfly.* New York: Crabtree Publishing.

Lasky, K. (1993). *Monarchs.* Photographs by Christopher G. Knight. San Diego, CA: Harcourt Brace.

Lavies, B. (1993). *Monarch butterflies: Mysterious travelers.* New York: Dutton.

Muther, C. (2000). *My monarch journal.* Photographs by Anita Bibeau. Nevada City, CA: Dawn Publications.

Pringle, L. (1997). *An extraordinary life: The story of a monarch butterfly.* Illustrated by Bob Marshall. New York: Orchard.

Rosenblatt, L. (1998). *Monarch magic! Butterfly activities and nature discoveries.* Charlotte, VT: Williamson Publishing Company.

Rylant, C. (2006). *The journey: Stories of migration.* New York: Blue Sky Press.

Schwartz, D. M. (2001). *La mariposa monarca: Life cycle.* Photographs by Dwight Kuhn. Strongsville, OH: Gareth Stevens Publishing.

Underwood, D. (2007). *Mexico or bust! Migration patterns.* Chicago: Raintree.

- **Learning Logs:** During reading workshop and independent reading, students write or draw about new ideas and concepts related to the monarch butterfly. At the end of each session, they share one idea from their learning logs with the class.
- **Compare and Contrast—Discovering Patterns of Animal Behavior:** During their study of the monarch butterfly, students learn about why the monarch migrates. They may select one other animal's migration patterns to compare and contrast with the monarch butterfly.
- **Story Boards:** Students use the story board approach to describe the life cycle of the monarch butterfly, from the laying of eggs to its flight south in the late summer, using only pictures from books or drawings.
- ***All About* Books:** Have students create their own *All About the Monarch Butterfly* book. Students may work in pairs or create their own book.

Historical Connections

Connecting to Our Past: Ellis Island

Fisher, L. E. (1986). *Ellis Island: Gateway to the new world.* Illustrated by Leonard Everett Fisher. New York: Holiday.

Houghton, G. (2003). *Ellis Island: A primary source history of an immigrant's arrival in America.* New York: Rosen Publishing Group.

Jacobs, W. J. (1990). *Ellis Island: New hope in a new land.* New York: Scribner.

Lasky, K. (2003). *My America: Hope in my heart: Sofia's Ellis Island.* New York: Scholastic.

Peacock, L. (2007). *At Ellis Island: A history in many voices.* Illustrated by Walter Lyon Krudop. New York: Atheneum.

Sanders, M. (2004). *Island of hope: The journey to America.* New York: Scholastic.

Woodruff, E. (1997). *Orphan of Ellis Island: A time-travel adventure.* New York: Scholastic.

- **Character Collage:** Students select a character from their readings and create a character collage with pictures that represent events in the character's life and symbols and words that represent the mood and personality of the character. Students may share their collages and describe their character.
- **New Cover, New Title:** Students create a new cover and title for the book they selected. The title represents the most important part of the story. The cover illustrates the main character and the scene that best shows what the story is about, and should appeal to others considering reading the book.
- **News, News, News . . . Read All About It!** The teacher has students select their favorite story or part of a story and write a news articles about it. Students may be prompted to use the five Ws—who, what, where, when, and why—to make their news article complete. Each article should have a headline. Students' articles may be published in the form of a newspaper about stories of Ellis Island.

Connecting to Freedom: The Underground Railroad

Bial, B. (1999). *The underground railroad.* New York: Houghton Mifflin.

Hamilton, V., & Dillon, L. (2002). *Many thousands gone: African Americans from slavery to freedom.* Illustrated by Diane Dillon. New York: Knopf.

Levine, E. (1993). *If you traveled on the underground railroad.* New York: Scholastic.

McDonough, Y. Z. (2002). *Who was Harriet Tubman?* Illustrated by Nancy Harrison. New York: Grosset and Dunlap.

McGovern, A. (1991). *Wanted dead or alive: The true story of Harriet Tubman.* Illustrated by R. M. Powers. New York: Scholastic.

Stroud, B. (2005). *The patchwork path: A quilt map to freedom.* Illustrated by Erin Suzanne Bennet. Cambridge, MA: Candlewick.

Weatherford, C. (2006). *Moses: When Harriet Tubman led her people to freedom.* Illustrated by Kadir Nelson. New York: Hyperion.

- **Quilt:** After their readings, students may express their feelings through pictures, words, or symbols on a square for the quilt. Students' collective responses may then be compiled to create a class quilt.
- **Cubing:** Students read a book on Harriet Tubman and engage in a discussion of her character and challenges that she faced. On five sides of the cube, students illustrate an event from her life or a character trait to describe her. On the sixth side of the cube, they draw her portrait and write her name.
- **Double-Entry Journals:** As students read, they select a quote from their book and write it in one column of their journal. In the other column, students make a personal connection, a text connection, or a world connection.

Global Connections

Mexican Americans Cross Borders to Make Connections

Herrera, J. F. (1995). *Calling the doves/El canto de las palamas.* Illustrated by Elly Simmons. San Francisco: Children's Book Press.

Jimenez, F. (2001). *Breaking through.* New York: Houghton Mifflin.

Johnston, T. (2001). *Any small goodness: A novel of the barrio.* New York: Blue Sky Press.

Medina, J., & Vanden Broeck, F. (2004). *My name is Jorge: On both sides of the river.* Illustrated by Fabricio Vanden Broeck. Honesdale, PA: Wordsong/Boyd Mills Press.

Perez, A. (2002). *My diary from here to there/Mi diario de aqui hasta alla.* Illustrated by Maya Christina Gonzalez. San Francisco: Children's Book Press.

Philip, N., & Mair, J. (2003). *Horse hooves and chicken feet: Mexican folktales.* New York: Clarion.

Ryan, P. M. (2000). *Esperanza rising.* Carmel, CA: Hampton-Brown.

- **Word Walls:** As students read books in the text set, they will learn Spanish words. They then add the new words to the word wall, say the words, and discuss their meanings.
- **Tea Party:** The teacher selects excerpts from a book for students to practice until they reach fluency in reading. The students participate in the tea party by forming pairs and taking turns reading the excerpt and discussing it. The tea party continues as students move into small groups to read and discuss their parts.
- **Grand Conversations:** After the whole class or small groups of students have read a book, they engage in a grand conversation. To prepare for the dialogue, students are directed to do a quickwrite, develop a set of questions with responses, or do a quickdraw. They then engage in a conversation on the book and share responses.

Asian Americans Cross Borders to Make Connections

Cheng, A. (2005). *Shanghai messenger.* Illustrated by Ed Young. New York: Lee and Low Books.

Engler, M., & Pei, I. M. (2005). *I. M. Pei.* Milwaukee, WI: Raintree.

O'Brien, A. S. (2006). *The legend of Hong Kil Dong: The Robin Hood of Korea.* Watertown, MA: Charlesbridge.

Pittman, H. (1995). *A grain of rice.* New York: Bantam Doubleday Dell.

Wong, J. S. (2002). *Apple pie fourth of July.* Illustrated by Margaret Chodos-Irvine. New York: Harcourt.

Yep, L. (2006). *The earth dragon awakes: The San Francisco earthquake of 1906.* New York: HarperCollins.

Yin. (2001). *Coolies.* Illustrated by Chris K. Soentpiet. New York: Philomel.

Young, E. (2003). *Voices of the heart.* New York: Scholastic.

- **Sketch to Stretch:** The class or a small group of students read one book. After a discussion of the themes of the story, students engage in a sketch to stretch activity by drawing personal reactions to the story. An important part the activity is the sharing of personal responses.
- **Open-Mind Portraits:** After reading a story, students reflect on the character's behavior and develop an "open-mind" portrait that includes drawings and words that represent the character.
- **Reading Logs:** As students read the story, they keep a reading log. They make a small booklet by fastening paper together, writing the title and author of their book on the first page, and making written entries of their readings on each page. Students' entries may include interesting words or quotes, self-to-text connections, text-to-text connections, or world connections.

Middle Grades

Natural Connections

Food Chains, Webs, and Pyramids—The Web of Life

Burnie, D. (2004). *Endangered planet.* Boston: Kingfisher.

Kalman, B. (1998). *What is a biome?* New York: Crabtree Publishing.

Kinney, K. (Ed.). (1999). *Our environment.* Richmond, VA: Time-Life Education.

Lantier-Sampon, P. (Ed.). (1995). *Endangered environments.* Milwaukee, WI: Gareth Stevens Publishing.

Pringle, L. (1975). *Chains, webs, & pyramids: The flow of energy in nature.* New York: Thomas Y. Crowell.

Silverstein, A., Silverstein, V., & Silverstein-Nunn, L. (1998). *Food chains.* Brookfield, CT: Twenty-First Century Books.

Wallace, H. (2001). *Food Chains & Webs.* Chicago: Heinemann.

- **Cause–Effect:** Students identify the threats to each level in a food chain/web/pyramid and create cause–effect maps to show what happens when a toxic substance enters the food chain.
- **Discussion Web:** Using a discussion web, students examine an environmental issue from a variety of perspectives.
- **Food Chain:** Students create a model to explain the relationships among the organisms at different levels of the food chain in a specific biome.
- **Debate Panel:** Students investigate a current environmental issue from the perspectives of environmentalists, industrialists, and governmental and nongovernmental agencies. Students then work in teams to prepare a debate.

Exploring Biomes

Allaby, M. (2006). *Biomes of the earth: Temperate forests.* New York: Chelsea House.

Brandenburg, J. (1995). *An American safari: Adventures on the North American prairie.* New York: Walker and Co.

Cochrane, J. (1987). *Water ecology.* New York: The Bookwright Press.

Johansson, P. (2004). *Biomes of the world: The temperate forest.* Berkeley Heights, NJ: Enslow Publishers.

Webb, S. (2000). *My season with the penguins: An Antarctic journal.* Boston: Houghton Mifflin.

Webb, S. (2004). *Looking for seabirds: Journal from an Alaskan Voyage.* Boston: Houghton Mifflin.

- **Data Charts:** Students participate in cooperative learning groups to research a specific biome (oceans, deserts, temperate forests, etc), using data charts to organize information from a variety of print and electronic resources.
- **Presentation:** Students create a PowerPoint presentation or written report to share information about a specific biome and describe how human interaction is threatening this environment.
- **Simulated Journal:** Students create a journal from the perspective of a scientist who is exploring a specific biome.

Historical Connections

Investigating Technological Advances

Clee, P. (2005). *Before Hollywood: From shadow play to the silver screen.* New York: Clarion.

DeAngelis, G., & Bianco, D. J. (2005). *Computers: Processing the data.* Minneapolis, MN: Oliver Press.

Graham, I. (2001). *The Internet: The impact on our lives.* Austin, TX: Raintree Steck-Vaughn.

Meltzer, M. (2003). *The printing press.* New York: Benchmark Books.

Richie, J. (2000). *Weapons: Designing the tools of war.* Minneapolis, MN: Oliver Press.

Wallace, J. (1999). *The lightbulb.* New York: Atheneum.

- **Open-Mind Portrait:** After reading one of the texts, students create an open-mind portrait (Tompkins, 2009) to explain daily life from the perspective of a person living before the technological advance.
- **Data Chart:** Using a data chart, students research the development and effects of a specific technological advance. They write a report to describe how the advance was developed, the role it played in improving people's lives when it was first introduced, and how it affects people's lives today. They predict how it may help improve lives in the future.

Examining Human Rights Issues

Cochrane, P. A. (1996). *Purely Rosie Pearl.* New York: Delacourt.

D'Adamo, F. (2005). *Iqbal.* New York: Aladdin.

Duffy, J. (1993). *Radical red.* New York: Maxwell Macmillan International.

Head, T. (2005). *Freedom of religion.* New York: Facts on File.

Kuklin, S. (1998). *Iqbal Masih and the crusaders against child slavery.* New York: Henry Holt.

Naidoo, B. (2004). *Out of bounds: Seven stories of conflict and hope.* New York: HarperCollins.

Winthrop, E. (2006). *Counting on Grace.* New York: Wendy Lamb Books.

- **Action Research:** Using print and electronic resources, students research the work of an organization that focuses on a specific human rights issue. They identify the activities of the organization and determine how students can get involved. Some examples include Human Rights Education Association at www.hrea.org and International Center on Child Labor and Education at www.knowchildlabor.org.
- **Position Paper:** Students prepare a position paper relative to a specific human rights issue.

Global Connections

Building Bridges to Understanding

Ellis, D. (2001). *The breadwinner.* Berkeley, CA: Publishers Group West.

Ellis, D. (2003). *Parvana's journey.* Berkeley, CA: Publishers Group West.

Staples, S. F. (1993). *Haveli.* New York: Dell Laurel Leaf.

Staples, S. F. (2003). *Shabanu, daughter of the wind.* New York: Dell Laurel Leaf.

Staples, S. F. (2005). *Under the persimmon tree.* New York: HarperTrophy.

Whelen, G. (2001). *Homeless bird.* New York: Farrar, Straus & Giroux.

- **Book Box:** Students create a book box (Tompkins, 2009) to describe the values of the culture of the main character and explain how the values affect the events in the story.
- **Double-Entry Journal:** Students create a double-entry journal to relate quotes to their own lives, to react to an event or challenge, to reflect on the main character's problems and his or her responses, or to make some other connection.
- **Reflection:** Students conduct research on the political and social issues that are the focus of the narrative and write a reflection on their views of the issue.

East Meets West: Understanding the Immigrant Experience

Banerjee, A. (2005). *Maya running.* New York: Random House.

Himelblau, L. (2005). *The trouble begins.* New York: Delacorte Books.

Na, A. (2002). *A step from heaven.* New York: Penguin Putnam.

Perkins, M. (2005). *The not-so-star-spangled life of Sunita Sun.* New York: Little, Brown.

Sheth, K. (2004). *Blue jasmine.* New York: Hyperion.

Yep, L. (1977). *Child of the owl.* New York: HarperCollins.

Yep, L. (1997). *Thief of hearts.* New York: HarperTrophy.

- **Narrative Account:** Students create a first-person narrative account of one main character's journey to America. The account should describe life in the home country, explain how and why the character comes to America, and the difficulties of adjusting to a new land and culture.
- **Story Quilt:** Students create a story quilt (Tompkins, 2009) to describe the theme, characters, setting, and conflicts the main characters experience in a new country and culture.

PROFESSIONAL REFERENCES

Allen, J. (2004). *Tools for teaching content literacy.* Portland, ME: Stenhouse.

Antonacci, P. A., & O'Callaghan, C. M. (2006). *A handbook for literacy instructional & assessment strategies, K–8.* Boston: Allyn & Bacon.

BBC News. (2007). *Sun and global warming: A cosmic connection?* Retrieved March 19, 2008, from http://news.bbc.co.uk/2/hi/science/nature/7092655.stm

Cunningham, J. W. (1982). Generating interaction between schema and text. In I. A. Niles & L. A. Harris (Eds.), *New inquiries in reading research and instruction: 31st Yearbook of the National Reading Conference* (pp. 42–47). Rochester, NY: National Reading Conference.

Muth, K., & Alvermann, D. (1992). *Teaching and learning in the middle grades.* Boston: Allyn & Bacon.

National Commission on Science Education Standards and Assessment & National Research Council. (1996). *NSES Science Standards.* Washington, DC: National Academy Press. Available at www.nap.edu/catalog.php?record_id=4962

National Council of Teachers of English & International Reading Association. (1996). *Standards for the English language arts.* Newark, DE: Author. Available at www.ncte.org/standards.

Oxford University Press. (2001). *The Oxford American desk dictionary and thesaurus.* New York: Berkley Books.

Taba, H. (1967). *Teacher's handbook for elementary social studies.* Reading, MA: Addison-Wesley.

Tompkins, G. E. (2009). *Fifty literacy strategies: Step by step* (3rd ed.). Boston: Allyn & Bacon.

Choices

In this age of global media, our students are bombarded daily with news stories about teenage celebrities or sports figures, which often leads to students admiring or emulating their behavior. Unfortunately, celebrities and sports figures often make terrible choices in their lives, and students do not always see the consequences of fame in newspaper accounts.

Chapter 6 will explore the theme of Choices and how we are often called in life to make difficult choices that may affect the direction of our lives. The National Council for the Social Studies (1994) recognized the importance of analyzing the consequences of actions and how our cultural backgrounds affect our interpretations of events. Through text sets, students across the grades will discuss how fictional and historical characters faced difficult or dangerous choices and how they came to their decisions.

In Dangerous Choices, primary grade students will read about historical figures such as John Quincy Adams or Sybil Ludington who chose to make dangerous journeys in the quest for freedom. Intermediate students will read about the authors of *Curious George,* Margaret and H. A. Rey, and their choice to escape war-torn Europe to make a new life elsewhere. The quest for freedom is also discussed in the middle school text set, which explores the 39 founders of America and their dangerous choice to risk all for the sake of liberty.

However, some of us may never be placed in a situation where we have to choose between life or death. Difficult Choices explores the many choices we face that may direct our lives for years to come. Primary grade students will read texts that address bullying and discuss ways to conquer playground aggressors in their own lives. Intermediate grade students will read about famous artists such as Henri Matisse and Georgia O'Keeffe, who chose to be different by focusing on the visual image. Middle grade students will discuss the difficult choices often present in their lives in texts such as *Scorpions,* which explores gang life.

The final sub-theme, Choices That Made a Difference, focuses on stories or historical accounts of choices that were made to make society or the world a better place. Primary grade students explore this sub-theme in an author study of Patricia Polacco. As students read stories such as *Pink and Say* or *The Butterfly,* they will discuss ways they can choose to reach out to others in their neighborhoods. In *Boxes for Katje,* intermediate grade students read about how a small effort to feed hungry Europeans after World War II saved many lives. Middle grade students read about Prudence Crandall and her choice to open a school for slaves despite the danger to her own life.

As students read about dangerous, difficult, or humanitarian choices made by historical or fictional characters, they will reflect on the daily choices they make in their own lives. It is not often that we are called on to make dangerous choices, but our students should be prepared to face the daily choices that form the pattern of our lives.

CHOOSING TO COME TO AMERICA

Text Set

Tattered Sails
William's House
I Was Dreaming to Come to America
Annushka's Voyage
Coming to America: A Muslim Family's Story
The Memory Coat

Outcomes

- Write a class wall story that retells one of the memories from an Ellis Island immigrant.

- Identify vocabulary words from the text set and use word cards to create sentences.

- Create your own simulated diary of a trip to America.

CHALLENGES IN THE SKY

Text Set

The Man Who Walked Between The Towers
Talkin' about Bessie: The Story of Aviator Elizabeth Coleman
Starry Messenger: Galileo Galilei
Flight: The Journey of Charles Lindbergh
The Glorious Flight: Across the Channel with Louis Bleriot

Outcomes

- Role play one of the main characters through a personal interview with a peer.

- Create a snapshot vignette that illustrates the key events in one of the texts.

- Retell one of the stories using felt board cutouts that are made from photocopied pictures of the text.

DEALING WITH BULLIES

Text Set

King of the Playground
The Recess Queen
Cody and Quinn, Sitting in a Tree
Stand Tall, Molly Lou Melon
Enemy Pie
The Bully Blockers Club

Outcomes

- Define and identify causes and effects of behavior.

- Create a T-chart to summarize Kevin's feelings.

- Role play responsive behaviors for dealing with bullies.

- Identify special qualities in yourself to use against bullying behavior.

- Construct rules for either the playground or classroom about behavior towards others.

CHOOSING FREEDOM

Text Set

Sybil Ludington's Midnight Ride
Dangerous Crossing: The Revolutionary Voyage of John Quincy Adams
Willy and Max: A Holocaust Story
Paul Revere's Ride: The Landlord's Tale
A Good Night for Freedom

Outcomes

- Construct display boxes based on your research on one of the historical figures or periods in the texts.

- Construct a character mobile that illustrates the brave choices made by the historical figures.

- Select one of the texts to illustrate through a story board and narrate it for the class.

Difficult Choices

Dangerous Choices

CHOICES

Choices That Made a Difference

REACHING OUT TO OTHERS

Text Set

The Butterfly
An Orange for Frankie
Mrs. Katz and Tush
Pink and Say
Thank You, Mr. Falker
Mr. Lincoln's Way

Outcomes

- Create a matrix that compares the story elements in the texts by Patricia Polacco.

- Construct a book box that illustrates the scenes from one of the texts and use it to retell the story.

- Write a story in the style of Patricia Polacco that is about reaching out to others.

PERSONAL CHOICES TO HELP OTHERS

Text Set

Martin's Big Words: The Life of Dr. Martin Luther King, Jr.
Passage to Freedom: The Sugihara Story
Good Queen Bess: The Story of Elizabeth I of England
Sequoyah: The Cherokee Man Who Gave His People Writing
Escape North: The Story of Harriet Tubman

Outcomes

- Create a diorama to illustrate how Harriet Tubman helped slaves through the Underground Railroad.

- Construct a character puppet of Elizabeth I and dramatize her life story.

- Research one of the historical figures in the text set and write an *All About* book for your peers.

▪ Primary Grades: Kindergarten–Grade 2

A favorite place for many young children to be is on the playground. Here children participate in all sorts of physical, social, and cognitive activities, including laughing, sharing, running, jumping, balancing, imagining and making new friends. Kevin, the main character in *King of the Playground* by Phyllis Reynolds Naylor, loves to go to the playground—except when Sammy is there. Each trip to the playground ends with Sammy, the self-proclaimed king, telling Kevin that he is not allowed to play there, and if he does Sammy will do all sorts of terrible things to him. Kevin must make the difficult choice of having fun on the community playground or being bullied to leave whenever Sammy is there.

Children begin to understand that choices are a part of their everyday lives in many different ways. As they explore this theme through their readings and discussions within the classroom, students will understand that sometimes choices may be difficult due to possible consequences of their decisions. In addition to the sub-theme Difficult Choices, students will also explore Choices That Made a Difference and Dangerous Choices, as illustrated in the graphic organizer.

SAMPLER ▪ Dealing with Bullies

In a first-grade classroom during the first week of school, Mr. Diamond introduces the following saying to his class: "Sticks and stones may break my bones but words will never hurt me." After a lively discussion about the different feelings that name-calling, teasing, and threats of physical harm create, the students begin to understand that words can hurt them. Mr. Diamond continues by explaining that when someone uses verbal or physical means to try to make us do something, it is called bullying, and the person that does this is called a bully. Mr. Diamond tells the class about a young boy named Kevin, who loves to go to the playground to play on the slides, swings, monkey bars, and sandbox, except when a boy named Sammy is there. Mr. Diamond explains, "Kevin was afraid to go to the playground because Sammy would threaten to do all sorts of mean things to Kevin if he wanted to play there." Kevin had to make the difficult choice of dealing with this bully or being afraid to go somewhere or do something he really enjoys. Mr. Diamond begins to read aloud *King of the Playground*.

Throughout the United States, Switzerland, Canada, England, Finland, Norway, Spain, Belgium, and Australia, schools are diligently working with educators, students, and parents to develop an awareness of and effective means to deal with bullying (Rigby, 2002). Though there are many different programs used by schools today, they all endorse a commitment by the whole school community to be effective. "Bullying behavior can be reduced by well-planned interventions. The likelihood of success appears to be greater when programs are implemented with younger students attending kindergartens and primary school" (Rigby, 2002, p. 3).

This text set provides opportunities for children to recognize the characteristics of bullying and become sensitive to the feelings of others. Several alternatives will also be presented for them to discuss and choose the most appropriate way to deal with such difficult situations. In *The Recess Queen,* another playground bully does not let any of her classmates play until she says so. Sometimes boys and girls become good friends, as in *Cody and Quinn, Sitting in a Tree,* and are teased about their relationship by the class bully. Children also see how a young girl who is different responds to the bully in her class in an effective and positive way in *Stand Tall, Molly Lou Melon.* Because

CHOICES
Dealing with Bullies

THE FOCUS LESSON

Conduct a read aloud to help students understand how to deal with bullies and to identify causes of behavior

READING WORKSHOP

Prepare the students for reading by discussing "bullying behavior." After reading the story, the students create a cause/effect graphic organizer that illustrates how the main character's behaviors cause reactions in others.

WRITING WORKSHOP

Students write about their own special qualities and how to use this information to respond to bullying behavior. They share their stories in the author's chair.

Text Set

Cody and Quinn, Sitting in a Tree
Stand Tall, Molly Lou Melon
King of the Playground
The Recess Queen
Enemy Pie
The Bully Blockers Club

SOCIAL STUDIES

Guide students in studying the rules and laws to preserve order. After a discussion on the importance of rules, the class will create their own rules for either the playground or the classroom.

COLLABORATIVE INQUIRY ACTIVITIES ACROSS THE CURRICULUM

ART

Students create a life-size portrait of themselves on rolled paper and write about their special qualities on the back of the portrait.

MATHEMATICS

Students create a bar graph to illustrate different ways to swing, jump rope or to use other playground equipment.

SCIENCE, MATH, AND TECHNOLOGY ACTIVITIES

SCIENCE

Students learn the role of gravity in the use of slides and other playground equipment. They study the force of motion and apply it to their everyday lives.

ON-YOUR-OWN ACTIVITIES

Students write possible responsive behavior when dealing with bullies and role play their scenarios for the class.

HOME–SCHOOL CONNECTIONS

Using the book, *King of the Playground*, the students conduct a shared reading with their parents and discuss ways to confront aggressive behavior from others.

children may find it difficult to stand up to a bully alone, *The Bully Blockers Club* presents another solution to deal with this problem. Readers have the opportunity to read and participate in several activities that will guide them through the difficult choices that dealing with a bully can present.

NCTE/IRA Standards for the English Language Arts

1. Students read a wide range of print and non-print texts to build an understanding of texts, of themselves, and of the cultures of the United States and the world; to acquire new information; to respond to the needs and demands of society and the workplace; and for personal fulfillment. Among texts are fiction and nonfiction, classic and contemporary works.
3. Students apply a wide range of strategies to comprehend, interpret, evaluate, and appreciate texts. They draw on their prior experience, their interactions with other readers and writers, their knowledge of word meaning and other texts, their word identification strategies, and their understanding of textual features.
4. Students adjust their use of spoken, written, and visual language (e.g., conventions, style, vocabulary) to communicate effectively with a variety of audiences and for different purposes (International Reading Association and National Council of Teachers of English, 1996).

Learner Outcomes

Students will be able to do the following:

1. Identify the main idea or essential message from text and identify supporting information
2. Read for information to use in performing and learning new tasks

Conduct a Focus Lesson

The text set for Dealing with Bullies includes award-winning literature that presents realistic situations about bullied characters who need to make a choice as to how to best respond to their situation. The focus lesson uses *King of the Playground* by Phyllis Reynolds Naylor to illustrate this scenario. Kevin really looks forward to going to the playground, but is threatened by Sammy if he should try to play there. Kevin chooses not to stay and returns home each time. After Kevin's father asks if he had a good time, he tells his dad about Sammy and what he threatens to do to him if he stays. Kevin's dad listens carefully before encouraging him to think about Sammy's empty threats. Kevin chooses to return to the playground each day, believing that Sammy cannot possibly hurt him, only to leave in response to a new threat. Finally Kevin chooses to confront the bully by challenging his threats. After the two boys exchange barbs, they finally decide to join together to play in the sandbox.

Establish a Purpose   The purposes of the focus lesson are to explore feelings about being bullied and identify personal traits needed for dealing with bullying behavior.

Engage in Read Aloud   The theme begins with a read aloud of *King of the Playground*. In order to prepare students for the text set, the teacher facilitates a discussion about bullying behavior and how being bullied makes them feel. During the read aloud,

FIGURE 6.1   Graphic Organizer for Kevin's Feelings

Feelings	Before Choosing to Act	After Choosing to Act
1		
2		
3		
4		
5		

the teacher stops at the midpoint and asks students how they would solve Kevin's dilemma. At the conclusion of the read aloud, students compare Kevin's solution to his problem with their previous discussion.

Conduct a Mini-Lesson   After the read aloud, the focus of the mini-lesson is to identify character traits of Kevin, the main character. Students are asked to provide words that describe how Kevin feels at the beginning of the story whenever he meets Sammy at the playground. Students then provide words that describe how Kevin feels after he chose to stay at the playground.

The focus lesson ends with a chart (shown in Figure 6.1) illustrating the words used to describe Kevin's feelings. Using the T-chart, students list Kevin's feelings before and after he makes the decision to confront Sammy in the playground. As a summation of the lesson, students discuss why Kevin's feelings changed and how he chose to respond to his feelings.

Additional Mini-Lessons

Character Traits

- As the students read about Kevin in *King of the Playground,* they create character hand portraits.
- The students outline their hand and then write a character trait on each finger.
- The students have to support their choices with examples from the text.

Identifying Story Elements

- When students have completed the text set, they use a matrix to compare story elements.
- The subheadings should be "Main characters," "Setting," "Problem," and "Solution."

Reading Response

- After students have finished reading each book in the text set, they respond to the stories in their learning journals.

■ Students' responses should focus on their text-to-self connections related to dealing with bullies.

Conduct a Reading Workshop

A longtime friendship between a boy and girl is challenged by the bully in a second-grade class in *Cody and Quinn, Sitting in a Tree*. After the teasing results in Cody becoming angry and taking out his frustration on his friendship with Quinn, he decides to do something. During a game of tag with some children, Royce was excluded and began to use his fists to threaten his classmates. Cody impulsively decides to come to Royce's aid by including him on his team, and the two boys quickly establish a friendship.

Before Reading   Before students read the book, the teacher discusses why two people become friends and if it matters if they are a boy and a girl. After students understand that friendship is always something special, they discuss why someone might not like these two people being such good friends.

During Reading   As students are reading the text, the teacher asks them to write a list of the things Royce does to bully Cody and Quinn. When the final situation arises in the playground during the game of tag, the teacher asks the class to predict what will happen next.

After Reading   The teacher creates a cause-and-effect chart, as illustrated in Figure 6.2. Using the list to identify one of Royce's actions, the students indicate the effect of these actions on Cody and Quinn. This can be done for as many actions as the teacher chooses and will work well for independent or small-group work.

The teacher discusses with the students if they feel that Cody and Quinn responded well to the bully in the story. The teacher facilitates a discussion with students of what they might have said or done in the same situation.

Conduct a Writing Workshop

In the text set, there are main characters that have to make a choice about responding to a class bully. In *Stand Tall, Molly Lou Melon*, Molly Lou was different from most

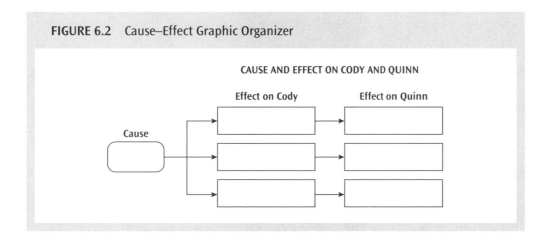

FIGURE 6.2   Cause–Effect Graphic Organizer

CAUSE AND EFFECT ON CODY AND QUINN

Effect on Cody   Effect on Quinn

Cause

ASSESS LITERACY

In order to assess students' understanding of cause and effect, the rubric presented below will serve as a guide. Students identify orally or in writing the specific actions by Royce, Cody, and Quinn and the reactions to these actions by one or more of these characters. Students understand that the actions are the *causes* and the reactions are the *effects* of these actions. Students respond by describing their feelings about the appropriateness of the characters' behavior.

Criteria	Independent	Proficient	Developing
Identification of Causes of Behavior	After reading the book, student identifies causes of behavior that lead to reactions by characters in the text. (3)	After reading the book, student begins to identify causes of behavior that lead to reactions by characters in the text. (2)	After reading the book, student needs assistance to identify causes of behavior that lead to reactions by characters in the text. (0–1)
Identification of Effects of Behavior	After reading the book, student identifies effects of behavior that lead to reactions by characters in the text. (3)	After reading the book, student begins to identify effects of behavior that lead to reactions by characters in the text. (2)	After reading the book, student needs assistance to identify effects of behavior that lead to reactions by characters in the text. (0–1)
Understanding Appropriate Behavior	Student is proficient at discussing appropriate behavior with evidence from text. (3)	Student is beginning to discuss appropriate behavior with evidence from text. (2)	Student needs assistance to discuss appropriate behavior with evidence from text. (0–1)
Accuracy of Information	Student's graphic organizer contains information that is complete and accurate. (3)	Student's graphic organizer contains information that is somewhat complete and accurate. (2)	Student's graphic organizer contains information that is not complete or accurate. (0–1)

Independent: 9–12

Proficient: 5–8

Developing: 0–4

children in many ways. Whenever Ronald, the class bully, would try to taunt Molly Lou, she would simply pay no attention. She responded with her usual charm and varied talents to successfully accomplish any task set before her. Katie Sue also paid no attention to the class bully, Mean Jean, in *The Recess Queen*. Both girls responded to their situation in a similar way and both were able to stop being bullied.

Before Writing   The teacher facilitates a discussion about self-esteem and how the two characters in these texts felt very good about themselves. Students are asked to think about some ways that they also feel very good about themselves and make a list of some of these qualities on a sheet of paper. The teacher lists these on the board or on chart paper for others to think about.

ASSESS LITERACY

When the writing workshop is completed, the teacher may use the rubric below to help the students evaluate their own writing.

What did you like best about this writing task?
What did you have to work at most?
How did you solve your problems?
What have you learned from this writing assignment?

Students are asked to write a paragraph describing one special quality about themselves and how this can help them respond to a bully. They are encouraged to describe an actual situation or can repeat one that was described in any of their texts.

During Writing   Students are required to use the format of a paragraph, including using complete sentences and indenting the first line. Word walls, dictionaries, vocabulary lists, and any other references are all encouraged to be used.

After Writing   Students are selected to read their paragraphs using the author's chair (Tompkins, 2009). The student calls on others to ask questions or offer comments about their writing.

Collaborative Inquiry Across the Curriculum

Extension to Mathematics   The setting in many of the texts includes the playground, which provides many opportunities to incorporate mathematics in the classroom. Working in pairs, students count the number of times they can swing, jump rope, and bounce a ball. They then develop a bar graph or circle graph to illustrate the results.

STANDARDS

Mathematics Standards
1. Number and Operation

Extension to Science   In the *King of the Playground, The Recess Queen,* and *The Bully Blockers Club,* the playground is a common setting. The teacher reviews or introduces the concept of gravity to the class and how gravity is important when playing in the playground. Students imagine what it would be like if there was no gravity when playing on the swing, slide, or seesaw. To illustrate the concept of gravity, the teacher provides a list of needed materials and a step-by-step procedure to construct a toy parachute. Students will have to follow directions to create and use their new toy.

STANDARDS

Science Standards
Physical Science, Content Standards B1 and B2

Extension to Social Studies   Students discuss the importance of laws and rules in their lives as the teacher leads a discussion on the ramifications of not having laws or rules. Many situations in this text set might have been resolved if certain rules were established by either the adults or the children in the story. The teacher asks the class to write a rule that may have helped one of the characters in their text effectively deal with a bully. From these rules, the students create their own playground rules for the class and post them in the room.

Home–School Connections   Parents need to become involved with their children and teachers and administrators when making such difficult choices about Dealing with Bullies, whether inside or outside of school. One way to accomplish this purpose is to invite parents to do a shared reading of *King of the Playground* with their child. As parents and students read about Kevin, they discuss their own experiences in dealing with bullying behavior and offer some positive ways to respond.

On-Your-Own Activities   *The Bully Blockers Club* by Teresa Bateman provides an alternative for children making Difficult Choices about dealing with bullies. Rather than responding to Grant, the class bully, Lotty enlisted the help of all the other children in her class to stand up together and call attention to Grant's behavior. With the help of their teacher, students formed a Bully Blockers Club where everyone was welcome. Their role was to speak out whenever they saw someone being bullied and also call the attention of any adult that was around. Since it was no longer possible to bully other children, Grant even decided to join the club.

Students will now be able to express their ideas about how to effectively respond to a bully, whether they are the victim or the observer. The class creates a simple list of responses and skills that everyone could follow when encountering a bully. Students then role play in order to practice their new skills.

Critical Literacy

When the Difficult Choices sub-theme has been completed, students synthesize and apply their new information about responding to bullying by creating poster boards for students in other classes that provide strategies for responding to bullies.

Collaborative Literacy

As a collaborative activity, students conduct a reader's theatre of *King of the Playground*. Students write their own version of the story, create costumes, and perform it for the kindergarten class. After the presentation, the second graders can discuss with their young guests how to make wise choices when dealing with a school bully.

The theme of Choices is continued in the intermediate grades as students discuss friendships. Through the sampler, Choices That Made a Difference: Choosing Friends, students read and discuss the daily choices that affect our lives.

■ Intermediate Grades: Grades 3–5

Children are able to understand that a choice in having a friend or being a friend is an important part of their lives in many different ways. As they explore this theme through their readings, discussions, and experiences in and out of the classroom,

CHOOSING TO BE DIFFERENT

Text Set

Leonardo: Beautiful Dreamer
A Bird or 2: A Story About Henri Matisse
Dreamer from the Village: The Story of
*   Marc Chagall*
Through Georgia's Eyes
Uncle Andy's

Outcomes

- Write a story about one of the artists and illustrate it with simulations of their paintings.

- Construct a K-W-L flip chart that summarizes new learnings about a selected artist.

- Create an open-mind portrait to identify a selected artist's character traits.

CHOOSING FREEDOM

Text Set

Let It Begin Here! Lexington & Concord:
*   First Battles of the American Revolution*
North Star to Freedom: The Story of the
*   Underground Railroad*
Delivering Justice: W. W. Law and the Fight for
*   Civil Rights*
Forging Freedom
Freedom on the Menu: The Greensboro Sit-Ins

Outcomes

- Discuss the stories through a tea party where students share responses.

- Create a cube which explores six dimensions of the topic.

- Construct a poster about the Greensboro Sit-Ins.

CHOOSING TO DEFY THE ODDS

Text Set

Celia Cruz, Queen of Salsa
A Strong Right Arm: The Story of Mamie
*   "Peanut" Johnson*
Mahalia: A Life in Gospel Music
Roberto Clemente: Pride of the Pittsburgh
*   Pirates*
Sixteen Years in Sixteen Seconds: The
*   Sammy Lee Story*

Outcomes

- Use a character cluster graphic organizer to identify character traits.

- Research one of the characters to create a collaborative book report.

- Create a quilt with symbols representing the traits of one of the characters.

CHOOSING TO JOURNEY AFAR

Text Set

The Journey that Saved Curious George:
*   The True Wartime Escape of Margaret*
*   and H. A. Rey*
Far Beyond the Garden Gate: Alexandra
*   David-Neel's Journey to Lhasa*
Everest: Reaching for the Sky
The Fantastic Journey of Pieter Brugel
The Travels of Benjamin Tudela: Through
*   Three Continents in the Twelfth*
*   Century*

Outcomes

- Use a REAP graphic organizer to summarize the story.

- Create and perform a script in reader's theatre based on a text.

- Write a collaborative story through interactive writing on one of the journeys.

Difficult Choices

Dangerous Choices

CHOICES

Choices That Made a Difference

CHOOSING FRIENDS

Text Set

Because of Winn-Dixie
Worlds Apart
Jennifer, Hecate, Macbeth, William McKinley,
*   and Me, Elizabeth*
It's Like This, Cat
Charlotte's Web

Outcomes

- Discuss the stories in the text set through a grand conversation.

- Construct hand puppets to retell one of the stories.

- Read the story with a partner and share your responses after each passage from the text.

CHOOSING TO CHANGE THE WORLD

Text Set

Boxes for Katje
Peace One Day: The Making of World Peace Day
Carl the Complainer
Tsunami: Helping Each Other

Outcomes

- Write a response to the texts in a double-entry journal.

- Create a wall story about the global response to the tsunami tragedy.

- Research a current global situation and create a *Box for Katje* to illustrate a solution.

students understand that some friendships can be a very important part of being a happy and healthy person. They will also understand that friendships thrive when people are able and willing to truly give of themselves.

In addition to the sub-theme Choices That Made a Difference, students also explore Difficult Choices and Dangerous Choices, as illustrated in the graphic organizer.

Choosing friends is an important sub-theme for students to understand in order for them to appreciate the importance of friendship in their lives. Skill in identifying the desired attributes they would like in their friends is important to a happy and healthy life. In order to provide children with the appropriate skills, this sub-theme provides numerous opportunities to explore a variety of familiar social situations.

SAMPLER ■ Choosing Friends

At the intermediate level, Choices are best studied by exposing students to different situations that require an appropriate decision to be made. Students will come to understand that though Choices must often be made, the best one may not be the same for everyone.

This text set provides opportunities for children to realize that true friendships are an important part of being a happy person. Children will find that friendships can be very strong even between children with very different backgrounds, as in *The Whipping Boy* by Sid Fleischman and *Jennifer, Hecate, Macbeth, William McKinley, and Me, Elizabeth* by E. L. Konigsburg. Being the new kid in school or the neighborhood is also a situation that many children have to deal with while growing up. In *Because of Winn-Dixie* by Kate DiCamillo, we learn how a girl living with her preacher father has to cope without being anywhere long enough to establish true friendships. In *Charlotte's Web* by E. B. White, students learn about a friendship that is based on the acceptance of differences, caring, understanding, love, and ultimately survival. Readers will have many opportunities to read, think, and discuss their feelings and understanding of the importance of Choosing Friends to not only themselves, but to other people as well.

NCTE/IRA Standards for the English Language Arts

1. Students read a wide range of print and non-print texts to build an understanding of texts, of themselves, and of the cultures of the United States and the world; to acquire new information; to respond to the needs and demands of society and the workplace; and for personal fulfillment. Among texts are fiction and nonfiction, classic and contemporary works.
5. Students employ a wide range of strategies as they write and use different writing process elements appropriately to communicate with different audiences for a variety of purposes.
12. Students use spoken, written, and visual language to accomplish their own purposes.

Learner Outcomes

Students will be able to do the following:

■ Read text and determine the main idea or essential message, identify relevant supporting details and facts, and arrange events in chronological order
■ Read and organize information for a variety of purposes

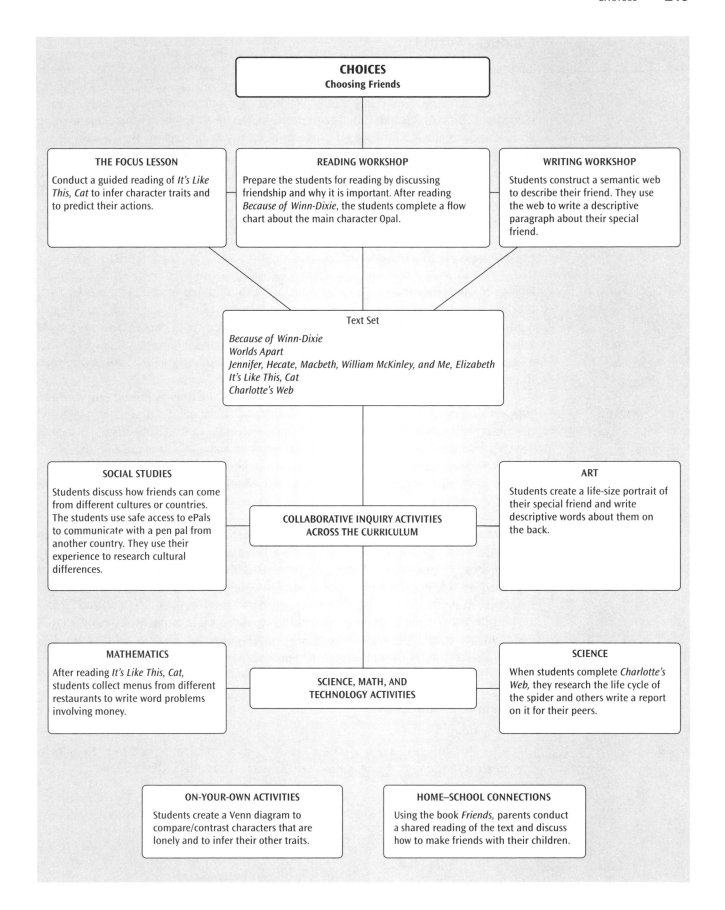

CHOICES
Choosing Friends

THE FOCUS LESSON

Conduct a guided reading of *It's Like This, Cat* to infer character traits and to predict their actions.

READING WORKSHOP

Prepare the students for reading by discussing friendship and why it is important. After reading *Because of Winn-Dixie*, the students complete a flow chart about the main character Opal.

WRITING WORKSHOP

Students construct a semantic web to describe their friend. They use the web to write a descriptive paragraph about their special friend.

Text Set

Because of Winn-Dixie
Worlds Apart
Jennifer, Hecate, Macbeth, William McKinley, and Me, Elizabeth
It's Like This, Cat
Charlotte's Web

SOCIAL STUDIES

Students discuss how friends can come from different cultures or countries. The students use safe access to ePals to communicate with a pen pal from another country. They use their experience to research cultural differences.

COLLABORATIVE INQUIRY ACTIVITIES ACROSS THE CURRICULUM

ART

Students create a life-size portrait of their special friend and write descriptive words about them on the back.

MATHEMATICS

After reading *It's Like This, Cat,* students collect menus from different restaurants to write word problems involving money.

SCIENCE, MATH, AND TECHNOLOGY ACTIVITIES

SCIENCE

When students complete *Charlotte's Web,* they research the life cycle of the spider and others write a report on it for their peers.

ON-YOUR-OWN ACTIVITIES

Students create a Venn diagram to compare/contrast characters that are lonely and to infer their other traits.

HOME–SCHOOL CONNECTIONS

Using the book *Friends,* parents conduct a shared reading of the text and discuss how to make friends with their children.

Conduct a Focus Lesson

The text set for Choosing Friends includes award-winning literature that presents realistic situations in which a character is lonely and in need of a friend. The focus lesson uses *It's Like This, Cat* by Emily Neville to illustrate this scenario. Dave, a young teenager, soon outgrows his only friend from childhood. Through his close relationship with Kate, a recluse who keeps a home full of cats, Dave decides that a stray tiger-striped tomcat is just what he needs. Through his day-to-day adventures with Cat, Dave encounters Tom, a young adult, and Mary, a girl from another neighborhood, with whom he builds special relationships that grow into true friendships.

Establish a Purpose   The purposes of the focus lesson are to explore the reasons people choose friends, understand that friends are special, and understand that a friend can be someone that is not your own age.

Engage in Guided Reading   The theme begins with a guided reading of *It's Like This, Cat* by Emily Neville. In a group setting, the teacher introduces the book, invites students to look at the illustration at the beginning of the first chapter, and to discuss what this chapter might be about. The illustration depicts a young boy happily holding a cat while an older man looks disagreeably on. The teacher asks the group why they think the two characters are feeling the way they do.

The teacher establishes the idea that friends are often able to provide us with the support or confidence we need to make important decisions. Students begin reading the chapter aloud until Dave, the young teenager, decides to visit Kate, his older friend. They then continue reading silently to find out why Dave and Kate are friends.

To prepare students for the text set, the teacher conducts a discussion about the value of choosing a good friend and how friendships can be made in different ways.

Conduct a Mini-Lesson   After the guided reading, the focus of the mini-lesson is to understand the special relationship between Dave and Kate. Students identify some of the needs of Dave and Kate and the teacher asks the students to think about some of the reasons Dave may be friends with Kate. The teacher then asks them to do the same for Kate. Students discuss the needs that are similar as well as different and, using a Venn diagram, they write these needs in the appropriate circle, noting the shared needs in the overlapping section of the Venn diagram. As a summation of the lesson, students discuss the value of this friendship and how they too may have similar needs.

Additional Mini-Lessons

Story Comprehension

- After the students have completed the text set on friendship, they work in pairs to create a diorama that illustrates a critical scene from their selected text.

Predicting

- Before they begin each text, the students do a five-minute quickwrite that focuses on their predictions.
- The teacher models how to use the book jacket and blurb to make predictions about chapter books.

Making Inferences

- After students have finished each text, they select one of the main characters to evaluate on a literature report card.
- The students list the main character's traits and give them a grade on each.
- The students must support their grades with evidence from the text.

Conduct a Reading Workshop

In the second text in the text set, *Because of Winn-Dixie* by Kate DiCamillo, a young lady named Opal adopts a stray dog that provides her opportunities to make many new friends. Opal lives with her preacher father, who has to move from one small town community to the next as his profession requires. Opal's mother abandoned her as an infant and Opal must also struggle to understand this as well as her difficulty in establishing new friendships with her peers. Through her dog, Winn-Dixie, Opal begins to meet several caring adults who help her choose new friends in her neighborhood.

Before Reading   Before students read the book, the teacher discusses why people become friends. The teacher asks students to discuss ways to make friends and keep a written list. Students then identify ways not to make friends and list these as well. The students create a classroom chart to use as a reference tool as they read *Because of Winn-Dixie.*

During Reading   As students are reading the text, the teacher asks them to identify the things that Opal does to either make friends or not make friends. The teacher refers students to their pre-reading chart to compare Opal's actions with their responses.

The teacher asks the class to discuss how they believe Opal's attitude will change about her choice of friends as the story unfolds.

After Reading   After students have completed the text, they create a graphic organizer as in Figure 6.3 to illustrate the people that Opal befriends throughout the story.

FIGURE 6.3   How to Make Friends

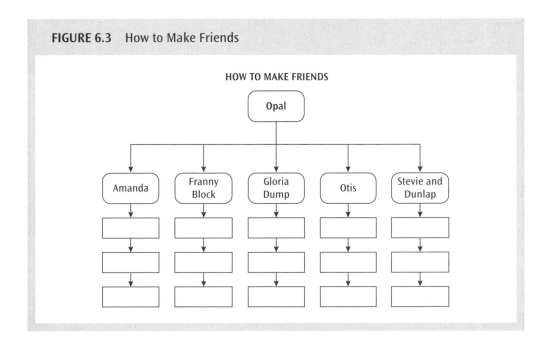

ASSESS LITERACY

To assess the students' comprehension of text and understanding of the actions of people that help to create friendships, the rubric presented below may be used as a guide.

Criteria	Independent	Proficient	Developing
Making Inferences	Student is proficient at making inferences in regard to character needs and reactions. (3)	Student is beginning to make inferences in regard to character needs and reactions. (2)	Student needs assistance in making inferences in regard to character needs and reactions. (0–1)
Making Connections	Student is proficient at making personal and text-to-text connections. (3)	Student is beginning to make personal and text-to-text connections. (2)	Student needs assistance in making personal and text-to-text connections. (0–1)
Identification of Causes of Behavior	After reading the book, student identifies causes of behavior that lead to reactions by characters in the text. (3)	After reading the book, student begins to identify causes of behavior that lead to reactions by characters in the text. (2)	After reading the book, student needs assistance to identify causes of behavior that lead to reactions by characters in the text. (0–1)
Identification of Effects of Behavior	After reading the book, student identifies effects of the character's behavior that resulted from a specific cause(s). (3)	After reading the book, student begins identifying the effects of the character's behavior that resulted from a specific cause(s). (2)	After reading the book, student needs assistance in identifying the effects of the character's behavior that resulted from a specific cause(s). (0–1)

Independent: 9–12
Proficient: 5–8
Developing: 0–4

Students use the flowchart to write the name of each friend Opal makes by the end of the story, and what specific actions of Opal's helped make them choose to become her friend.

Conduct a Writing Workshop

In *Charlotte's Web* by E. B. White, Wilbur's final thought was "It is not often that someone comes along who is a true friend and a good writer. Charlotte was both" (p. 184).

Before Writing   The teacher leads a discussion about Charlotte's writing ability. Through the discussion, students understand that Charlotte has a large vocabulary, using such words as *sedentary, gullible, salutations, radiant, versatile,* and even the Latin term *magnum opus.* A brief review of the meanings of these words in context would

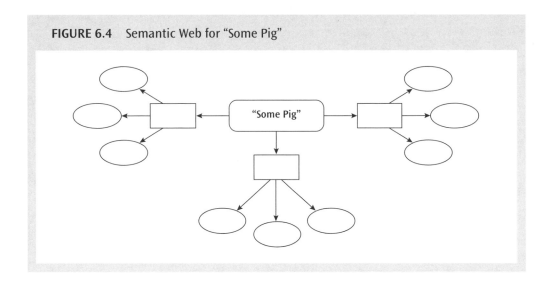

FIGURE 6.4   Semantic Web for "Some Pig"

be appropriate. The teacher reviews the scene where Charlotte spins her first web with the words "Some Pig" and presents this in a semantic web, as in Figure 6.4.

The teacher asks students to identify words that describe Wilbur as "Some Pig" and to write them in the semantic web. Using the words in this web, students write a descriptive paragraph about their special friend.

During Writing   Students work independently using any resource they wish (dictionary, thesaurus, computer) to identify new words that describe their friend. When the new words are identified, students write their descriptive paragraph using their words appropriately. Before beginning to write their paragraph, the teacher models a standard format and displays it on chart paper.

After Writing   When students have completed their descriptive paragraph, they create a portrait of their friend to accompany the text. Students are asked to share their writing and drawing with each other in either a small group or with the entire class.

Collaborative Inquiry Across the Curriculum

Extension to Mathematics   In *It's Like This, Cat,* the main character found his spending money to be a concern whether he is eating out, traveling by train or bus, or paying for some form of entertainment. Students collect menus from their favorite neighborhood restaurants to use in math problems. The teacher presents different scenarios where students have a set amount of money to spend.

STANDARDS
Mathematics Standards 4. Measurement

Another opportunity to explore money and mathematics related to this text is the change in the value of money—a Coke costs only 15 cents in this story. Explore how the prices of things have changed from years ago.

Extension to Science   *Charlotte's Web* has an intriguing spider as a central character. Students find studying the life cycle of spiders and how they spin their webs to be fascinating. Students use the Internet to create a poster of spiders from different regions. This activity can be coordinated with social studies as students explore the types of spiders found through different regions of the globe.

STANDARDS
Science Standards Life Science, Content Standards C2 and C3

ASSESS LITERACY

Teachers may use the rubric below to monitor student progress after they have completed their descriptive paragraph.

Criteria	Independent	Proficient	Developing
Paragraph Structure	Paragraph is well developed and has a logical sequence with supporting sentences. (3)	Paragraph is somewhat developed and has a logical sequence with supporting sentences. (2)	Paragraph is not developed and does not have a logical sequence with supporting sentences. (0–1)
Sentence Structure	Student employs varied types of sentences in writing, using some complex structures when appropriate. (3)	Student uses sentences that are somewhat simple, but accurate. (2)	Student uses sentence structure that is simple and not always accurate. (0–1)
Vocabulary	Student consistently uses content and descriptive vocabulary with a high degree of accuracy. (3)	Student uses some of the content and descriptive vocabulary but may use words incorrectly. (2)	Student does not use the content or descriptive vocabulary. (0–1)
Language Mechanics	No errors in language mechanics are present. (3)	Some errors in language mechanics are present but do not interfere with meaning. (2)	Many errors in language mechanics appear throughout. (0–1)
Independent: 9–12 Proficient: 5–8 Developing: 0–4			

STANDARDS

Social Studies Standards
III. People, Places, and
Environments

Extension to Social Studies   Throughout the text set, characters establish friendships with others who are quite different from them. A spider befriends a pig in *Charlotte's Web*; a young adolescent develops his first friendship with a girl, as well as with an older male, in *It's Like This, Cat*; a misbehaving prince and his whipping boy build an unlikely friendship in *The Whipping Boy*; and two lonely young girls struggle to make new friends in *Because of Winn-Dixie* and in *Jennifer, Hecate, Macbeth, William McKinley, and Me, Elizabeth*.

Learning about other people who are different is a wonderful way to build friendships. Students are encouraged to search the Internet for an international friend, or ePal. A good place to begin is ePALS SchoolMail (www.epals.com), which is a safe and secure environment for students. This website also offers a multilingual translation feature to help students communicate with one another. There are also many other sites available to build international friendships that teachers can explore before introducing to students.

Students read and write letters to each other to begin to build friendships with others from different cultures, backgrounds, and languages. These letters can be used in endless ways in the classroom while exploring social studies units and building literacy throughout the intermediate grades.

Home–School Connections   Parents need to become involved with their children and teachers to guide children to make good choices in their friends. Often we focus on simply encouraging children to be friends with certain children instead of teaching children how to both make new friends and be a good friend.

Parents can not only read aloud to their children in the intermediate grades, but can share a book by reading it at the same time independently. Parents can share *Friends!* by Elaine Scott with their children or *Make Friends, Break Friends* by Peggy Burns to initiate discussions. Peggy Burns shows that while making friends makes life much more interesting, making and keeping friends is not always easy. Discussions should emphasize the importance of Choosing Friends and how to be a good friend.

On-Your-Own Activities   *The Whipping Boy* by Sid Fleischman is a tale about Jemmy, a common boy, selected to receive punishment on behalf of a young, arrogant, and disrespectful prince. The lonely and bored prince decides to run away and commands his whipping boy to accompany him. After being kidnapped and pursued by outlaws, the two boys learn to depend on one another and eventually became true friends.

In *Jennifer, Hecate, Macbeth, William McKinley and Me, Elizabeth* by E. L. Konigsburg, Elizabeth, another lonely young girl, tries to become friends with Jennifer, who is African American, likes pretending she is a witch, and also has no friends.

Both stories present characters who are lonely yet independent youngsters. Their choice in friends seems unusual until a situation develops that forces behavior that provides the foundation for friendship.

After reading both stories, students compare and contrast Prince Brat and Jennifer and Jemmy and Elizabeth. Using Venn diagrams, students identify the similarities and differences between these characters, and then write a paper discussing the importance of friendship, the basis for friendship, and the attributes desired in a friend.

Critical Literacy

After the completion of the sub-theme, the teacher leads the class in a closing activity regarding the qualities of special friends. Working in pairs, students consolidate the information from their readings and other activities to complete the compare/contrast graphic organizer illustrated in Figure 6.5.

Collaborative Literacy

Students share their own special friends in a "Celebrate Special Friendships" class session. Students create hand puppets of their friends and explain how they chose their friends and how their special qualities cement their relationship. Students also display the descriptive paragraph they wrote about their special friend. After everyone has shared their friendship story, the class can discuss how they maintain their friendships.

Middle grade students, similar to their intermediate grade peers, are also struggling with life's daily choices. Through the sampler Difficult Choices: Life's Daily Struggles, young adolescents will discuss fictional characters and their search for wisdom and discernment.

FIGURE 6.5   Compare–Contrast Graphic Organizer

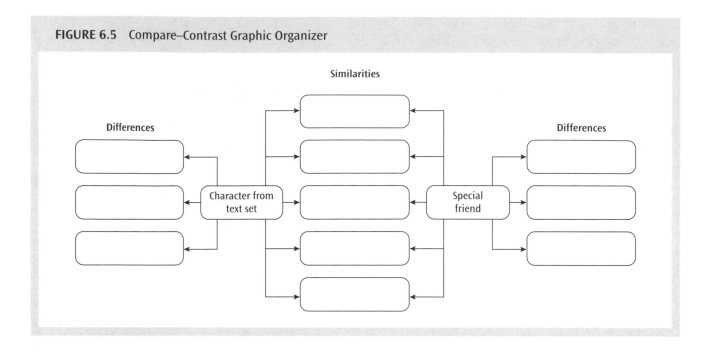

■ Middle Grades: Grades 6–8

The theme Choices will offer students opportunities to read and discuss how life is often disrupted by difficult or dangerous choices that must be made. Dangerous Choices will offer students the opportunity to read about Oskar Schindler, who chose to harbor Jews from the Nazis during World War II. In the text set Freedom's Founders, young adolescents will discover how America was founded based on the risk of a few courageous citizens to choose liberty rather than the yoke of tyranny. For Difficult Choices students read literature such as *Heat* and *Scorpions* to discuss the difficulties and struggles that all young adolescents face on a daily basis. Taking a Stand explores texts that focus on brave individuals such as Nelson Mandela who chose to take a stand against injustice to improve the lives of their fellow human beings. In the final sub-theme, students develop an understanding of Choices That Made a Difference by reading about how famous inventors such as Thomas Edison changed our lives for the better through their research. As students read and discuss the Choices theme, they begin to reflect on their own lives and the direction they wish it to take.

SAMPLER ■ Life's Choices

Every day the young adolescent learner faces choices that can affect their lives for years to come. It can be difficult to know which path to take, as life often presents problems that are not clearly defined but require discernment and wisdom in order to solve them.

This sampler will explore difficult choices made by fictional young adolescent characters faced with the same problems of daily life as their readers. As students read about the characters and discuss their lives, they will find opportunities to explore how they would react in similar situations. In their literature discussion groups, students explore how the choices we make in our daily lives will define us and determine our future.

LIFE'S CHOICES

Text Set

Heat
Bud, Not Buddy
Tuck Everlasting
Hoot
Kira-Kira
Miracle on 49th Street
Scorpions

Outcomes

- Use the book-a-day graphic organizer to discuss main characters in texts.
- Write a simulated memoir about a hero.
- Graph the tension in the text by using a plot profile graphic organizer.

FIGHT OR FLIGHT

Text Set

Oskar Schindler: Saving Jews from the Holocaust
Code Talker: A Novel About the Navajo
  Marines of World War Two
I Will Plant You a Lilac Tree:
  A Memoir of a Schindler's List Survivor
Hidden Child
Remember World War II
The Secret Seder

Outcomes

- Use a REAP graphic organizer to summarize the fight for freedom.
- Create hero cards to depict the lives of the historical figures they have read about.
- Research the Navajo code and create one for the class to decipher.

TAKING A STAND

Text Set

Demanding Justice: A Story about Mary
  Ann Shadd Cary
Fight On! March Church
Terrell's Battle for Integration
Ida B. Wells: Mother of the Civil Rights
  Movement
Dream Freedom
Peaceful Protest: The Life of Nelson
  Mandela
Abby Takes a Stand

Outcomes

- Discuss whether they would risk their lives for a just cause.
- Research current injustices and brainstorm possible ways to be involved in solutions.
- Create a quilt about one of the characters.

FREEDOM'S FOUNDERS

Text Set

The Real Revolution: The Global Story of
  American Independence
Ben Franklin's Almanac: Being a True Account
  of the Good Gentleman's Life
The Founders: The 39 Stories Behind the U.S.
  Constitution
The Signers: The 56 Stories Behind the
  Declaration of Independence
Let It Begin Here! Lexington and Concord:
  First Battles of the American Revolution

Outcomes

- Summarize knowledge of American Revolution in a Learning Log.
- Use the ReQuest strategy to deepen knowledge about the American Revolution.
- Construct a story board to illustrate one of the texts.

Difficult Choices

Dangerous Choices

CHOICES

Choices That Made a Difference

CHOOSING TO CHANGE THE WORLD

Text Set

Leonardo: Beautiful Dreamer
Amelia to Zora: Twenty-Six Women Who
  Changed the World
Airborne: A Photobiography of Wilbur and Orville Wright
Inventing the Future: A Photobiography
  of Thomas Edison
The Man Who Made Time Travel

Outcomes

- Create a data chart to compare/contrast lives of inventors.
- Use an open-mind portrait to infer traits of characters.
- Brainstorm possible inventions that can help society and the world.

CHOOSING TO HELP OTHERS

Text Set

Portraits of African-American Heroes
50 American Heroes Every Kid Should Meet
The Forbidden Schoolhouse: The True and Dramatic
  Story of Prudence Crandall and Her Students
Heroes and She-Roes: Poems of Amazing
  and Everyday Heroes
A Good Night for Freedom

Outcomes

- Evaluate characters in text through a literature report card.
- Create a timeline depicting events in the life of one of the heroes.
- Discuss the heroes in the text set through a grand conversation.

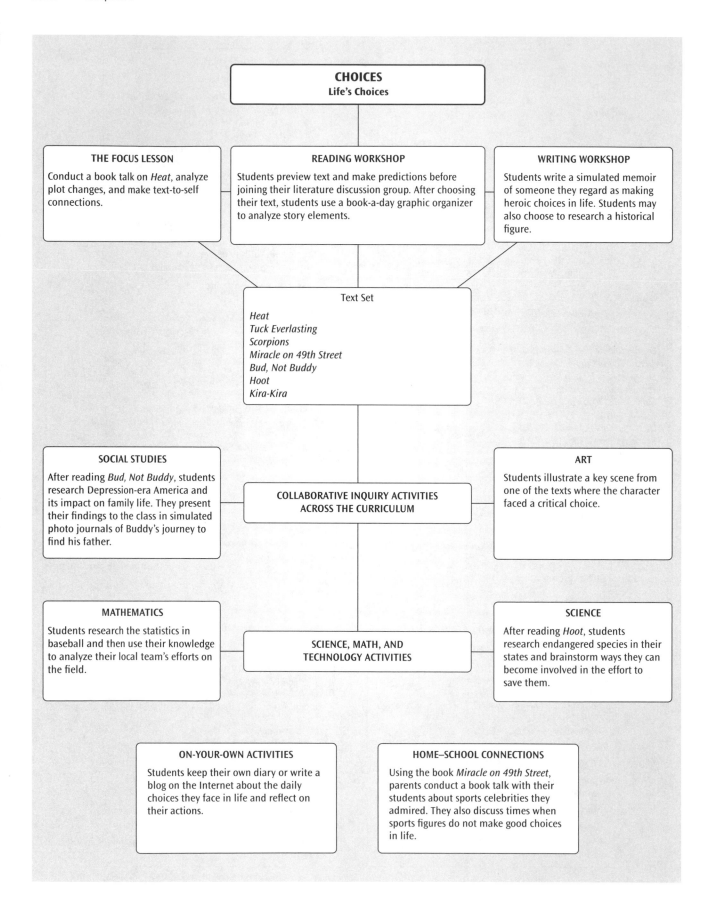

CHOICES
Life's Choices

THE FOCUS LESSON

Conduct a book talk on *Heat*, analyze plot changes, and make text-to-self connections.

READING WORKSHOP

Students preview text and make predictions before joining their literature discussion group. After choosing their text, students use a book-a-day graphic organizer to analyze story elements.

WRITING WORKSHOP

Students write a simulated memoir of someone they regard as making heroic choices in life. Students may also choose to research a historical figure.

Text Set

Heat
Tuck Everlasting
Scorpions
Miracle on 49th Street
Bud, Not Buddy
Hoot
Kira-Kira

SOCIAL STUDIES

After reading *Bud, Not Buddy*, students research Depression-era America and its impact on family life. They present their findings to the class in simulated photo journals of Buddy's journey to find his father.

COLLABORATIVE INQUIRY ACTIVITIES ACROSS THE CURRICULUM

ART

Students illustrate a key scene from one of the texts where the character faced a critical choice.

MATHEMATICS

Students research the statistics in baseball and then use their knowledge to analyze their local team's efforts on the field.

SCIENCE, MATH, AND TECHNOLOGY ACTIVITIES

SCIENCE

After reading *Hoot*, students research endangered species in their states and brainstorm ways they can become involved in the effort to save them.

ON-YOUR-OWN ACTIVITIES

Students keep their own diary or write a blog on the Internet about the daily choices they face in life and reflect on their actions.

HOME–SCHOOL CONNECTIONS

Using the book *Miracle on 49th Street*, parents conduct a book talk with their students about sports celebrities they admired. They also discuss times when sports figures do not make good choices in life.

NCTE/IRA Standards for the English Language Arts

1. Students read a wide range of print and non-print texts to build an understanding of texts, of themselves, and of the cultures of the United States and the world; to acquire new information; to respond to the needs and demands of society and the workplace; and for personal fulfillment. Among texts are fiction and nonfiction, classic and contemporary works.
5. Students employ a wide range of strategies as they write and use different writing process elements appropriately to communicate with different audiences for a variety of purposes.
12. Students use spoken, written, and visual language to accomplish their own purposes.

Learner Outcomes

Students will be able to do the following:

- Use background knowledge of subject and related content areas, prereading representations, and knowledge of text structure to make and confirm complex purposes
- Compare and contrast elements in multiple texts

Conduct a Focus Lesson

Heat by Mike Lupica is the fictional account of a 12-year-old Cuban American boy with remarkable pitching abilities. Despite Michael Arroyo's amazing talent, he faces many challenges off the field as he and his brother Carlos try to stay together as a family. Through book talks, a shared reading, and a mini-lesson on plotting story tension, the teacher helps students to discuss the texts in the sampler and to make text-to-self connections.

Establish a Purpose   In order for students to understand the text in the sampler, they must be able to draw on their knowledge of baseball and life in Cuba. Therefore, the English language arts teacher begins the sequence by asking students to do a five-minute quickwrite to record their knowledge about the topics. After the allotted time, the teacher takes their responses and records them on a descriptive graphic organizer, as illustrated in Figure 6.6.

Engage in a Book Talk   The teacher introduces *Heat* by writing the title on the board and asking the students to read the blurb on the jacket.

Students are directed to read the first chapter of the text and to record any questions they raise during their reading. After the class has read the first chapter, they discuss the following questions in their literature discussion groups:

- Who is Michael Arroyo?
- What dilemma does he face?
- How do you think you would have acted if you were in his place?

Students also bring their Post-it note questions and share them in their small groups. One member of the group will act as a recorder and chart their responses.

Conduct a Mini-Lesson   After students have completed the text, the teacher conducts a mini-lesson exploring the book's themes and the daily choices that Michael Arroyo and his brother must make in order to survive.

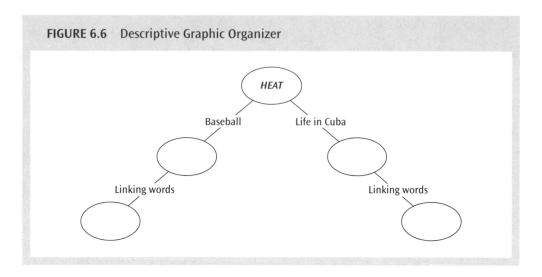

FIGURE 6.6 Descriptive Graphic Organizer

The teacher uses the plot profiles strategy (Antonacci & O'Callaghan, 2006) to facilitate comprehension of text by plotting the story tension. The students remain in their discussion groups to complete the following task:

- After discussing the story, the group charts the story events and numbers them in correct sequence.
- Using chart paper, the group creates a graph and lists the story events along the horizontal *(x)* axis by using the number of the story event.
- The vertical *(y)* axis is used to rate the degree of tension or excitement attached to each event from 0 to 10.
- When the graph is complete, the teacher directs the students to discuss the varying levels of tension and how the author crafted the plot.

When the groups are ready, the class reconvenes and one member of each group presents their graph and response. After each group has responded, the teacher asks the students to compare their responses and support any disagreements regarding story events with passages from the text.

Additional Mini-Lessons

Think-Pair-Share

- Students read about Michael Arroyo in *Heat* and work in pairs to respond to the question, Should Michael tell Mr. Gibbs the truth?
- After they come to consensus on a group response, students share their responses with the class.

Connect It

- When students have completed the text set, they use the connect it strategy to respond to the stories.
- The graphic organizer asks them to identify personal and world connections that they make with their readings.

Story Pyramids

- After students have completed their readings, they select a book from the text set to complete the story pyramid graphic.

■ The graphic is completed with the name of the main character, two words describing the character, three words describing the setting, four words stating the problem, five words describing the first story event, seven words describing the middle story event, eight words describing the final event, and nine words describing a personal response to the ending.

Conduct a Reading Workshop

During reading workshop, students remain in their literature discussion groups to read additional texts about fictional characters who are dealing with difficult choices. Since the groups will be reading several texts, this reading workshop will occur over two weeks.

Before Reading   The students choose one of the following texts for their literature discussion group: *Scorpions* by Walter Dean Myers, *Miracle on 49th Street* by Mike Lupica, *Tuck Everlasting* by Natalie Babbitt, or *Hoot* by Carl Hiaasen.

The teacher directs students to preview their books before reading. Before beginning the text, students use their journals to record their predictions and any questions they have regarding the text.

During Reading   As students read each text, the teacher walks around to monitor their progress and to intervene if any student is struggling. Students record their predictions and any new vocabulary words in their journals as they read.

After Reading   After the literature groups finish each text, they share their responses with the whole class and new vocabulary words are defined and placed on a wall chart. New groups are formed with one reader from each literature group for the after-reading activity. As groups discuss the texts, students will take notes with a book-a-day graphic organizer (Allen, 2004). This graphic organizer allows students to compare and contrast characters as well as story elements across texts. As illustrated in Figure 6.7, students record how the character of Michael Arroyo and the plot of *Heat* compare to the story they chose from the text set.

Conduct a Writing Workshop

During writing workshop, the teacher engages the students in the genre of memoirs. In the text set, students read several fictional accounts of courageous actions by characters faced with life's daily struggles and choices. For example, Roy Eberhardt in *Hoot* defies corporate bullies to help endangered miniature owls. In the opening chapter of *Heat*, Michael Arroyo comes to the aid of an elderly neighbor who was robbed of her food money. These heroic actions are excellent discussion points for exploring how life events often call us toward heroic choices. During writing workshop, students are given the choice of interviewing a family member who they regard as a hero or researching a famous historical figure.

Before Writing   To begin the writing workshop, the teacher asks students to define the word *hero* and to list two people they would identify as heroic. After students have recorded their responses, the teacher lists their answers on a brainstorming chart and asks the class to summarize their definition of a hero. When students have the concept

FIGURE 6.7   Book-a-Day Organizer

Titles		
■ *Heat* by Mike Lupica ■ *Hoot* by Carl Hiaasen		

EX	**P**	**L**
Example of Genre, Author, and Style	**P**urpose for Writing	What Are the Key **L**ines?
■ Young adult fiction ■ Christopher Curtis	■ To tell the story of a young pitcher ■ To engage young readers in a story about the environment	■ "And you're telling me that you got him with this from home plate? . . . that's some arm, kid."

O	**R**	**E**
Organizational Features that Support Reading	**R**elate to Reading	**E**valuate My Thinking
■ Already knowing about baseball and the Yankees made it easy to begin. ■ The book jacket and cover gave an idea of the story.	■ All teenagers have problems talking to boys/girls like Michael. ■ All kids get picked on by bullies.	■ Will Michael ever become a Yankee like El Grande? ■ What will happen to Roy next?

of heroic actions and choices, the teacher gives them the option of writing about a hero in their families or a famous figure in history who risked their lives for others. Heroes in their own families might be police officers, firefighters, or veterans.

During Writing   Students who choose to write about a family hero will interview the person and take notes about his or her life and work. If they choose a historical figure they use research materials to gather information for the memoir. Before students begin to interview or research their heroes, they record five questions they would like answered. After students have gathered their information, the teacher helps them to categorize the data in order to answer their questions. When their data is organized, the teacher reviews the characteristics of memoir writing and reminds students to write the account as a first-person narrative from the hero's perspective. The class discusses "voice" and how they will write their hero's account.

After Writing   When students have completed their memoirs, they give them to a partner to edit and critique. The partner will raise questions for clarification and also comment on the voice of the memoir. After revising their work, students may illustrate their memoir with photographs or drawings.

Collaborative Inquiry Across the Curriculum

Extensions to Mathematics   In *Heat* students read about the world of baseball and the importance of batting averages and the pitcher's earned run average (ERA). In

ASSESS LITERACY

The teacher assesses students' skills in the following areas: (1) making a text-to-self connection, (2) locating information in text after reading, (3) summarizing information and recording their responses, (4) articulating their responses in a discussion, and (5) using their graphic organizers to share their information with the group.

Criteria	Independent	Proficient	Developing
Text-to-Self Connections	After reading their books, students make text-to-self connections that illustrate their comprehension of text. (3)	After reading their books, students begin to develop text-to-self connections that illustrate their comprehension of text. (2)	After reading their books, students need assistance to develop text-to-self connections that illustrate their comprehension of text. (0–1)
Locating Information in Text	Students are proficient at locating information from their books. (3)	Students are beginning to find information from their books. (2)	Students need assistance in order to find information from their books. (0–1)
Summarizing Information and Using It in Discussions	Students are proficient at paraphrasing the information from the text and using it during discussions. (3)	Students are beginning to paraphrase the information from the text and to use it during discussions. (2)	Students need assistance to paraphrase the information from the text and to use it during discussions. (0–1)
Use of Graphic Organizers	Students apply information from text that is complete and/or accurate. (3)	Students apply information from text that is somewhat complete and accurate. (2)	Students' graphic organizers include information that is not complete and/or accurate. (0–1)

Independent: 9–12
Proficient: 5–8
Developing: 0–4

this activity, students research the origin of the two statistics in baseball and how the averages are calculated. In groups, students plot the ERAs of the pitchers on their local home teams to evaluate their effectiveness.

Extension to Science The character Roy Eberhardt in *Hoot* is drawn into the fight to save endangered miniature owls in Florida. In this group activity, students research one of the endangered species in their home state and discuss how they can become involved in attempts to save them.

Extension to Social Studies In *Bud, Not Buddy* by Christopher Paul Curtis, students read about a 10-year-old boy growing up in Michigan during the Depression. He runs

STANDARDS
Science Standards
Life Science, Content Standards C2 and C3

STANDARDS
Social Studies Standards
II. Time, Continuity, and Change

It is critical to monitor student progress throughout the instructional sequence. When students have completed their memoir, teachers may use the rubric below to evaluate their writing performance.

Criteria	Independent	Proficient	Developing
Planning	Student carefully plans prior to writing, taking into account all of the memoir parts. (3)	Student engages in planning throughout the writing of the memoir. (2)	Student shows little or no planning prior to constructing a draft of the memoir. (0–1)
Drafting	Student engages in the careful construction of a draft developed through planning; drafting occurs throughout writing as needed. (3)	Student develops an adequate draft that demonstrates planning for memoir was considered. (2)	Student develops a simple draft that does not account for planning for memoir. (0–1)
Revising	Student makes substantial changes in the memoir. (3)	Student makes adequate changes in the memoir. (2)	Student makes no or very few changes in the memoir after being prompted. (0–1)
Editing	Student edits carefully for errors and systematically edits for a wide array of language conventions. (3)	Student edits many errors and attends to some language conventions. (2)	Student pays little attention to errors and focuses on a single error type, such as spelling. (0–1)
Vocabulary	Student uses many descriptive and complex words with accuracy and incorporates the language of the literature. (3)	Student uses some descriptive words with accuracy. (2)	Student uses simple vocabulary. (0–1)
Spelling	Student's writing exhibits no or few spelling errors. (3)	Student's writing exhibits some spelling errors. (2)	Student's writing exhibits many spelling errors. (0–1)
Capitalization	Student's writing has no or few errors in capitalization. (3)	Student's writing has some errors in capitalization. (2)	Student's writing has many errors in capitalization. (0–1)
Punctuation	Student's writing has no or few punctuation errors. (3)	Student's writing has some punctuation errors. (2)	Student's writing has many punctuation errors. (0–1)
Sentence Structure	Student's writing exhibits a variety of sentence structures that are used appropriately within the story. (3)	Student's writing has some errors with sentence structure and attempts at writing complex sentences. (2)	Student's writing contains incomplete and simple sentences. (0–1)
Independent: 19–27 Proficient: 10–18 Developing: 0–9			

away from foster care in an attempt to find his father, who he believes to be a jazz musician. Bud's choice to search for his father brings him across the railway stations and roadways of America during the Depression. In this group activity, students create fictional photo journals of Bud's journey to find his father based on photographs of Depression-era United States that can be found at the History's Channel's website (www.historychannel.com).

Home–School Connections   In *Miracle on 49th Street* and *Heat,* Mike Lupica writes about the world of sports and the devotion of fans towards their teams. Teams such as the New York Yankees and the Boston Celtics have generations of fans that revere their sports heroes and follow their lives on and off the fields. Students use the texts as vehicles for a talk with their parents to discuss sports teams they followed and the sports celebrities that captured their imaginations. It also provides an opportunity for families to discuss how sports celebrities often choose the wrong path in life.

On-Your-Own Activities   In *Kira-Kira* by Cynthia Kadohata, students read about a Japanese American family struggling to survive in Georgia during the 1950s. Katie Takeshima admires her eldest sister Lynn and her "glittering, shining" approach to life. When Lynn loses her battle with lymphoma, Katie must face the most difficult choice one can be called to make in life: How does one go on after such a tragic loss? Katie finds the strength to choose life rather than sorrow by reading Lynn's journal.

After reading the texts in the sampler, students begin to compose their own daily account of life's choices and worries. Many adolescents keep their own blogs for friends to view on the Internet. However, they often don't see their blog as a written diary. Journaling is a way for young adolescents to have an internal dialogue about the daily choices they must face. The diary is for their personal use and reflection. However, they may share entries in class meetings or post them on a blog if they so desire.

Critical Literacy

As a closure activity to the Choices theme, students synthesize and evaluate their new knowledge about heroes by creating a multimedia presentation. Students work in groups of three to outline the character traits shared by their chosen heroes and the key choices in their lives that led to destiny. The groups may choose to create a PowerPoint slideshow or a podcast to present their information.

Collaborative Literacy

Students share their memoirs through a classroom celebration entitled "Everything We Do Is a Choice." The students perform a dramatic reading of their memoir in their literature discussion groups and share their photographs or illustrations. When everyone has participated, the group discusses the choices made by their chosen heroes and how they have gained insight by studying their lives.

RESOURCE GUIDE: CHILDREN'S LITERATURE REFERENCES AND ACTIVITIES

Primary Grades

Dangerous Choices

Challenges in the Sky

Burleigh, R. (1991). *Flight: The journey of Charles Lindbergh.* Illustrated by M. Wimmer. New York: Philomel.

Gerstein, M. (2004). *The man who walked between the towers.* Brookfield, CT: Roaring Brook.

Grimes, N. (2002). *Talkin' about Bessie: The story of aviator Elizabeth Coleman.* Illustrated by E. B. Lewis. New York: Orchard.

Provensen, A., & Provensen, M. (1983). *The glorious flight: Across the channel with Louis Bleriot.* New York: Viking Press.

Sís, P. (1996). *Starry messenger: Galileo Galilei.* New York: Farrar, Straus & Giroux.

- **Personal Interviews:** After reading about the many heroes presented in this text set, students role play one of the main characters and are "interviewed" by their classmates.
- **Snapshot Vignettes:** This summary activity allows students to consolidate their knowledge about one of the heroes in the text set. Working in groups, students illustrate the key events of the person's life. The students write a caption for each event and arrange them in chronological order.
- **Retelling:** The students use cutouts from one of the stories to retell the plot for their peers. After they have orally told the story, they write their summary in a reader's response journal.

Choosing Freedom

Amstel, A. (2000). *Sybil Ludington's midnight ride.* Illustrated by Ellen Beir. New York: Carolrhoda.

Krensky, S. (2005). *Dangerous crossing: The revolutionary voyage of John Quincy Adams.* New York: Dutton.

Littlesugar, A. (2006). *Willy and Max: A Holocaust story.* Illustrated by William Low. New York: Philomel.

Longfellow, H. (2003). *Paul Revere's ride: The landlord's tale.* Illustrated by Charles Santore. New York: HarperCollins.

Morrow, B. (2003). *A good night for freedom.* Illustrated by Leonard Jenkins. New York: Holiday.

- **Display Boxes:** After the students have read about the perilous journeys of Sybil Ludington, Paul Revere, and John Quincy Adams, they select one hero to research. After they have gathered the facts about their freedom journey, they use a cereal box to create a display case of scenes depicting the person's life.

- **Character Mobile:** After the students have completed the text set, they create a character mobile with a cutout for each person. Students write about the character's choice for freedom on the other side of the cutout and display their mobile.
- **Story Boards:** The students work in groups to create a story board about one of the heroes they have researched. The story board illustrates the hero's actions and emphasizes the dangerous choices that needed to be made.

Difficult Choices

Dealing with Bullies

Bateman, T. (2006). *The bully blockers club.* Morton Grove, IL: Albert Whitman & Co.

Burns, P. (2005). *Make friends, break friends.* Milwaukee, WI: Raintree Publishers.

Larson, K. (1996). *Cody and Quinn, sitting in a tree.* Illustrated by Nancy Poydar. New York: Holiday.

Lovell, P. (2001). *Stand tall, Molly Lou Melon.* Illustrated by David Catrow. New York: Putnam.

Munson, D. (2000). *Enemy pie.* San Francisco: Chronicle.

Naylor, P. (1991). *King of the playground.* Illustrated by N. Malone. New York: Atheneum.

O'Neill, A. (2002). *The recess queen.* Illustrated by Laura Huliska-Beith. New York: Scholastic.

Scott, E. (2000). *Friends!* New York: Atheneum.

- **T-Chart:** Students use a T-chart to discuss the protagonist's character traits and provide supporting evidence from the text.
- **Reader's Theatre:** Students create their own script for *King of the Playground* and perform it for younger students.
- **Cause–Effect:** Students explore the effects of characters' actions in a cause–effect chart.

Choosing to Come to America

Howard, G. (2001). *William's house.* Illustrated by Larry Day. New York: Millbrook Press.

Kay, V. (2001). *Tattered sails.* Illustrated by Dan Andreasen. New York: Putnam.

Lawlor, K. (1997). *I was dreaming to come to America: Memories from the Ellis Island Oral History Project.* New York: Puffin.

Tarbescu, E. (1998). *Annushka's voyage.* Illustrated by Lydia Dabcovich. New York: Clarion.

Wolf, B. (2003). *Coming to America: A Muslim family's story.* New York: Lee & Low Books.

Woodruff, E. (1999). *The memory coat.* New York: Scholastic.

- **Wall Story:** After their readings, students work with the teacher to create a wall story retelling the journey of one of the families depicted in the text set.
- **Word Study:** Students use a set of word cards based on vocabulary from the text set to recreate sentences from the stories as well as create new ones.
- **Simulated Diaries:** As a culminating activity, students write their own simulated diaries of their family's journey to America. It can be based on their actual immigration to this country or a fictional account based on one of the texts.

Choices That Made a Difference

Personal Choices to Help Others

Kulling, M. (2000). *Escape north: The story of Harriet Tubman.* New York: Random House.

Mochizuki, K. (1997). *Passage to freedom: The Sugihara story.* Illustrated by Dom Lee. New York: Lee & Low Books.

Rappaport, D. (2001). *Martin's big words: The life of Dr. Martin Luther King, Jr.* Illustrated by Bryan Collier. New York: Hyperion.

Rumford, J. (2004). *Sequoyah: The Cherokee man who gave his people writing.* New York: Houghton Mifflin.

Stanley, D. (1990). *Good Queen Bess: The story of Elizabeth I of England.* New York: Far Winds Press.

- **Diorama:** As students read about Harriet Tubman, they create a diorama to illustrate how she helped slaves escape to the North.
- **Character Puppets:** After the students have read about Queen Elizabeth I, they create hand puppets of Elizabeth I and her court to role play her life story.
- *All About* **Books:** After the whole class or small groups of students have read a book, they choose one of the heroes presented in the text set and create an *All About* book to share their story.

Reaching Out to Others

Polacco, P. (1994). *Mrs. Katz and Tush.* Illustrated by P. Polacco. New York: Philomel.

Polacco, P. (1994). *Pink and Say.* Illustrated by P. Polacco. New York: Philomel.

Polacco, P. (2000). *The butterfly.* Illustrated by P. Polacco. New York: Philomel.

Polacco, P. (2001). *Mr. Lincoln's way.* Illustrated by P. Polacco. New York: Philomel.

Polacco, P. (2001). *Thank you, Mr. Falker.* Illustrated by P. Polacco. New York: Philomel.

Polacco, P. (2004). *An orange for Frankie.* Illustrated by P. Polacco. New York: Philomel.

- **Author Study:** The class discusses Patricia Polacco's books and constructs a matrix highlighting the features of her stories. After the matrix is completed, the class discusses how the stories share similar features.
- **Book Boxes:** Students select one of the texts and create a book box. Each side of the shoebox is decorated with a scene from the story and inside are props to retell the text.
- **In the Style of:** Working in groups, students create their own story in the style of Patricia Polacco. This culminating activity is the application of their knowledge about the writer's craft.

Intermediate Grades

Dangerous Choices

Choosing to Journey Afar

Borden, L. (2005). *The journey that saved Curious George: The true wartime escape of Margaret and H. A. Rey.* Illustrated by Allan Drummond. New York: Houghton Mifflin.

Brown, D. (2002). *Far beyond the garden gate: Alexandra David-Neel's journey to Lhasa.* New York: Houghton Mifflin.

Masoff, J. (2002). *Everest: Reaching for the sky.* New York: Scholastic.

Shafer, A. (2002). *The fantastic journey of Pieter Brugel.* New York: Dutton.

Shulevitz, U. (2005). *The travels of Benjamin Tudela: Through three continents in the twelfth century.* New York: Farrar, Straus & Giroux.

- **Read, Encode, Annotate, and Ponder (REAP):** After reading about the many historical figures, students use the REAP strategy (Allen, 2004) to comprehend texts. The students read the text and jot down the title and author (R). They encode the text by putting the main idea in their own words (E). Students annotate the text by writing important points (A). Finally, they ponder what they have learned (P).
- **Interactive Writing:** After the students have completed the text set, they choose one dangerous journey, such as climbing Mount Everest, and write an interactive story about it.
- **Reader's Theatre:** Working collaboratively, the students write a script for one of the texts and perform it for their peers.

Choosing Freedom

Fradin, D. (2005). *Let it begin here! Lexington & Concord: First battles of the American Revolution.* Illustrated by Larry Day. New York: Walker and Company.

Gorrell, G. (2000). *North star to freedom: The story of the Underground Railroad.* Illustrated by Clement Oubrerie. New York: Delacorte.

Haskins, J. (2005). *Delivering justice: W. W. Law and the fight for civil rights.* Illustrated by Benny Andrews. New York: Candlewick Press.

Talbott, H. (2000). *Forging freedom.* New York: Puffin.

Weatherford, C. (2005). *Freedom on the menu: The Greensboro sit-ins.* Illustrated by Jerome Lagarrigue. New York: Dial Books.

- **Tea Party:** A tea party is another format for discussing literature. The teacher makes cards with excerpts from the text. The students pair up to read and discuss their excerpt and then move on to share another section with other peers. To close the activity, the teacher calls all the students together to discuss their responses.
- **Cubing:** This strategy may be used as a culminating activity for a selected text. The students may choose to study the American Revolution or Civil Rights Movement. Working in groups, the students address the following six dimensions of the topic: description, comparison to another topic/concept, association with another topic/concept, analysis of the topic, application of the topic, and argument for/against the topic.
- **Posters:** After studying the Greensboro sit-ins, the students work in pairs to design and create posters that illustrate the historical event.

Difficult Choices

Choosing to Defy the Odds

Chambers, V. (2005). *Celia Cruz, queen of salsa.* Illustrated by Julie Maren. New York: Dial Books.

Green, M. (2002). *A strong right arm: The story of Mamie "Peanut" Johnson.* New York: Dial Books.

Orgill, R. (2002). *Mahalia: A life in gospel music.* New York: Candlewick.

Winter, J. (2005). *Roberto Clemente: Pride of the Pittsburgh Pirates.* Illustrated by Raul Colón. New York: Atheneum.

Yoo, P. (2005). *Sixteen years in sixteen seconds: The Sammy Lee story.* Illustrated by Dom Lee. New York: Lee & Low Books.

- **Character Cluster:** Working in groups, students use a graphic organizer to discuss the character traits of one of the historical figures in the text set. Using a cluster map, the students write the person's character traits and support their choices with citations from the text.
- **Collaborative Book Reports:** After students have completed a text, they further research the historical figure on the Internet and write a collaborative book report that expands on their chosen book.
- **Quilt:** This activity would be appropriate as a closing instructional strategy for this text set. Working in groups, the students create quilts representing the men and women they have read and written about in this text set. Each square in the quilt represents a symbol for their chosen historical figure.

Choosing to Be Different

Byrd, R. (2003). *Leonardo: Beautiful dreamer.* New York: Dutton Children's Books.

LeTord, B. (1999). *A bird or 2: A story about Henri Matisse.* Grand Rapids, MI: Eerdmans Books for Young Readers.

Markel, M. (2005). *Dreamer from the village: The story of Marc Chagall.* Illustrated by Emily Lisker. New York: Henry Holt.

Rodriquez, R. (2006). *Through Georgia's eyes.* New York: Henry Holt.

Warhola, J. (2003). *Uncle Andy's.* New York: Putnam Juvenile.

- **In the Style of:** After their readings, students create their own version of an artist's life by illustrating their text with simulations of their paintings.
- **K-W-L Flip Chart:** When students have finished reading about one of the artists, they create a flip chart using the K-W-L format. The students write about what they knew about the artist, what they wanted to learn, and new knowledge they acquired after reading.
- **Open-Mind Portraits:** Students create an open-mind portrait for each artist depicted in the text set. The students write the artist's character traits on the other side of the portrait.

Choices That Made a Difference

Choosing Friends

DiCamillo, K. (2000). *Because of Winn-Dixie.* Cambridge, MA: Candlewick Press.

Fleischman, S. (2003). *The whipping boy.* New York: Greenwillow Books.

Karr, L. (2002). *Worlds apart.* New York: Marshall Cavendish.

Konigsburg, E. (1967). *Jennifer, Hecate, Macbeth, William McKinley, and me, Elizabeth.* New York: Atheneum.

Neville, E. (1963). *It's like this, cat.* New York: HarperCollins.

White, E. B. (1952). *Charlotte's web.* Illustrated by Gareth Williams. New York: HarperCollins.

- **Grand Conversation:** As a culminating activity, the students can discuss the texts about friendships in a grand conversation. The teacher opens the conversation with a quote from one of the texts or a question and the students share their responses. The grand conversation concludes with the students writing their summations in their reading logs.

- **Hand Puppets:** Students select one of the texts about friendship and create hand puppets on popsicle sticks for the main characters. The students use their puppets to retell the story plot in their own words.
- **Say Something:** Students are paired with a reading buddy to read one of the texts. They read a few pages to themselves and then stop to discuss their responses. The reading buddies can continue to finish one chapter or a designated amount of text.

Choosing to Change the World

Fleming, C. (2003). *Boxes for Katje.* Illustrated by Stacey Dressen-McQueen. New York: Farrar, Straus & Giroux.

Gilley, J. (2005). *Peace one day: The making of world peace day.* Illustrated by Karen Blessen. New York: Putnam.

Knudsen, M. (2005). *Carl the complainer.* Illustrated by Maryann Cocca-Leffler. New York: The Kane Press.

Morris, A., & Larson, H. *Tsunami: Helping each other.* New York: Millbrook/Lerner Publishing.

- **Double-Entry Journals:** As students read the texts about characters that chose to help others, they use a double-entry journal to respond to passages from the text.
- **Wall Story:** After reading about the tsunami disaster, the class writes a collaborative wall story about the tragedy focusing on how the global community came to the aid of the countries damaged by the tsunami.
- **Boxes for Katje:** After reading *Boxes for Katje,* the students work in groups to research a global campaign to help others on the Unicef or American Red Cross websites. The students then create Boxes for Katje that symbolically illustrate how they can come to the aid of their fellow citizens of the globe.

Middle Grades

Dangerous Choices

Fight or Flight

Byers, A. (2005). *Oskar Schindler: Saving Jews from the Holocaust.* New York: Enslow Publishers.

Bruchac, J. (2005). *Code talker: A novel about the Navajo marines of World War Two.* New York: Dial.

Hillman, L. (2005). *I will plant you a lilac tree: A memoir of a Schindler's list survivor.* New York: Atheneum.

Millman, I. (2005). *Hidden child.* New York: Farrar, Straus & Giroux/Frances Foster Books.

Nicolson, D. (2005). *Remember World War II.* Washington, DC: National Geographic Children's Books.

Rappaport, D. (2005). *The secret Seder.* Illustrated by Emily A. McCully. New York: Hyperion.

- **Read, Encode, Annotate, and Ponder (REAP):** After reading about the many heroes of World War II, the students use the REAP strategy (Allen, 2004) to comprehend texts. The students read the text and jot down the title and author (R). They encode the text by putting the main idea in their own words (E). Students annotate the text by writing important points (A). Finally, they ponder what they have learned (P).
- **Hero Cards:** In this activity, students create their own deck of cards by drawing a World War II hero's face on one side and recording his or her heroic action on the other side.
- **Code Talker:** Using the Internet, the students research the Navajo code used during the war to save American lives. After studying how to create codes based on patterns, the students create their own version for their peers to decipher.

Freedom's Founders

Aronson, M. (2005). *The real revolution: The global story of American independence.* New York: Clarion.

Fleming, C. (2003). *Ben Franklin's almanac: Being a true account of the good gentleman's life.* Illustrated by Ann Schwartz. New York: Atheneum.

Fradin, D. (2003). *The signers: The 56 stories behind the Declaration of Independence.* Illustrated by Michael Mc-Curdy. New York: Walker and Company.

Fradin, D. (2005). *The founders: The 39 stories behind the U.S. Constitution.* New York: Walker and Company.

Fradin, D. (2005). *Let it begin here! Lexington and Concord: First battles of the American revolution.* Illustrated by Larry Day. New York: Walker and Company.

- **Learning Logs:** During reading workshop and independent reading, students write about the founders of our country and the dangerous choice they made to risk their lives and homes in the quest for liberty.
- **ReQuest:** During their study of the founders of America, students can use the ReQuest strategy (Allen, 2004) to deepen their knowledge of American history. In this strategy, the teacher first models higher-order thinking and the students work in pairs to generate questions as they read texts. After the reading, the students ask the teacher their questions. The teacher responds by modeling how to research answers or refer back to the text. The process is repeated throughout the text set.
- **Story Boards:** The students work in groups to create a story board about one of the founders they have researched. The story board illustrates the founder's life and emphasizes the dangerous choices that needed to be made.

Difficult Choices

Taking a Stand

Ferris, J. (2003). *Demanding justice: A story about Mary Ann Shadd Cary.* Illustrated by Kimanne Smith. New York: Carolrhoda Books/Lerner Publishing.

Fradin, D. B., & Fradin, J. B. (2000). *Ida B. Wells: Mother of the civil rights movement.* New York: Clarion.

Fradin, D. B., & Fradin, J. B. (2003). *Fight on! March Church Terrell's battle for integration.* New York: Clarion.

Levitin, S. (2000). *Dream freedom.* New York: Silver Whistle.

McDonough, Y. (2002). *Peaceful protest: The life of Nelson Mandela.* New York: Walker and Company.

McKissack, P. (2005). *Abby takes a stand.* Illustrated by Gordon James. New York: Viking Children's Books.

- **Discussion Web:** Working in groups, students use a graphic organizer to discuss the question, Would you risk your life to save another? The group must come to agreement in their response.

- **Taking a Stand:** Students research human rights offenses around the world at the United Nations website and present their findings to the class. The class then discusses how they can take action against those offenses.

- **Quilt:** This activity would be appropriate as a closing instructional strategy for this text set. Working in groups, the students create quilts representing the courageous men and women they have read and written about in this text set. Each square in the quilt represents a symbol for a man or woman who took a stand against injustice.

Life's Choices

Babbitt, N. (2007). *Tuck everlasting.* New York: Square Fish Publishers.

Curtis, C. P. (2001). *Bud, not Buddy.* New York: Yearling.

Hiaasen, C. (2002). *Hoot.* New York: Knopf.

Kadohata, C. (2006). *Kira-Kira.* New York: Aladdin.

Lupica, M. (2006). *Heat.* New York: Puffin Books.

Lupica, M. (2006). *Miracle on 49th Street.* New York: Philomel.

Myers, W. D. (1996). *Scorpions.* New York: Amistad.

- **Book-a-Day:** After their readings, students use this graphic organizer to explore the story elements and main characters in the text set.

- **Memoirs:** Students interview a family member or research a historical figure that they regard as a hero and write an account of the person's life as a memoir.

- **Plot Profiles:** As students read *Heat*, they graph the story tension as it unfolds and discuss the author's writing style.

Choices That Made a Difference

Choosing to Help Others

Bolden, T. (2003). *Portraits of African-American heroes.* Illustrated by Ansel Pitcairn. New York: Dutton.

Denenberg, D., & Roscoe, L. (2005). *50 American heroes every kid should meet.* New York: Millbrook Press/Lerner Publishing.

Jurmain, S. (2005). *The forbidden schoolhouse: The true and dramatic story of Prudence Crandall and her students.* New York: Houghton Mifflin.

Lewis, J. P. (2005). *Heroes and she-roes: Poems of amazing and everyday heroes.* Illustrated by Jim Cooke. New York: Dial.

Morrow, B. (2003). *A good night for freedom.* Illustrated by Leonard Jenkins. New York: Holiday.

- **Literature Report Card:** As students read books in the text set, they use the literature report card strategy (Antonacci & O'Callaghan, 2006) to discuss the heroes who chose to help others. In this strategy, students list the heroes' names and rate them against character traits.

- **Timelines:** As students read about African American heroes who made a difference, they work in groups to create a timeline that compares the events in the hero's life with what was going on in the United States at the time.

- **Grand Conversations:** After the whole class or small groups of students have read a book, they engage in a grand conversation. To prepare for the dialogue, students are directed to do a quickwrite, develop a set of questions with responses, or do a quickdraw. They engage in a conversation on the book and share responses.

Choosing to Change the World

Byrd, R. (2003). *Leonardo: Beautiful dreamer.* New York: Dutton.

Chin-Lee, C. (2005). *Amelia to Zora: Twenty-six women who changed the world.* Illustrated by M. Halsey and S. Addy. New York: Charlesbridge Publishing.

Collins, M. (2003). *Airborne: A photobiography of Wilbur and Orville Wright.* Washington, DC: National Geographic Society.

Delano, M. (2002). *Inventing the future: A photobiography of Thomas Edison.* Washington, DC: National Geographic Society.

Lasky, K. (2003). *The man who made time travel.* Illustrated by Kevin Hawkes. New York: Melanie Kroupa Books/Farrar, Straus & Giroux.

- **Data Charts:** Using a data chart, the students create a graphic organizer comparing inventors with the periods they lived in, resistance to their findings, their inventions, and outcomes.

- **Open-Mind Portraits:** After reading about an inventor, the students create an open-mind portrait that illustrates the character on one side and describes their thinking/feelings on the other side.

- **Brainstorming:** Working in groups, students brainstorm possible inventions that would affect our daily lives. Students may choose a field such as medicine or technology and present their choices to the class.

PROFESSIONAL RESOURCES

Allen, J. (2004). *Tools for teaching content literacy.* Portland, ME: Stenhouse.

Antonacci, P., & O'Callaghan, C. (2006). *A handbook for literacy instructional and assessment strategies: K–8.* Boston: Allyn & Bacon.

National Council of Social Studies. (1994). *Expectations for excellence: Curriculum standards for social studies.* NCSS Bulletin No. 89. Baltimore: Author.

National Council of Teachers of English & International Reading Association. (1996). *Standards for the English language arts.* Newark, DE: Authors. Available at www.ncte.org/standards

Rigby, K. (2002). *A meta-evaluation of methods and approaches to reducing bullying in pre-schools and in early primary school in Australia.* Canberra, Australia: Commonwealth Attorney-General's Department.

Tompkins, G. E. (2009). *50 literacy strategies: Step by step* (3rd ed.). Boston: Allyn & Bacon.

Index